NEW STUDIES IN BIBL

A mouth full of fire

Titles in this series:

An index of Scripture references for all the volumes may be found at http://www.thegospelcoalition.org/resources/nsbt.

NEW STUDIES IN BIBLICAL THEOLOGY 29

Series editor: D. A. Carson

A mouth full of fire

THE WORD OF GOD IN THE WORDS OF JEREMIAH

Andrew G. Shead

APOLLOS

INTERVARSITY PRESS
DOWNERS GROVE, ILLINOIS 60515

APOLLOS
An imprint of Inter-Varsity Press, England
Norton Street
Nottingham NG7 3HR, England
Website: www.ivpbooks.com
Email: ivp@ivpbooks.com

InterVarsity Press, USA
P.O. Box 1400
Downers Grove, IL 60515-1426, USA
Website: www.ivpress.com
Email: email@ivpress.com

InterVarsity Press®, USA, is the book-publishing division of InterVarsity Christian Fellowship/USA® <www.intervarsity.org> and a member movement of the International Fellowship of Evangelical Students.

Inter-Varsity Press, England, is closely linked with the Universities and Colleges Christian Fellowship, a student movement connecting Christian Unions throughout Great Britain, and a member movement of the International Fellowship of Evangelical Students. Website: www.uccf.org.uk

Unless otherwise specified, all Bible translations are the author's, and all references give the English numbering and reflect the Masoretic form of the text as used in English versions.

Scripture quotations marked ESV are from The Holy Bible, English Standard Version, published by HarperCollins Publishers © 2001 by Crossway Bibles, a division of Good News Publishers. Used by permission. All rights reserved.

Scripture quotations marked HCSB have been taken from the Holman Christian Standard Bible®, copyright © 1999, 2000, 2002, 2003 by Holman Bible Publishers. Used by permission. Holman Christian Standard Bible®, Holman CSB® and HCSB® are federally registered trademarks of Holman Bible Publishers.

Quotations marked NETS are taken from A New English Translation of the Septuagint, © 2007 by the International Organization for Septuagint and Cognate Studies, Inc. Used by permission of Oxford University Press. All rights reserved.

Figure 3.1 (p. 113) used by permission, © SIL, Biblical Hebrew and Discourse Linguistics, 1994.

First published 2012.

Set in Monotype Times New Roman
Typeset in Great Britain by Servis Filmsetting Ltd, Stockport, Cheshire

USA ISBN 978-0-8308-2630-8
UK ISBN 978-1-84474-596-8

British Library Cataloguing in Publication Data
A catalogue record for this book is available from the British Library.

Library of Congress Cataloging-in-Publication Data

Shead, Andrew G.
  A mouth full of fire : the word of God in the words of Jeremiah / Andrew Shead.
    p. cm.—(New studies in Biblical theology ; 29)
  Includes bibliographical references and index.
  ISBN 978-0-8308-2630-8 (pbk. : alk. paper) 1. Bible. O.T. Jeremiah—Criticism, interpretation, etc. 2. Word of God (Christian theology) 3. Word (Theology) I. Title.
  BS1525.6.W73S54 2013
  224'.206—dc23
                                                                           2012018986

| P | 19 | 18 | 17 | 16 | 15 | 14 | 13 | 12 | 11 | 10 | 9 | 8 | 7 | 6 | 5 | 4 | 3 | 2 | 1 |
| Y | 28 | 27 | 26 | 25 | 24 | 23 | 22 | 21 | 20 | 19 | 18 | 17 | 16 | 15 | 14 | 13 | 12 |

To my colleagues on the faculty of
Moore Theological College

I am about to set my words
    on fire in your mouth;
these people are tinder,
    and it will consume them.

                  (Jer. 5:14)

When I say, 'I will not call him to mind
    or speak any more in his name,'
there is in my heart something like a fire
    burning, bottled up in my bones.

                  (Jer. 20:9)

Contents

Figures

Tables

11

Series preface

New Studies in Biblical Theology is a series of monographs that address key issues in the discipline of biblical theology. Contributions to the series focus on one or more of three areas: (1) the nature and status of biblical theology, including its relations with other disciplines (e.g. historical theology, exegesis, systematic theology, historical criticism, narrative theology); (2) the articulation and exposition of the structure of thought of a particular biblical writer or corpus; and (3) the delineation of a biblical theme across all or part of the biblical corpora.

Above all, these monographs are creative attempts to help thinking Christians understand their Bibles better. The series aims simultaneously to instruct and to edify, to interact with the current literature, and to point the way ahead. In God's universe, mind and heart should not be divorced: in this series we will try not to separate what God has joined together. While the notes interact with the best of scholarly literature, the text is uncluttered with untransliterated Greek and Hebrew, and tries to avoid too much technical jargon. The volumes are written within the framework of confessional evangelicalism, but there is always an attempt at thoughtful engagement with the sweep of the relevant literature.

It is extraordinarily rare for a reading of a biblical book to be simultaneously creative and convincing, but Dr Andrew Shead has managed it in this work on Jeremiah. It is even more extraordinary for a book that exemplifies careful exegesis and the best of one kind of biblical theology to speak authoritatively to the discipline of systematic theology, but Dr Shead's work manages that, too. Characterized by tight and disciplined writing and careful thought, this volume deserves careful study. You will never again read Jeremiah exactly the same way you have read it in the past. No less important, as you work carefully through the pages of this volume you will see, in Jeremiah's doctrine of the word of God, a convincing anticipation of one who is called the Word of God – but

13

without the artificial links that frequently characterize attempts to read Old Testament books Christologically. This is an important and stimulating book.

D. A. Carson
Trinity Evangelical Divinity School

Author's preface

As with most books this one has a number of parents, each discernable in various features of its child. The focus on Jeremiah owes its existence to doctoral studies completed under Professor Robert Gordon; the concern with biblical theology comes from years of teaching at Moore Theological College; the interest in exploring how the Old Testament may contribute to systematic reflection was generated by the interdisciplinary fellowship of a wonderful faculty; the particular shape it has taken in the following pages derives from a series of public lectures, in 2007, that the principal invited and enabled me by grant of study leave to deliver. The same principal, John Woodhouse, with the governing board, has granted me further study leave to write this book, and his predecessor, Peter Jensen, was responsible for my venturing into doctoral study in the first place. Almost from first to last, then, what you are about to read is a child of Moore College and its faculty. While I could mention some individuals specifically – Mark Thompson, Robert Doyle, David Höhne, Michael Jensen for their guidance in matters theological; David Peterson, Peter O'Brien, Bill Salier for their insights into the New Testament (and the Old) – it is the faculty as a whole, whose Christian fellowship and sense of common scholarly endeavour is singular in my experience, to which I feel I owe the greatest debt of gratitude, and to whom this book is dedicated. Its achievements are theirs; its failings I politely accept.

In addition to these my dedicatees I should mention Andrew Robinson, who gave useful research assistance in the final stages, Graeme Goldsworthy and Scott Newling, whose comments led me to re-examine my argument at a number of points, and especially my father, Geoff Shead, whose keen perusal of drafts with a layman's eyes is responsible for countless improvements of every kind. Before and after these helpers came D. A. Carson, the series editor, whose invitation to join the series and encouragement thereafter was instrumental to the book's existence. And finally, special mention must go to Philip Duce, my long-suffering editor at Inter-Varsity Press, whose kindness and patience with an author whose one-year project stretched out into five will not soon be forgotten.

Not even my colleagues have had to live with Jeremiah the way my wife, Jean, has over the past fifteen years. I am grateful for her patience, and for the good-natured tolerance of my children, over the adoption of an unplanned prophet into our family. And to the God who speaks, who makes us an 'us', like him, may these endeavours return as an act of praise.

Andrew G. Shead

Abbreviations

AB	Anchor Bible
AbOTC	Abingdon Old Testament Commentaries
AnBib	Analecta biblica
AOTC	Apollos Old Testament Commentaries
ATD	Das Alte Testament Deutsch
ATSAT	Arbeiten zu Text und Sprache im Alten Testament
AV	Authorized (King James) Version of the Bible (1611)
BAR	*Biblical Archaeology Review*
BaST	Basel Studies of Theology
BBB	Bonner Biblische Beiträge
BBR	*Bulletin for Biblical Research*
BETL	Bibliotheca ephemeridum theologicarum lovaniensium
BHS	*Biblia Hebraica Stuttgartensia*, ed. K. Elliger and W. Rudolph, Stuttgart: Deutsche Bibelstiftung, 1983
BIS	Biblical Interpretation Series
BKAT	Biblischer Kommentar Altes Testament
BST	The Bible Speaks Today
BThSt	Biblische Theologische Studien
BZ	*Biblische Zeitschrift*
BZAW	Beiheft zur Zeitschrift für die alttestamentliche Wissenschaft
CBET	Contributions to Biblical Exegesis and Theology
CBQ	*Catholic Biblical Quarterly*
CBSC	Cambridge Bible for Schools and Colleges
CD	*Church Dogmatics* (Barth 1977)
CSCD	Cambridge Studies in Christian Doctrine
DG	*Davidson's Introductory Hebrew Grammar: Syntax* (J. C. L. Gibson 1994)
DJD	Discoveries in the Judaean Desert

DTIB	*Dictionary for Theological Interpretation of the Bible*, ed. K. J. Vanhoozer, Grand Rapids: Baker Academic, 2005
ESCT	Edinburgh Studies in Constructive Theology
ESV	English Standard Version (2001)
ETSMS	Evangelical Theological Society Monograph Series
EvT	Evangelische Theologie
FAT	Forschungen zum Alten Testament
Gk.	Greek
HAT	Handbuch zum Alten Testament
HBM	Hebrew Bible Monographs
HBV	Hebrew Bible and its Versions
HCSB	Holman Christian Standard Bible (2003)
HS	*Hebrew Studies*
HSAT	Die Heilige Schrift des Alten Testaments
HSM	Harvard Semitic Monographs
HTIBS	Historic Texts and Interpreters in Biblical Scholarship
ICC	International Critical Commentary
IJST	*International Journal of Systematic Theology*
Inst.	*Institutes of the Christian Religion* (Calvin 1960)
IRT	Issues in Religion and Theology
ISBL	Indiana Studies in Biblical Literature
ITC	International Theological Commentary
JBL	*Journal of Biblical Literature*
JFSE	*Journal of Faith and Science Exchange*
JNES	*Journal of Near Eastern Studies*
JSOT	*Journal for the Study of the Old Testament*
JSOTSup	Journal for the Study of the Old Testament, Supplement Series
JPSTC	JPS Torah Commentary
JTI	*Journal of Theological Interpretation*
KHC	Kurzer Hand-Commentar zum Alten Testament
LCC	Library of Christian Classics
LHBOTS	Library of Hebrew Bible/Old Testament Studies (formerly JSOTSup)
LXX	Septuagint
LXXV	The parent Hebrew text from which the LXX was originally produced: the LXX *Vorlage*
M	The parent text from which the MT emerged: the proto-Masoretic Text

MT	The Masoretic Text of the Hebrew Bible, sometimes used interchangeably with M
NDBT	*New Dictionary of Biblical Theology: Exploring the Unity and Diversity of Scripture*, ed. B. S. Rosner, T. D. Alexander, G. Goldsworthy and D. A. Carson, Downers Grove: InterVarsity Press; Leicester: Inter-Varsity Press, 2000
NETS	*New English Translation of the Septuagint* (2007)
NIBC	New International Biblical Commentary
NICOT	New International Commentary on the Old Testament
NIV	New International Version (1984)
NJPSV	Tanakh, the Holy Scriptures: The New JPS Translation According to the Traditional Hebrew Text (1985)
n.p.	no page number
NS	New Series
NSBT	New Studies in Biblical Theology
NT	New Testament
NTSup	Supplements to Novum Testamentum
OAN	Oracles Against the Nations (Jeremiah MT 46 – 51)
OBO	Orbis biblicus et orientalis
ÖBS	Österreichische Biblische Studien
OT	Old Testament
OTG	Old Testament Guides
OTL	Old Testament Library
OTS	Old Testament Studies
OtSt	Oudtestamentische Studiën
pl.	plural
PNTC	Pillar New Testament Commentaries
RB	*Revue biblique*
Rem.	remark
RSV	Revised Standard Version (1973)
RTR	*Reformed Theological Review*
RV	The Revised Version of the Bible (1885)
SBLDS	Society of Biblical Literature Dissertation Series
SBLMS	Society of Biblical Literature Monograph Series
SBT	Studies in Biblical Theology
SE	*Studia evangelica*
sg.	singular
SHBC	Smyth & Helwys Bible Commentary

SJOT	*Scandinavian Journal of the Old Testament*
SNTSMS	Society for New Testament Studies Monograph Series
SOFS	Symbolae osloenses fasc supplet
SOTBT	Studies in Old Testament Biblical Theology
SOTI	Studies in Old Testament Interpretation
SOTSM	Society for Old Testament Studies Monographs
SSN	Studia semitica neerlandica
TDOT	*Theological Dictionary of the Old Testament*, ed. G. J. Botterweck, H. Ringgren and H.-J. Fabry, 15 vols., Grand Rapids: Eerdmans, 1974–2006
TNIV	Today's New International Version (2005)
tr.	translation
TU	Texte und Untersuchungen zur Geschichte der altchristlichen Literatur
TynB	*Tyndale Bulletin*
VT	*Vetus Testamentum*
VTSup	Supplements to Vetus Testamentum
WBC	Word Biblical Commentaries
WMANT	Wissenschaftliche Monographien zum Alten und Neuen Testament
WUNT	Wissenschaftliche Untersuchungen zum Neuen Testament
ZAW	*Zeitschrift für die alttestamentliche Wissenschaft*

Introduction: an exercise in theological interpretation

The aim of this book

In this book I aim to present a reading of the book of Jeremiah that makes good sense of its apparently chaotic structure and flow of thought. My solution is not the only way of reading Jeremiah, but as a teacher and preacher I have found it a satisfying and fruitful one. It is also an overtly theological reading from the start. I did not set out to read Jeremiah in this way, but have become convinced that this is the way the book expects to be read. And so my initial quest to read Jeremiah coherently has been captured by a grander question, the question of what it might look like to read Jeremiah (or any other biblical text) as a work of theology or even – daringly – as an expression of Christian doctrine. The doctrine in this particular case, for reasons that will become evident, is the doctrine of the word of God.

Doctrine and biblical studies are two disciplines we are used to thinking about quite separately. Many, perhaps most, graduates of theological schools have been trained to approach each as a distinct field of study with its own modes of thought and its own body of literature. While there are good reasons, both historical and practical, for doing so, I hope that this book will demonstrate the value of blurring the boundaries between them. The boundary-blurring I have in mind is a species of what has come to be called 'theological interpretation of the Bible', and in this introduction I shall address some of the challenges and opportunities this type of interpretation brings with it.

Unlike most studies of a biblical-theological nature, however, I shall not be broadening the biblical basis of this study beyond Jeremiah. It is all too easy for preachers schooled in biblical theology to move from an Old Testament passage to the grand story of redemption and on to Christ, without giving enough time to reflecting on the character of God and, dare I say, the character of Christ, as presented in the passage in its own right. We need to take the Old

Testament seriously in itself as a source of Christian doctrine. After all, this is precisely where the earliest church found its Christology.[1]

The plan of this book

Because of my dual aim, namely, to explore the book of Jeremiah and the doctrine of the Word of God, readers of a theological bent may find themselves impatient with the amount of biblical exposition I have included, not all of which is necessary to establish Jeremiah's word theology. This includes a detailed study of the book's overall structure and message, and close readings of Jeremiah 1, 14 – 15, 26 – 28, 30 – 31, 36 and 50. I do not apologize for this, however; theologians often extract ideas from Scripture and leave behind the messy incidentals of persons, places and times so as to construct well-organized general truths. I hope to demonstrate, by contrast, that theology viewed 'from below' can have a refreshingly different character.

From this reading process I have drawn the following 'heads' of a Jeremianic 'doctrine' of the Word of God. While there is no neat correlation between each of these elements and the chapters opposite them in table 1 below, there is a sense, as we shall see, that new elements come into successive focus as the book unfolds. Each is also present in Jeremiah's programmatic opening chapter.

Table 1 Elements of word theology in Jeremiah's unfolding story

Elements of Jeremiah's word theology	Parts of the book where the present investigation is focused	
Word and words	Jeremiah 1 – 52	(1:1–3)
Word and speaker	Jeremiah 1 – 20	(1:4–8)
Word and hearers	Jeremiah 21 – 29	(1:13–19)
Word and power	Jeremiah 30 – 51	(1:9–12)
Word and permanence	Jeremiah 36	(1:1)

My own opening chapter, on word and words, provides a justification for the entire project, and an analysis of Jeremiah's use of word language. After it I have inserted a chapter on the book's structure, important because the success of my reading strategy depends on the validity of my observations about Jeremiah's overall shape and direction as a narrative. The third chapter, on word and speaker,

---

[1] On this see the fine work by Ronald Heine, and especially his chapter on the gospel in the Prophets (Heine 2007: 97–141).

examines some of the literary techniques by which the book controls our perception of who is speaking, and moves on to consider Jeremiah the person. Each of these chapters moves from relatively technical discussions of mechanics to more accessible observations and conclusions; by the second half of chapter 2 biblical exposition starts to be thrown into the mix. When appropriate I have provided signposts to help readers navigate this *mélange*.

In chapters 4–6 there are fewer technicalities and more exposition, and theological discussions begin to make their presence felt, sometimes leaving Jeremiah behind altogether. A final chapter brings Jeremiah into an extended conversation with Karl Barth, and offers some assessment of the contribution Jeremiah makes both to the doctrine of the Word of God and to some of the questions about the nature of theological reading raised in this introduction.

The great bulk of incidental scholarly debate has been relegated to the footnotes, and for readers who do not wish to participate in this particular conversation the book should make perfect sense without them.

In the remainder of this introduction I wish to add my voice to the petition to allow theology to enter the domain of biblical studies, and to have a say in how Scripture is read; and to allow biblical studies to return the favour, by shaping the way theology is organized and articulated. Far from this resulting in mystical, dehistoricized readings of Scripture, and disorderly, skewed theological formulations, I hope to show that each discipline can breathe a new type of life into the other.

Biblical theology or theological interpretation? Reading Jeremiah as a theological book

The series preface to this volume avoids defining biblical theology too closely. Indeed, the first designated focal area for volumes in the series is 'the nature and status of biblical theology'. The other two focal areas – articulating the structure of a biblical author's thought and delineating a biblical theme across many books – are firmly planted in biblical soil without being overtly theological. This vagueness reflects a general lack of agreement in the academic community as to how biblical theology ought to be defined.[2] Historically,

---

[2] For a good survey of the history and methods of biblical theology see Scobie (2003: 3–102).

the term has been understood in two distinct ways: 'a theology contained within the Bible, or a theology which accords with the Bible'.[3]

'Neutral' biblical theology

The first of these senses dates back to the emergence of biblical theology as a modern discipline, linked with a now-famous lecture given by Johann Gabler in 1787.[4] This definition limits biblical theology to description of the theology of biblical texts or, ideally, of the ancients who wrote them. Today this view is ably represented by James Barr:

> The term 'biblical theology' has clarity only when it is understood to mean theology as it existed or was thought or believed within the time, languages and cultures of the Bible itself. Only so can its difference from doctrinal theology, from later interpretation, and from later views about the Bible be maintained.[5]

This type of biblical theology (and those who practise it) can be called 'neutral' because it does not concern itself with whether the Bible's theological content is true or not.[6]

'Confessing' biblical theology

Biblical theology in the second sense is constructive and theological. It can be traced back to a desire to rejuvenate the discipline in the wake of its virtual collapse by the early twentieth century. Brevard Childs is perhaps its most well-known champion, though Childs himself credits Gerhard Ebeling as the pioneer of this new biblical theology,[7] and picks out some of its salient features in Ebeling's thought: it begins with a descriptive component, it seeks to account for the inner unity of Old and New Testaments as a whole, and it understands the Bible 'not simply as a cultural expression of ancient peoples, but as a testimony pointing beyond itself to a divine reality

---

[3] Childs 1992: 3, citing G. Ebeling.
[4] Gabler 2004.
[5] Barr 1999: 4.
[6] The labels 'neutral' and 'confessing' come from John Barton (whose work will be discussed below); I retain quotation marks throughout to signify that these terms describe an approach to reading and not the theological convictions of the author.
[7] Ebeling 1963.

to which it bears witness'.[8] For Childs this divine reality is ultimately Christological, and behind this conviction we can detect the seminal work of Karl Barth, whose Romans commentary in particular emboldened many biblical scholars to read the Bible once more as a book through which 'the reader is confronted with the Word of God who is Jesus Christ'.[9] Add to this a strong focus on an overarching narrative as the vehicle for conveying Childs's 'inner unity of Old and New Testaments' and one gets the sort of biblical theology that volumes in the present series (NSBT) generally seek to develop: one that seeks 'to analyze and synthesize the Bible's teaching about God . . . on its own terms, maintaining sight of the Bible's overarching narrative and Christocentric focus'.[10] Such is the overt theological nature of this enterprise that Brian Rosner can describe it as 'theological interpretation of Scripture'.[11]

Variations on a theme

Biblical theologians in Childs's sense are members of a broad church, however, especially on the question of the relation between the Testaments. They are particularly divided over the way in which, and the extent to which, the Old Testament bears witness to Jesus. Childs himself is caught between those who think he goes too far, and those who think he does not go far enough. So John Goldingay for example, though he reads the Old Testament as Christian Scripture, avoids reading it as 'witness to Christ' in favour of reflection on its 'more central witness to Yhwh'.[12] Francis Watson, on the other hand, complains that 'Childs is in practice so concerned to preserve the integrity of the Old Testament that its dialectical relationship to the New virtually disappears.'[13] For Watson biblical theology effectively comes to mean Christian theology centred and founded on 'the particular truth attested in the biblical texts' – which ought to

---

[8] Childs 1992: 6–9, quoting from p. 9.
[9] Childs summarizing Barth (ibid. 22). In similar vein, Childs maintains that 'the specific characteristic of the canonical shaping of the two testaments into one Christian Bible lay in the preservation of two distinct witnesses to a common subject matter who is Jesus Christ' (91). Walter Brueggemann goes so far as to credit Barth with 'the re-creation of the possibility of a biblical theology' (Brueggemann 1997: 18).
[10] Rosner 2000: 10.
[11] Ibid.
[12] Goldingay 2003: 26; cf. Goldingay in Rae et al. (2008: 7–11). An even more disapproving position is taken by Rolf Rendtorff (2005: 751–756).
[13] Watson 1997: 14.

'describe all Christian theology'.[14] While Watson still holds out for a specialized biblical theology, others are happy to see it absorbed into plain theology: 'if "biblical theology" is anything coherent at all, it is just "theology" . . . and it will not fare well if it is not pursued by the means proper to theological reflection'.[15]

While there are a number of factors at work in the shifting and conflicting use of terms here, what I judge to be the major issue can be expressed as a question about initial and final meanings. To what extent does the final meaning of the one, divinely authored Scripture shape the initial meaning of its various parts read in their own right? Some interpreters are particularly concerned not to collapse the two so that the meaning intended by the Old Testament author is lost. This can be seen by comparing (for example) the false statement 'In the light of the New Testament we see that Nathan in 2 Samuel 7 spoke to David about the birth of Jesus' with the true statement 'In the light of the New Testament we see that Nathan's prophecy is *finally* fulfilled only with the birth of Jesus.' There is a process, an etiquette, by which God's revelation unfolds across Scripture, and this must be honoured. Other interpreters, by contrast, are particularly concerned to point out that the meaning an Old Testament text turns out to have when read in the light of the New is the meaning it had all along. Without distorting it, the final meaning is contained within the initial meaning.

One way to distinguish between these uses of the Old Testament might be to use the terms 'biblical theology' and 'theological interpretation' to describe two approaches to reading Scripture – or, perhaps, two variations on a way of reading it – so that biblical theology describes reading oriented towards the initial meaning, and theological interpretation describes reading oriented towards the final meaning. A good example of this can be found by comparing the contents of two eponymous dictionaries: the *NDBT* and the *DTIB*. Well over half the entries in the former volume have their analogues in *DTIB*, but in the later volume they receive a more theological treatment. Thus for example 'God', 'Man and Woman' and 'Word' become 'Doctrine of God', 'Male and Female' and 'Word of God' respectively. In practice the respective entries show substantial overlap; the main difference is that the 'biblical theology' entries stay more closely within the confines of the Bible, and traverse those con-

[14] Ibid. 2.
[15] Yeago 1997: 97.

fines methodically from end to end. They thus correspond to what Charles Scobie calls an 'intermediate biblical theology', standing 'between the historical study of the Bible and the use of the Bible as authoritative Scripture by the Church'.[16]

However, the question remains of just what it means to call this sort of activity 'theology', and in my opinion it is neither very accurate nor very helpful to treat biblical theology and theological interpretation as if they were two analogous ways of reading. There is more to be gained by recognizing that 'biblical theology' and 'theological interpretation' relate to one another as two quite distinct types of activity. At the risk of sounding obvious, they relate as 'theology' and 'interpretation' respectively. This realignment is not mere pedantry, for it is precisely the failure to conduct the two activities in proper relation to one another that makes biblical theology prone to theological flatness and predictability, and theological interpretation prone to disparate methods and theological unpredictability.

Biblical theology: knowledge of God as the God of the Bible

Ultimately, the theological character of the NSBT volumes does not derive from statements in the series preface about biblical theology; it derives rather from the next paragraph's assertion that they are 'written within the framework of confessional evangelicalism'. In the first instance this assertion is a way of referring to those convictions about Scripture – about what the Bible *is* – that put this type of biblical theology into the 'confessing' camp. Confessions are inescapably foundational.[17] However, the assertion also makes room for what happens next, when biblical theology (whatever we understand that to mean) itself becomes the framework on which theological interpretation grows, interpretation that in its turn nourishes confessional evangelicalism. And it is in this sense that I wish to use the term 'biblical theology' in the present book – a theology that creates a framework, or method of reading and understanding, out of which theological interpretation is the result.

Biblical theology in this sense may be defined as *knowledge of God as the God of the Bible*. What it means for God to be the God of the

---

[16] Scobie 2003: 8.

[17] 'Our confession regarding the nature and role of Scripture within the divine economy as the living voice of God surely influences, if not determines, the way one engages the material' (Gignilliat 2010: 220).

Bible is something that develops progressively as we read Scripture with an ear to what it says about God and about itself.

First of all, the God of the Bible is the God *in* the Bible, the God of whom the Bible speaks. And by the testimony of Scripture this God turns out to be the God *behind* the Bible, the one whose word the Bible is. And as a result of this fact, God also turns out to be the God who addresses us *from* the Bible.

This biblical theology generates a commensurate way of reading and understanding. First, we read for knowledge of the God in the Bible, that is, for its theological message. Along the way it will yield other sorts of information, but they are important only as they throw light on the God of the Bible. Secondly, the God of whom the Bible speaks is not a fiction or a myth but the God who creates and redeems, who acts and speaks in history. To speak of this God as God of the Bible means that though we read the Bible as a book written by many hands over many years, behind all these hands we see God's creative power and speaking voice. We read it as Scripture. In its diverse words we expect to find one word, and by the clear testimony of the New Testament this one word is Christ.[18] *How* Scripture in its diversity conveys this word to us is perhaps the single question that most exercises biblical theologians, and how to discern this message without descending into bad reading practices is the challenge of biblical criticism. Thirdly, because God is the God of the Bible in this strong sense, the message of Scripture is one by which he makes himself present to us in judgment and salvation. And so we do not value objectivity and scholarly detachment in quite the same way that those who read the Bible as a secular book do. We read prayerfully, in the Spirit and as part of the body of Christ. Only this way does knowing about God become knowing God.

The result: biblical-theological interpretation

This way of understanding amounts to a hermeneutic,[19] and the result of putting this hermeneutic to work – that is, of practising biblical-theological reading – is biblical-theological interpretation, which is a type of what its modern-day practitioners call 'theological

---

[18] The contention that Christ, or the gospel, forms the organizing centre of biblical theology tends to be honoured more in the breach than the observance. For a helpful discussion see Goldsworthy 1997, who defines biblical theology as 'the study of the gospel in the context of its antecedents and its effects as these are set out in the whole canon of Scripture' (43).

[19] See Childs 1992 and Watson 2010.

interpretation of the Bible'. This is not a purely intratextual activity, but pushes behind and in front as the God of the Bible does. In John Webster's words, 'theological interpretation of Scripture is interpretation informed by a theological description of the nature of the biblical writings and their reception, setting them in the scope of the progress of the saving divine Word through time'.[20] The current practice of 'theological interpretation of the Bible' is rather heterogeneous in its methods, with some making more of the 'rule of faith' in the interpretative process, others emphasizing the role of the church as a reading community, and so on; by *biblical*-theological interpretation' I mean to indicate a set of restraining parameters that guide and shape the activity of theological interpretation.

If theology needs to be biblical, the Bible needs equally to be read theologically. For example, I have heard many preachers, rightly convinced that biblical theology is built on a grand narrative of salvation with Christ at its centre, preach as though that grand narrative is itself biblical theology, and not just one of the conditions that shape biblical theology and the interpretation that flows from it. The result is that Old Testament texts are read as if they were relating the gospel story in code, and they are 'explained' by going to the New Testament and finding passages to serve as the 'plaintext' which deciphers that code. One would hope that when biblical theology is grasped as a way of thinking about the God of the Bible, which in turn generates a way of reading the Bible, 'biblical-theological' Old Testament preaching will not so much 'tell the gospel story' as 'tell the gospel-shaped God'. The proper end of biblical theology is not narrative but theology.

Can biblical studies admit theological readings and remain intact?

The battle for Scripture in the post-Enlightenment university

It will be evident by now that theological interpretation gets underway from the moment biblical theology starts shaping the reading of Scripture: the fruits of theological interpretation grow from the soil of 'initial meaning', watered and nourished by the hermeneutic that flows from knowledge of God as the God of the Bible. That the two

---

[20] Webster 2010: 116.

expressions overlap as much as they do is no surprise. Yet over the past decade or so the expression 'theological interpretation of the Bible' (or 'Scripture') has acquired a distinctive usage, reflecting a particular set of concerns. This usage has emerged from a conversation taking place mainly in the English-speaking world, which some would even describe as a movement.[21] The conversation partners are made up of biblical scholars and theologians, from a range of confessional backgrounds, who share the desire to bring the academic disciplines of biblical studies and theology back together. This desire flows from the recognition not only that the Bible is a theological book, unlike any other, by which God addresses us, but from the belief that it can be interpreted as such in a publically meaningful way. Both of these truths are hotly contested; their encroachment into the academy is perhaps another symptom of the decline of the so-called 'Enlightenment project'.[22]

In an engrossing study of German scholar Johann David Michaelis (1717–91) Michael Legaspi has shown how Enlightenment thinkers created an academic 'Bible' in sharp distinction to the 'Scripture' of believers. They did so out of the conviction that religious readings of Scripture were the source of 'war, fraud and superstition in modern life', and that if there were to be any hope of a happy and moral society, then 'new conceptual frameworks for biblical interpretation' had to be created.[23] The result was the transformation in universities of *theologica exegetica* into 'biblical studies'; its relocation in the philosophical faculty; its adoption of a host of new interpretative frameworks including ethnography, history, comparative Semitics, textual criticism and biblical poetics; all of which 'allowed practitioners to create a *post*-confessional Bible by reconstructing a *pre*-confessional Israel'.[24]

The resulting divide between Bible and Scripture is just as strong

---

[21] So Treier 2010: 145. My preference for the title Theological Interpretation of 'the Bible' rather than 'Scripture' is because it more clearly expresses the goal of legitimizing the reading of Scripture precisely in its humanity, as a cultural artefact – in a word, as the Bible – as the text in and by which God addresses us. For an introduction to recent writing on the theological interpretation of the Bible, see *DTIB* and Treier 2008. For his inclusion of scholars from beyond the English-speaking world, see the survey by Trimm 2010.

[22] A term that goes back to Alasdair MacIntyre (1981: 58–59). (Joel Green's claim that the Enlightenment project has failed would no doubt be just as hotly contested: Green 2000.)

[23] Legaspi 2010: 164.

[24] Ibid. 165, italics original; cf. Fowl 1998: 13–21.

in universities today, as pithily demonstrated by Philip Davies's book title *Whose Bible Is it Anyway?*[25] Fresh evidence of this conflict appears regularly. Even as I was writing this chapter the internet was buzzing with the noisy resignation of Ronald Hendel from the Society of Biblical Literature, in protest against its tolerance of 'faith' in biblical scholarship. Hendel complained that the Society had compromised Pascal's

> wise distinction between religious faith and intellectual inquiry. The two have different motivations and pertain to different domains of experience. They are like oil and water, things that do not mix and should not be confused. . . . That is to say, facts are facts, and faith has no business dealing in the world of facts.[26]

Needless to say, equally strident and uncompromising voices could be sampled from the 'faith' side of the divide, for feelings run high on this question.

John Barton and the hermeneutics of theological interpretation

A less vociferous but much more substantial argument for laying questions of faith to one side before engaging in biblical criticism has been put forward recently by John Barton.[27] I propose to engage his argument in some detail as a way of illustrating the issues involved in getting from the Bible back to Scripture. Like many others I am indebted to Barton for his writings on biblical criticism over many years, writings that have shaped my understanding of what it looks like to read well. Indeed, one of his most valuable insights is that the art of reading well is what biblical criticism basically is.[28]

Neutral reading brackets out truth questions
Where I must respectfully part company with Barton, however, is over the question of what difference it makes, if any, that it is the

---

[25] Davies 1995. Watson has provided a trenchant response to Davies's book under the heading 'Bible, Theology and the University' (Watson 1996).

[26] Hendel 2010: 74. Francis Watson mentions similar criticisms of his own interdisciplinary work (Watson 1997: vii). For further examples and a gloomy forecast for the future of 'secularistic study of the Bible' see R. B. Hays (2007: 7–11).

[27] Barton 2007: 137–186. On reading Jeremiah with faith to one side see Holt 2007.

[28] Barton 2007: 5.

Bible we are criticizing. The essence of his argument is that critical method is fatally flawed unless questions of theological truth are 'bracketed out' during the process of criticism. 'One cannot establish what the Bible means if one insists on reading it as necessarily conforming to what one already believes to be true – which is what a theological reading amounts to.'[29] This is slightly ambiguous, as we shall see, but Barton makes himself clearer as the argument unfolds. 'There are two stages involved in understanding a text. One must establish what it means; one may then ask whether what it means is true. This is an elementary point, which in reading texts other than the Bible almost everyone takes for granted.'[30] 'The attitude that thinks the text must be read as saying something one personally already believes to be true is quite fatal to the critical endeavour.'[31] Barton reassures us that there is a place for belief, but it belongs with application. If introduced at the start, exegesis will be 'controlled by a theological or religious vision, so that the meaning found in the text in the course of exegesis is determined by prior theological commitments'.[32]

There is much wisdom in what Barton says here, but he fails to make a crucial distinction between two different types of truth claim, which leaves him attacking a straw man. For there is a difference between a commitment to the *fact* that the Bible is true, and a commitment to the *way* in which it is true. It is clear by the way the argument unfolds that Barton means the second of these.[33]

Commitment to the fact that the Bible is true

By 'commitment to the fact' I mean a belief about what the Bible *is* – at one and the same time a human book and a divine book. This is a foundational (though not unalterable) commitment, and though others will have different beliefs about what the Bible is, no reader begins the task of criticism without one particular foundational commitment or another. While Barton is surely right to insist that focusing on the Enlightenment as the source of biblical criticism

---

[29] Ibid. 164.
[30] Ibid. 171.
[31] Ibid. 173.
[32] Ibid. 177.
[33] Just once Barton appears clearly to be describing the first type of truth claim, when he speaks in the broadest terms of 'a prior conviction that anything that is in the Bible must be true (in some sense or other)' (172). But this does not serve his argument well, as I shall go on to demonstrate.

ignores the existence of criticism from the patristic period onward,[34] it remains true that it was the Enlightenment that finally changed the object of criticism from (theological) 'Scripture' to (secular) 'Bible'. And with a new set of beliefs about what the Bible is – a cultural artefact through and through, which illuminates an ancient people and their culture(s) as any other ancient book might – comes a new set of foundational truth commitments that are essentially rationalist and 'modern' in nature.[35] In this sense, Barton's strictures on reading the Bible 'as necessarily conforming to what one already believes to be true' apply to his own biblical criticism as much as to anybody else's. Barton does not describe his foundational commitments here (though they may perhaps be inferred), but for many 'neutral' readers they involve the belief that the Bible is true and false in just the same way that other texts are true and false; that the events to which it testifies are as open (or closed) to scrutiny as any other events in history; that the statements made in it are subject to the same rules of evidence and verification as any other statements; and so on.

Commitment to the way the Bible is true

By 'commitment to the way' I mean beliefs not about the *fact* that the Bible is true, but about *how* it is true, about how a specific text gives expression to the general fact of the Bible's truthfulness. And concerning this sense of theological truth – the precise sense Barton accuses 'confessing' readers of abusing – I have no quarrel with him at all, and embrace critical method with as much enthusiasm as he. For the Scriptures I read, though the word of God, remain human texts and must not be read 'flat' simply because they serve as divine address. Theological interpretation is not a matter of listening for the divine voice while ignoring the human words. I therefore accept that reading a text well involves determining what it meant as the product of a certain time and place, working with comparative material inside and outside the Bible to establish the all-important judgment of genre, making diachronic judgments when called for, even struggling against the headwinds of postmodernism towards a recovery of authorial intention. And – a crucial point for this response to Barton – this process can and regularly does yield unexpected

---

[34] Ibid. 9–30.
[35] See Green's remarks on the 'predispositions of modernity' (Green 2000: 29; cf. Vanhoozer 2008b: 18–19).

readings, challenging readings even, that do not necessarily conform to what the reader already believed to be true.[36] Indeed, this is the only way in which theology can be held accountable to the norm of Scripture.

All reading is constrained reading

Having said this, it is of course true that not every reading is permissible. Commitment to the fact of a divine book brings certain constraints into the reading process, just as commitment to the fact of a non-divine book brings its own reading constraints. Of Barton's complaint that 'confessing' readings produce eisegesis because 'Only certain readings are permissible, and what these are can be known in advance,'[37] the same mixed response applies equally to 'confessing' and 'neutral' ways of reading: yes, only certain readings are permissible, but no, although one can know in advance the *types* of reading that will and will not be allowed, one cannot know in advance what a given text will be judged to mean.[38]

Thus – by way of example – there are texts that offer fewer interpretative possibilities for 'confessing' critics. If God identifies himself as the God of the exodus, then the possibility that an exodus did not in fact occur is ruled out at the start.[39] Other texts, however, offer fewer interpretative possibilities for 'neutral' critics. If the Philistines were not yet settled in Canaan, then the possibility that someone prophetically sang 'pangs have seized the inhabitants of Philistia' (Exod. 15:14) is ruled out at the start. Yet in neither of these examples is the actual reading determined: the 'neutral' critic in the first instance might conclude that the best reading involves a historical exodus of some sort, while the 'confessing' critic in the second instance might conclude that the best reading involves Philistia being specified by a later tradent[40] acting as a curator of the text.[41]

In other words, all reading is constrained reading, constrained

---

[36] Barton comes close to conceding this when he points out that 'The most conservative reader still believes that truth is to be *discovered* in the pages of the Bible, not imputed to them' (172, italics original). Against Barton, however, this need not be a sign of inconsistency.

[37] Ibid. 188.

[38] For a warning to confessing readers not to rush into judgment over what constitutes a theologically inadmissible reading, see Gordon (2006: 169–179, esp. 172–173).

[39] Cf. Goldingay 2003: 869.

[40] That is, a scribe or the like acting to preserve and pass on the textual tradition.

[41] Cf. Sailhamer 2002.

by the attitudes the reader brings to what he or she reads.[42] In the case of theological reading, this is the first element of a theological hermeneutic. In particular, the hermeneutic I have advocated is that of biblical theology, and it will be biblical-theological considerations that ultimately provide criteria for choosing the best readings.

Biblical theology in the hermeneutical spiral

We have seen that Barton's argument against 'confessional' reading turns on his judgment that such reading breaches the required separation of understanding and evaluation. If one brings a pre-packaged meaning to the text then one is agreeing with oneself, not the text.

While proper biblical-theological method avoids this solecism, a point of evaluation may well arrive when a 'best choice' needs to be made from among a number of readings arrived at without prior commitment to how they must be true.[43] All readers, whatever they read the Bible as, regularly need to make choices of this kind, and at this point in the reading process their evaluation must needs be guided by some overarching principle of meaningfulness, whether it be the historian's principle of analogy, or the postmodernist's principled suspicion of power. For the biblical-theological interpreter, the ultimate meaning will determine the immediate meaning. This is not a *sensus plenior*, if by that is meant additional new meanings not to be found in the text when it is read on its own terms. Rather, it is the selection of such readings as are meaningful and productive when read not just against the immediate context, but also as a piece of the canon-wide, Christ-shaped story in which all Scripture is caught up, and by which the divine author addresses us now.

The point may be restated thus: a 'confessing' critic uses critical tools, but, like every reader, applies them to an object conceived of

---

[42] A full treatment of this question would need to take matters further. For a start, readers may draw incorrect conclusions about what is and is not permitted within their starting commitments. An example would be 'confessing' readers who insist that, say, Gen. 1 must be a flat empirical account of creation, lest God be made out to be a liar. It should be evident that a different understanding of genre would open out the interpretative possibilities for those readers without altering their commitment to what they are reading. They simply needed to grow more proficient as readers. On the other hand, it is also possible (and not infrequently occurs) that the reading process may bring about a change in a reader's beliefs about what the Bible is.

[43] Admittedly, the existence of a basic assumption that they are true in some sense (perhaps as yet undetermined) will colour the procedure of discovering how they are true, but this is equally the case for a reader with e.g. a materialist assumption, which will colour the discovery procedure in its own way.

in a particular way – in this case, 'Scripture', not 'Bible' – and this subtly alters the process of reading to fit the altered nature of the object. In particular, the three-way interaction of literature, history and theology will be different in the case of 'Scripture' than it is in the case of the 'Bible'. For a 'neutral' reader, historical and literary considerations modify one another recursively. Thus awareness of historical context generates increased genre sensitivity, which in turn makes one better able to assess the text's quality as a historical document.[44] It is even possible for theology to enter the equation, by recognizing that the literature in question is theological literature, and reading it accordingly.[45] For a biblical-theological reader, however, theology cannot be confined to the text, because the God of the Bible is also the God behind the Bible, and the world outside the text is a world whose living and active God is the God revealed in the Bible. The resurrection of Jesus is the most obvious case in point, but the inseparability of theology from history is general. 'Statements about God's acts are not only the *basis* for belief in Yhwh but also constitute the *content* of belief in Yhwh.'[46] This means that a 'scandalous particularity' may perhaps attach to some of the events the Bible records, leaving them closed to investigation by historical method. As Daniel Treier puts it, '"behind" the text advocates face crucial ambiguities regarding whether they focus dogmatically on the divine Author or hermeneutically on the human author(s) in historical

[44] E.g. does the text of Jeremiah code for conflict between postexilic factions (Seitz 1989b)? Are there statements of hope in the book 'that would have been impossible for the person of Jeremiah himself' (Brueggemann 2007: 9)? Are there inconsistencies of theological outlook from verse to verse that betray layers of successive redaction (Schmid 1996: 43–45 and *passim*)? The answers to these questions depend to a large extent on how well the reader judges the book of Jeremiah to hold together as a piece of coherent writing.

[45] Cf. Westermann 1985, who demonstrates that the OT's 'comprehensive understanding of history as a totality' (218) is fundamentally at odds with the Enlightenment idea of history that must be documented and follow 'a verifiable course governed by causal laws' (207).

[46] Goldingay 2003: 869, italics original. For this reason, biblical-theological interpretation needs to resist the temptation to follow the 'cultural-linguistic turn' pioneered by Hans Frei and George Lindbeck, in which the Bible is read as a theological book, but the God of the text remains in the text (Frei 1974; Lindbeck 1984; cf. Vanhoozer 2005: 3–12). Such readers resist 'any venture outside or behind the text, either to critical possibility or to metaphysical essence. Yahweh is a player in the life of Israel, only as long as Yahweh is "played" in the drama of Israel' (Brueggemann 1997: 70). While reading as a Christian (p. 1, n. 1), Brueggemann chooses 'to exposit the theological perspectives and claims of the text itself, in all its odd particularity, without any attempt to accommodate to a larger rationality, either of modernity or of classical Christianity' (86).

context(s)'.[47] This does not mean that in every case of doubt we offer a piece of divine special pleading and ignore any counter-testimony from other sources. Rather, it means that more readings are available to the 'confessing' critic to help her or him read better.

Whether or not this is superior to Barton's 'neutral' criticism, it is certainly closer to the sort of criticism the Bible itself expects its readers to perform. For in a variety of ways Scripture makes claims about itself that only 'confessional' readings can honour. To read the Bible as divine address does not mean ignoring its rootedness in human language and culture, but it does mean that these human texts are read in a particular way, and with a particular attitude of humble listening, that suggests that the best readings of Scripture will not only be confessional but will take place in confessional contexts, and in prayer and by the illumination of the Holy Spirit.[48]

Can theology made from retold narrative still be called theology?

Having considered what it looks like to read Jeremiah as Scripture, we must return to explore the implications for theological interpretation of the fact that the literature in question is narrative.

As with the Bible as a whole, narrative is not the only literary form in Jeremiah, and every form within its pages is richly generative of theological reflection. But while narrative must not be privileged as a source for theology, it does form the framework by which Jeremiah holds its diversity of theological material together.[49] For Paul Ricœur, 'laws, prophecies, wisdom sayings, and hymns, by contributing to the full *meaningfulness* of biblical narratives, start the transfer from mere storytelling to the grasping of the enduring significance of the stories themselves'.[50] However, Ricœur is not sure how we recognize a 'principle of meaningfulness', or that we have figured out how to derive the 'regulative concepts' that would

---

[47] Treier 2010: 148.

[48] Webb 1997: 68–73. On theological interpretation of Jeremiah see Job (2006: 201), Osuji (2010: 75–85) and especially Polk (1984: 174), who argues that 'the transformed life of a competent reader becomes a guide to interpretation'.

[49] As Ricœur (1995: 197) points out, 'the teaching of these narratives, their truth for us today, requires the mediation of all the other literary genres and all the other acts of discourse interweaving through the canonical texts. This is why the project of a merely narrative theology is a chimera.' Cf. Vanhoozer 2005: 29; R. B. Hays 2008.

[50] Ricœur 1995: 246, italics original.

determine the confessional statements necessary to theology.[51] In Jeremiah we shall see that the narrative framework generally functions to give meaning to the non-narrative material contained within it, so that meaningfulness is reinforced by the consonance of narrative and non-narrative material.

However, this still begs the question of how one draws theology from narrative. Goldingay's words would be echoed by many: 'There is no method for doing this . . . It requires a more-or-less inspired guess as to what the theological freight of the narrative might be.'[52] Whatever this looks like – and it should reflect both the historically determined literary shape of the text, as well as its canonically determined theological context – the larger narrative should not simply provide the context for establishing what the 'theological' verses are saying; it must be recognized as the vehicle of the text's theology in and of itself.

A theological protagonist

What is the shape of Jeremiah's story? And what is the organizing principle of a book that most conclude defies reading?[53] I shall argue that 'the word of the LORD' is the book's protagonist. This is not God himself but a divine attribute and self-communication. In this sense it is accurate to call Jeremiah a narrative about a theological idea.[54] We might describe it as the story of what happened when the word of the LORD came to Jeremiah.

This is not yet theology. How may we move from a theological story to theology itself? How can we provide an orderly account of the book's word theology without sanitizing it to the point of unrecognizability? N. T. Wright imagines the biblical story as a play to which the theologian appends a final act, an act whose successful 'making sense of' the previous text authenticates it.[55] Kevin Vanhoozer writes of cultivating 'the mind of the canon', which is done 'not by systematizing Scripture's concepts, nor by extracting

---

[51] Ibid. 246–248.

[52] Goldingay 2000: 127.

[53] 'The book of Jeremiah is indeed unreadable unless one can allow for the plurality of voices that are shrill, disjunctive, and in conflict with one another, for that is what is given us in the book' (Brueggemann 2006: 86).

[54] Of course God himself in the story is a theological idea, a textual representation of an extra-textual reality, but I use the term 'theological idea' in a narrower sense when I attach it to the word of God, to mark it as an abstraction, or an action, over against the person of God.

[55] Wright 1992: 141.

(i.e. decontextualizing) principles, but rather by discerning and continuing a pattern of judgment rendered in a variety of linguistic, literary, and conceptual forms'.[56]

In the case of Jeremiah, however, we are able to map the book's word theology onto the narrative far more directly than is usually possible. Jeremiah has presented us with a protagonist, the word of the LORD, and our first task, *at once literary and theological,* is to perform a character study of this protagonist. Who or what *is* the word of the LORD? Verbal sentences immediately take us forward.[57] The word of the LORD comes to Jeremiah. Jeremiah speaks the word of the LORD. The word of the LORD is heard (or not heard). The word of the LORD tears down. The word of the LORD builds up. Because 'the word of the LORD' is an idea as well as a character, we can think of it as a theme – the theme – of Jeremiah, developed in the form of these thematic sentences.

In what follows I shall attempt to read Jeremiah as an authoritative story whose many and varied elements advance the progress of the word of the LORD in their own way and, by so doing, yield a portrait of God that no simpler collocation of elements could do justice to. From this retelling, arguably the first form theological discourse ought to take,[58] we immediately see that general truths about words and the way they work are being instantiated. Words are first thought of, then spoken, then heard, then acted upon. The question of Jeremiah's word theology will therefore be, what does each of these situations look like when the words in question are God's words?

From theology to doctrine

A 'doctrine', in Watson's words, is 'a communally acknowledged norm, classically defined at some point in the past in a form that continues to shape the present. . . . In contrast, a theology is an

---

[56] In Marshall 2004: 93; cf. Vanhoozer 2005: 16–33; O'Collins and Kendall 1997. For examples of theological readings of narrative see the essays on Exodus in Fowl 1997.

[57] Cf. Goldingay 2003: 32.

[58] 'But it would be fatal to our understanding of Israel's witness if we were to arrange it from the outset on the basis of theological categories which, though current among ourselves, have absolutely nothing to do with those on whose basis Israel herself allowed her theological thinking to be ordered. Thus, re-telling remains the most legitimate form of theological discourse on the Old Testament' (Von Rad 1965: 121).

individual proposal for the future development of doctrine.'[59] To speak of *Jeremiah's doctrine*, rather than simply his theology, points in the first instance to the community within which his book was preserved, the people of God in exile to whom God was present in word alone. Perhaps it is anachronistic to speak of doctrine in that connection; we cannot be certain. In the context of the Christian canon, to speak of *doctrine in Jeremiah* suggests that its theology of the word of God, though pre-Christian, gives expression in a singular way to the doctrine normed by the apostolic discourse.[60] It may not contain all the ingredients of a fully fledged doctrine of the Word of God, but it is nevertheless that same fully fledged doctrine to which Jeremiah contributes. My main interest in this volume is *doctrine from Jeremiah*, brought as a distinctive voice to the church's conversation about the doctrine of the word of God.

Some years ago the philosopher Nicholas Wolterstorff could observe that talk about 'the Word of God' had fallen out of fashion among theologians, and that the idea of divine speech had instead either been equated with, or subsumed under, the idea of divine revelation.[61] My chosen conversation partner, Karl Barth, is the theologian of the Word of God par excellence in the modern era, and his influence has only waxed stronger since Wolterstorff wrote his book.[62] My modest goal is to suggest some ways in which a doctrine of the word of God from the book of Jeremiah can contribute to ongoing conversations between biblical studies and dogmatic theology on the subject.

So much for questions of introduction and method. One ought to be conscious of such questions, but in themselves they do not advance the quest for biblical-theological exegesis. It is time to take up R. W. L. Moberly's challenge: 'There tends to be more discussion about the nature of theological interpretation and theological hermeneutics than there is demonstration in persuasive and memorable readings of the biblical text.'[63] I hope to keep readings of the text at least as prominent as talk about those readings, and so trust that readers will, if nothing else, find themselves enriched through exposure to the words and word of God.

[59] Watson 2010: 122–123; cf. McGrath 1990: 12.
[60] Vanhoozer 2008a.
[61] Wolterstorff 1995: 9–10.
[62] E.g. Childs 1992; Brueggemann 1997; Morrison 2006. See further the survey in Treier (2008: 14–20).
[63] Moberly 2009: 169.

Chapter One

Word and words in Jeremiah

What makes Jeremiah, of all books, so well suited to being read for its theology of the word of God? If we can answer this question we shall have cleared the ground and shall be ready to begin the theological reading I have proposed. The next task will then be to begin that reading by getting the lie of the land, as it were, both thematically (in this chapter) and structurally (in the next chapter). This will mean examining the rather sophisticated way in which Jeremiah speaks about the word of the LORD.[1] And it will mean sketching out the structure and flow of thought of the book of Jeremiah when conceived of as a narrative about the word of God.

The suitability of Jeremiah as a source for word theology

The book's heading

Jeremiah's distinctive theology of the word of God – its 'word theology', in shorthand – begins to show itself in the book's opening verses, where we find two subjects introduced: the words of Jeremiah (v. 1) and the word of the LORD (v. 2). The way these two subjects are related to one another is important, and deserves careful examination:

> The words of Jeremiah son of Hilkiah, one of the priests living in Anathoth in the territory of Benjamin, being the word of the LORD that came to him ['ăšer hāyâ děbar-yhwh 'ēlâw] in

---

[1] On the use of names: (1) the ambiguity attached to the word 'Jeremiah' – the person, or his book – is not one I always wish to resolve. The book links the two so closely together, as we shall see, that I often choose to follow its lead. When necessary, 'the prophet' or 'the book' will be added for clarification. (2) Throughout this book I follow the convention of indicating the divine name, *yhwh*, by the capitalized 'LORD'.

the thirteenth year of the reign of Josiah son of Amon, king of Judah.

The opening of verse 2 contains some unusual syntax, and in the four other places in Jeremiah where this atypical expression is found (Jer. 14:1; 46:1; 47:1; 49:34), it clearly functions as a new sentence, as in the TNIV/NIV: 'The word of the LORD came to him'. But here in Jeremiah 1:2 it is in the wrong place to be a new sentence, because the relative particle *'ăšer* does not act as an absolute beginning (as it does in 14:1), but rather subordinates what follows to verse 1. As a result, versions like the ESV/RSV have made it a relative clause: 'to whom the word of the LORD came'. However, this solution also has its problems, as it wrongly makes Jeremiah the focus of the verse. The referent of the relative particle *'ăšer* is not Jeremiah, but the words of Jeremiah, as the Septuagint version suggests.[2]

In my judgment verse 2 is not an opening after the atypical pattern of Jeremiah 14:1, but rather follows the pattern of one of the most common headings used throughout the book, such as at Jeremiah 1:4: 'the word of the LORD came to me' (*wayĕhî dĕbar-yhwh*). It has lost its normal shape, however, because it has been attached to another heading in verse 1, giving the book a double title. In other words, two titles have been joined into one, and the second title has been altered so as to prevent it from being read as a second and subsequent statement. These are two different ways of saying the same thing.

We may conclude that the double title of the book is making a close identification between two things: the words of Jeremiah, and the word of God that came to him.[3] At one level this is not a difficult

---

[2] By choosing the nominative particle *hos* to represent *'ăšer* at the start of v. 2 the translator has made the most obvious antecedent, Jeremiah, an impossible choice ('who became the word of God to him'). The less immediate antecedent, namely, the subject of v. 1, is the only viable reading, despite the gender mismatch. As it happens the subject of v. 1 in the LXX is not the words of Jeremiah but the word of God (*to rhēma tou theou*), and the result reads as follows: 'The word of God which came to Jeremiah ... which was the word of God to him in the days of Josiah ...' The other possible antecedent is found later in v. 2: 'a word of God which came to him' (so *NETS*) – still not Jeremiah.

[3] For A. J. O. van der Wal the inclusion 'words of Jeremiah' in 1:1 and 51:64 must be rendered 'history of Jeremiah' since the intervening material contains deeds as well as words (Wal 2004: 17; cf. Rudolph 1967: 2). However, the category of words arches over both in a manner that is both hermeneutically and theologically significant. Hermeneutically, it shows us that the deeds must be interpreted by the words that surround them, and theologically it is the word of God rather than his mighty acts

idea, and a phrase such as 'Hearing the Word of God in the words of Isaiah' can be used with no further qualification.[4] And yet, Jeremiah challenges us to take a closer look. What precisely does it mean to identify the words, plural, of Jeremiah with the word, singular, of God? Does this restrict the word of God in this book to the words of Jeremiah, so that only those things Jeremiah said count as the word of God? On the contrary, the sense is quite different: verse 1 implies that every word in the book that follows is one of the words of Jeremiah, whether Jeremiah is reported as having said it or not. This implication is borne out by the addition in the Masoretic version of an inclusio to bind together the material between Jeremiah 1:1 ('The words of Jeremiah') and Jeremiah 51:64 ('The words of Jeremiah end here'). This clearly demarcates the limits of the words of Jeremiah, embracing the entire book except for its final chapter, a version of 2 Kings 25.[5]

'The word of the LORD' in verse 2, as we shall see, means the message from God, and so we are being told that Jeremiah's words – that is, the words contained in the book of Jeremiah – make up this message. But how closely is this message tied to the words of Jeremiah? Was Jeremiah free to express the message he received from God in any words he liked, or is there an exact form of words that count as the word of God? Most of us read Jeremiah in translation, and in replacing Jeremiah's words with English equivalents inevitably something of the original meaning will be lost or altered. For Muslims this would be unacceptable, and the Qur'an cannot be translated. But for Christians the Bible is translatable. So what is it about Jeremiah's words that make them count as the word of God? Is it their divine origin? Is it their particular content? Is it the person who says them?

Whatever the answers to these questions – and we shall return to them – Jeremiah unmistakeably draws our attention to the theology of the word of God at the very outset.

---

that is singled out in Jeremiah as the universal and irresistible force for destruction and reconstruction. John Job believes the phrase originally meant 'the sayings of Jeremiah' (Job 2006: 172; cf. McKane 1986: 2); while this fits the range of meaning for the word as used in Jeremiah it clearly no longer carries this meaning here, if it ever did.

[4] Goldingay 1995: 189.

[5] Some commentators, following Duhm (1901: 2), restrict the scope of 'the words of Jeremiah' to chapters 1–25, since the bulk of Jer. 26ff. is not spoken by Jeremiah but refers to him in the third person. The fact of the inclusio should exclude such an interpretation.

The prevalence of the word of God in the book of Jeremiah

Jeremiah abounds in 'word of the LORD' language, more so than in any other book. This abundance takes three main forms: a general affinity for word vocabulary, the prominent use of markers of direct speech, and a frequent emphasizing of divine speech.

First, the vocabulary of word and words is used more liberally in Jeremiah than in any other major Old Testament book.[6] In the rest of the Old Testament we can identify a second tier of word-heavy writings consisting of Deuteronomy – which is a major source for Jeremiah's language and theology – and books with significant Deuteronomic influence.[7]

Secondly, Jeremiah is replete with formulas that mark and give formal structure to direct speech, mostly the speech of God. The three most important formulas are used to introduce poetic oracles, narrative episodes and major book divisions respectively. The first of these formulas is usually labelled the Messenger Formula; the latter two are variously labelled, but because I shall be referring to them often I have given them informal labels: the Narrative Formula and the Disjunctive Heading, respectively.

• The most well known of these formulas is the phrase 'Thus says the LORD'. Its label, the Messenger Formula, is somewhat misleading since it is not always used by messengers; it is a simple formula to mark a citation of another's words.[8] It is used to introduce prophetic oracles, in both poetry and prose, as well as the

---

[6] The Accordance software programme (Accordance 2008) reveals that Kings is the only major book that comes close to Jeremiah's frequency of word language; Haggai, Jonah and Esther exceed Jeremiah's use of the singular 'word'. Of the rest of the OT, only Samuel–Kings, Deuteronomy and Ezekiel achieve even half the frequency of Jeremiah. The plural noun 'words' is even more peculiar to Jeremiah and Kings, with Deuteronomy the only other major book with even close to the frequency of usage. Surprisingly, even with the verbal form *dbr* the same books feature, though this time the rest of the Pentateuch comes into play. Finally, when compared with Isaiah, *dbr* in the singular occurs thrice as often in Jeremiah, and *dbr* in the plural, five times as often. If we combine the verbs of speech *dbr*, *ngd*, *nb'* and *'mr* (excluding the *wayyiqtol* forms) Jeremiah's prominence becomes even greater.

[7] However, if Jeremiah's love for the language of word and words reflects a debt to Deuteronomy (cf. Lundbom 1999: 110–114), Jeremiah has nevertheless made the vocabulary his own, and its significance within the book must be assessed on its own terms, notwithstanding any assistance the Deuteronomic context may provide (cf. Meier 1992: 141–161).

[8] As demonstrated by Meier (1992: 277–298).

interpretation of symbolic actions. It is quite strikingly abundant, being found 155 times in Jeremiah, which is more often than the rest of the Old Testament books combined.[9]

- The principal Narrative Formula is the phrase 'The word of the LORD came to Jeremiah, saying' or, if Jeremiah is the speaker, 'The word of the LORD came to me, saying'.[10] This phrase is used to introduce new episodes within the main storyline of the narrative,[11] and it occurs some 23 times in Jeremiah. Ezekiel uses it twice as often, but it occurs almost nowhere else in the Old Testament.
- Perhaps the most important of these formulas is 'the word that came to Jeremiah from the LORD'; I shall call this the Disjunctive Heading.[12] It is not a sentence proper but a heading that stands over a divine word or a narrative leading up to a divine word. It is completely unique to Jeremiah, and marks a major break, or disjunction, in the narrative. Its function is to link the material it introduces into the overarching narrative framework of the book.[13]

We shall return to these formulas, especially the Disjunctive Headings, in our next chapter, because they have been used to structure the final form of the book. As Mark Biddle has argued, they 'subsume entire discourses under the heading of YHWH speech' and ultimately convert what were once oracles, sermons and narratives addressed to a range of audiences into a single written message from the LORD.[14]

Thirdly, the expression usually translated 'declares the LORD', or 'oracle of the LORD' (*ně'um yhwh*) deserves separate mention. It has no structuring significance, but simply adds emphasis to a divine word. And once again it is strikingly preponderant in Jeremiah:

---

[9] This formula often goes by its German name *Botenformel*. It occurs 74 times in the rest of the Latter Prophets. For a fuller description of the way it functions, see Shead (2002b: 42–44).

[10] This formula is variously labelled the *Wortempfangsformel* (word reception formula) after Reventlow 1961, or *Wortereignisformel* (word occurrence formula), after Zimmerli (1969: 89). It is sometimes abbreviated WEF.

[11] All cases are followed by 'saying', except 42:7, where the following narrative clause makes it inappropriate (Shead 2002b: 31, n. 23).

[12] This formula is labelled the *Wortgeschehensformel* (word event formula) after Neumann 1973. It is sometimes abbreviated WGF, and is widely held to indicate the redactional unity of the following material (Seidl 1979).

[13] There are minor variations in the form of both this formula and the preceding one, and some of them show variations and mixed features. For a full analysis see Shead (2002b: 26, 31, 45–53).

[14] Biddle 1996: 121–122.

with 167 uses Jeremiah accounts for over 60% of all cases of this expression in the Bible.[15] There is another reason for noting this third feature of the book's word language, and that is the fact that many of the structural formulas mentioned above are associated with a later stage in the composition of the book; they are more frequent in the MT edition than in the earlier edition which underlies the Septuagint (the LXXV); and their Deuteronomic flavour is pronounced. It might be possible to conclude from this that Jeremiah's word theology was a late development, not native to the prophet's thought. However, the prominence of the expression 'declares the LORD' in every level and stage of the book suggests that this is not the case. We might say that the book's interest in the word of God grew along with the book itself, but this growth was nothing more than the continuation of an interest central to the book from the beginning. This point will become increasingly clear as we examine more of the book in later chapters.

Let me summarize this welter of statistics. The book of Jeremiah, even more so than its spiritual parent Deuteronomy, is rich in the language of word and words. And when it comes to expressions referring to the speech of God, Jeremiah is unparalleled in the richness and diversity of its language. What is more, this language is not randomly scattered throughout, but serves two main functions. It provides a structure within which the poems, sermons and narratives are contained, and it throws a spotlight on the direct speech of God. A survey like this actually underestimates the prominence given to divine speech in the book, for as we shall see in chapter 3, the oracles spoken by Jeremiah are generally reshaped in their written form to eliminate human speakers from the narrative as much as possible. In short, Jeremiah is arguably the book above all others in the Old Testament that lends itself to systematic reflection on the word of God. And while a complete doctrine of the word of God obviously needs to draw upon all of Scripture, what we have in Jeremiah is an unusually complete expression of an individual's theology of the word of God.[16]

---

[15] Other instances: Isaiah uses it 21 times, Ezekiel only 4 times – in contrast to moderately full usage by Ezekiel of other formulas. Amos, Haggai and Zechariah are the only other heavy users, as they and they alone also are for the formula 'thus says the LORD'.

[16] This reflects the conclusion of Ulrich Mauser (Mauser 1971: 83) that in Jeremiah we find reflections on the meaning of the LORD's speaking that come to us with such intensity and scope that one may speak of a Jeremianic theology of the word of God.

Having established the general importance of language referring to the word of God in Jeremiah, we must move to a closer examination of the way this language is used. The question of what precisely it means to identify the words, plural, of Jeremiah with the word, singular, of God, lies before us still. First, however, the pressing question of *which* words we are discussing must be addressed.

Which words? The history of writing and rewriting in Jeremiah

One of the most valuable features of the book of Jeremiah is its extensive descriptions of the writing down of the prophet's words. And as far as we can tell, writing and rewriting characterized the growing book of Jeremiah from the beginning, not stopping until the final form of the book was fixed within the Jewish canon. The textual history of this book is complex, and there are gaps in our knowledge, but it is an important starting point for anybody interested in Jeremiah's word theology.

As with so many features of the book we may discern Deuteronomy in the background, whose first command to write (Deut. 6:9) stipulates doorposts rather than papyrus or leather. But by Deuteronomy 31 Moses has written down 'all the words of this law' and charged that they be read aloud in public every seven years during the Feast of Booths. In this way Moses will die but his words live on. Some scholars, notably William Holladay, believe that the septennial reading of Deuteronomy marked significant events in Jeremiah's career and perhaps prompted some of his own sermons.[17] Be that as it may, the Deuteronomic concern with writing and reading pervades the book of Jeremiah, and we shall explore it systematically in chapter 6. The aim of the present section is simply to provide a sketch of the way the book grew into its present shape, and to indicate some of the theological implications that follow.[18]

The book of Jeremiah is made up of prophetic oracles, sermons and biographical material.[19] The oracles and sermons were originally spoken by the prophet Jeremiah during the course of a long ministry lasting around forty years (627–586 BC or shortly after).

---

[17] Holladay 1985: 326–328.

[18] I have laid the foundations for my view of Jeremiah's literary and textual history elsewhere (Shead 2002b), and in its basic outline it reflects the work of many – though by no means all – contemporary Jeremiah scholars (e.g. Brueggemann 2007; Goldman 1992; Lundbom 1986, 1999; McConville 1993b; Stulman 1998; Tov 1998, 2001).

[19] Mowinckel 1914.

The biographical material was most probably written by Baruch, Jeremiah's scribe, perhaps in collaboration with other scribes (Baruch's brother Seraiah is mentioned in Jer. 51:59), and it is reasonable to assume that Baruch was also responsible for writing down and collecting Jeremiah's oracles and sermons as they were delivered over the years (Jer. 36:1–4; 43:6; 45:1).

There are several direct indications within the book of the contemporaneous writing down of the prophet's words, in distinct collections or 'scrolls':

> This is what the LORD, the God of Israel, says: 'Write for yourself all the words I have spoken to you on a scroll.' (Jer. 30:2)

> Jeremiah wrote about all the evil that would come to Babylon, on one scroll – all these words written against Babylon. (Jer. 51:60)

> 'I will bring upon that land all my words I spoke against it, all that is written on this scroll, which Jeremiah prophesied against all the nations.' (Jer. 25:13)

In addition there are blocks of material that show signs of having been written at different times or by different people. To give one example, in Jeremiah 27 – 29 the names 'Jeremiah' and 'Nebuchadnezzar' are spelled differently from the way they are spelled in the rest of the book.[20]

In other words, it is clear that the book of Jeremiah has been constructed out of a collection of smaller documents. And in chapter 36 we are given concrete evidence of a *growing* collection. After Jehoiakim destroyed a scroll of Jeremiah's prophecies, God commanded Jeremiah to write the scroll again. The new scroll is not a mere copy of the first, but an expansion:

> Then Jeremiah took another scroll and he gave it to Baruch, son of Neriah, the scribe, and as Jeremiah dictated he wrote on it all the words of the scroll that Jehoiakim king of Judah

---

[20] Martin Kessler suggests one or two words that seem to be favoured by Jer. 37 – 39, and judges the term 'remnant' (*š'ryt*) to be favoured by Jer. 40 – 44 (Kessler 1968: 84).

had burned in the fire. And in addition many similar words were added to them. (Jer. 36:32)

The contents of this scroll probably covered much of the material in Jeremiah 1 – 25, as well as perhaps 46 – 51.[21] This process of rewriting and expanding continued until the end of Jeremiah's life, and perhaps beyond. There are large gaps in our knowledge at this point, but what we do have is documentary evidence of more than one surviving edition of the book of Jeremiah, preserved both in ancient translations and in scroll fragments recovered from the Judean desert during the last century. From this evidence the following reconstruction can be made. After Jeremiah went with Baruch to Egypt (Jer. 43:4–7) an edition of the book of Jeremiah was produced for local circulation, assembled and carefully edited from the written records Baruch had been collecting over the years. This edition was preserved and transmitted, and eventually became the source of the Greek translation of Jeremiah known as the Septuagint. It remains the canonical version of the book in the Eastern Church to this day. This Egyptian edition of Jeremiah is therefore referred to as the LXX *Vorlage*; some fragments of a version very close to it have been found at Qumran, dating to the third century bc.[22]

This was not the final version of the book, however. A new, revised and expanded edition – about one seventh longer than the LXXv – was created from the same source materials (plus one or two new sources, such as Jer. 33:14–26). The name of Seraiah, Baruch's brother, has been linked to this edition by some scholars.[23] Its intended audience seems not to have been the local Egyptian community, but the exilic community in Babylon.[24] After the Babylonian exiles returned and the biblical canon began to take final shape, it was this edition of Jeremiah that was included in the Prophets, and that eventually became part of the Masoretic Hebrew text (MT) that forms the basis of every English Bible version in common use today. Because of its eventual incorporation into the MT, we give this final edition of the book of Jeremiah the label 'M' or – because M does not exist any more and MT is accepted as basically the same text – 'MT'. This text, like the LXXv, survives in fragments from Qumran.[25]

[21] Cf. Holladay 1989: 16–19.
[22] Ulrich et al. 1997: 145–208.
[23] Lundbom 1986: 108.
[24] Shead 2002b; Stulman 1986: 143.
[25] The suggestion that the final version of Jeremiah can be placed within the

It is important to recognize that the differences between the final edition (M) and its predecessor (LXXV) are not random, but the result of careful shaping and editing.[26] Most strikingly, the 'Oracles Against the Nations' (OAN), which occupy Jeremiah 25:14 – 31:44 in the LXX, were shifted to the end, to become Jeremiah MT 46 – 51, and they were internally rearranged to place the Egypt oracle at the beginning of the collection, and the Babylon oracle at the end. The movement from Egypt to Babylon that was created by this revision is reflected in many small additions in MT Jeremiah, such as the expansion of personal names, that serve to bring Babylon and its king into greater prominence as the place where God's plans for the future are centred.[27] As Louis Stulman concluded in his study of the extra M material added to the sermons of Jeremiah, 'it accentuates the role of Babylon and its king in the divine programme and favors the exiles in Babylon over against Zedekiah and those with him in Jerusalem'.[28]

Not only is MT Jeremiah more interested in Babylon, its king and the exiles living there, but it is also concerned to tighten the structure of the book. This is seen both in structural additions made within units,[29] as well as in the way multiple units are held together within a book-wide structure.[30] A striking example of this is the book-wide

exilic period is not popular among scholars. The process of literary development is thought by many to have required much more time to reach completion. Some scholars suggest the postexilic period (Janzen 1973; Tov 1985: 236–237); for others, the book was complete only by the third (Schmid 1996) or even second (Piovanelli 1997) centuries. Three types of reason underlie these judgments. The first is textual: the differences between MT and LXXV could not have emerged over just a few decades. However, internal textual grounds for positing a long separation between MT and LXXV are more slender than is often thought (Shead 2002b: 260). The second is the provenance of texts on which Jeremiah draws, especially Deuteronomy: if they are late (exilic and beyond) then Jeremiah must be later. For contrasting views see Tov (1985: 215); McConville 1991, 1993a. The third is internal to Jeremiah: where its message is judged contradictory or incoherent, multiple authors across centuries make for a good explanation (Schmid 1996; McKane 1986).

[26] A number of scholars would argue that differences between the Greek and Hebrew texts of Jeremiah are the result of piecemeal scribal additions (Janzen 1973; Stipp 1994; McKane 1986) rather than intentional literary editing. But the evident purposefulness of the MT additions has caused the consensus to shift towards the latter view (Bogaert 1981a; Gosse 1986; Shead 2002b; Stulman 1984; Tov 1985).

[27] E.g. the name Nebuchadnezzar appears thirty-six times, compared to fourteen in the Greek edition.

[28] Stulman 1986: 143.

[29] Biddle 1996: 121; Shead 2002b: 246–247.

[30] To borrow the example of Jer. 8 – 9 from Biddle 1996: 121, MT and LXXV agree in marking divine speech at Jer. 8:4, 13; 9:6, 8, 11, 14, 16, 19, 22, 24; but MT adds markers at 'key points': Jer. 8:17; 9:2, 5, 21. The general development of structural markers in

inclusio unique to Jeremiah MT, which was referred to earlier in this chapter. In the LXXv the book's opening verse began with the conventional title 'the word of God which came to Jeremiah'. In the MT, however, the conventional title is replaced by the phrase 'the words of Jeremiah', the same phrase that has been added to the last verse of MT Jeremiah 51 (see table 1.1 below).

What is the relevance of this literary and textual history for the present study? First, it validates an exegetical method that treats the book as carefully composed, in spite of what can often appear to be a rather chaotic jumble of material. We may expect the book to be going somewhere as a narrative, and conveying a message to its readers. Secondly, as will be seen below, the changes made in MT Jeremiah over against LXXv suggest that the word formulas used by the author to introduce new units should be the starting point in our efforts to delineate its overall shape and purpose.

Thirdly, and more pertinent to the narrower question of Jeremiah's word theology, *which* words of Jeremiah should we treat as the word of God? Which Church has the true Jeremiah, the East or the West? At one level, of course, the answer must be both of them; Jews and Christians in the New Testament period and before do not seem to have been troubled by this question, and their attitude seems to have been to accept as Scripture whatever version they had to hand, or whatever version best lent itself to their purpose in citing it.[31] If we follow the example of the New Testament authors, we ought to be happy to receive and read the Greek version of Jeremiah as the word of God. Yet at the same time I would suggest that the Masoretic version has a special place as Jeremiah's words *to us*. Not only was it his last and final version, but its target audience, the exilic community in Babylon, was in Jeremiah's eyes the one group of people with a future in the divine plan of salvation. The seeds of the church were planted in Babylonian soil.[32]

MT over against the LXXv is a further piece of evidence for the priority of the latter, since the difference is quantitative, not qualitative.

[31] Cf. Gordon 2006: 176.

[32] From these brief remarks a vast field of discussion opens up, around questions of text (e.g. Tov 1985), canon (e.g. Flint 2001), the use of the OT in the NT (e.g. Silva 1993), authority (e.g. J. D. Hays 2004), etc. More work needs to be done in pursuing the implications of the two recensions of Jeremiah for a doctrine of Scripture. Daniel Hays (2004), for example, while reflecting helpfully on possible implications of the editions of Jeremiah for a doctrine of inspiration, limits himself by trying to accommodate the data within a general theory of inspired original autographs. It would be better to let the facts modify the theory, and my suggestion that we take into account

Finally, if the inclusio of Jeremiah 1:1 and 51:64 is allowed to have its full force, the words of Jeremiah must be seen to encompass not only the oracles given him directly by God, but also the stories about his life that were, at best, written under his supervision. Moreover, even the oracles are not only words put by God into the prophet's mouth (Jer. 1:9), but also words carefully shaped and reshaped to convey a total message. The word of God with which these words are identified is, ultimately, the final message of the book as a whole.

Table 1.1 References to the written book surrounding Jeremiah MT

Jeremiah LXX*		Jeremiah MT	
1:1–2	The *dictum of God* (*to rhēma tou theou*) which came to Ieremias the son of Chelkias of the priests, who was living in Anathoth in the land of Beniamin; which *word of God* (*logos tou theou*) came to him in the days of king Iosias son of Amos of Iouda, in the thirteenth year of his reign.	1:1–2	The *words of Jeremiah*, the son of Hilkiah, one of the priests living in Anathoth in the territory of Benjamin, being *the word of the* LORD that came to him in the thirteenth year of the reign of Josiah son of Amon, king of Judah.
51:64	[lacking in LXX]	51:64	Here end *the words of Jeremiah*.

* The translation is taken, with a minor revision, from *NETS*.

The textual history of Jeremiah gives us an almost unique insight into the care with which large narratives were shaped by the biblical authors, and provides strong supporting evidence for my suggestion that the book is intentionally presented to us as a narrative about the word of God.

The distinctive shape of Jeremiah's word theology

The meaning of 'word' in Jeremiah

The opening sentence of the book identified the words of Jeremiah with the word of the LORD. A cursory reading of the book suggests that the singular *word* of the LORD is a message made up of constituent *words*, which are identified with Jeremiah in Jeremiah 1:1. In English the word 'word' can have a wide range of meanings. In common use we might say its basic meaning is a piece of vocabulary, a group of

the recipients of a text is relevant here. Nevertheless, my aim at this stage is simply to justify the choice of Jeremiah MT as the source for my theological interpretation; the discussion of words and word in the next section will begin to provide a framework for theological reflection on the textual history of the book.

letters between two spaces. Linguists would not agree that these are the smallest units of speech, and like atomic physicists they like to 'split the word' into its morphemes and so forth. In everyday usage 'word' can also mean a larger unit of speech: 'Could I have a word with you?' 'She sent word that she would be late.' 'He kept his word.'

The Hebrew word *dābār* is similarly flexible,[33] and when it is definite – 'the word', 'this word' – it refers in Jeremiah to a word about something, a message. This sense, which we might call the 'whole' sense of the word *dābār*, is the normal meaning of 'the word' in Jeremiah:

You shall speak this word to them:

'Let my eyes overflow with tears,
night and day may they not cease,
for with a great blow is shattered
the virgin daughter of my people –
a wound most grievous.'

(Jer. 14:17)

While *dābār*, when singular, usually means a 'whole' message, it can also have a 'partial' meaning. Once or twice it is used to denote a single 'word' in the sense of normal English usage:

So Jeremiah the prophet said to them, 'I have heard. I am about to pray to the LORD your God according to your words, and it will happen that every word [sg.] the LORD answers you I will declare to you; I will not withhold a word [sg.] from you.' (Jer. 42:4)

More often, however, its 'partial' sense denotes what we might think of as a word cluster, or clause. In the following example the 'word' in question would be equivalent to a short sentence in English: 'Speak this word to them: Thus says the LORD, the God of Israel: "Every jar shall be filled with wine"' (Jer. 13:12a). One further 'partial' sense of *dābār* is worth mentioning, namely, an individual law from a legal code.[34] When more than one law is referred to, the plural 'words' is used:

[33] This breadth of meaning applies to the term across the OT (Schmidt 1978: 103).
[34] Cf. Schmidt 1978: 116.

> I did not speak with them or command them . . . concerning
> words [pl.] of burnt offering and sacrifice. However, this word
> [sg.] I did command them: 'Obey my voice, and I will be your
> God, and you will be my people.' (Jer. 7:22–23)

In the case of the plural, 'words' or 'these words', Jeremiah refers either to the individual words of which a message is made up, or perhaps to the smaller parts into which a larger message divides.[35]

The meaning of *dābār* alone does not resolve the relationship between Jeremiah's words and the LORD's word. We are no closer, for example, to discovering whether Jeremiah freely expressed God's word in his own words, or whether the word of God was made up of the precise words given to the prophet by God. We need to move from meaning to consider usage. The way Jeremiah uses the vocabulary of word and words is quite distinctive, especially when it comes to the choice of singular versus plural forms. Indeed, it will prove foundational for our understanding of the book's word theology.

The usage of 'word' in Jeremiah

Before embarking on an analysis of word language in Jeremiah, two preliminary comments are in order. First, it should be remembered that Jeremiah's words were ordinary human ones. The notion that human language can be an adequate vehicle for the divine word is a bone of contention among theologians, and yet the remarkable implication of the book's opening paragraph is that the inescapable imprecision of human language does not prevent it from conveying the word of God. This impression is only strengthened by the striking imagery of Jeremiah 1:9, towards the end of the prophet's call narrative: 'Then the LORD reached out his hand and touched my mouth. The LORD said to me, "I have just put my words in your mouth."' Clearly, it was not merely a general message that Jeremiah received. We can safely conclude that the message from God came to Jeremiah in words. To put it in theological terms, this act of revelation was *verbal*. Three other verses (Jer. 5:14; 15:16; 23:9) refer to God's 'words' (pl.) being received by Jeremiah, and, interestingly, all of them use language of ingestion, involving a range of metaphors – fire, food, wine. Significantly, however, the language of God giving

---

[35] I have excluded from this discussion the occasional usage of *dābār* with the sense 'matter', 'thing' or 'deed' (Jer. 5:28; 32:8, 27; 38:5, 24; 40:3, 16; 42:3; 44:4). It is not always clear what the best English gloss is for *dābār*, and I have erred on the side of caution.

words (pl.) to Jeremiah is not found outside these verses. In particular, Jeremiah is never said to 'hear' God's words.[36] It is always the 'word' of the LORD, singular, that comes to Jeremiah. We shall explore the implications of this presently.

Secondly, the book of Jeremiah is not a work of systematic theology; its use of language is fluid, reflecting the span of years over which it was written and the range of genres by which its message is conveyed. The aim of the following analysis is not to deduce rules governing supposed technical terminology; it is not that sort of literature. Rather, I am seeking to examine the text carefully enough to provide confirmation of a tendency that may be discerned behind the way in which language of word and words is used. There appears to be a conception of the nature of the word of God that leads to a normal way of speaking and writing about it in Jeremiah. This normal usage is not inviolable, and, if needs must, it can be departed from in the interests of effective communication. The reasons for such departures are generally evident from examination of the relevant contexts. Nevertheless, it remains demonstrable that the use of the singular and plural forms of the word 'word' is strongly and significantly differentiated in the book of Jeremiah.[37]

The singular, 'word'
We shall first consider the singular. When Jeremiah uses the expression 'the word', *it is almost always the word of God, not the word of humans, and it is almost always heard, rather than spoken.*

The most prominent examples of this usage are found in the word formulas that structure the book: 'the word that came to Jeremiah from the LORD' and 'the word of the LORD came to me/Jeremiah, saying';[38] 'this word came from the LORD';[39] 'hear [pl.] the word of the LORD!'[40] In all these cases the word is heard, or intended to be heard. Mostly, the word itself is the subject, and 'comes' to its hearer;

---

[36] For details see the analysis below.

[37] This tendency is seen outside Jeremiah as well. Scholars have tended to ignore or discount a possible distinction between word and words; e.g. Rendtorff (2005: 205): 'no fundamental distinction is made between statements about the "word" and the "words" of God'. It is my contention, however, that a careful examination of the evidence provides grounds for revising earlier scholarly impressions.

[38] The Disjunctive Heading and Narrative Formula, respectively. The verses where they appear are listed in chapter 2, nn. 7–9.

[39] An idiosyncratic narrative opening device found only in Jer. 26:1; 27:1; 36:1.

[40] Jer. 2:4; 7:2; 9:19 (variant); 10:1 (variant); 17:20; 19:3; 21:11; 22:2 (sg.), 29 (sg.); 29:20; 31:10; 34:4 (sg.); 42:15; 44:24, 26.

sometimes it is the object of the imperative 'Hear!' In addition to these there are three unusual cases where the word is 'seen'.[41] This striking metaphor should not be taken to contradict the verbal mode of revelation implied by Jeremiah 1:9; rather, as Jeremiah 23:18 suggests, vision, when present, is accompanied by words. Whatever the mode, the sense of what this type of word language conveys is the same: the reception of the word of the LORD by a human hearer. In all of Jeremiah there is only one verse (the poetic Jer. 8:9) that speaks of the word of God, singular, being rejected.[42]

Almost as rare as the word of God being rejected are cases of the word of God being spoken, by him or anyone else. There are just four clear instances. Two are variations on a word formula: 'The word which the LORD spoke to Jeremiah/to Babylon' (Jer. 46:13/50:1). The OAN, where both these verses are found, are full of atypical word formulas. The main interest of this particular pair is that they demonstrate that the LORD can indeed be described as speaking his word; it is therefore of considerable interest that he almost never is. The third case is Jeremiah 14:17, cited above, and the fourth is Jeremiah 34:5, '"For I have spoken a word," declares the LORD.' The other instances of the word (sg.) being spoken may be excluded, because they make indirect reference to a particular word of God, and do not actually speak or introduce it. For example, Jeremiah 44 begins, 'The word that came to Jeremiah', and continues with an oracle. Afterwards the people respond by saying, 'the word which you spoke to us in the name of the LORD: we will not hear you!' (Jer. 44:16). Such indirect references to the word (sg.) may also be found without the involvement of verbs of speech.[43] The *idea* of the word

---

[41] Jer. 2:31; 23:18; 38:21 – which last verse may be translated, 'this is the word that the LORD has caused me to see'.

[42] In the remaining cases where the word of God (sg.) is the object of a verb with a human subject, the verb is either a verb of speech or a verb of obedience (Jer. 22:4, 'who has paid attention to his word and obeyed?'; cf. Jer. 23:18). The only other verse that might be argued to depict the word of the LORD's being rejected is Jer. 6:10, 'The word of the LORD has become a reproach to them; they take no delight in it.' However, these are people unable to hear, whose reaction is the result of divine judgment. The fact that the same word, 'reproach', is used of Jeremiah in Jer. 20:8, 'the word of the LORD has become a reproach to me', supports the view that human rejection is not involved in these verses.

[43] E.g. Jer. 17:15, 'They said to me, "Where is the word of the LORD"?'; Jer. 37:17; 38:14, 'Is there a word from the LORD?' (cf. 13:2; 32:8). Such indirect references to a word of the LORD can involve verbs of speech when pointing to a formal speech formula and subsequent word from God, e.g. Jer. 22:1–2, 'Speak this word and say, "Hear the word of the LORD . . ."'

of God is an idea that may be clear to anybody, whether or not they are disposed to receive the word when it comes.

In short, the *word*, when singular, is a message that comes from God and is received by humans (Jeremiah, for the most part). When this message is spoken by humans – as we shall see – it is generally described as *words*, plural. Interestingly, the three occasions on which the *word* (sg.) is attached to Jeremiah rather than to the LORD[44] are all moments when Jeremiah's special status as the true emissary of God is at the forefront of the discourse. These exceptions serve only to point to the general rule, that the *word* (sg.) in Jeremiah is God's word, God's message, and it is received by humans.[45]

The plural, 'words'

In the case of 'words', plural, the picture is more heterogeneous, but a clear pattern nevertheless emerges: *the words of God are normally spoken or written down, and they are normally rejected by their listeners.*

First, the 'words' of God are either attached to verbs of speaking, or verbs of hearing. Speaking is more common, with the typical scenario being a human instructed by God to 'speak these words'.[46] The correlation with hearing is a negative one: that is, the words are 'not heard' but are rejected.[47] There are just three possible cases of the words of the LORD being heard receptively, and two of them are causative: 'I will cause you to hear my words' (Jer. 18:2; 23:22). Arguably, the focus in these cases is on the act of divine speech that causes the hearing. The remaining case is Jeremiah 35:13, and the context here implies that the words mentioned therein are laws.[48]

---

[44] 'The word of Jeremiah' or equivalent: Jer. 28:7–9; 45:1; 51:59; cf. Jer. 23:36 and 29:23, in which the word of the prophets masquerades as the word of God.

[45] The foregoing analysis of *word* (sg.) has omitted a small number of references that I judge to be using 'word' in its partial sense, i.e. a single lexical item or grammatical phrase. Cases in point are Jer. 5:14, 31:23 and 23:38, referring to human words, and Jer. 13:12, referring to a divine word. Strictly speaking, this last example belongs in a treatment of 'words' (pl.), because it is just one of the many words that add up to a complete message, or 'word'.

[46] Jer. 3:12; 7:27; 11:6; 16:10; 19:15; 25:30; 26:2, 7, 12, 15, 20; 27:12; 34:6; 37:2; 38:1, 5; 42:4–5; 43:1. A variety of verbs is used in these verses: the words are spoken, proclaimed, prophesied and answered.

[47] Jer. 6:19; 7:27; 11:10; 13:10; 16:10; 18:18; 19:15; 22:5; 23:30, 36; 25:8; 26:5; 29:19; 37:2. The verbs used are negative: 'did not hear', 'do not obey', 'steal' and 'pervert'.

[48] As mentioned earlier, a 'word' can denote a piece of legislation, and 'words' can signify many laws. Jer. 11 provides unambiguous examples of this usage (Jer. 11:2, 3, 6, 8; also 34:18).

Secondly, God's words can be written and read out.[49] The picture is entirely consistent in these cases: it is only 'words' that are written, never 'the word', and written words are heard unreceptively in Jeremiah.

Finally, human words are mentioned, though surprisingly infrequently. Most belong to Jeremiah or the false prophets, which gives them a theological dimension. And like God's words, human words are generally heard unreceptively.[50]

To summarize: while one may sometimes find word or words mentioned simply to be described (e.g. Jer. 23:29, 'is not my word like a fire, like a hammer that breaks the rock?'), nearly always words are spoken or written or read, and then heard and obeyed, or else rejected. And while there are one or two exceptions, mostly in poetry, the normal language in Jeremiah for describing the process is that the word of God (in the singular) comes to the prophet, and as part of the divine message there is a command to speak these words (in the plural), meaning the specifics of the word, or message. The 'word' of the LORD is heard and obeyed, but the 'words' of the LORD are rejected by their listeners.

This normal pattern of usage is borne out by the few times words do things other than being spoken and heard. In the singular the word of the LORD can be said to stand (Jer. 29:10), to be established for good (Jer. 33:14; 44:28) or to be enacted by the LORD (Jer. 1:12). All these uses stress the irresistible power of the word to accomplish God's good purposes. In the plural, however, the words of the LORD are 'brought against' and 'stand against' their addressees to destroy them (Jer. 39:16; 44:29). It would appear to be no accident that when words (pl.) have a positive effect on their recipient (the prophet) they are said to be eaten or drunk (Jer. 1:9; 5:14; 15:16; 23:9). Rather than destroying from without, they enter in and transform.

---

[49] Jeremiah's words written: Jer. 1:1; 29:1; 36:10, 17, 18, 27; 45:1; 51:60, 61, 64; God's words written: Jer. 30:2; 36:2, 4, 6, 8, 11, 13, 16; written words with no specified author: Jer. 36:20, 24, 28, 32. Finally, in Jer. 25:13, written words and covenant curses come together: 'I shall bring on that land all my words I have spoken against it, all that is written in this book which Jeremiah prophesied.'

[50] Jer. 7:4, 8; 23:16; 27:14, 16; 28:6; 35:14; 38:27; 42:4; 44:17. In some cases the positive 'hear' is used of Jeremiah's words, but the action that accompanies the hearing is negative, usually murderous (Jer. 26:7, 21; 38:1). Twice, in Jer. 26:10, 12, words are heard receptively.

Some examples

The data presented above can be assembled into the following 'normal' process: *The* word *of the* LORD *comes to Jeremiah. Jeremiah is told to proclaim 'these* words'. *He says, 'Hear the* word *of the* LORD!', *and the people disobey 'these* words'. *The* words *of the* LORD *(or of Jeremiah) are eventually written down, read and generally rejected.* To illustrate this process I have chosen a number of examples. In the first we see the word that comes to Jeremiah and the words he speaks as a result:

> At the beginning of the reign of Jehoiakim son of Josiah, king of Judah, this *word* came from the LORD: 'Thus says the LORD: Stand in the courtyard of the LORD's house and speak against all the cities of Judah that are coming to worship in the LORD's house all the *words* I have commanded you to speak to them. Do not hold back a *word*.' (Jer. 26:1–2)

In the next we see the words Jeremiah speaks being – hopefully – heard as a word:

> Thus says the LORD: 'Go and buy a potter's earthenware jar. Take some of the elders of the people and some of the elders of the priests and go out to the Valley of Ben Hinnom near the entrance of the Potsherd Gate. Proclaim there the *words* I will speak to you. Say: Hear the *word* of the LORD, kings of Judah and inhabitants of Jerusalem.' (Jer. 19:1–3a)

The third example is of words written: 'The *word* that came to Jeremiah from the LORD: Thus says the LORD, the God of Israel: write down all the *words* that I have spoken to you, on a scroll' (Jer. 30:1–2). The last two examples show how subtly the author shifts between word and words according to whether obedience or disobedience is being envisaged:

> 'Instead, diligently carry out this *word*, and kings sitting on David's throne will come through the gates of this house riding on chariots and horses – they, their officials, and their people. However, if you do not obey ['hear'] these *words*, then by myself I swear' – oracle of the LORD – 'that this house will become a ruin.' (Jer. 22:4–5)

From the thirteenth year of Josiah son of Amon, king of Judah, until this very day, namely, 23 years, the *word of the* LORD *has come to me, and I have spoken to you* time and again, but you have not obeyed ['heard']. . . . Therefore, thus says the LORD of Hosts: '*Because you have not obeyed ['heard']* my words, I am about to send and take all the families of the north . . .' (Jer. 25:3, 8–9)

Conclusions: the relationship of word and words in Jeremiah

This picture will be sharpened in later chapters. But at this stage we can present as normative the following way of speaking about word and words in Jeremiah: *what is heard and obeyed is the word of the* LORD; *what is spoken or written are the words of the* LORD. *What is* not *heard, that is, disobeyed, are the words of the* LORD.

I have raised the question of whether we should imagine Jeremiah expressing God's word freely in his own words, or whether God gave precise words to him. And the evidence is somewhat conflicting. On the one hand we have verses like Jeremiah 1:9 in which a situation almost of dictation is implied. But on the other hand the strict distinction that runs throughout the book between the word heard and the words spoken seems to suggest an intentional distancing. We are being told that the words Jeremiah speaks are in exact correspondence not so much with the particular words he heard, but with the word, or message, that he heard. Jeremiah might express that message in different words on different occasions. However – and this is the force of Jeremiah 1:9 – whatever words he chose to use on each occasion would be not just his words, but the words of God.

We find an analogous situation in Jeremiah 32, where the prophet tells us the contents of a prediction that the word of the LORD brought him, and proceeds to narrate its fulfilment. Hanamel gives Jeremiah the same message that the word of the LORD predicted, but his words are not the same. The variations are italicized:

And Jeremiah said, 'The word of the LORD came to me: "Look! Hanamel, the son of Shallum your uncle, is coming to you to say, 'Buy *for yourself* my field in Anathoth, for yours is the right of redemption to buy it.'" Then Hanamel my uncle's son came in accordance with the word of the LORD to the court of the guard and said to me, "*Please* buy my field in Anathoth *in the land of Benjamin*, for yours is the right of

inheritance and yours is the redemption. Buy it *for yourself."*
Then I knew that this was the word of the LORD.' (Jer. 32:6–8)

What do we make of this? We should immediately exclude the possibility that God's prediction was wrong or, to put it more harshly,
that God did not tell the exact truth about what Hanamel would say.
A second possibility is that God did not actually use those precise
words to Jeremiah, or that Hanamel did not use those precise words
in his speech, and that Jeremiah or his scribe has made a mistake in
recording God's words, or Hanamel's, or both. But this merely shifts
the problem from the veracity of God's word spoken to the veracity
of God's word written. Are these words in the Bible the words of
God or not?

However, such lines of argument carry weight only if we believe
that any change to the words must inevitably change the word, or
message. Yet the scriptural version of this episode presents both
forms of words, God's and Hanamel's, as the word of God – indeed,
as the same word of God. It is clear that the determinative reality
is the message, the word from God, and that the words can change
without changing the word. Even more than this, Jeremiah would
assert that all the words here, variable as they are, were the very
words of God.[51]

To recapitulate: *what is heard and obeyed is described in Jeremiah
as the word of God, and when that word is spoken or written by the
prophet the words that come out are the words of God.* And this
remains true whether or not those words were the precise ones given
in the initial revelation. We shall see in chapter 3 that situations
where the originally given words are reshaped are not uncommon.
The determinative reality is the message: the word from God. And
the words that Jeremiah chooses when he conveys this message
are the words of God. When I receive them in obedience, I have
received the word of God; if I reject them, I have rejected the words
of God – as though they did not gel together into a message that had
the power to save.

In the next chapter we shall explore the question of whether we
can find a way of describing the words of the book of Jeremiah, in
their Masoretic form, as a coherent whole, a single message.

---

[51] Note that even though the words of the fulfilment are words in Hanamel's, not
Jeremiah's, mouth, the broader context claims them for Jeremiah.

First elements of a word theology

At the end of each 'word' chapter I shall gather together some theological reflections to serve as building blocks for a Jeremianic theology of the word of God. The four reflections that follow can be no more than tentative at this stage; in subsequent chapters I shall aim to reinforce and extend them.

1. *The word of God is the subject of the book of Jeremiah, addressing us just as it once addressed him.* In the opening two verses of Jeremiah the book presents itself to us both as the written words of Jeremiah, and as the spoken word of God that addresses us so that we may hear it, just as it once addressed Jeremiah himself. What is this word of God? It does not lend itself to a neat definition as if it were a concept in philosophy.[52] It is more like a human character, and indeed it is effectively the main character in the book of Jeremiah. It is the subject of the narrative framework that structures the book, and it is the voice we hear, displacing and supplanting the book's human speakers. We shall examine this feature of Jeremianic discourse in more detail in chapter 3. The book of Jeremiah, more than any other book in the Old Testament, demands to be understood as a systematic exposition of the word of God.

2. *The word of God determines the words of God.* What can we say about the relationship between the words of Jeremiah and the word of God? Are they to be exactly identified with one another? In the normal usage of the book, the *word* of God is that which is heard, and the *words* of God are those which are spoken or written. The word heard is not necessarily spoken forth by the hearer in identical words to those that were given him, as the incident of Hanamel and the field indirectly demonstrates. After all, the words received are not magical incantations, but a message from a divine Person. And when the prophet relays that message, perhaps in identical words to those received, or perhaps not, the hearers hear not the words of Jeremiah but the word of God. Indeed, as we shall explore in chapter 4, when hearers in the book of Jeremiah refuse to hear, it is not the word they hear but words, as if some vital ingredient in the message has not got through.

---

[52] For Moberly, 'The singularity of the divine word [in Jeremiah] may also suggest a communication that is intrinsically simple, in the sense of being a wholistic reality of a kind that involves the total range of human awareness in the task of comprehension' (Moberly 2006: 44). With the note of caution Moberly supplies, a conceptual description of this nature can sit happily alongside Jeremiah's presentation.

The *word* is heard, the *words* are spoken or written. But the word that is heard is not less than the words that are spoken. It comes to the prophet in words, not as a vague impression or mystical enlightenment. The word heard is not less than the words spoken, but perhaps it is more. We do not know exactly what Jeremiah experienced when he received the word of the LORD, but we do know what the people experienced when they received the word of the LORD from Jeremiah. It was not just words they heard, not just disembodied propositions; they received a person along with those words. We shall examine the person of Jeremiah in chapter 3.

3. *The fact that the words of Jeremiah are human words does not prevent them from conveying the word of God.* What is the nature of the identity between the word heard and the words spoken? Whatever it is, it is an identity that is not damaged by the inescapable imprecisions of human language. If the word of God could be dimmed by being conveyed in human words, then our translations of many times copied manuscripts would be faint echoes indeed. Yet the story that unfolds in the book of Jeremiah demonstrates that the word of God, spoken from frail human lips, written down and revised and rearranged, this word of God carries all before it in an irreversible tide of destruction and recreation. Why frail human lips? Can they not be done without? And how can words, mere vibrations in the air, exert real power in the physical world? To these questions we shall return in chapter 5.

4. *As we read the words of the prophet we read them as God's words, but ultimately the word of God that comes to us determines the way we read them.* We do not know whether the words written by Baruch are identical to those Jeremiah spoke; we do not know whether the words Jeremiah spoke were identical to those God revealed to him, but we do know that the words we read are the words of God, the direct product of the infilling of his prophets with his words. And so when we read them we must take them seriously as the words of God. We may not try to get behind them and alter their message to fit our understanding of history, or theology, or ethics. On the other hand, we must read those words very carefully indeed as fully human words, pressing them for meaning.

And as we do this, we must make sure that our close reading is always determined by the word, the message, that we hear in the reading of the words. For Jeremiah this word is ultimately the message of the book as a whole. For Christian readers this word is ultimately the revelation of God in the person of his incarnate Son.

Chapter Two

Structuring Jeremiah as a narrative about the word of God

As we have seen in the previous chapter there are solid grounds for inferring from the peculiar shape of Jeremiah MT 1:1–2 + 51:64 that the book in its final incarnation ('the words of Jeremiah') was presented to its readership as a single narrative about the word of God. The aim of the present chapter is to assume the truth of this inference and see whether a coherent structure emerges as a result.[1]

Jeremiah is long, full of repetitions, non-linear in its chronology, and constantly cycles from one genre to another. A number of commentaries over the years have taken the extreme step of rearranging all the parts, usually into chronological order, and commenting on the result.[2] However, there has been a growing consensus among scholars that the book's arrangement is far from random, and while this is not the type of literature that lends itself to having every detail pigeonholed, the general flow of its thought is discernable with careful reading. While the following reading is my own, it shares much in common with the work of a number of contemporary scholars whose thoughts have run along similar lines – especially as regards Jeremiah 1 – 24.[3]

When it comes to the structure and thrust of the book's second half, however, there is much less agreement. For one scholar, who has written more on Jeremiah's structure than most, the role of chapters 26–45 'may well be the most vexing problem in Jeremiah

---

[1] By naming the 'word of the LORD' as the book's subject I am not suggesting either that the word of God is a person, or that the book's author conceived of it as a person. It is true to call God himself the book's subject; however, the fact remains that this subject is referred to as 'the word of the LORD', and this renders 'word-shaped' the type of theology we extract from God's activities in the book. David Pao, who argues that the word of the LORD is the main 'actor' in the book of Acts, conceives of it there as a 'hypostatization' at the centre of a conquest narrative (Pao 2002).

[2] E.g. Cornill 1895; Leslie 1954; Bright 1965.

[3] Stulman (1999, 2005) stands out among these, with Clements (1993) and Carroll (1986: 86–87) also worthy of note.

studies'.[4] For this reason we shall need to take some pains to examine transition points and connections in the text of chapters 25–52, especially where a structure built around word of God language yields unconventional results. Nevertheless, due to the nature of the present study a host of issues will have to be left unexplored, and the preliminary sketch that results is just that: a sketch that would need to be filled out before one would want to claim definitively that this is the way its final author conceived of his book, still less that it is the only valid way of reading it.[5] And yet I do hope to show that it is a successful, even compelling, reading strategy.

The plan of the chapter

The present chapter is divided into two parts. The first part deals mainly with the important task of establishing Jeremiah's structure. It devotes most of its energy to chapters 25–52, and takes note of relevant scholarly debates on the various questions that arise. Readers who are happy to take this structure as read and 'get on' with my larger argument will lose little by skipping to the second part (beginning on p. 86), which presents a concise reading of the narrative that emerges from structuring Jeremiah as a book about the word of the LORD. It provides the context within which the exegetical studies that appear in succeeding chapters will be conducted.

Establishing the structure of Jeremiah

Criteria for structuring the narrative

The first criterion for thinking about structure is caution. It is important to remember that few biblical texts have been written so tightly that one and only one structure can be meaningfully assigned them. The narrative of Jeremiah does not slot neatly into a single structural scheme at every small point, and some statements about its structure will feel more tentative than others. It is also evident that the book has a history of growth and development, from which older structural schemes remain, sometimes incorporated into the structural framework of the final product and sometimes superseded

---

[4] Kessler 1999: 66.

[5] To take just one example, Leslie Allen's recent commentary provides an interesting reading of macrostructure based on the theological relationship of judgment and hope, and taking its structural cues from observations made by Ronald Clements about the make-up of other prophetic writings (Allen 2008: 12–14).

by it. In the end, the purpose of structural analysis is to throw light on the shape and purpose of the narrative, and the most convincing arguments will be cumulative ones, in which diverse features of the text are seen to point in the same direction. To this end I have chosen four clearly identifiable features of the book to examine in parallel, in the hope that a measure of cross-correlation will help to reduce the arbitrariness of my conclusions.[6]

First and foremost among these features are the structural 'word of the LORD' formulas, especially those I have labelled Disjunctive Headings and Narrative Formulas.

Disjunctive Headings are more significant structurally, as they make a clean break from what came before; they are in bold type in figure 2.1 on page 69 (as is the double heading of 1:1–3). Grammatically they are not complete sentences but headings, or superscriptions, and they are typically translated 'The word that came to Jeremiah from the LORD.'[7] In addition to these are four variant word formulas that do not correspond to the standard Disjunctive Heading, but lack a main verb and so act as superscriptions (i.e. disjunctively) in the same way.[8] These 'atypical Disjunctive Headings' are mostly in the OAN. By and large, the final (M) edition of the book of Jeremiah appears to have been built by joining together units introduced by Disjunctive Headings. As much as anything else, it is this prominent use of 'word of the LORD' headings that supports a reading of Jeremiah as a narrative whose protagonist is the word of the LORD.

Narrative Formulas incorporate a discrete unit into the larger unfolding narrative, and have not been marked in figure 2.1. Grammatically, they form complete narrative sentences, translated 'The word of the LORD came to Jeremiah [or, to me], saying'.[9] There are indications that these formulas, especially in Jeremiah 1 – 24,

---

[6] It is precisely the presence of these four features that lead some scholars to conclude the book lacks 'a coherent theme or plot or any systematic historical framework' (Davidson 1993: 344). Davidson makes specific reference to the second, third and fourth features discussed below. It is because of my belief that the book possesses an overall coherence that derives both from the proto-Masoretic editor (by observation) and from the divine author (by conviction) that I take the time to search for coherence in these other features as well.

[7] Jer. 7:1; 11:1; 18:1; 21:1; 30:1; 32:1; 34:1, 8; 35:1; 40:1. Also Jer. 25:1; 44:1 (lacking 'from the LORD').

[8] Jer. 45:1; 46:13; 50:1; 51:59. 'The word which the LORD spoke' (Jer. 50:1) is an example.

[9] Jer. 1:2 (variation), 4, 11, 13; 2:1; 13:3, 8; 16:1; 18:5; 24:4; 25:3 (in a speech); 28:12; 29:30; 32:6 (in a speech), 26; 33:1, 19, 23; 34:12; 35:12; 36:27; 37:6; 39:15 (transposed); 42:7; 43:8.

are designed to echo and develop themes set forth in the opening chapter.[10]

There are four variant Narrative Formulas that share some features of the Disjunctive Heading, but grammatically they are sentences rather than headings.[11] However, I have counted three of them as disjunctive, namely, those that fall within the OAN, because the other three unit-opening formulas in these chapters are both atypical and genuinely disjunctive (see n. 8). This brings to seven the number of atypical Disjunctive Headings, all to be found between Jeremiah 45:1 and Jeremiah 51:59; they are underlined in figure 2.1.[12]

After the structural word formulas the second feature of note is the markers of time, person and place. These are usually of structural significance in the Hebrew Bible, and in Jeremiah we see them occurring when oracles and events are dated relative to kings' reigns.

The third feature, also fairly straightforward to identify, is the three different types of literary genre: poetry, sermonic material in the style of Deuteronomy, and biographical narratives.[13] The chronological markers and the parts of the book that are mostly or all poetry are represented in figure 2.1, and their correlation with the word formulas will combine to shape my judgment about the book's overall shape and direction.[14]

The final feature is the less objective one of subject matter: major themes, key words and strategic repetitions of words and phrases that tie together the intervening material.[15] These have not been plotted in figure 2.1, but have been taken into account together with the data of speech formulas, chronology and genre to arrive at the

---

[10] Lawlor 2004.

[11] Jer. 14:1; 46:1; 47:1; 49:34. The classification of these verses is debated; for a discussion see Shead (2002b: 31, n. 21). For a fuller analysis of all the formulas discussed here see Shead (2002b: 26–31).

[12] Jer. 14:1 will be discussed further in the section on the structure of Jer. 1 – 24 below. Also noteworthy are Jer. 26:1, 36:1, which introduce blocks of narrative with non-formulaic temporal sentences whose second half is similar to an atypical Narrative Formula.

[13] As first elaborated by Sigmund Mowinckel (Mowinckel 1914).

[14] For ease of reading I have chosen not to represent the literary genres of poetry, prose sermon and prose narrative in any detail; Joel Rosenberg, who pays close attention to these, has generated from them a different (and chiastic) structure for the book (J. Rosenberg 1987: 190–192). It should also be noted that while there is less poetry in Jer. 11 – 20 than there is in Jer. 2 – 10, the prose in those chapters generally takes the form of prophetic oracles rather than narratives about the prophet or Deuteronomic sermons.

[15] These repetitions are mostly useful for delimiting smaller units (Lundbom 1999: 76–84).

Chronology (Josiah, Jehoiakim, Zedekiah) and blocks of poetry (▨)

1	2 – 20	21 – 24
	mostly poetry; some sermons and symbolic actions	
Jos, Jeh, Zed	▨▨▨▨▨	Zed (+ sons of Josiah)

Disjunctive headings (bold) and progression of thought

Jer. 1		Jer. 2 – 24: The word of the LORD tears down the nation (1:10)				
1:1 –3	1:4– 19	2:1 – 6:30	**7:1** – 10:25	**11:1** – 17:27	**18:1** – 20:18	**21:1** – 24:10
Frame	Call	Judah rejects the God who brought them out of Egypt (2 Kgs 17:7)	Judah defiles the temple with idolatry (2 Kgs 17:8–14)	Judah abandons the covenant (2 Kgs 17:15–17)	Elect Judah is torn down (2 Kgs 17:18–20)	Judah's kings will never again sit on David's throne

Chronology (Jehoiakim, Zedekiah) and blocks of poetry (▨)

25 – 26	27 – 29	30 – 31	32 – 34	35 – 36	37 – 39	40 – 44	45	46	46:13 – 49:33	49:34 – 52:34
Jeh	Zed	▨	Zed	Jeh	Zed	Nebuzaradan		Jeh	▨	▨ Zed

Disjunctive headings (bold) and progression of thought

Jer. 25 – 51: The word of the LORD vindicated and triumphant among all nations							52
25:1 – 29:32	**30:1** – 34:22	**35:1** – 39:15	**40:1** – 43:13	**44:1**– 30	45	46:1 – 51:64	52:1 –34
True prophecy is tested and found to be on the lips of Jeremiah	A true and revolutionary hope lies in the future, not the present	The word exerts its power and the kingdom falls	The indestructible word	The word is silent while the remnant self-destruct / No escape: God's word will stand	Baruch's hope	The word of the LORD tears down nations and draws Israel, alive, from the jaws of death	Frame (2 Kgs 25)
	32:1; 34:1, 8			[6 variants]			

Figure 2.1 Structural features of Jeremiah

progression of thought around which I have ordered the book's plot as I read it.

The aim of the present study is not an exhaustive analysis of the book of Jeremiah, so the structural observations and other comments in the following section will be selective. The intention is to confirm the shape and thrust of the overall narrative, and to commend the coherence and critical value of reading Jeremiah around the word of the LORD as its organizing centre.

Establishing the two halves of 'this book'

We have already seen the way the 'words of Jeremiah' (Jer. 1:1; 51:64) create a book-wide frame for the M edition. Within this vast arch the pivot point is Jeremiah 25. There is broad agreement about this fact; Martin Kessler, for example, suggests that chapter 25 functions as a hinge, looking both back to the first half of the book (Jer. 25:1–7) and forward to coming judgment at the hand of Babylon (vv. 8–11), followed by the judgment of Babylon itself (vv. 12–14).[16]

That Jeremiah 25 begins a major new unit, however, is more contentious. In the first instance there is a good case for seeing chapters 1 and 25 as 'bookends' framing the intervening material. It may even be that these chapters once existed as a 'book' in themselves.[17] In the second instance, the similarities between chapters 26 and 36 suggest to many scholars that they ought to make up a second large unit. Once again, the evidence is real, but – as I shall argue shortly – whatever status these units may have enjoyed in earlier versions of the book, the final edition has incorporated them within an overarching word structure of its own. In particular, the Disjunctive Heading is found in Jeremiah 25:1 but not 26:1, suggesting that the unit begun in Jeremiah 25 continues into chapter 26 and beyond.[18] Yes, the links back to the first part of the book are strong, but, as we shall see, there is a strong tendency in Jeremiah 25 – 52 for new units to look back before they move forward. Jeremiah 25, then, functions in the MT less as a bookend than as a recapitulation, a chapter in which the book regathers itself ready to launch into its second phase. That this chapter has been adapted to take its place in a book-wide structure can be seen from verse 13, where reference is made to a written book: 'I am going to bring upon that land all my words that I spoke against it, everything written in this book, which Jeremiah prophesied against all the nations.' To which book does 'this book' refer? Some argue that since Jeremiah 26 and 36 are both set in the fourth year of Jehoiakim we should link 'this book' to the scroll written by Baruch and burned by the king according to

---

[16] Kessler 1999: 65–66.

[17] Stulman 1999: 44, nn. 38, 46–47.

[18] Jer. 25 also marks a new departure with its chronological scheme (see below). For some literary connections between Jer. 25 and the succeeding chapters, see Fischer (2005: 1.732).

Jeremiah 36.[19] However, the scroll of chapter 36 spoke of Judah's destruction at Babylon's hand (36:2, 29), whereas the words of 'this book' in chapter 25 were directed against Babylon herself. Others, therefore, take 'this book' to refer to the Babylon oracle which, in an older edition of Jeremiah (the LXXV), followed soon after.[20] In support of this, Jeremiah 51:63 refers to the Babylon oracle as 'this book', the only other use of the phrase in Jeremiah. However, since the Babylon oracle is dated in Jeremiah 51:60 to Zedekiah's reign, some ten years after chapter 25 is set, supporters of this view must treat Jeremiah 25:13b as a later addition.

Another solution is to take 'this book' as a reference to Jeremiah 25:15–38, in which brief oracles against the nations are set forth (and where the complete OAN were positioned in the LXXV). However, the relative clauses in Jeremiah 25:13 convey retrospective information, and are not naturally forward looking; also, the matching reference to 'this book' in Jeremiah 51:63 remains to be reckoned with.[21]

The best solution, in my opinion, is to take 'this book' as a reference back to the entire book of Jeremiah as introduced to us in chapter 1, and to recognize in the book-wide structure of word formulas a reappropriation of material from across Jeremiah's entire ministry to serve in the proclamation of his final message.

The connection back to Jeremiah 1 is very strong. As Georg Fischer points out, the thirteenth year of Josiah is mentioned only in 1:12 and 25:3, and the tribes of the north feature only in 1:15 and 25:9;[22] most significantly, he argues that the relative clause in 25:13 ('which Jeremiah prophesied against all the nations') – absent from the LXX – makes a clear link to his commission as a prophet to the nations in 1:5. The result of this, in the M edition, is to turn 25:13 into a claim that 'this book' of Jeremiah corresponds to the preaching

---

[19] So Holladay (1986: 664), who goes on to expound the widely held view that the book referred to in Jer. 36 went through at least three stages of expansion to keep up with changes in Judah's circumstances: first, a call to repent or be destroyed; then, an announcement of destruction and seventy-year exile; then, a promise that Babylon will be destroyed after seventy years. Holladay remarks (669), 'If God is the God of the living and not of the dead, then his Scripture must at all costs be kept current.'

[20] So McKane 1986: 631; Lundbom 2004a: 238–239. The Babylon oracle appears in chs. 27–28 of the LXX, and chs. 50–51 of the MT.

[21] Lundbom deals with this by arguing that originally the oracle against Babylon stood alone after Jer. 25, and the other oracles against the nations were included only at a later stage (Lundbom 2004a: 239); there is no direct evidence for this.

[22] Fischer 2005: 1.731–732. Other links mentioned by Fischer include Jer. 25:32, 34 with 6:22, 26; Jer. 25:33 with 8:2; Jer. 25:23 with 9:26. For another helpful discussion, alert to contrasts between spoken and written words, see Stulman (2005: 223–225).

of the prophet.[23] We can put these observations together into the following account of Jeremiah 25.

After twenty-three years of warnings which the people completely ignored, the announcement of a seventy-year exile in Jeremiah 25:11 fell like a thunderclap, and it precipitated Jeremiah's confrontations with the establishment in chapters 26–28. There is no reason to doubt that Jeremiah also announced the ultimate destruction of Babylon in the same speech: it offered no personal hope to the listeners, and though it was a new development, it was implicit in the message of Jeremiah 1 – 24, not only in positive oracles like 3:16b–18,[24] but in the call narrative itself, in which Judah turns out to be just one among the nations that God will tear down and build up through Jeremiah. The new message about Babylon in 25:12–14 is therefore doing no more than include Babylon, like Judah, among the nations subject to the divine word. Ten years later the long Babylon oracle underlined this truth; it was written down as 'this book' and a copy thrown into the Euphrates; then, in composing the final edition of Jeremiah the oracle was moved to the end and the phrase 'this book' turned to serve a broader purpose; and at the same time the words 'which Jeremiah prophesied against all the nations' were added to 'this book' in Jeremiah 25:13, turning it to serve the same broader purpose – namely, to refer to and encompass the entire book of Jeremiah.[25]

In short, Jeremiah MT has structured itself by interconnected references to the book of Jeremiah in chapters 1, 25 and 51. There are other 'books' contained within the large book, composed at various stages in Jeremiah's career, and as befits Jeremiah's call they are all alike concerned with the nations, or with Judah's deliverance from among them.[26] Like 'this book', these other books have been caught up into the book of the words of Jeremiah; however, they have not

---

[23] Fischer 2005: 1.743–744.

[24] The judgment of many scholars that 3:16–18 post-dates the fall of Jerusalem is made on the grounds that it presupposes the exile of Judah (Bright 1965: 27), and that Jer. 3 holds contradictory views about northern Israel and Judah (Thiel 1973: 93). Neither of these grounds holds up in a biblical-theological reading, so long as the internal coherence of the chapter can be demonstrated (as ably done by David Jobling 1978, though he concurs with Thiel and Bright about dating).

[25] Robert Carroll, though he does not share the historical conservatism of my reconstruction, judges that 'a synchronic reading of the book of Jeremiah will always associate Babylon with Judah–Jerusalem's vindication and will read 25.8–14 as the turning-point in the tradition' (Carroll 1999: 81).

[26] See the references to books (variously translated 'scroll' or 'letter' or 'deed', but always the same Hebrew word) at Jer. 29:1; 30:2; 32:10; 36:2; 45:1; cf. 46:1. Cf. Stulman 1998: 100–103.

been given the same structuring role. For it is the spoken word, not the written words, that the written book is mainly concerned with, and the division of the book at chapter 25 creates the two main movements by which the book's story is organized: the tearing down of the nation by the word of the LORD (Jer. 1 – 24), and the triumphant vindication of the word of the LORD among all the nations (Jer. 25 – 51).

Establishing the divisions of Jeremiah 1 – 24

The call of Jeremiah in chapter 1 culminates in the job description of verses 9–10, 'Look, I have just put my words in your mouth. See, today I have set you over nations and kingdoms to uproot and tear down, to destroy and demolish, to build and plant.' This job description is picked up and repeated frequently throughout the book, and it sets the program for the first half of Jeremiah, in which the word of God tears down the nation.[27]

In Jeremiah 1 – 24 the Disjunctive Heading is relatively rare, as most of this half of the book is poetic. But each that occurs introduces a major piece of prose that contains Deuteronomic material, and functions as a sermon preached by Jeremiah to the people.[28] This observation implies a principle of interpretation that applies to the first half of the book with its tightly interwoven prose and poetry. The principle is that the prose interprets the poetry; in particular the prose sermons introduced by a Disjunctive Heading establish the general theme the remainder of the section develops.[29]

The third and fourth sections into which figure 2.1 divides Jeremiah 2 – 24 are further subdivided by prose units, to wit, accounts of prophetic sign acts in 13:1–11; 16:1–13; 19:1–15. Finally, a fifth sermon, in 17:19–27, serves as a counterpart to the sermon in 11:1–17, by which means the book's longest section is demarcated.[30]

---

[27] Though the focus, as established in Jer. 1:13–19, is the nation of Judah, it is clear from the start that the implications of her tearing down extend to all the nations; the actual spelling out of these implications, however, is saved for the second phase of the book in chs. 25–52.

[28] As observed by Stulman (1998: 39). The prose units are Jer. 7:1 – 8:3; 11:1–17; 18:1–12; 21:1–10. Note that Jer. 14 begins with a heading that looks a little like a variant of the Disjunctive Headings of Jer. 7:1, etc. However, it is probably best taken as a sentence proper (as does the LXX) rather than as a heading, and in any case does not introduce prose, but comes in the middle of a long stretch of poetry – which might be enough to explain its lack of the narrative marker *wayĕhî*.

[29] Ibid. 52–55.

[30] The use of sign acts to subdivide sections in this way is essentially similar to Stulman's most recent work on the book (Stulman 2005).

These observations dovetail with a creative suggestion made by Ronald Clements, that the major sections of Jeremiah 2 – 25 keep in close step with the explanation for the fall of the northern kingdom in 2 Kings 17:7–23.[31] An awareness of 2 Kings 17 in the background makes the presence of Jeremiah 52, which is virtually identical with 2 Kings 25, all the more satisfying as an epilogue to the book.

Three other features make Jeremiah 1 – 24 cohere as a distinct block. First of all, undated material dominates this half of the book. No king is mentioned until Zedekiah in 21:1, and even then no regnal year is mentioned, and the section that follows touches indiscriminately on all the kings of the period. There is no chronological narrative framework until Jeremiah 25:1. Secondly, despite the variety of literary genres in Jeremiah 2 – 24, poetry predominates across the section, though this dominance fades after chapter 16, and is lost after chapter 21. Even so, 35% of Jeremiah 16 – 24 is poetry, and this characteristic mixture of prose and poetry is not found in the second half of Jeremiah. And thirdly, a number of inclusios help to demarcate this half of the book. Jeremiah 24 bears strong resemblance on the one hand to chapter 21:1–10, forming a closing frame to that particular unit,[32] and on the other hand to Jeremiah 1:11–19, forming a bookend to the first half of the narrative. The similarity between 1:11–19 and 24:1–10 is particularly striking, as they make up a pair of units whose form is unique in the book. Each consists of a dialogue in which God asks Jeremiah, 'What do you see?', and gives him a vision leading to an oracle. Between the first vision and the last there is a major shift of emphasis, which prepares us for the developments that will occur in chapters 25–52.[33]

The specific units into which figure 2.1 divides the first half of the book will be elaborated below in the section entitled 'Narrating Jeremiah 1 – 24'. Suffice it to say here that there are good grounds for dividing these units into two groups, consisting of chapters 2–10 and 11–24 respectively.[34] These two 'mini-movements' emerge from

---

[31] Clements 1993: 94–107.

[32] See e.g. Applegate 1998: 149–150.

[33] This shift of emphasis, plus similarities of date and setting between 24:1 and 29:2, leads Lundbom to make Jer. 24 the start of a major section (Lundbom 2004a: 222–223). However, while a historical connection between Jer. 24, 27, 28 and 29 is possible (Lundbom's so-called 'Zedekiah cluster'), the lack of a Disjunctive Heading for ch. 24 shows that in the present form of the book it has been put to use as a closing unit (see Rofé 1989: 394).

[34] See e.g. O'Connor 1988: 118–148; Lundbom 1999: 615; Henderson 2007; Jindo 2010: 59–62.

the third and fourth levels of structural organization I have identified above. For example, the balance of prose and poetry shifts
after chapter 11 in the favour of prose; prose accounts of prophetic
symbolic actions are not found before chapter 13; and the 'confessions of Jeremiah' (see below) are found only in chapters 11–20.[35] In
addition, Job Jindo has argued that the motif of 'devouring Israel/
Jacob' binds together chapters 2–10 (2:3; 10:25), while the covenant
formula 'you shall be my people and I shall be your God' binds
chapters 11–24 by a second inclusio (11:4; 24:7).[36]

Establishing the divisions of Jeremiah 25 – 45

Methods of reading

The chronological and thematic complexities of these chapters
provide a wide scope for the imagination when it comes to accounting for their present shape. For this reason it is essential that any
remarks on their formation and structure be both cautious and
modest. And yet, given the rich evidence in Jeremiah itself of a series
of writings, rewitings and expansions, the existence of earlier versions of the book will inevitably be a consideration in discussions
of its present structure. At least, they will be for any reader who is
interested in establishing a connection to the book's author(s) and
historical point of origin, and this will certainly include those readers
who read the text as the word of God it claims to be.

Cautious reading, in my opinion, does not press beyond such
evidence as is directly present in the text; modest reading treats
the results with a certain provisionality, at least until such time as
usage has tended to strengthen or weaken the conviction they carry
with them. The three features of the text I have chosen to be guided
by in my analysis of these chapters are, in order, the Disjunctive
Headings, the dated introductions, and the literary framing devices
that unify blocks of material.

This last feature is potentially troublesome because of the different ways in which repetitions can be interpreted. Often two similar
passages serve to contain a larger unit, providing a neat delimitation
of its boundaries. An example of this is the pair of verses describing
a reversal of gender roles, in Jeremiah 30:6 and 31:22, that serve to
delimit the intervening song cycle. But things are not always as simple
as this, and a passage may serve not only to frame an earlier unit,

---

[35] O'Connor 1988: 128.
[36] Jindo 2010: 60.

but at the same time to launch a new unit. We have seen Jeremiah 25 operating along these lines, and for some readers chapter 25 is best described as a 'hinge', belonging equally in both halves of the book. However, I have argued that formally it belongs in the second half, and its backward references function to gather up the threads of the message and move from there into the next phase of the narrative. It is important that we construe literary devices in a way that is sympathetic to the experience of reading. For example, while large-scale chiasms and other concentric structures can be pondered on the page from the centre to the outside, or vice versa, when read or listened to they are experienced from beginning to end, and what looks like a chiasm will sound like a narrative arch, or a journey 'there and back again'.[37] In the case of Jeremiah the Disjunctive Headings and chronological structure work together to take the reader repeatedly back to the same starting point – the ominous fourth year of Jehoiakim – from which the unfolding events of Judah's downfall can be viewed again, from a new angle, and understood with ever-increasing sophistication.

In the rest of Jeremiah I propose that three units of text, namely, chapters 25–26, chapters 35–36 and chapters 45–46, function as starting points for the iterative unfolding of Jeremiah's narrative about the word of the LORD. They are not fresh starts, but regatherings that look back in order to move the story forward.

Methods of assembling small units

Starting from the data available from the two surviving recensions (LXXV and M), I have argued elsewhere that rather than M being an expanded version of LXXV, each recension has revised a common text base, albeit less extensively in the case of LXXV.[38] This suggests that rather than a single definitive edition (or 'book'), which was expanded when the occasion of making a new copy permitted, successive 'books' were constructed as needed from the raw materials gradually accumulated and stored over the course of Jeremiah's ministry. These raw materials would consist of scrolls on which were recorded collections of oracles, reports of speeches, accounts of incidents in Jeremiah's life. How extensive each document was we cannot be sure, but in many cases we can guess, as I shall suggest shortly.

---

[37] Tolkien 1966.
[38] Shead 2002b: 258–260; J. G. Eichhorn was the first to propose a theory of this type (Eichhorn 1803: 154).

Although such a theory does not depend on a particular view of date and authorship, with Jack Lundbom I am content to accept Baruch as the principal author of the LXXV, and either him or his brother Seraiah (mentioned in Jer. 51:59) as the author of the final edition.[39] Most scholarly interest in this process is focused on the scroll described in Jeremiah 36, which, it has been suggested, was an early version of Jeremah 1 – 20.[40] Judging which parts of this scroll were produced when, and how it grew, is an uncertain exercise, and Lundbom offers some helpful and suitably cautious suggestions that work from indications within the text such as catchwords, inclusio, and so forth.[41] However, when it comes to the second half of the book, his theories about the text's prehistory sometimes get in the way of his analysis of the final form. Before engaging Lundbom's theories it would be well to set out the probable 'raw materials' from which Jeremiah 25 – 52 has been constructed.

In approximate chronological order, the following units of text have the appearance, by their dated introductions and narrative cohesiveness, of being independent accounts that were incorporated into the book of Jeremiah in its various editions: from the time of Jehoiakim, chapters 26, 25, 36, 45 and 35;[42] from the time of Zedekiah, chapters 49:34–39; 27; 28; 29; 50–51 (by implication from 51:59–64); 34:8–22; 34:1–7; 37–38; 32–33; 39;[43] from after the fall of Jerusalem, chapters 40–43; 44; 52. The collections of oracles in Jeremiah 30 – 31 and 46:1 – 49:33 are undated. However, we can go a little further than this, for it appears that some of these units were already gathered together into smaller collections, which effectively functioned as discrete building blocks from which to construct the final editions of Jeremiah. Two of these small collections are significant for the present discussion. The first is Jeremiah 27 – 29, and the second, Jeremiah 30 – 34.

---

[39] Lundbom 1986.

[40] Cf. Holladay 1976; Rietzschel 1966 restricted this to chs. 1–6.

[41] Lundbom 1999: 92–101.

[42] The date of Jer. 35 is unspecified and much debated (Lundbom 2004a: 571–572); into this period we may also place Jer. 19:14–15; 20:1–6. For a concise scheme of Jeremiah's internal chronology see Bright (1965: viii); for a more ambitious attempt, Parenti (1930: 59–62).

[43] On the date of Jer. 27 see below, nn. 45, 55. Jer. 29 is not precisely dated; I have followed the argument of Holladay (1989: 140) in linking it with the situation of the previous chapter. The undated unit 34:8–22 has been placed in 588 BC by Holladay's theory of septennial readings of Deuteronomy (Holladay 1989: 239). Into Zedekiah's reign we may also place Jer. 24; 21:1–10.

Regarding Jeremiah 27 – 29, the heading of chapter 28, 'in that same year', already connects it to chapter 27 as a continuous narrative. Although Jeremah 29 is not connected in this way, but starts with a new heading ('these are the words of the letter'), it is tied to the previous chapters by a striking linguistic feature: the name 'Nebuchadnezzar' is spelled this way only in these three chapters. Everywhere else in Jeremiah (and once in this unit, Jer. 29:21) it has its Babylonian spelling, 'Nebuchadrezzar'. Why the spelling 'Nebuchadnezzar' is used here is hard to say, given that all but two occurrences of the king's name between Jeremiah 21 and 29 (spelled either way) were added to the text in the course of a single late revision.[44] Be that as it may, the appearance given by their orthography is that the text of chapters 27–29 has been assembled and revised en bloc, an appearance reinforced by the fact that these three chapters unfold in a coherent and logical way.[45]

The unit Jeremiah 30 – 34 is more complex, and the following suggestions are offered in a more provisional spirit.[46] The oracles of hope in chapters 30–31, traditionally called 'The Book of Consolation', consist of a song-cycle capped by a series of more prosaic oracles, whose climax is the promise of the new covenant. Jeremiah 32 reports a symbolic action from the end of Zedekiah's reign, whose unlikely message of hope prompts a puzzled prayer from Jeremiah and new oracles of hope from the LORD, including another promise of a future, eternal covenant. Jeremiah 33 is a series of miscellaneous

---

[44] We know this because they are absent from the LXX, and were almost certainly newly added in the preparation of the final edition as part of its special interest in Babylon (see Stulman 1986: 141–144).

[45] Of course, many interpreters judge that these chapters cannot be read as a unit because e.g. of the way in which verses like 27:19–22, 29:10–14, 16–19 contradict the hope, expressed in the bulk of the unit, that the remnant who were not exiled will enjoy continued existence in the land (Seitz 1989b: 222–225). However, one reader's contradiction is another reader's qualification, and it does not seem to me that Jeremiah's listeners during Zedekiah's reign would have been incapable of understanding a nuanced message, whether or not they gave heed to it.

[46] On the whole, interpreters struggle to know what to do with chs. 34 and 35, which tend to be orphaned by units that end at ch. 33 and begin from ch. 36. Lundbom's 'clusters' leave ch. 34 to be explained away as 'inserted for polemical purposes' (Lundbom 2004a: 254); Stulman relegates chs. 34 and 35 to 'moral instruction' (Stulman 2005: 286–287). For Allen chs. 34–36 share the theme of 'failure to listen to Yahweh's manifold revelation' (Allen 2008: 383); for Lundbom they are united by virtue of presenting contrasting 'covenants' (e.g. Lundbom 2004a: 548); however, the language of ch. 35 is all of 'commands' (*miṣwâ*); there is no covenant in view. While there is, of course, a contrast between the obedience modelled in ch. 35 and the disobedience of ch. 34 (and ch. 36, for that matter), Jer. 35 points us in other directions than the previous chapter, as I shall argue below.

hopeful oracles, all linked by verse 1 to the previous chapter, as if the symbolic action and what followed released a stream of hopeful words.[47] Although Jeremiah 32 – 33 is prose linked to a specific time and place, so that it contrasts starkly with the undated poetry of chapters 30–31, the two units are tightly bound by numerous features, culminating in parallel covenant assurances in 31:35–37 and 33:25–26.[48] Jeremiah 34:1–7 has close links to 32:1–5, each beginning with what looks like the same oracle, until 34:4–5 introduces a surprising twist. Having established the connection to what precedes, the final unit, Jeremiah 34:8–22, closes the collection with an account of a broken covenant and its consequences; aside from an echo of chapter 32 in Jeremiah 50:5, this is the last appearance of a covenant in the book of Jeremiah. Covenants thus bring to a close chapters 31, 32, 33, 34, binding the whole composite together. (The story they tell will be sketched out in my next section.) Finally, one more unusual feature of these chapters should be noted, namely, that the Disjunctive Heading is used four times in quick succession, at the head of each constituent element of the group (30:1; 32:1; 34:1; 34:8). In my judgment this represents an independent deployment of the Disjunctive Heading to provide internal connection points within a composite unit. Whether it is earlier or not is impossible to say, but at the point when the book of Jeremiah was drawn together into its final versions (LXXV and M), this heading, which binds 30 – 34 together, was the heading chosen to bring narrative unity to the whole book.[49]

This brings us back to Lundbom's account of the structure of Jeremiah's second half. Lundbom observes that if the Jehoiakim chapters 25, 26, 35, 36 are extracted from the rest, they form a chiasm by date and subject matter. Since this arrangement seems so much more satisfying than their present placement Lundbom concludes 'that the Jehoiakim cluster was originally an independent collection of prose narrative written *and arranged* by Baruch'.[50] He draws the same conclusion for a 'Zedekiah cluster' made up of Jeremiah 24,

---

[47] I have overlooked the fact that Jer. 33:14–26 is missing from the LXX; as Emanuel Tov has argued, this does not mean that its contents originated only after the LXXV was finished; they could as easily be genuinely Jeremianic documents that were not incorporated until the final edition (Tov 1981: 154).

[48] Biddle 1988.

[49] The use of a distinctive structural formula to hold together a composite unit within the larger book can also be seen in the OAN, where seven word formulas, all of them atypical, are used to introduce the various oracles (see n. 8 above).

[50] Lundbom 1975: 109, my italics.

27, 28, 29 (pp. 109–111). As a result he makes chapters 24 and 36 the boundaries of a major section within the book of Jeremiah.

The problem with this sort of analysis is that if the history of Jeremiah's growth involved assembling large documents from individually preserved units, it is not meaningful to speak of older *arrangements* of narratives as if they had a fixed nature. To be sure, when units are bound up into a composite whole in the way chapters 27–29 are, we may postulate their pre-existence as a whole. However, the possession of common features such as date and subject matter does not amount to evidence that texts now separate were once neighbours, attractive as the possibility may seem. It is therefore ill-advised to make Jeremiah 24 the start of a unit running to chapter 36 on the grounds of a putative 'Zedekiah cluster' having once existed. The structure of the book as we now have it has its own integrity and should not be decided on the basis of old structures that no longer exist, if indeed they ever did.

From Jeremiah 25/26 to Jeremiah 35/36
The technique of framing units, large and small alike, by inclusio and similar devices recurs frequently across the book, as Lundbom in particular has convincingly demonstrated. We have seen it at work in the way references to 'this book' frame chapters 25 and 51, in the way references to covenant tie chapters 32–33 to chapters 30–31, in the way the question 'What do you see?' balances chapters 1 and 24, and so forth. And yet the attempt to discern not just framing devices but concentric 'ring compositions' is more problematic. The best candidate for ring composition is the unit Jeremiah 26 – 36, as set out by Stulman,[51] but the suggested points of internal correspondence are based on thematic elements that are not without alternatives, nor do they match up with chronological or syntactical breaks in the text. However, the claims of chapters 26–36 to be read as a unit remain strong, and need to be addressed.

The similarity of Jeremiah 26:1–3 and 36:1–3 is the first of several parallels that prompt many to regard Jeremiah 26 – 36 as a unit.[52]

[51] Stulman 1998: 86–88; for a more ambitious scheme cf. J. Rosenberg (1987: 190–194).

[52] Kessler 1968; Holladay 1989: 22–23; Carroll 1989: 509–510; and others. For Kessler, ch. 26 legitimizes Jeremiah as a true prophet; chs. 27–29 concern rival ideas of *šālôm* (peace), with the prophet's own version in ch. 29 attracting more *šālôm* oracles in chs. 30–33. Finally, chs. 34–36 return to focus on the motif of hoped-for obedience, first introduced in ch. 26. Other scholars accept Jer. 36 as ending a unit,

Indeed, the impressive opening of Jeremiah 26, which starts (like Gen. 1) without a narrative verb form or even a connective waw, has the appearance of launching a narrative, and the echo of its word language in Jeremiah 36:1 points to another bookend.[53] However, even if we accept these arguments – and the frame created by Jeremiah 36:1 and 45:1 militates against it in the minds of some[54] – the neatness of such a unit has been spoiled by the addition in MT of a new verse at the start of Jeremiah 27 that echoes Jeremiah 26:1 in every respect.[55] More importantly, after the conclusion of the supposed unit, Jeremiah 37:1 not only lacks the heading required to launch a new unit, but it lacks any sort of narrative structural formula at all. Yes, a new king is introduced, but his reign continues the narrative sequence, filling the throne vacated by the son of Jehoiakim (who is named in 37:1, strengthening the link to the preceding material). It is my contention that, irrespective of any structural significance the parallels between chapters 26 and 36 may once have had, the contours imposed on the book by its final editor are determined by the Disjunctive Headings, and reinforced in Jeremiah 25 – 52 by its chronological scheme.[56] While we have little information about the literary history of these chapters, it may well be that an older, atypical Narrative Formula (Jer. 26:1) has been subsumed in the book's final editions within the unit beginning at Jeremiah 25,

but extend its beginning back to ch. 24 (Lundbom 2004a) or even ch. 21 (Nötscher 1934).

[53] Both verses end with 'this word came [to Jeremiah] from the LORD'.

[54] Those who see Jer. 36 as primarily linked, through the character of Baruch, with what follows, tend to make each chapter the beginning of a unit, namely, Jer. 26 – 35 and 36 – 45 (Rudolph 1967: xix–xxi; cf. Brueggemann 1991: 121; Fischer 2005: 1.85). As a result, Jer. 26 – 35 tends to be broken down into smaller units. Stulman's solution is to regard ch. 36 as a 'hinge', doing double duty (Stulman 1998: 84–85).

[55] Jer. 27:1 MT is anarthrous, and differs only in the addition of Jeremiah's name. Most commentators, and almost all modern English Versions (NJPSV is a rare exception), emend the name Jehoiakim to Zedekiah (cf. 27:3), supposing that a scribe has accidentally assimilated Jehoiakim's name from the otherwise identical Jer. 26:1. Although I have followed this practice in the present book, it is not traditional – Rashi's reading, followed by Calvin, AV, RV and others, is that 'three years prior to Nebuchadnezzar's ascent to the throne, he prophesied about him that he would reign' (A. J. Rosenberg 1989: 217) – and some strong arguments have recently been made against it (Fischer 2005: 2.49–50; Wells 2007: 327–328; cf. Leuchter 2006: 7–8). Which king's name heads the chapter does not materially affect the present structural discussion.

[56] It is worth noting that the Disjunctive Headings are not a novel feature in the final edition, but are present in the LXX as well, with the exception of Jer. 7:1. Some of the atypical headings are missing from the Greek version of the OAN, whose complicated structural reorganization for the M edition we cannot examine here.

a unit in which Jeremiah 26:1 and 27:1 mark subdivisions. A new Disjunctive Heading at Jeremiah 30:1 marks the start of the next unit. Such a conservative approach to older material characterizes the entire work, in which we have seen spellings not regularized, and atypical headings left intact.

In the same way the Disjunctive Heading at Jeremiah 35:1 sets in train a unit that runs into chapter 36. Jeremiah 36 does not have a conventional formulaic opening, but the way it begins preserves its narrative continuity with the preceding chapter.[57] Chapters 35 and 36 are already unified by the name of Jehoiakim and as a unit they look forward to chapter 45 and back to chapters 25–26.[58] Thus the framework of Disjunctive Headings suggests that we treat Jeremiah 35 – 39 as a unit within which Jeremiah 36:1 and 37:1 mark subdivisions.

In other words, while the connection noticed by scholars between chapters 26 and 36 is real and strong, in the final versions of the book these chapters do not relate to one another as single chapters, but as members of two pairs of chapters dating from Jehoiakim's reign. A number of cross-connections bear this out. Beginning with Jeremiah 25, we see first that it is linked to chapter 35 by the theme of drinking wine,[59] and especially by the almost verbatim repetitions of 25:3b–5 in 35:14b–15.[60] However, in terms of its message, chapter 25 is more like chapter 36, as is its setting in time (Jehoiakim's fourth year). Thus the theme of a scroll containing God's word against all nations (25:13) is picked up in 36:2, where Jeremiah fills a scroll with 'all the words I have spoken to you against Israel and Judah and all the nations'. And in 36:29 Jehoiakim is outraged that the

---

[57] While Jer. 36:1b has something of the look of the Disjunctive Headings of Jer. 25:1, 35:1, etc., the verse as a whole begins with the macrosyntactic marker *wayĕhî* plus a time margin; as it stands it is an atypical Narrative Formula (see n. 11 above). Even if an earlier version of Jer. 36 began with a fully fledged Disjunctive Heading, the subsequent alteration has introduced a sense of narrative continuity with ch. 35, and if we are to pursue the notion that the framework of the book was the result of careful editing, then this connectedness to ch. 35 must be taken with due seriousness. Jeremiah scholarship has almost always read chs. 34 and 35 together, and we shall further explore the viability of reading them separately in the sections covering narrating Jer. 25 – 52, below.

[58] Cf. Lundbom 2004a: 238.

[59] Is the pointed way in which Jeremiah is to bring the Rechabites to the house of the LORD before offering them wine supposed to remind us of the drinking of the cup of the wine of God's wrath in ch. 25, by which Judah and the nations become a wasteland?

[60] Thiel 1973: 267; Fischer 2005: 1.732.

scroll announced destruction at the hands of Babylon's king – a pronouncement that Jeremiah makes in chapter 25 but not in chapter 26, whose word is directed primarily against the temple, and does not mention Babylon.

Moving on to Jeremiah 26, despite its aforementioned links to chapter 36 its message is more like that of chapter 35, as is Jeremiah's location (in the temple). Thus in chapter 26 the LORD urges the people to listen him and walk in his law (*tôrâ*, v. 4), and 'to listen to the words of my servants the prophets whom I send to you urgently, though you have not listened' (v. 5). In Jeremiah 35 the Rechabites' obedience to their father's command (*miṣwâ*, v. 14) leads to the charge that the people by contrast have not listened, even though 'I have sent to you all my servants the prophets, sending them urgently' (v. 15).

From Jeremiah 39 to Jeremiah 40

While some commentators make a division after Jeremiah 39, it is just as common to find the division made at 40:6, or not at all.[61] My decision to divide at 40:1 is clear-cut, because of the Disjunctive Heading, but in this instance there is no chronological marker to go with it, and it is best treated as a new episode in the narrative that begins in chapter 35. This division is borne out by the way chapter 40 draws to a close. It gives us a flashback to a word received in Jeremiah's captivity, promising Ebed-Melech his life, 'because you have put your trust in me'. The promise is strikingly phrased: 'you shall have your life as a spoil of war' (39:18). It refers us back to a previous oracle, recorded first in 21:8–10 and again in 38:2–3, offering life to any person who surrendered to the Babylonian army. And so the unit in chapters 35–39 is bracketed by two acts of faithfulness carried out by people on the margins of society – the Rechabites and Ebed-Melech – who in their actions point to a future that lies outside and beyond the present order.

Jeremiah 40:1–6 functions as we have come to expect: it recapitulates earlier material and launches us into a new phase of the narrative. Looking back, it rehearses the reason Jerusalem fell, and with the mention of Jeremiah's continued survival alludes back to a line of thought begun in 1:19. The way in which it does these things is far from expected, however. The word about Jerusalem

---

[61] Dividing after Jer. 39: McConville 1993b; Fischer 2005; Allen 2008; dividing after Jer. 40:6: Lundbom 2004b; Stulman 2005; Roncace 2005; Longman 2008.

comes, unprecedentedly, from the lips of a Babylonian officer, while Jeremiah himself is mute for two chapters. His continued presence 'among the people who were left in the land' in 40:2 is significant because it establishes that Jeremiah is not absent from 40:7 – 41:18, and neither is God; they are silently present, withholding the life-giving word.

From Jeremiah 44 to Jeremiah 45 and beyond

That Jeremiah 44 brings a story to its close is well recognized. Which story, however, is less clear. By repeating God's accusation that 'they/you neither listened nor lent their/your ears' (44:4–5) a frame is created with Jeremiah 35:15, but the phrase is also used at the start and end of the previous section (25:4; 34:14); the original use of the phrase comes in 7:24–25.[62] The idolatry of the fugitives evokes the sin that precipitated Jeremiah's ministry in the beginning, a point underlined by the first appearance since chapter 7 of the Queen of Heaven. Stulman is correct to label Jeremiah 44 'a summarizing speech in Deuteronomic style that functions in a manner similar to Jeremiah 25'.[63]

It is when we get to the brief chapter that follows that things get more difficult. Jeremiah 45 clearly does not continue on from the previous chapter, being set in Jehoiakim's reign, although it does take us back to the start of the story that chapter 44 concludes. This has prompted a wide variety of suggestions, most of them concerned to account for the placement of the three chapters set in Jehoiakim's fourth year.[64] In the other direction, the relation of chapter 45 to Jeremiah 46 – 51 (the OAN) is complicated by the varying placement of these oracles in MT and LXX. Was chapter 45 originally the end of the whole book (as it is in the LXX), or was it placed here to make a link to the OAN?[65]

---

[62] The only other occurrences of the phrase are in 11:8; 17:23. In the first half of the book it refers to their ancestors' rejection of the covenant; in the second half the connection to Jeremiah's listeners is made explicit.

[63] Stulman 1998: 61, who sees Jer. 25 as a conclusion to the unit 1 – 25.

[64] On the history of interpretation see Taylor (1987: 79–86). Alexander Rofé has drawn attention to the fact that 'the compiler of the book put the events of the 4th year of Jehoiakim at the beginning of all the dated prose chapters of Jeremiah (ch. 25), at their very end (ch. 45) and in the middle [ch. 36]': a ring-composition device that Rofé judges was designed to draw attention to the theological significance of the year in which Babylonian dominion began (Rofé 1989: 394).

[65] Lundbom argues the former case (Lundbom 1986) and Christopher Seitz the latter (Seitz 1989a: 22); the current consensus about the book's textual history favours Lundbom's view. However, the allusion to Jer. 25:31 ('he is entering into judgment

I have argued that when Jeremiah is read around its word formulas the Jehoiakim chapters become starting points for new sections of the book. And yet in the case of Jeremah 45 we have a chapter that comes closer to being a bidirectional 'hinge' than any other. As the closing chapter of the LXXV edition, Jeremiah 45 forms a conclusion in a way the other Jehoiakim chapters (in my opinion) do not. First, the word formula of 45:1 is not a normal Disjunctive Heading. Secondly, 'these words' that Baruch wrote (45:1) clearly refer back to the scroll of chapter 36. For numerous interpreters Jeremiah 45 serves to conclude a 'Baruch narrative' that began in chapter 37, or perhaps to conclude a scroll beginning in chapter 25.[66] Thirdly, Baruch's fate, to have his life 'as a spoil of war', makes him the only other beneficiary, apart from Ebed-Melech, of the hope held out by the oracles of 38:2–3. These two men are the Joshuas to Jeremiah's Moses, the Elishas to his Elijah.[67] Fourthly, the reference to building, destroying, planting and plucking up (45:4) ties the chapter back to the programme announced in 1:10.[68]

At the same time, when the OAN were moved to their present position, chapter 45 was brought into service as an introduction, and this is how I believe it primarily functions in the book's final edition. First, in the reading sequence of the book we are taken back to 'ground zero', the fourth year of Jehoiakim, as if to begin cycling through the history of Judah's fall for a fourth time. Secondly, the word formula that begins Jeremiah 45, while clearly not a normal Disjunctive Heading, functions in the same way (see n. 8 above) and, moreover, shares its atypical form with the disjunctive headings that form subdivisions within the OAN. Thirdly, of these atypical word formulas, 45:1 has an especial connection to 51:59: these are the only word formulas whose speaker is given as Jeremiah rather than the LORD; while the first addresses Baruch, the second addresses his brother Seriah; one introduces and the other concludes the OAN. In short, 45:1 and 51:59 frame this section of the book of Jeremiah.[69]

---

with all flesh, and the evil he will put to the sword') in the words 'I am bringing evil upon all flesh' (Jer. 45:5) offers an interesting point of connection back to the older (LXX) placement of the OAN.

[66] Scalise 2007, who argues, following a suggestion of W. Thiel, that Baruch is a model for the reader: 'Baruch's lamenting response to the scroll is exemplary in some way' (298).

[67] Seitz 1989a.

[68] Jer. 45:4 has special affinity with 24:6 and 42:10 (Taylor 1987: 91).

[69] Cf. Wanke (1971: 133–134), who argues that Jer. 45 + 51:59–64 constitute a single complex of tradition.

Fourthly, the internal rearrangement of the OAN has placed two discrete Egyptian oracles at the start, which combine to relate the history of the previous unit from an Egyptian perspective. (1) The first oracle starts from the fourth year of Jehoiakim (46:2), arguably creating another pair of Jehoiakim chapters. It shows that the fate of Judah, begun in that year, was being experienced in Egypt at the same time. (2) The second oracle repeats the thrust of Jeremiah's prophecy in 43:8–13, and its opening (46:14) names three of the four places settled by the Jewish fugitives according to 44:1: Migdol, Tahpanhes and Memphis. (3) At the end there is hope after judgment, both for Egypt (46:26b) and, in context, the Jews exiled in her (46:27–28).

In conclusion, it is best to read Jeremiah 45 as a unit that gathers up the threads of the book so far, and launches a final phase of the story concerning the word of the LORD. This Baruch word then forms a frame that is closed at the other end by the hopeful word to his brother Seraiah concerning Babylon. In between, the Oracles are subdivided by their atypical Disjunctive Headings into the two Egyptian oracles mentioned above (headings in 46:1, 13), the oracles against the surrounding nations in chapters 47–49 (headed by 47:1), the oracle against the distant nation Elam (headed by 49:34) and the Babylon oracle (headed by 50:1).[70]

A narrative about the word of God

Having settled on a structure for the book, it remains to provide a concise account of the book that emerges from this structure.[71] Although the book divides into two distinct halves, Jeremiah's story about the word of God unfolds in four successive movements, consisting of chapters 1–24, 25–34, 35–44 and 45–52, and subdivided

[70] In the LXXV the Elam oracle was the first of the OAN, and 49:34 as we have it in the MT was split up and bracketed the oracle, with the Zedekiah reference at the end (Jer. LXX 25:14 + 26:1); for a discussion see Lundbom (2004b: 360–362). One ought not, therefore, to write off the Disjunctive Heading in Jer. MT 49:34 as a vestigial structural element from the previous edition, because the combining of the LXXV subscriptions and superscriptions by the compiler of the M edition shows that its continued presence is intentional, and may well have been prompted by two considerations: (1) Elam was not one of the surrounding nations, but lay East of the Tigris, opposite Babylonia; (2) the mention of Zedekiah links the oracle to the Babylon oracle, and turns the OAN into a journey from Egypt to Babylonia that runs parallel to the journey from Jehoiakim to Zedekiah.

[71] This account forms the context for the close readings that feature in chapters 3–6 below.

by the Disjunctive Headings as described above. I have presented an outline of this four-movement narrative in tables 2.1–2.4 below. Each movement picks up on themes from previous movements and carries them further. And each movement tends to present the word of God and its speaker, Jeremiah, from a different angle, or point of view. To develop this idea I have chosen an analogy from cinema.

Jeremiah goes to the movies

The effect of Jeremiah's structure upon the reader may be illustrated by an analogy to film-making, in which camera position is used to

Table 2.1 A narrative about the word of the LORD: first movement – the word of the LORD announces Judah's destruction and its speaker is crushed

Jer. 1	Prelude
	Jeremiah's call and commission as speaker (1:1–10)
	The word, its speaker and their respective tasks (1:11–19)
Jer. 2 – 6	The fruitless appeal to an adulterous wife, to return to her husband
	The pleas of a scorned husband (2:1 – 4:4)
	The wrath of a warrior aroused (4:4 – 6:30)
Jer. 7 – 10	The tragic corruption of the temple into a doomed pagan shrine
Jer. 11 – 17	The painful consequences of covenant-breaking
	Covenant-breakers fall under a curse and Jeremiah feels the pain (11 – 12)
	The pride of being God's people will perish; Jeremiah is preserved (13 – 15)
	As a warning to Judah, life in God loses its joy for Jeremiah (16 – 17)
Jer. 18 – 20	The freedom of God to reject his elect evokes a violent response
Jer. 21 – 24	The throne of David in Judah will be vacant
	Your kings cannot save you; one day God will raise up his own king (21 – 22)
	Your prophets cannot save you (23)
	The kingdom of Judah is past saving; exiles will one day be replanted (24)

Table 2.2 A narrative about the word of the LORD: second movement – the word of the LORD vindicates its speaker and offers true hope to deaf listeners

Jer. 25 – 29	True prophecy is tested and found to be on the lips of Jeremiah
	The true extent of God's wrath is revealed (25)
	God preserves Jeremiah and destroys the speakers of rival words (26 – 29)
Jer. 30 – 34	A true and revolutionary covenant lies in the future, not the present
	A radically new covenant emerges from the present darkness (30 – 33)
	Its promises lie entirely in the future (34)

Table 2.3 A narrative about the word of the LORD: third movement – the word of the LORD destroys the nation it created and plants seeds of new life

Jer. 35 – 39	The indestructible word exerts its power and the kingdom falls
	Godly outsiders earn a future by their obedience (35)
	The word enters in and takes away the king's future (36)
	Jeremiah kept safe while the word he speaks tears down the nation (37 – 39)
Jer. 40 – 43	The word is silent while the remnant self-destruct
Jer. 44	No escape, even back in Egypt: God's word will stand

Table 2.4 A narrative about the word of the LORD: fourth movement – the word of the LORD sends a tide of judgment across the earth and draws a new nation from the wreckage

Jer. 45	Baruch, whose scroll preserved the word, will himself be preserved
Jer. 46:1 – 51:58	The word of God tears down the nations and draws Israel, alive, from the jaws of death
	The word destroys Egypt even as Judah falls; in her destruction lies hope (46)
Jer. 51:59–64	The nations around Judah share her wickedness and her fate (47 – 49)
Jer. 52	Babylon dies and the mystery of Israel's future hope is revealed (50 – 51)
	Seraiah, whose scroll secures Babylon's end, ends Jeremiah's book
	Back to the present, where the word of the LORD lives on

convey the 'point of view' (POV) the director wishes the viewer to share. For example, the camera might look over the shoulder of the main character to gaze into the face of her husband, with whom she is conversing; we thus share her POV, and when the camera looks away we interpret the camera movement as if it were made by her, and we invest it with the same emotional significance as we would if we could see her face. And the reactions we see in her husband's face show us how we might react in his place, and – more importantly – show us, with her POV, how 'we' are being perceived. Alternatively, the director might position the camera further off and to the side, with one character at each edge of the screen. Our POV is now that of an observer. We see the conversation more objectively, and are more ready to think about the fact of the conversation, and its implications, rather than simply experience it from one side or the other. Sometimes the director might place the camera high above the couple, or far away from them, so that they themselves become objects in the centre of the screen, and their surroundings will play an important role in conveying the mood of the encounter. From this POV we might be more conscious of the conversation as an element in a larger story, affecting and being affected by external parties and events.

To apply this to reading Jeremiah, the first movement of the book gives us the prophet's POV, so that we see as he sees and feel as he feels. It is in this part of the book that his inner life is laid bare before us. And because of the blurring of voices (a phenomenon we shall explore in the next chapter) we are looking out not only from inside Jeremiah, but from inside the word of the LORD, and experiencing its rejection first hand.

In the second movement the camera begins with a long shot, showing us the surroundings (people, places and times), and panning across the nations of Jeremiah's world to anticipate the vast canvas the final movement will fill. From chapter 26, however, the camera settles down alongside the action, and we observe Jeremiah on one edge of the screen in conflict with a series of opponents on the other edge. Thus, while the chapter starts very much as chapter 7 did, in 26:7–8 the new camera position is clearly established. For the first time, we hear others speaking for themselves, even taking Jeremiah's words onto their lips in accusation (26:9). And so Jeremiah 26 – 29 turns into a war of words. It is a war Jeremiah wins, and though further battles are fought in chapter 29, in the Book of Consolation the word of the LORD is unrivalled and uninterrupted, so that we could almost forget that Jeremiah has (silent) listeners.[72] The listeners speak up again in chapter 32, and we are again aware of the camera alongside the speakers, giving us a ringside view of their encounter.[73]

As we move into the third movement the camera begins in the same position; Jeremiah 35, for example, is similar in its discourse structure to chapter 32.[74] However, the conflict is much more intense this time. The words of the LORD have taken on written form, and

---

[72] It may be, of course, that the poetry of Jer. 30 – 31 is formally identical to that of Jer. 2ff., but in its present placement in the book's reading sequence it attracts an implied audience on the other edge of the screen, as it were.

[73] Cf. the way in which Jeremiah's first-person account in 32:6–25 is framed within a third-person narrative, as opposed to the account of, say, Jer. 18, which is pure autobiography. The narrative quality of Jer. 32 is less marked in the LXX, and some interpreters have minimized its narrative structure (esp. Migsch 1996), but this is unjustified, as I argue elsewhere (Shead 2002b: 53–66).

[74] Migsch 1997.

their opponent is now the king himself. The battle to establish the legitimacy of the word of the LORD and of his prophet was won in the previous movement; now the battle concerns the power of the word to do what it says versus the power of the king to impose his will. From chapter 37 our camera starts to pull back, and though the war of words continues, words are slowly overtaken by events, and Jeremiah shrinks to a figure in a wide-angled landscape shot of destruction until, in chapter 39, he is reduced to an incidental character, caught up with the rest of Judah in the destructive power of the word of God, finally unleashed on his feckless people.

In the final movement of the book the camera rises as high as it can go, and we see the word of the LORD sounding across all the nations of the earth. The whole story in its universal setting is now clearly seen for the first time since being announced in chapter 1 and foreshadowed in chapter 25. As the book closes we see the remnant of God's people in Babylon, but know that the word of the LORD has promised a future transformation that will have eternal consequences for the whole earth.[75]

Narrating Jeremiah 1 – 24

Following the patterns observed in the interweaving of prose and poetry and in the Disjunctive Headings, Jeremiah 2 – 24 divides into five sections. Before they get underway, the opening chapter provides two beginnings to the work. In the first, Jeremiah's identity as the speaker of the word is established, and the scope of the word's activities among the nations laid out (vv. 1–10). In the second, Jeremiah receives his orders along with some words of assurance (vv. 11–19). This opening chapter anticipates every major theme of the book and foreshadows the course the word of the LORD will follow over the next thirty years and fifty chapters.

1. *Jeremiah 2 – 6* unfolds in two parts. Jeremiah 2:1 – 4:4 makes up a third beginning to Jeremiah, one that expresses God's anguish over Israel by the metaphor of a broken marriage. Stulman argues that this collection is positioned here to control the way we read the rest of the book:

---

[75] A sensitivity to perspectival shifts of this nature, especially between the personal immediacy of the first movement and the greater distance of the next three, may well underlie the decision of the Septuagint translators to alter their translation equivalents for the Messenger Formula from *tade legei kyrios*, 'this is what the LORD says', to the more historical *houtōs eipen kyrios*, 'thus did the LORD say' (Pietersma 2007: 7–8).

To some degree, all subsequent God-talk is rooted in this initial metaphor. One might even argue that the theological discourse of the LORD as scorned lover *generates* the rich tapestry of symbolic constructions in the following chapters. Just as grief gives rise to many discordant expressions, so Israel's rejection of the LORD fuels a wide range of divine emotions, responses, musings and strategies.[76]

God longs to pour out his affection on his intransigent nation; but after repeated appeals meet with lukewarm response, his tone changes to one of resolute anger. And from Jeremiah 4:4 until the end of chapter 6 the poetry is unrelentingly cold, dark and savage, as the controlling metaphor shifts to one of military aggression.

The second half of this section is a vast poetic indictment that is matched in its scale only by the poetry of chapters 30–31 in the middle, and 50–51 at the end of the book. After a series of terrible visions of invasion in chapter 4, 'the balance between event and comment alters, as God builds up the case against his people, punctuating it only with the last three visions of the coming ordeal'.[77] And yet, at the very point when God's anger places him at a distance, Jeremiah's voice enters to bridge the gap, showing us through his experience of both divine love and divine wrath that the God who judges so harshly is filled with an anguish equal to that of the beloved nation he is judging.

2. *Jeremiah 7 – 10* begins with the famous temple sermon and announces the tearing down of the evil people whose temple worship is a prop for their complacence (7:1 – 8:3). As with the previous section, idolatry is at the heart of the problem, and the nation's leaders are chiefly culpable. Where the previous section brought judgment in grand and mythic terms, chapter 7 is couched in terms of Judah's daily realities, and isolates the institution of the temple and its worship as the target of the terrifying oracles of chapters 4–6. The poetry that follows in chapters 8–10 is filled with despair over the people's refusal to repent, regret over the way their leaders betrayed them, and profound grief over the fate that awaits them:

> Is there no balm in Gilead?
> is there no healer there?

[76] Stulman 2005: 61, italics original.
[77] Kidner 1987: 39.

So why has there not welled up
health for my dear people?
Oh, that my head were a well of water
and my eyes a torrent of tears,
that I might weep both day and night
for the slain of my dear people.

(Jer. 8:22 – 9:1)

Together, these two sections comprise a 'mini-movement' that runs from Jeremiah 2 to 10, in which the opening legal drama and the people's refusal to repent (chs. 2–3) leads inexorably to the judgment of invasion from the north (chs. 4–6), whose chief anticipated effect is the destruction of the temple (ch. 7), a destruction that precipitates national anguish (chs. 8–9) and eventually spreads to destroy the very nations who oppressed Israel (ch. 10).[78] For Joseph Henderson this mini-movement dramatically portrays the history of God and his people Israel from the exodus to the exile. Jeremiah 9 – 10 thus reflects the destruction of Jerusalem, the subsequent contrast between chastened exiles and the devastated, grieving city, and the hope of a final judgment of the nations so as to prevent the complete annihilation of God's people (10:22–25).[79] The point of view of chapters 2–10 is very much that of God himself.

3. *Jeremiah 11 – 24 as a whole* makes up the second 'mini-movement'. The camera angle is the same as for chapters 2–10, but we are more conscious now that it is Jeremiah's eyes through which we see. The theme of covenant, though concentrated in chapters 11–17, is present at one level or another right through to the hoped-for new covenant of 24:7. Whether there is a distinct plot to this 'mini-movement' is harder to say; for O'Connor, chapters 11–20 are about the rejection and triumph of the prophetic word; for Jindo, chapters 11–24 are about Jeremiah's emotional reactions to his contemporaries, in ever-widening circles from the people of Anathoth through to the royal house.[80] I have argued above, with the help of Clements,[81] that we see in these chapters the progressive dismantling of the

---

[78] Jindo 2010: 60–61.

[79] Henderson 2007: 150–151. Henderson draws a false dichotomy between seeing these chapters as crafted to tell a story and seeing them as windows onto the historical Jeremiah. More convincing is his criticism of the methods and assumptions by which traditional critical interpreters reconstructed Jeremiah's biography.

[80] O'Connor 1988: 128; Jindo 2010: 61.

[81] Clements 1993.

nation, its institutions and its covenantal privileges, a dismantling that is seen in concrete in the life of the prophet himself.

In narrating these chapters it must not be forgotten that the prose both structures and interprets the poetry. We have seen the way a sermon initiates each of the units beginning at 7:1; 11:1; 18:1; 21:1; we have also seen that prose accounts of prophetic sign acts (13:1–11; 16:1–13; 19:1–15) serve to subdivide two of these units. It remains to be observed that in each of the five units thus created within chapters 11–20 there is a lament, or 'confession', of the prophet (11:18 – 12:6; 15:15–18; 17:14–18; 18:18–23; 20:7–18). Through these laments we see a 'light-expelling despair breaking into the prophet's inner being'.[82] The final unit ends not with a lament but with a vision (ch. 24).

4. *Jeremiah 11 – 17* is the longest and most complex of the sections in the first movement. It consists of three prose accounts, each with poetry attached to it, and a closing warning. The first prose passage is a sermon on the dangers of covenant unfaithfulness, as is the final warning (17:19–27). An inclusio binds these sermons: 'yet they neither listened nor lent their ears' (11:8; 17:23); it refers to the covenant-breaking of their ancestors, and serves to warn Jeremiah's listeners of the dangers of disobedience. Within this frame the intervening material is very diverse, but is punctuated by two symbolic actions: the spoiling of the loincloth (13:1–11) and Jeremiah's prevention by the word of the LORD from marrying, having children or mourning the dead (16:1–9). Each of these brings home in its own way the reality of the covenant curses Judah is bringing down on their head by 'refusing to listen or lend their ears'. And each is followed by turbulent poems of lament spoken by Judah, God and – most of all – Jeremiah.

The cruel treatment Jeremiah suffers evokes a series of laments – known as the 'confessions of Jeremiah', though they involve no confession of sin – that run through this and the following section. As these confessions grow more terrible in their pain and desperation, Jeremiah the righteous sufferer becomes a mirror in which the sufferings of both the people and their God are reflected.[83] By the

---

[82] Von Rad 1983: 97.

[83] They are called 'confessions' rather than 'laments' to draw attention to their intensely personal character, as opposed to the more generic and liturgical flavour of the psalms of lament. Of the substantial literature on the confessions the following works in English may be noted: Baumgartner 1988 [1917]; Diamond 1987; O'Connor 1988; Smith 1990; for brief remarks see von Rad (1965: 2.201–206), and especially McConville (1993b: 61–78).

end of this section we are left with the conviction that despite the terrible warnings, threats and exhortations to repent that punctuate the early chapters, the people are afflicted with a fatal deafness to the word of the LORD, the consequences of which they will not be able to escape:

> Deceitful is the heart above all,
> and incurable. Who can know it?
> I, the LORD, search the heart
> and probe the inmost being,
> to give to each as their path,
> as the fruit of their deeds decree.
>
> (Jer. 17:9–10)

5. *Jeremiah 18 – 20* is largely concerned with the symbolic action of the buying and smashing of a pot, representing the sovereign freedom of God to make or destroy nations as he pleases. The key word 'relent' (*niḥām*) brackets the section (18:8–10; 20:16), showing that God is free to relent of the good he promised if a nation does not amend their ways.[84] If the second section attacked the temple as a source of spiritual security, and the third section announced the end of covenant blessings, this section effectively ends the assurance Judah placed in their status as God's treasured possession, his elect from among the nations. The loss of their status as the elect has already been suggested by their demotion to the level of one of the nations (e.g. 9:25–26; 17:4), but here it is made explicit. The only source of security left to them now are the promises made to the Davidic monarchy, and in the fifth section they will be removed as well.

The narrative of the pot is divided into two sections, each followed by an account of attacks against Jeremiah (18:18; 20:1–3) and a subsequent lament (or confession) of the prophet. The first mention of Babylon in the book (20:4) lends a particularly ominous tone to the closing verses of the section. The result of God's choice to destroy his people is foreshadowed by Jeremiah's own rejection, which leads him to voice on his own account the despair of a rejected people.

> Cursed be
> the day on which I was born,
> the day my mother bore me:

---

[84] Allen 2008: 212.

let it never be blessed!
Cursed be
the man who brought news to my father,
saying 'Born to you is a man-child,'
bringing him such joy!
Make that man like the towns
the LORD overturned unrelenting;
make him hear screaming in the morning,
a battle cry at midday –
he who did not kill me in the womb
so that my mother could have been my grave,
her womb pregnant for ever.
Why is it that from the womb I have come
to see struggle and sorrow,
then end my days in shame?

(Jer. 20:14–20)

6. *Jeremiah 21 – 24* stands somewhat apart from what has preceded it. It is more prosaic, and features the first dated material, though it does so in order to drive home its judgment of the Davidic monarchy. After an account of Zedekiah's appeal to Jeremiah for divine assistance against Babylon, which anticipates similar encounters between king and prophet in the second half of the book (21:1–10),[85] a series of oracles against the house of David and the (generic) king of Judah follow (21:11 – 22:10), eventually picking 'the sons of Josiah' out one by one (22:11–30). The final denunciation is a death knell rung over the institution of Judean kingship:

Earth, earth, earth,
hear the word of the LORD!
This is what the LORD says:
Write down this one as childless,
a man who will not advance in his lifetime.
For not one of his offspring will advance
to sit on the throne of David
or rule once more in Judah.

(Jer. 22:29–30)

---

[85] On the relationship between Jeremiah and Zedekiah, and the way it resonates with the relationship between earlier prophets and kings, especially Samuel and Saul, see Roncace (2005: 146–159).

95

The final two chapters launch attacks on the prophets (ch. 23) and record the vision of good and bad figs. This sets the stage for the second half of the book by locating Israel's future in Babylon and denying any future to the present order (ch. 24). From this point on Jeremiah will be in constant conflict with Judah's kings and the prophets that serve them.

And yet, this section is not without notes of hope. Jeremiah 23:5–8 looks forward to a wise king, the righteous branch of David, by whom both Judah and Israel will return from exile. This is no ordinary king, and cannot be taken as a contradiction to the previous anti-monarchic material (just as it need not be read as a late insertion): 'This is the name by which he will be called, the LORD our righteous saviour' (23:6). In similar vein, the good figs of chapter 24 are promised an inward transformation by which their return to the land as God's true and faithful covenant partners will be enabled, so that God's intention to build as well as tear down (1:10) will finally be fulfilled. It is the word of the LORD, we are reminded, that is the active power both for destruction and reconstruction:

> I will set my eyes upon them for their good,
> and I will bring them back to this land;
> I will build them and I will not destroy;
> I will plant them and I will not uproot.
>
> (Jer. 24:6)

These notes of hope are fleeting and distant, of no immediate bearing on the dire present situation as the word of the LORD progressively announces the tearing down of his people, Judah, institution by institution, while opportunities to repent are offered and rejected, until eventually no good thing remains to be salvaged in all the land, and what hope remains is entirely invested in the 'good figs' in exile.

Nevertheless, we do not actually see any tearing down (with the exception of the persecutions of Jeremiah himself). In fact we see hardly anything apart from the word itself. The viewpoint of this half of Jeremiah is intensely subjective. Jeremiah delivers oracles in the first person and narrates events in his own life. Even poetic oracles with no introduction, which seem to come straight from God, contain the odd verse that betrays Jeremiah's subjective presence (e.g. 10:23–25; 17:14–18; 23:9). Apart from the narrative framework of third-person Disjunctive Headings, Jeremiah is spoken about in the third person just four times. In Jeremiah 14:1 and 18:18 it is just a single verse that triggers a first-person speech (cf. 14:11; 18:19); only in Jeremiah 19:14 – 20:6 and 21:1–10 do we have genuine narratives about the prophet such as we find in the book's second half. In short, Jeremiah 1 – 24 focuses exclusively on the word and its speaker, with everything else – the people spoken to, the events spoken about – refracted through the eyes of the speaker and the word, second-hand images of themselves.

The second half of the book unfolds in three movements, each beginning in the fourth year of Jehoiakim, the year in which Nebuchadnezzar's defeat of Egypt at Carchemish marked the start of a new world order.

Narrating Jeremiah 25 – 34

The second movement of Jeremiah unfolds in two phases. Jeremiah 25 – 29 begins by condensing Jeremiah's entire ministry to date, as preserved in chapters 1–24, into a concise indictment of Judah's refusal to hear the word of the LORD (vv. 1–7), followed by an announcement of judgment that identifies the foe from the north with Nebuchadnezzar for the first time (vv. 8–11).[86] It is not the name Nebuchadnezzar that precipitates the ensuing conflict, but the specifying of seventy years that closes out verse 11. The last part of this programmatic speech (vv. 12–14) offers no personal hope to the listeners, but it does foreshadow the direction of the book of Jeremiah by drawing out the significance of Jeremiah's commission as prophet to the nations: 'Upon the completion of seventy years I will punish the king of Babylon and that nation – oracle of the LORD – for their iniquity' (Jer. 25:12a). Jeremiah 25:1–14 anticipates the shape of the rest of the book in much the same way that chapter 1 does for the first half. In the rest of chapter 25 the cup of God's wrath is poured out on all nations, and the true extent of God's destructive word is finally made clear.

> The tumult comes to the ends of the earth,
>   for the LORD lays charges against the nations.
> He is entering into judgment against all flesh,
>   and the wicked – he gives them to the sword.
> (Jer. 25:31)

---

[86] In the LXX this is the first time Nebuchadnezzar is named as Judah's nemesis; the MT has added in that information to 21:7 and 22:25.

There is no word of hope yet, which must surely raise a question in the mind of a listener (or reader) who remembers that God's word was to have built and planted as well as torn down and plucked up; only at the very end of this section, in Jeremiah 29:14, will it be time to consider what happens after judgment.

Jeremiah 26 then opens with a reprise of the temple sermon of chapter 7. If the date of 25:1 did not, then this encourages us to read the section that follows as a new perspective on old material. Jeremiah 2 – 20 was very personal, mostly told from Jeremiah's point of view. But now we look on from outside as Jeremiah's seventy-year prophecy precipitates an intense debate about the validity of his prophetic calling. The people look on as Jeremiah and the prophet Hananiah battle over their rival visions of the future. At the centre of Jeremiah's message in chapter 27 is the claim that the word of the LORD determines the fate even of Nebuchadnezzar, who becomes a tool in God's programme of tearing down the nations.[87] After Hananiah's vision dies with him, Jeremiah is free to turn his attention to the exiles, identified in chapter 24 as the seed of future hope. The oracle in 29:10–14 marks the victory of the word of the LORD in the battle of the prophets, and culminates by introducing the phrase 'I will restore your fortunes', which will punctuate the section that follows with a sevenfold repetition.

Jeremiah 30 – 34 begins by taking us forward in time to a glorious future of reversal and restoration, in which images and phrases are drawn from across the book and inverted in a cycle of six poems that forms the high point of Jeremiah. The prose conclusion to chapter 31 presents a radically new covenant (31:31–34), which God swears by his creation that he will keep (31:35–37). To this 'Book of Consolation' is added an anthology of hopeful oracles that contain fresh images of God's new future, and that also finish with an oath sworn by the creation (33:20–22, 25–26). This anthology opens with words that place it into the very last days of Judah (32:1–5), so that the contrast between present darkness and future hope is made as strong as it can be. Jeremiah 34:1–7 reinforces this location in time. Taken together, this pair of words to Zedekiah helps 'to crystallise the theological movement of Jeremiah xxxii 1–xxxiv 7 from threatening punishment to the proclamation of uncondi-

[87] Cf. Stulman's presentation of 'Yahweh reigns' as a root metaphor in ch. 27, which gives rise to two conflicting visions of the future for all nations, especially including Judah (Stulman 1998: 73–74, 109–115).

tional salvation'.[88] However, despite this hint of personal hope for Zedekiah, the overwhelming effect of the intrusion of 'the tenth year of Zedekiah' (32:1) into the oracles of chapters 32–33 is to highlight the sense of discontinuity between God's hope and the present age. It is precisely this distancing of present and future that the broken covenant of 34:8–22 reinforces, with its contrast to the future covenants of chapters 30–33.[89]

Read as part of a movement spanning from Jeremiah 25 to 34, the oracles of future hope are not at all the intrusive presence that so many judge them to be. As chapter 25 deferred its word of hope away from the listeners to a future generation, and as chapter 29 (foreshadowed by ch. 24) deflected all its hopeful words away from Jeremiah's listeners to the 'good figs' in Babylon, so chapter 34 extinguishes any hope that the promised new covenant might find a toehold in Judah's present experience.[90] And when the oracles of the Book of Consolation are themselves examined, they turn out (as we shall see in a later chapter) to be shot through with dark threads alongside the bright, giving expression to a deep tension between present and future. Such is the depth of Judah's depravity that for restoration to be real it must be marked by a fundamental discontinuity with the present order. The word of the LORD must 'create a new thing on the earth' (31:22).

In short, this second movement of Jeremiah depicts the word of the LORD doing battle with a people, led by their prophets, priests and kings, who have shut their ears to it because they prefer words of cheap grace and false comfort. Having vindicated Jeremiah as God's true prophet, the word of the LORD then proclaims true comfort in words filled with the pain of costly grace. At the end of the movement the narrative of the broken covenant reconnects us to the wider story by its allusions to the broken covenant of 11:1–13 and the sabbath violation of 17:19–27.[91] And so Jeremiah's words of hope

---

[88] Applegate 1998: 152; cf. Applegate 1997.

[89] Anthony Osuji correctly cautions against finding 'a clear cut demarcation' between judgment in the first half of Jeremiah and hope in the second (Osuji 2010: 117); however, 'motifs that contradict the hope of salvation' in this part of Jeremiah have not received the scholarly attention they deserve.

[90] Cf. Rannfrid Thelle's observation that ch. 34 'serves to bring readers back to the gloomier mood of the book, which has temporarily been lifted and deflected by the promise of a more hopeful future [in ch. 32]' (Thelle 2009: 203).

[91] The connection is created by the unusual Jeremianic phrase 'neither listened nor lent your ears' in 11:8, 17:23 and 34:14 (the remaining uses of the phrase are dealt with in my paragraph on Jer. 35 below), and the fact that the covenant broken in

are played into the bleak reality of Jeremiah's listeners, whose deafness is as profound as ever.

Narrating Jeremiah 35 – 44

Jeremiah 35 returns to Jehoiakim's time to take us through the story again in a movement that stretches to chapter 44. Its references back to the previous movement show that it is not a fresh start, but rather a fresh perspective on the activities of the word of the LORD in this crucial time. The main unchanging factor is the deafness of the people to the word of the LORD, as conveyed by the phrase, peculiar to Jeremiah, 'you have neither listened nor lent your ears to hear'. The four occurrences of this phrase in Jeremiah 25 – 52 serve to frame the second (25:4; 34:14) and third (35:15; 44:4) movements, with particularly strong parallels at the start of each movement:

Table 2.5 New movement, old starting point

Jeremiah 25:3b–5	Jeremiah 35:14b–15
I have spoken to you day in and day out, but you have not listened. The LORD has constantly, diligently sent you all his servants the prophets – to whom you *neither listened nor lent your ears to hear* – saying, 'Turn now, each of you, from your evil path and your evil deeds, and remain on the land the LORD has given you and your ancestors from ages past and for ever.'	I have been speaking to you day in and day out, but you have not listened to me. I constantly, diligently sent you all my servants the prophets, saying, 'Turn now, each of you, from your evil path, and reform your deeds, and stop pursuing other gods to serve them, and remain in the land I have given you and your ancestors.' *But you neither lent your ears nor listened to me.*

The other motif chapter 35 picks up from the second movement is found in the narrative of the title deed, related in 32:6–15. The climax of that narrative is an oracle promising that 'houses and fields and vineyards shall again be purchased in this land' (32:15); and it is only in chapter 35 that houses, fields and vineyards all appear again (35:9), as the very things the Rechabites promised not to possess. In their obedient renunciation of these blessings the Rechabites foreshadow the requirement to wait, dispossessed, for the ulti-

---

ch. 34 is a covenant of sabbatical release. The word used in 34:8, 15, 17 (release) suggests that the covenant is not the seven-yearly remission of Deut. 15:12–18, but the permanent return granted in the jubilee (Shead 2002a: 20–24). In the understanding of the Chronicler, it was just this type of refusal to grant a sabbatical return of slaves to family and land that led to God giving the land a seventy-year sabbatical (2 Chr. 36:20–21).

mate restoration of blessing when fortunes are restored (cf. Jer. 32:42–44).[92] And so, with notes of present judgment and future hope picked up, Jeremiah 35 launches a new movement. As we retraverse the period covered by the second movement our attention is now tightly focused onto the monarchy.[93] In the Rechabites we are presented with the first of the movement's 'godly outsiders', whose obedience acts as a foil for the rebellious kings of the following chapters. Jeremiah's oracle begins fairly generally, by targeting the residents of Judah and Jerusalem for refusing to obey the divine words (v. 13), the plural anticipating the plurals of the written words rejected in the next chapter. However, by the time it ends, the oracle has sharpened its claws. The final word of the chapter, 'Jonadab the son of Rechab shall never lack a man to stand before me' (v. 19), stands in bleak contrast with the final word to Jehoiakim, 'he shall have none to sit on the throne of David' (36:29).

Jeremiah himself is on the sidelines in the power struggle of chapter 36, as the word of the LORD penetrates the king's chamber and does battle on its own account. The relevance of this incident to the fall of Jerusalem should not be missed: verses 30–31 establish that it was Jehoiakim's rejection of the word that sealed the fate of Zedekiah and the nation, and verse 32 brings the word back into play so that its power can finally be unleashed:

'Therefore thus says the LORD regarding Jehoiakim king of Judah: None shall he have sitting on David's throne; his carcass shall be flung out into the daytime heat and the night-time frost. And I will punish him, his offspring and his servants for their iniquity. I will bring upon them and Jerusalem's residents, and on the people of Judah, all the disaster I have spoken against them, which they would not hear.'
Then Jeremiah took another scroll and gave it to Baruch, son of Neriah, the scribe, and he wrote on it at Jeremiah's

---

[92] Another possible link between these chapters is the word 'commands' (*miṣwôt*), which describes both the contents of the title deed (32:11) and the paternal command the Rechabites are determined to obey (35:14–18); the word is found nowhere else in Jeremiah. Both the promise of future fields and the renunciation of present fields have a command behind them.

[93] Where Jer. 23 foreshadows the conflict between the word of God and the prophets in the second movement, Jer. 21 – 22 foreshadows the conflict with the house of David in the third movement.

dictation all the words of the scroll that Jehoiakim king of Judah had burned in the fire. And many words like them were added in addition to them. (Jer. 36:30–32)

In Jeremiah 37 a new king is introduced, filling the throne vacated by the son of Jehoiakim. The words of the LORD are mentioned immediately, to establish that neither Zedekiah nor any of his subjects listened to them (v. 2). In the narrative that follows, Jeremiah's treatment reflects a concerted attempt to silence the word of the LORD. The empty cistern into which Jeremiah is thrown takes us back to images from early in the book of a land caught in a drought of the word of God (e.g. 14:3); as Else Holt has shown, the muddy pit codes for Sheol.[94] And yet, even as he is caught in the midst of the historical process, a lonely figure now in a landscape of destruction, Jeremiah is kept safe while the word he proclaims inexorably disintegrates the nation around him (39:11–14).

If the section from chapter 25 had been about the testing and vindication of God's prophet, then this section from chapter 35 is about the triumph of the prophetic word, as we see every prediction made by Jeremiah come true, one by one, beginning from the moment when the king's burning of the words fails to destroy it. The theme of the unit is the preservation and fulfilment of the divine word.[95]

The transition to the next section, Jeremiah 40 – 43, is made with the help of two more godly outsiders. Jeremiah 35 – 39 closes with a word to Ebed-Melech the Ethiopian, who receives his life not so much for his act of saving Jeremiah, but for the trust in the LORD that prompted it (39:18); and the next unit opens with a remarkable incident in which Jeremiah receives a prophetic word from Nebuzaradan, the captain of the Babylonian guard (40:2–5). These outsiders are used, in Holt's words, 'to underline the complete sin of the originally chosen people. Those from whom they had been set

---

[94] Holt 1999: 165; cf. Pss 28:1; 30:4; and others.

[95] For a number of scholars this part of Jeremiah (and esp. chs. 36–45) aims to present a 'passion narrative' of the prophet in which he is held up as the model of a righteous sufferer (Kremers 1953); for others, it is a narrative about the word of God and the way its rejection leads to judgment (Nicholson 1970: 39–57). With Brueggemann I want to minimize the difference between these readings, recognizing that one cannot easily separate the person of Jeremiah from a story about the word of God (cf. Brueggemann 1991: 124–125). Against Brueggemann, however, the reading I offer here does not see opposition to the word of God as a focus of interest in this part of Jeremiah; much as this is a true depiction of the book's earlier movements, it is the triumph of the word in the face of opposition that takes centre stage here.

apart through Election and Covenant in the end became the elected instruments of the God of the Covenant.'[96] The word of the LORD has disappeared from Judah but is alive among the nations. In the long stretch of narrative from 40:7 to 41:18 Jeremiah is entirely absent. Murder and mayhem follow, the Judean remnant self-destruct, a cistern appears again, this time filled with dead bodies, and when Jeremiah finally reappears it is to preside over the final demise of the remnant. In the encounter that follows (chs. 42–43) Johanan's implacable resolve to return to Egypt is shown for what it is by means of two oracles (each introduced by a Narrative Formula[97]), one at journey's beginning and one at journey's end. In the final section of this movement (ch. 44), which looks back over the entire history we have now rehearsed three times, we see the word of the LORD alive and well in Egypt. The end of the movement crystallizes the nature of the conflict between God's word and Judah's kings: 'the whole remnant of Judah will know, all who came to the land of Egypt to live as aliens, whose word shall stand: mine or theirs' (44:28b).

In short, this third movement of Jeremiah shows the word of the LORD protecting his prophet while all his words are fulfilled in a tide of destruction. As the remnant scatters among the nations the word of the LORD disperses as well, and begins to create new life there. The nations cannot afford to be complacent, however; the fate of Judah stands as a sobering warning of what awaits a nation in whom the word of God dwells.

Narrating Jeremiah 45 – 52

Jeremiah 45 opens the final movement by taking us back to the scroll written by Baruch in Jehoiakim's fourth year; to the programme of demolition announced in 1:10; and to the hope given to some (Baruch himself, in this case) of surviving judgment. However, it is not as a survivor that Baruch, the third godly outsider, earns his place here in the narrative. Rather, he is celebrated here because, like Ebed-Melech, he saved the prophetic word from destruction.[98]

---

[96] Holt 1999: 166.

[97] Kessler suggests that the verb form *wayyiqtol* takes over as the prominent structuring device in chs. 37–45 (Kessler 1968: 84); true though this may be (and it would be more accurate to say chs. 36–44), *wayyiqtol* is generally a lower-order structuring device that slots into units demarcated by macrosyntactic markers such as the two formulas on which I have focused.

[98] In Elena Di Pede's persuasive analysis, Baruch features at the pivotal points

And it is that same powerful word which will now sound across the nations until Babylon herself has fallen, the victim of another scroll, this time from Zedekiah's fourth year (51:59–64). And so Jeremiah 45 establishes the context and provides the opening frame for a quite different retelling of the story, beginning in chapter 46. The fourth year of Jehoiakim provides the link (46:2), effectively creating a movement that might be narrated as follows: 'We have seen what Jehoiakim's behaviour precipitated in Judah. Meanwhile, in Egypt, the LORD has been at work also.' In the second Egypt oracle the word of the LORD announces Egypt's exile (v. 19), and although the use of the title 'the LORD of hosts, the God of Israel' (v. 25) suggests an Egyptian audience, one cannot help but think of the Judean fugitives hearing their new home towns named for destruction (v. 14).

At first sight the presence of an oracle of hope for Jacob and Israel at the end of chapter 46 seems out of place. And yet, just as Babylon was God's tool for Judah's judgment in chapters 25–44, Babylon is thrice named as Egypt's nemesis here (46:2, 13, 26); and just as seeds of new hope sprang from the ruins of exile in earlier movements, so the exile of Egypt is not the end for her (v. 26b) or the Judeans in residence within her (vv. 27–28). In this final movement the international context in which God's people suffer death and new hope carries fresh possibilities. If Judah is but one of the nations, might not her eventual hope of life beyond death become an international hope? Such universal notes are muted in Jeremiah, but they are there all the same, and they grow stronger as the final movement progresses to its denouement.

From Egypt the word of the LORD sounds across nation after nation, tearing down sinful peoples as fearsomely as it did God's own rebellious people. And even as Nebuchadnezzar arrives at the gates of Jerusalem, while Zedekiah cowers within, the word of the LORD passes through Elam and assails Babylon herself. For it turns out that Baruch's deliverance from affliction was a foretaste of the new work the word of the LORD was to do among all the nations, beginning in Egypt and culminating in Babylon, to call out a people for himself. The majestic malediction of Jeremiah 50 – 51 is matched in scale only by the opening salvo of chapters 2–6 and the song of hope in chapters 30–31. Indeed, there are surprising similarities

(chs. 32; 36; 45) of a narrative she classes as 'la passion de Jérémie'. In this narrative, while Ebed-Melek and Baruch both save Jeremiah, what they really save is his message, his word, and it is that for which Baruch receives an oracle in his praise (Di Pede 2004: 77). In Jer. 45 Jeremiah himself is absent, but Baruch continues to proclaim the prophet's oracles. Cf. also Seitz 1989a: 23–24.

between chapters 50 and 30, with both of them drawing on language of reversal, until we see that Babylon's final downfall will be nothing less than the birth pangs of a new Israel, raised among the nations by the word of God to a life beyond death. This oracle is the climax of the book, to which all else has been leading since the programmatic commissioning in 1:10, and Judah's relegation to the level of one of the nations. Only now can we see how the dissonant chords of the book's alternating themes of judgment and hope resolve themselves. This final triumph of the word is enacted by the throwing of a scroll containing written words into the Euphrates.

After these great heights the historical epilogue in Jeremiah 52 is a huge anticlimax, but that is exactly the way the book needs to end, just as the book of the new covenant ended with the anticlimax of Zedekiah's broken covenant. For hope needs to operate in the real, anticlimactic world, or it is no hope at all, and the final verse, with its account of Jehoiachin's favoured treatment, is a call to the book's readers, still in exile themselves, to put their trust in the mighty word of the LORD.[99]

Concluding reflections

I have argued in this chapter that Jeremiah can indeed be read as a narrative about the word of God. Whatever the shape and thrust of earlier editions of the book may have been,[100] the final edition as preserved in the Scriptures of the Western church tells a coherent and compelling story. It is the story of God's word addressing his people with the utmost urgency, over matters of life and death, with patience and longsuffering, until at last that divine word puts into effect all that it had declared, with devastating results. The suffering that was initially felt only by the speaker of the word (both God and Jeremiah) was ultimately poured out upon his deaf audience and, in the end, every nation on earth. And yet, all along – glorious twist in the plot! – it turns out that it is precisely and only through this very devastation that God's longed-for future can be created. And so the word of God triumphs twice over.[101]

---

[99] On Jer. 52 see Stulman (1998: 69–71).

[100] Michael Shepherd argues that Jeremiah LXX was edited to convey a more strongly eschatological message than the more 'historicized' MT (M. B. Shepherd 2011: 91–102).

[101] For a fuller treatment of the message of the book, which shares much in common with the present account, see McConville (1993b: 43–148).

With this story in mind we turn now to examine selected portions of the book of Jeremiah in greater detail, with a view to examining the theology of the word of God that emerges from it. I have chosen texts that can help us reflect on the speaker of the word, on its listeners, on its power and on its written form, with the hope that by reflecting on these 'attributes' we may come to a deeper understanding of the word itself, and of the God who has spoken it.

Chapter Three

Word and speaker

In chapter 1 we began to explore the relationship between the words of Jeremiah and the word of God. Although there is a fundamental identity between the words and the word, I suggested that there is not a complete congruence between them. In the book of Jeremiah the *word of the LORD* normally describes that which is heard and obeyed, while what is spoken or written is normally described as the *words of the LORD* (or, for that matter, of Jeremiah). The determinative reality is the word.

In chapter 2 we began to examine the role the word of God plays in the book itself. The written words of Jeremiah present the word of the LORD to us not as a philosophical idea, but as the main 'character' in the book of Jeremiah. It is the subject of the narrative framework that structures the book, and we follow it on a journey of destruction and rebuilding that spans the earth.

The goal of the present chapter is to examine Jeremiah's role as the speaker of God's words, and to ask whether the identity of the speaker should be a significant factor in a theology of the word of God. Somewhat paradoxically, then, this chapter will begin by establishing Jeremiah's absence from the book that bears his name.

The word of God is the speech of God

The Scriptures have been around for a long time. They are first referred to in the Bible when God writes the law on stone tablets at Sinai. The written law is appealed to explicitly in places like Joshua 8:34; 2 Kings 14:6; Ezra 3:2. Yet there is a sense in which the Scriptures are, and have always been, a derivative thing, a substitute for speech. Though theologians traditionally describe the Bible as 'God's word', or the word of God written,[1] it is not an

---

[1] In both popular textbooks (e.g. Milne 2009: 35–41) and classic theological texts, such as Karl Barth: '[Scripture] too can and must – not as though it were Jesus Christ,

identification that Scripture itself makes, for in the Bible's usage the word of God is an oral category (remember that in Jeremiah, when written, it is called the words of God). There are a couple of occasions when the New Testament cites a single Old Testament verse as a 'word' (John 15:25; 1 Cor. 15:54), and Hebrews 4:12 uses 'word of God' to indicate a portion of Psalm 95 (vv. 7–11), but the Scriptures as such are not described as 'the word of God', which is a category reserved for spoken proclamation.[2]

Even Scripture itself, once written down, is designed in general to be spoken aloud. The poetry of which so much of the Old Testament is made up is, of course, an intensely aural medium (occasional literary features such as acrostic notwithstanding), and both the preaching style of Deuteronomy and 1 John and the narrative style of Samuel and Luke were designed for speech. To be sure, it is hard to imagine genealogies or legal material being made to be read aloud, but even there we find the meditation of the psalmist on the law of the LORD in Psalm 1 is a vocalized meditation – the verb *hgh* (v. 2) is a verb of speech, or at least of sound, whether it be only mumbling.[3]

The word of God in the thought of the Old Testament is the product of divine speech produced, in the language of metaphor, by the shaping of breath into words:

> The heavens were made by the word of the LORD,
> and all the stars, by the breath of his mouth.
>
> (Ps. 33:6)

Occasionally, the reception of the divine word is couched in language of vision (Gen. 15:1; 1 Sam. 3:1; Jer. 2:31; 23:18), but even

---

but in the same serious sense as Jesus Christ – be called the Word of God: the Word of God in the sign of the word of man, if we are going to put it accurately' (*CD* I/2: 500).

[2] Once (2 Chr. 34:21) the word of God is linked to the written book of Moses, but the claim made by William Schniedewind that the 'word of the LORD' comes in the books of Chronicles to refer to the written law of Moses (Schniedewind 2004: 188–189) is not supported by the evidence; of eighteen references, only 2 Chr. 34:21, 35:6, 36:21, 22 make clear reference to a written word, and the last two stress the spoken origins of that word.

[3] Perhaps the most literary material in the OT are the royal histories in Kings, where three different written sources are frequently cited as authorities for the details of kings' reigns, and in Chronicles, where a large number of different written sources are mentioned, many of them the writings of otherwise unrecorded prophets. Even here, however, the prophetic service into which the histories have been pressed gives the resulting narrative a 'proclamatory', even didactic, feel.

then it is the 'word' of God that the person 'sees'. And the word of God always comes to a prophet (with Abraham and Joshua being the only exceptions, if indeed they are exceptions). Indeed, this effectively defines what a prophet is: someone to whom the word of God is spoken directly (as Jer. 18:18 illustrates: 'Surely the law is not going to be lost to the priest, nor counsel to the sage, nor the word to the prophet!').[4] In dreams God 'speaks' to Jacob, and 'reveals' mysteries to Daniel, but the receiving of the 'word' of God is an exclusively prophetic function.[5]

It follows that Scripture is not the word of God in the sense of being God's speech. It is not any sort of speech, but rather words written on a page. The person who reads Scripture is not like a prophet to whom the word of God comes, but like Baruch reading Jeremiah's words, that is, the LORD's words, from the scroll, or like Aaron in Exodus 4:30, passing on the words God spoke to Moses. This idea will be explored at greater depth in chapter 5, when we come to examine Jeremiah 36.

None of this is to suggest that we stop calling Scripture the word of God. That is a theological term, and has its own value as part of the ordering of truth which is the art of dogmatic theology. It is important, however, to recognize that in the usage of biblical writers the words spoken are the word of the LORD as and precisely because God is speaking them. Every subsequent speech event that relays God's word is derivative from that original act of divine speaking.

When we look at Jeremiah, then, we should not be surprised to see the original spoken event made prominent in the written discourse. And in the next part of this chapter we shall examine some literary techniques by which this is achieved.

The shape of Jeremianic discourse

Each of the three literary techniques we shall now survey is essentially a way of shaping words so that they take us back with as much directness as possible to the original word, that is, the original

---

[4] Cf. Grether (1934: 59), who shows that with few exceptions the expression 'the word of the LORD' is a technical term for 'the prophetic word of revelation' throughout the OT.

[5] The only exceptions do nothing to displace this rule. In Amos 8:12 the people will seek the word of the LORD but not find it. In Mic. 4:2 (Isa. 2:2) the word of the LORD will go out from Jerusalem in future days. In Ps. 33:6 the word of the LORD goes out directly to create the heavens.

speech event. It is important to the writer that in reading his book we hear God speak to the full extent that written words permit this.

Embedded discourse

Jeremiah's discourse, in common with all Hebrew discourse, almost never contains indirect speech. One hardly ever finds a sentence in Hebrew along the lines of 'God says he wants you to repent.' Instead, God's voice will always come directly in the form of an embedded speech: 'God says, "I want you to repent."' This phenomenon is labelled embedded discourse, and it can lead to passages of labyrinthine complexity, such as the following example from Jeremiah 27:

Narrator:	¹In the beginning of the reign of Zedekiah, the son of Josiah, king of Judah, *this word came to Jeremiah from the* LORD:
Jeremiah:	²Thus said the LORD to me:
The LORD:	Make straps and yoke bars for yourself and put them on your neck. ³Send word to the king of Edom, the king of Moab [etc. . . .] by their messengers who come to Jerusalem to Zedekiah, ⁴and command them to go to their masters and say,
'Jeremiah'?	Thus says the LORD of hosts, the God of Israel:
"'The LORD'"?	Thus you shall say to your masters:
"''The LORD'"'	⁵By my great strength and outstretched arm I have made the earth [etc. . . .]. ⁹Do not listen to your prophets, your diviners [etc. . . .] who say to you:
?	You shall not serve the king of Babylon. ¹⁰For they prophesy a lie to you.

Verse 1 is straightforward: it is narrated by the book's author, and refers to Jeremiah in the third person. In verse 2 we hear the voice of Jeremiah ('Thus said the LORD to me'), and then Jeremiah quotes the words of the LORD directly. From there it begins to get complicated. The second line of verse 4 ('Thus says the LORD') looks like the LORD quoting the words he is instructing Jeremiah to give to the messengers to say, in which case the next line ('Thus you shall say to your masters') is the LORD's voice again, coming from Jeremiah's lips, and instructing the messengers to speak to their masters. But verses 3–4 do not stand on their own: they are subordinate to verses 1–2, that is, a speech of Jeremiah given him to say by the LORD. So the proper description of the LORD's words in verse 5 is Jeremiah quoting the LORD quoting Jeremiah quoting the LORD quoting himself! No English translation even tries to keep up with the multiply nested quotation marks.

Fortunately for us readers, the narrator has made everything simple by the heading I have italicized in verse 1. It simply dumps everything that follows into the single category of divine speech, including Jeremiah's opening 'Thus said the LORD to me'. As we read through the passage, then, we see a lot of lips moving – Jeremiah's, the messengers as they pass on the message, the false prophets in verse 9 who tell them to resist the king of Babylon – but we only hear a single voice on all those lips: the voice of God.

This habit biblical Hebrew has of constant direct speech has the effect of creating immediacy. We are there listening to Jeremiah in verse 1; we are there listening to the foreign messengers in verse 5; we are there listening to distant soothsayers counselling resistance. But in every time and place we visit it is God's voice we hear.[6]

Drift of speaker

Not only are God's words presented to us in a way that preserves their original orality, but in Jeremiah the spoken words we hear are made as much as possible into the words of God. One of the techniques by which this is achieved may be dubbed 'drift of speaker', whereby the prophet's voice is displaced without notice by the encroaching voice of God. An example of this may be seen in Jeremiah 25:[7]

---

[6] In two valuable studies Christof Hardmeier demonstrates the way in which embedded discourse interrupts the narrative flow, bringing the original scene of the discourse into the narrative present, and thereby imposing a basic structure onto the narrative (Hardmeier 1993: esp. 61–62; cf. Hardmeier 1995).

[7] The discourse structure of this passage is significantly different in the LXX, which omits 'the word of the LORD has come to me' in v. 3, and the other references to 'the LORD' in vv. 4–7, and turns the whole into a speech of God. This has occasioned much critical speculation about the textual history of the passage, of which we need notice only one aspect. If I am right in suggesting that drift of speaker and the blurring of Jeremiah's and God's voices are conscious literary devices in Jeremiah (for other examples see Shead 2002b: 23–52), then critics ought to be cautious about the conclusions they draw from shifts of speaker in the text, however jarring they may feel. What may be plainly stated about the two versions in the case of Jer. 25:1–7 is

[1]The word that came to Jeremiah ... [2]which Jeremiah the prophet spoke ... saying,
[3]'For twenty-three years the word of the LORD has come to me, and I have spoken to you, but you have not listened. [4]And the LORD has sent to you his servants the prophets again and again ...
[7]'Yet you would not obey me', declares the LORD, 'in order that you might provoke me to anger ...'
[8]Therefore thus says the LORD of Hosts, 'Because you have not obeyed my words, [I will exile you to Babylon. Then, seventy years later,] [13]I will bring upon that land all my words I have spoken against it, all that is written in this book that Jeremiah prophesied against the nations.'

There is no indication of a change of speaker at verse 7. We simply slip into hearing God's speech directly, and we are not sure who is saying 'thus says the LORD': it could be Jeremiah, or it could be God himself. But by verse 13 the drift has reached the point where Jeremiah can now be referred to in the third person, even though strictly he is the one speaking. It makes for confusing reading at times, but there is a strong theological imperative in Jeremiah to have the reader encounter God's words directly, even if it means that the voice of Jeremiah himself must slip into the background.[8]

Telescoping

The third technique for bringing God's voice to prominence has been noted by A. van Selms, and called by him 'telescoped discussion'.[9] It relates to the way the biblical author selects from the events that occurred when he chooses what to write down for posterity. As it happens, telescoping is but one of a number of ways in which disparate voices in the text are blended together, and we shall encounter

that a straightforward proclamation in the LXX begins in the MT as a reminiscence by Jeremiah; speculation about the history of this passage should begin from this point. Cf. the approaches of Stipp (1994: 112–115), McKane (1996: 619–622) and Goldman (1992: 200–207); cf. also de Regt 2004.

[8] As the LXX shows, Jeremiah could have been relegated to the background from the start; in the MT edition, however, Jer. 25:3 is an important reflection on the failure of Jeremiah's ministry, and it prepares for his encounters with priests and prophets in the following chapters (chapters that do not follow in the LXX).

[9] Van Selms 1976. The author suggests that this literary technique preserves the divine word at the expense of the human (103); that it is unique to Jeremiah (111); and that it is probably to be attributed to Baruch (112).

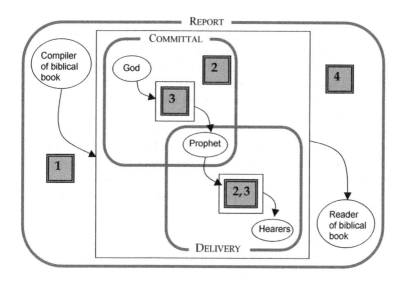

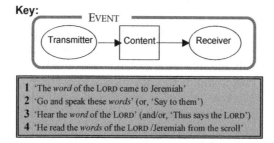

Figure 3.1 Communication events in prophetic oracles and the 'word of the LORD'

this blending of voices frequently as we come to read selected texts more closely.

In order to see how telescoping exemplifies the wider phenomenon of blending of voices, an explanation of the way prophetic discourse normally works is necessary. To do this I have borrowed and adapted a diagram from H. Van Dyke Parunak that displays the various communication events involved (figure 3.1).[10]

The first of three separate communication events reflected in the book of Jeremiah is the REPORT, which is the author's account

[10] Parunak 1994: 494.

of the whole episode, written down for us to read. It will be cast as a narrative and refer to Jeremiah in the third person. (Sometimes Jeremiah himself writes or dictates the report, in which case it will be a first-person narrative in the style of Ezekiel.) It is often introduced by the form of words labelled '1' in figure 3.1.

In the REPORT we read of a second communication event, the COMMITTAL, where God speaks to the prophet. It may begin with instructions about where to go, and whom to address (labelled '2' in the figure). Jeremiah 26:2 is an example: 'Stand in the gate of the LORD's house and speak all the words I have commanded you to speak to all the cities of Judah who have come to worship there.' God then tells Jeremiah what to say (labelled '3'), which often begins with the words 'thus says the LORD', and moves from there into the oracle proper. Both elements of the COMMITTAL can be seen in Jeremiah 11:2: 'Speak to the men of Judah and to the inhabitants of Jerusalem and say to them, "Thus says the LORD, the God of Israel: 'Let a curse be on the man who does not obey the words of this covenant.'"'

The third communication event is the DELIVERY, in which Jeremiah duly goes and relays the oracle to its target audience. He will say 'thus says the LORD' to signal to his listeners that the next words he utters are not going to be his, but God's. However, Jeremiah often repeats not only the substance of God's message ('3'), but also the things God said to him before the message ('2'). Perhaps Jeremiah always did this. But the author rarely gives a full narration of this chain of events. More often than not the whole DELIVERY stage is omitted, and we simply assume that Jeremiah complied with God's instructions.[11] And sometimes two communication events are blended, or 'telescoped', together. This brings us back to van Selms's observations, which I shall reframe with the help of figure 3.1 above.

Perhaps the best example of telescoping is Jeremiah 45, which is reproduced in full in figure 3.2 below. The rather confusing sequence of clauses that go to make up this chapter can be best understood in terms of two separate words committed to Baruch by the LORD. Instead of reporting each COMMITTAL separately, the two have been 'telescoped' into a single event for the purposes of the written REPORT. This has created a disconcerting jump at verse 4, where the 'you' in 'this is what *you* are to say to him' is no longer Baruch but,

---

[11] Or else there is a very brief summary, such as Jer. 19:14a, after a prophecy in Topheth, where we read, 'Then Jeremiah came from Topheth, where the LORD had sent him to prophesy.'

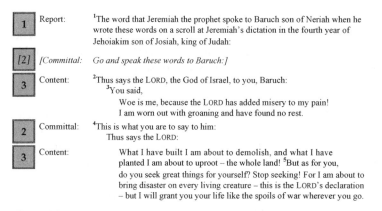

1	Report:	[1]The word that Jeremiah the prophet spoke to Baruch son of Neriah when he wrote these words on a scroll at Jeremiah's dictation in the fourth year of Jehoiakim son of Josiah, king of Judah:
[2]	[Committal:	*Go and speak these words to Baruch:]*
3	Content:	[2]Thus says the LORD, the God of Israel, to you, Baruch: [3]You said, Woe is me, because the LORD has added misery to my pain! I am worn out with groaning and have found no rest.
2	Committal:	[4]This is what you are to say to him: Thus says the LORD:
3	Content:	What I have built I am about to demolish, and what I have planted I am about to uproot – the whole land! [5]But as for you, do you seek great things for yourself? Stop seeking! For I am about to bring disaster on every living creature – this is the LORD's declaration – but I will grant you your life like the spoils of war wherever you go.

Figure 3.2 Two communication events telescoped together in Jeremiah 45

we must presume, Jeremiah. The italicized line before verse 2 is not part of the biblical text, but presumably something like it was said to Jeremiah.[12]

What is the effect of composing the chapter in this way? The omission of a fresh REPORT before verse 4 (e.g. 'And Jeremiah added, "The LORD said to me . . ."') means that God's becomes the only voice in this word spoken by Jeremiah. The phrase 'thus says the LORD', as elsewhere in the book, brings all three communication events together so that we cannot really say which one is being described: God's COMMITTAL of the message to Jeremiah, Jeremiah's DELIVERY of the message to Baruch, or the narrator's REPORT of these events. Through a blending of voices every effort is made to stress the identity of the words spoken to Jeremiah with the words spoken by Jeremiah, and the identity of the words once spoken to Jeremiah with the words now written down.[13] In short, the author uses the technique of telescoping to bring us back into the original event of

---

[12] We can reconstruct a possible sequence of events behind this. Perhaps Jeremiah dictated words of judgment to Baruch, who was distressed by them. Later on, God revealed Baruch's distress to Jeremiah and instructed Jeremiah to tell Baruch that God knew of his distress. Then, in a separate word from God, Jeremiah is given a fresh committal: to relay to Baruch a stark but comforting word (van Selms 1976: 100–103). Van Selms's reconstruction was much more colourful and speculative than this, leading to a dubious reception by later commentators (e.g. Holladay 1989: 309, n. 7; Keown et al. 1995: 271; Fischer 2005: 2.458, n. 2); Lundbom has provided a more sober account (Lundbom 2004b: 176), which makes unnecessary the traditional practice of simply excising the beginning of v. 4 (as recommended by the *BHS* footnote and McKane 1996: 1096).

[13] Cf. Shead 2002b: 44.

the COMMITTAL, and dulls all other voices so as to make God's voice predominate. Did Jeremiah paraphrase the message he heard? Did the author of the book reshape it? These questions are unanswerable because we are hearing the words as if freshly spoken.[14]

Summary

Whether by the embedding of speech, by drift of speaker, by telescoping, or by other techniques for blending voices in the text, we readers are consistently taken back into the event of the committal, just as were the prophet's original hearers. The voice of the prophet is replaced by the voice of God.

Alongside this observation we should remember the way in which the Disjunctive Heading serves to bring large units of the book, not only oracles but entire narratives, under the rubric of the word of the LORD. By this means even the narrator's voice in the report is replaced by the voice of God.

For a book that gives such prominence to the person and works of Jeremiah, there is an irony to the fact that we hear so little of his voice. It is Jeremiah's life we see, but God's voice we hear. Biddle has also recognized this feature of the book, which he characterizes as a 'retraction of the prophetic persona'.[15] The literary techniques we have surveyed not only bring God's words to life as spoken realities, but also render invisible the prophet who brings those words to us. He becomes like a transparent vessel through whose glass we have an unimpeded vision of the spoken words contained within. Those words, of course, make up the word of the LORD, the protagonist of the book as a whole.

Jeremiah in his times

Jeremiah may be a book whose discourse structure aims to make the prophetic speaker as transparent as possible, but Jeremiah the man

---

[14] Telescoping may also be used to control the discourse structure. It is impossible to know why the author chose to retain the second committal, apart from the indication this gives of two original words from God to Jeremiah. However, it is suggestive that its inclusion adds a level of embedding to vv. 4–5, which brings God's second word onto the same level as Baruch's initial word in v. 3. The result, not only for the reader but also for the listener, is that God's word stands structurally and rhythmically as a direct answer to Baruch's complaint. The insertion of the first committal would have spoiled this rhythm just as much as the deletion of the second.

[15] Biddle (1996: 120), following Seitz's work on Isaiah. In the LXX the prophet is even less visible, both speaking less and being mentioned less explicitly (de Regt 2004).

is startlingly prominent. He was anything but transparent in his day, and his book contains more biography than any other prophet's.[16] For the present purposes only a very brief sketch of his life and times is needed.[17]

As described in Jeremiah 1:3, the years of Jeremiah's ministry were tumultuous ones. After the tremendous discovery of the lost law book in Josiah's reign and the religious reforms that filled his remaining years, there were to be just twenty-two more years left in the life of the nation while the shallowness of their repentance was exposed.

Table 3.1 The last kings of Israel

Dates	Kings
640–609	Josiah
609	Jehoahaz (Shallum), deported by Pharaoh Neco after 3 months
609–597	Jehoiakim installed by Pharaoh Neco
?Jan. 597	Jehoiachin (Jeconiah)
15 Mar. 597	Defeat of Jerusalem: Jehoiachin and nobles deported
597–587	Zedekiah installed by Nebuchadnezzar
587	Sack of Jerusalem: Zedekiah and many others deported
587	Gedaliah appointed provincial governor

His prophetic calling precipitated Jeremiah from a rural priestly family into the political chaos of Jerusalem. The book's opening verse is the only time Jeremiah's parentage and profession are mentioned. There is a rabbinic tradition that Hilkiah was the same high priest who found the lost book of the law during Josiah's reign (2 Kgs 22:8), and although this is quite speculative, as many since Calvin have been quick to point out,[18] it would provide a nice context for Jeremiah's profound debt to the book of Deuteronomy. Some scholars also propose, even more speculatively, that a childhood growing up in the village of Anathoth – to which Abiathar the priest of David was exiled in ancient times – could have imbued Jeremiah with an antipathy to the Davidic establishment.[19]

---

[16] Where Isaiah is mentioned by name 17 times in his book, and Ezekiel just twice in his, Jeremiah is named 125 times.

[17] Scholarly treatments of the life of Jeremiah abound, from John Skinner's spiritual biography (Skinner 1948) and William Holladay's historical reconstructions at one end of the spectrum (Holladay 1989: 25–35; 1990; cf. Lundbom 1999: 107–120), to Carroll's complete rejection of a historical Jeremiah at the other (Carroll 1981: 5–30), with Brueggemann and many others occupying the middle ground (e.g. Brueggemann 2007: 27–35; Fretheim 2002: 11–16).

[18] Calvin 1950a: 1.32–33.

[19] Cf. Brueggemann 2007: 29.

Be that as it may, and the fact is we do not know anything certain of his family, Jeremiah had a lot to say against the two big institutions of Jerusalem, the temple and the monarchy. And he said it in two distinct modes of speech. We encounter poetic oracles typical of the pre-exilic prophets, but there is also a lot of material that is not poetic at all. Jeremiah was a powerful preacher of sermons in the style of Deuteronomy, and it is probable that he had a public preaching ministry, at least for a while.[20] In addition to his preaching, Jeremiah was given a number of striking sign acts to perform, pieces of public drama that must have made him a well-known figure in all levels of society.

As a public figure opposed to the Jerusalem establishment during a time of war it is natural that Jeremiah should have been considered a security risk. Constantly under suspicion for being in the pay of the Babylonian enemy, imprisoned several times, and the victim of outright hatred from powerful priests and members of the royal family, Jeremiah's troubled personal life is a memorable part of his book. Other prophets feature in the books named after them, such as Hosea and Ezekiel. But the book of Jeremiah is unique in the extent and significance of its biographical material. While some of this is presented as autobiography, the bulk is written about Jeremiah by a biographer, named in the book as Baruch son of Neriah. This biographical material forms the third type of literature in the book, combining with the poetry and the sermons to form a three-stranded whole. Not only was Baruch a scribe for Jeremiah; he was that rare thing in Jeremiah's life, a trusted ally (as may be inferred from 36:8, 19; 43:3). Actually, despite his marginalization, Jeremiah was not completely without friends and supporters, of whom the family of Shaphan, the court secretary, was the most significant politically (cf. 2 Kgs 22:8–14; Jer. 26:24; 29:3; 36:10–13; 39:14). It appears that this family was opposed to both the policies of the royal house and the practices of the temple establishment, and after the conquest of Jerusalem it was a member of this family, Gedaliah, who was installed by Nebuchadnezzar as governor of the conquered province. It was from within the support of this group that the words of Jeremiah were written down, collected, assembled and (probably) disseminated.[21]

---

[20] After the accession of Jehoiakim in 609 BC the reforms of Josiah came to an end (cf. Jer. 7) and Jeremiah's years of freedom were numbered.

[21] Cf. Brueggemann 2007: 31–32.

Against this background there were a number of prophecies made by Jeremiah that precipitated acute trouble for him. In the early days of Jehoiakim's reign it was Jeremiah's prediction of the temple's destruction that put his life in danger (26:7–9); in the last days of Zedekiah's reign it was Jeremiah's exhortations to surrender to the enemy (e.g. ch. 38); but between these there was one prophecy which the book's compiler has put at the very centre of the book as the turning point of its message, a prophecy that was seen as precipitating, directly or indirectly, all the troubles that followed. The prophecy, made in the first year of Nebuchadnezzar's reign, is recorded in Jeremiah 25:11: 'This whole land will become a desolate ruin, and these nations will serve the king of Babylon for seventy years.' Not two or three years, but two generations. This announcement polarized society, and it precipitated the nation into a war with the word of God.

Even these sketchy biographical details are enough to underscore the paradox of the prophet: Jeremiah as depicted in his book is among the most highly visible personalities since king David, and there is every reason to see this prominence as reflecting the state of affairs in his day. And yet he appears to have no profile at all when it comes to the real subject of his book, the word of God. As a speaker of the words of God Jeremiah is an enigma. Everything is done to make the prophet transparent before the word of God. So why does the author bother to leave Jeremiah the man in Jeremiah the book?

I shall address this question by examining two units of text from the first half of the book: Jeremiah 1:4–19 and Jeremiah 14 – 15.

Jeremiah's call and commissioning

Jeremiah 1:4–10

Isaiah and Ezekiel open with their respective prophets seeing a vision, but Jeremiah does not open with the prophet doing anything. He is entirely passive, and the active subject is the word of God, which comes to Jeremiah and addresses him in Jeremiah 1:4–5. This first word is highly poetic: assonant, rhyming, rhythmically balanced and entirely arresting. Its language of 'shaping' echoes Genesis 2:

> Before I shaped you in the belly I knew you,
> before you emerged from the womb I had sanctified you:
> a prophet to the nations I have appointed you.
>
> (Jer. 1:10)

Jeremiah's life is reduced to three stages: before his conception, in the womb and prophet.[22] God's involvement with him also progresses as he enters into relationship with Jeremiah, sanctifies him for the task ahead, and launches him into his vocation.

To what does Jeremiah's sanctification refer? We should probably understand this as preparing him to be a fit vessel for God's words, the words put into his mouth in verse 9. We get another insight into this from Jeremiah 23:9, where Jeremiah says:

> My heart is broken within me;
> all my bones shake;
> I am like a drunken man,
> like a man overcome by wine,
> because of the LORD and because of his holy words.

(Isaiah's unclean lips and the burning coal of Isa. 6 also spring to mind in this connection.) In addressing Jeremiah the word of the LORD defines him, it constitutes him as a person; the word of the LORD makes him fit to receive the word of the LORD. These are foundational verses for our study of Jeremiah as speaker of the word, for they establish him from the start as someone who in his being is a creature of the word of God.

In the conventions of Hebrew narrative the first words of a major character open a significant window onto their character, and Jeremiah's reply in verse 6 opens not one window but two. First, his words draw our minds immediately to the reluctant Moses, called by God in Exodus 3. And with this connection made, we may well ask whether this is in fact the prophet like Moses whom God promised to raise up in Deuteronomy 18:18. This possibility will be confirmed by the end of Jeremiah's call, as both parts of Deuteronomy 18:18 are quoted: 'I will put my words in his mouth' is echoed in Jeremiah 1:9, and 'he shall speak to them all that I command him' is echoed in verse 7.[23] Secondly, Jeremiah's inability to speak foreshadows

---

[22] Some scholars have suggested that the thirteenth year of Josiah's reign mentioned in v. 2 was the year of Jeremiah's birth, and read v. 5 as if proclaimed in the delivery room (Holladay 1989: 25–26). But this verse does not help us date the start of his ministry, for its sole concern is Jeremiah's appointment as prophet.

[23] Like Moses, Jeremiah will straddle two generations: a generation under judgment, and a generation living in hope. As Seitz has shown, the parallels with Moses continue throughout, so that in Jeremiah's life we see many Mosaic elements: the prophet as intercessor, the death of a generation in the wilderness (seventy years to Moses' forty), the destruction and rewriting of divine words (a scroll for Moses'

the relative absence of his voice in the chapters that follow. In God's reply in verse 7 he is not troubled by Jeremiah's speech phobia, for Jeremiah's speech will not be his own to control.

Left to himself, Jeremiah is mute. Like his contemporary Ezekiel he has no words of his own; instead, the word of God compels him. The stress in verse 7 is on '*everywhere*' and '*all* that I command you'. There is nothing left of Jeremiah – his identity, his will, the events of his life – that has not been possessed by the word of God. Verse 8 then depicts God himself acting to prevent his voice from being silenced. To be so thoroughly possessed by the word of God must be unnerving, and Jeremiah needs to be assured that God will accompany his word. It is no doubt rather disconcerting to be told one will be rescued when one did not know one would need to be rescued in the first place! This is the first hint the book gives us that Jeremiah may be in for a rough time.

The final stage of Jeremiah's call begins in verse 9 with the description of an experience that is perhaps visionary, though it is not described as such. Perhaps we should see it as the first of many symbolic actions in the book, albeit performed here by God. The touching of Jeremiah's mouth is described in the same words used for Isaiah's calling, but where the burning coal removes Isaiah's sin, here the touch puts God's words into Jeremiah's already-sanctified mouth. It is clear from the next verse that having God's words in his mouth does not mean that Jeremiah has been given divine knowledge, but that he has been endowed with the power of the Creator.

The word of the LORD that has addressed Jeremiah, that has defined and compelled him, will now issue from Jeremiah's lips to judge the nations and to save the nations. Verse 10 is Jeremiah's job description. It is referred to or alluded to about a dozen more times throughout the book, mostly in connection with symbolic actions.[24] Clearly, it is God rather than Jeremiah who will physically destroy and create these nations – but he does it by his word, and his word is conveyed by the words placed in the mouth of Jeremiah. God

tablets), the election of a Caleb and Joshua (in Ebed-Melech and Baruch) and, at the end, a promised land glimpsed from afar by a prophet who dies in the wilderness (Seitz 1989a; cf. Holladay 1964). Jeremiah was being seen as a Mosaic figure as early as the time of the Qumran scrolls (Brooke 1997: 191).

[24] Jer. 12:14–17 (followed by the symbolic action [SA] of the loincloth); 18:6–10 (followed by SA); 24:5–7 (part of a SA-vision); 29:5, 28 (a SA in itself); 31:27–30, 40; 35:6–7 (a SA itself); 39:8 (fulfilment); 42:10–11 (also references 1:8; SA in 43:8); 45:4; 50:15 (reversal); 52:14 (fulfilment).

in Genesis 1 creates the universe by the power of his word; here, however, it is not the words God speaks but God's words Jeremiah speaks that have this same creative and uncreative power.[25]

In these early stages of the speaker's portrait, then, we see a man specially formed and fitted to be a vessel for the word of God, a word that will emerge from his mouth with the same power and effectiveness as if God had spoken unmediated.

Jeremiah 1:11–19

This is such an astounding commission that God confirms it in verses 11–12 by another word, the 'sign of the almond'. Its point is in verse 12: Jeremiah will be able to tear down nations not because the words he speaks have magical power of their own, but because God guarantees to do what they say. The point is driven home in a typical Hebrew wordplay between 'almond' (*šāqēd*) and 'watching' (*šōqēd*). Through long years of preaching to no apparent effect one can imagine the prophet remembering, each time he saw an almond tree, God's vivid promise to watch over his word.[26]

In the rest of chapter 1 Jeremiah receives the first of those words for the nations to which verses 9–10 referred. The word consists of a second vision (v. 13), this one of a boiling pot in the north, tilting dangerously southwards.[27] To this vision is attached a word (vv. 14–16) in which God explains that judgment is about to pour over all who live on the earth. Most versions translate the word *'ereṣ* in verse 14 as 'land', but, given the international nature of the commission in verse 10, 'earth' is the more natural reading. It is only when the following verse springs its surprise, namely, that the target of this word is not the nations but Judah and Jerusalem, that one retrospectively 'corrects' the natural reading 'earth' to 'land'. Either way, the ominous implication of this is that Judah is being classified here as just one more of the nations. And this recategorizing of Judah is in fact precisely what we find later in the book, as God declares that circumcision that is only skin-deep does not count as true circumcision:

---

[25] On the question of who does the actions of v. 10, cf. Holt (2007: 177–178).

[26] The vision may also have put Jeremiah in mind of the other 'sign of the almond', namely, the miracle of Aaron's staff in the wake of Korah's rebellion (Num. 17:8–10). The fulfilment of God's word on that occasion led to the death of many thousands of rebels. By the sign of the almond Jeremiah is assured that rebellion will be just as surely punished if his words are ignored by the people.

[27] The expression 'a second time' in v. 13 is ambiguous taken by itself, because there are two previous words of the LORD in the chapter (vv. 4, 11); however, the qualifying 'what do you see?' makes it clear that v. 11 is in mind.

Look! days are coming – oracle of the LORD – when I will punish all those circumcised in the flesh only: Egypt, Judah, Edom, the Ammonites, Moab, all who crop the sides of their head, the residents of the wilderness. For all these nations are uncircumcised, and all the house of Israel are uncircumcised in heart. (Jer. 9:25–26)[28]

This identity of Judah and the nations has already been subtly asserted in chapter 1 by attaching to the northern peoples and to the people of God alike the same word, 'evil'. Thus the evil that will pour from the north (v. 13) is linked to 'all the peoples of the northern kingdoms' (v. 14), so that when they come to Jerusalem, whose residents are 'evil' worshippers of other gods (v. 16), we have the sense that Judah is being given into the hands of its own kind. Hence we see Jeremiah fulfilling his vocation as prophet to the nations in every chapter of the book, not just in the closing OAN.

The real focus of this passage is not Judah, however, but Jeremiah. If verse 10 was the commission he was empowered to perform, then verses 17–19 show us what performing it will look like. We see that the oracle of the boiling pot is only the beginning, just one typical sample of 'all which I command you' (v. 17), and it gives us a quick taste of the ministry of the new Moses: a ministry of bringing down the covenant curses on the heads of an unfaithful people, just as the first Moses at the end of his life had foretold would happen (Deut. 31:29).

In the same way that the general call to tear down and build up the nations was made particular in this section, so the general assurances of verses 7–8 are made particular in verses 17–19. For a start, these two paragraphs share commands to go, to speak and not to fear. And then the promise of verse 8 is repeated word for word at the end of verse 19.

As table 3.2 shows, this is not a case of simple repetition. First, the common verbal ideas are expressed in more intense language the second time around ('go'/'get to work'; 'afraid'/'terrorized'). And secondly, God adds to Jeremiah's task ('as for you', v. 17) a self-appointed task of his own ('as for me', v. 18). In particular, Jeremiah's task is not to give in, no matter what; and God's task is to make Jeremiah able to withstand anything. What is of interest about God's task is the way he picks up the language of walls and cities that was used to describe Jerusalem in verse 15, and applies

---

[28] In view of Jer. 4:4, 'in the flesh' in 9:25 means 'flesh *only*'.

Table 3.2 Some verbal parallels in Jeremiah 1

Jeremiah 1:7–8 [and 15b]	*Jereremiah 1:17–19*
The LORD said to me, 'Do not say, "I am only young." For to all to whom I send you, you shall go, and all that I command you, you shall speak.	'As for you, get to work, get up, and speak to them all that I command you.
Do not be afraid of them,	Do not be terrorized by them, or I will terrorize you before them. As for me,
[v. 15b . . . each shall set his throne at the entrance of the gates of Jerusalem, against all its surrounding walls and against all the cities of Judah.]	I have made you today into a fortified city, an iron pillar, a bronze wall against the whole earth – against the kings of Judah, her officials, her priests and the people of the land. They will fight against you and they
for I am with you to rescue you,' declares the LORD.	will not prevail, for I am with you,' declares the LORD, 'to rescue you.'

it to Jeremiah in verse 18.[29] The implications of this identification point in two directions. As the city fortified 'against the whole earth', Jeremiah himself is made the implied target of the northern hostility described in verse 15. At the same time, he is the explicit target of the Judean people. This is the first hint that Jeremiah will in some fashion stand in the place of the embattled people of God while at the same time standing in the place of the word of God that has embattled them in the first place.

In all the horrific unravelling of covenant relationships that was going on around him, Jeremiah alone was cruelly kept intact (v. 19). And yet, if Jeremiah truly stands in the place of the people in some sense, the fact that he received promises from God of personal deliverance may well offer some sort of hope to the people in whose place he stands. To adapt the words of the apostle Paul, Jeremiah was to be 'persecuted, but not forsaken; struck down, but not destroyed; always carrying around in his body the death of Israel, so that the life of Israel also may be manifested in his body' (2 Cor. 4:9–11, ESV adapted).

If the word of the LORD is the book's main 'character', it is Jeremiah who gives this character its flesh and bones, as his entire life embodies the message he has been created to deliver.

---

[29] Both verses begin with the attention-grabbing word traditionally rendered 'behold'. And each speaks of a city and its walls. Again I read *'ereṣ* in v. 18 as 'earth', not 'land', and see the same sort of Judean specifying of international concepts as we have seen elsewhere. See Holt 2007: 179.

Some questions about the speaker, his words and his deeds

What can we say, so far, about Jeremiah as the speaker of God's words? First of all, there is a real sense in which Jeremiah is a non-person. The entire purpose of his existence is to be a vessel for the words of God. He has no speech of his own, no freedom of his own; he is entirely possessed. God brought this one speaker into being to give voice to a particular group of words, and the words he speaks are powerful and effective not because he speaks them, but because they are God's words. This raises a question for us: does the prophet have any words of his own left to him? Can Jeremiah ever point to a statement he has made and say of it, 'I, not the LORD'? For Gerhard von Rad the answer to this was clearly positive:

> On the one hand, [Jeremiah] was bound to Jahweh and remained subject to him more than any other prophet; on the other, however, he had to let his thought have free range. And the seriousness with which he took this intellectual state, which of course lay outside his prophetic calling proper, is shown precisely by the wide range of his reflexion on theological problems.[30]

Our reading of Jeremiah 1 leads us to question the certainty of von Rad's 'of course'. However, von Rad had in mind Jeremiah's complaints and protests against God, and we cannot answer him until we have considered the prophet's 'Confessions'.

Secondly, Jeremiah 1 leads us to consider not just the speaker's words but the speaker's life, his deeds. For at the same time as he is presented to us as mute, Jeremiah is depicted as a giant whose coming was foretold in ages past, a new Moses who stands not on a mountaintop but astride the whole earth, with its nations and kingdoms. Is it proper, then, to incorporate Jeremiah's deeds somehow into a theology of the word of God, or are they strictly adjunct to it, being after all not words in themselves?

A third question follows directly on. The clearest examples of the incorporation of Jeremiah's actions in some manner into the word of the LORD are the sign acts he is commanded to perform, such as the linen loincloth of chapter 11, or the broken pot of chapter 18. However, there is much else that he does, and the same question

---

[30] Von Rad 1965: 2.205.

we asked of Jeremiah's words might again be asked here: Does the prophet have any deeds of his own left to him? Or is everything he does, all his choices and responses, co-opted into the service of the word of the LORD?

Finally, should we see in Jeremiah an embodiment of the word of God in its reception as well as in its speaking? A brief perusal of Jeremiah 2 – 6 and 14 – 15 suggests that we should.

The voice of God in Jeremiah 2:1 – 6:30

While it is accurate to describe the prophet as a vessel for the word of the LORD, he is not a passive, unresisting one. Though he has no choice about speaking the word, his feelings and personality have not been tampered with, and gradually we become aware of a voice, rising from within the words of God Jeremiah utters, that belongs peculiarly to the prophet. This Jeremianic voice begins to make itself heard in the first main section of the book.[31]

The divine voice is rich and complex, and when we first hear it, it is remembering the idyllic early days of marriage (2:2). All too soon, however, we see God's disappointment and even incredulity at what his bride has done, as he institutes divorce proceedings (2:11–13). There are no winners here. God's anguish becomes more palpable as the marriage unravels. The opening verses of chapter 3 refer to the law of Deuteronomy 24:1–4, according to which remarriage to her first husband is illegal if a divorced wife has married and divorced someone else in the meantime. Yet so strong is God's tender love that against every likelihood, even against his own law, he invites this prostitute who was once his bride to return home. Language of turning dominates chapter 3, where the people are called 'children of turning', that is, people predisposed by nature to turn away from God. And in the climactic verse all the turning language comes together into a triple pun:

> Return, children of turning,
> I will cure you of turning back.
>
> (3:22)[32]

---

[31] O'Connor 1999: 389–395. For thoughtful analysis of Jer. 2 – 3 and the metaphor of marriage, see Diamond and O'Connor (1999: 126–134), and especially Abma (1999: 234–260).

[32] Holladay 1958; McConville 1993b: 35.

The LORD longs to pour out his affection on this rogue nation; he offers her a golden future, he longs to lavish gifts upon her, but after repeated appeals fall on deaf ears his tone changes in the space of half a verse to one of resolute anger, as God the abandoned husband becomes God the military avenger:

> Circumcise yourselves to the LORD;
>   remove the foreskins of your hearts,
>   people of Judah and residents of Jerusalem,
> lest my wrath flare forth like fire
>   and burn unquenchable
> in the face of the evil of your deeds.
>
> (Jer. 4:4)

As Amy Kalmanofsky has shown, these chapters aim to horrify their readers, and drive them 'to alter their behavior before they confront angry God or become abject Israel'.[33] The depiction of God here is violent and terrifying. Yet this is not the sadistic violence of a tyrant; God never ceases to be the husband whose perfect love for his bride is infinite and unquenchable. It is not easy to grasp how strong anger and strong love might coexist intact. But it is at precisely this point that the person of Jeremiah begins to find his way into the discourse, showing us that wrath has not obliterated anguished love. It is just a single verse at first, offering a reaction: 'Then I said, "Alas, LORD God, how surely and utterly you have deceived this people and Jerusalem by saying, 'Peace will be yours,' when the sword has reached the throat"' (Jer. 4:10). Soon we have an impassioned intrusion (4:19–22), as Jeremiah's pain at what is happening cannot be held in any longer:

> My stomach, my stomach! I'm writhing!
>   My constricted heart!
> Such a noise my heart is making.
>   I cannot keep silent
> since I heard the blast of trumpets –
>   my soul! – the battle shout.
>
> (Jer. 4:19)

At least, it might be Jeremiah's pain, though by the end it feels more like God speaking. Scholars struggle in vain to identify the

[33] Kalmanofsky 2008: 138.

speaker unambiguously, and indeed it is a vain struggle, because what God has done to Jeremiah in making him a prophet has meant that Jeremiah now feels God's feelings.[34] And out of this shared emotional response to the disaster, Jeremiah issues desperate and increasingly frustrated warnings:

> To whom shall I speak,
>   shall I warn, so that they hear?
> They have uncircumcised ears!
>   they are unable to pay attention.
> The word of the LORD is now a reproach to them,
>   they take no delight in it.
> But the wrath of the LORD fills me
>   and I am weary of containing it.
>
> (Jer. 6:10–11a)

Does the prophet have a voice of his own? Not yet. For although Jeremiah reacts in horror and anguish to God's wrathful judgment – emotions no doubt genuinely his own – his anguish serves in the text to carry God's own anguish through into these chapters of warfare. Jeremiah is in no way resisting the word of God inside him, but serving it by showing that the 'root metaphor' of the abandoned husband remains active. However, this is only the beginning: the intrusion of the prophet into his own message is a central feature throughout the book, and we see it developed in a number of directions over the first twenty chapters. We shall examine just one case.

The voice of the prophet in Jeremiah 14 – 15

These chapters follow on from Jeremiah's first symbolic action, the spoiling of a linen loincloth in chapter 13. The word this action conveys, that God will destroy his people without pity, evokes a storm of laments, prayers, divine actions and complaints that involve all parties. At the end of the unit we hear Jeremiah's own voice raised in a very personal cry of distress (15:15–18), the second of the so-called confessions of the prophet.[35] These are chapters in

---

[34] Abraham Heschel speaks in this connection of 'the nexus between prophetic emotion and divine pathos' (Heschel 1962: 119).

[35] The others are found in Jer. 11:18–23 + 12:1–6; 17:14–18; 18:18–23; 20:7–13 + 14–18.

which we see with great clarity the complex nature of Jeremiah's double identity.

God's voice is heard through Jeremiah in a variety of forms in chapters 11–20: prose sermons, poetic oracles, oracles given to explain the significance of symbolic actions. Jeremiah's confessions stand out from all of these, because in them we seem to be hearing Jeremiah's own voice and not God's at all. For an older generation of interpreters this was precisely what we were hearing – the prophet pouring out his heart in private, expressing a deep spirituality he possessed quite apart from his prophetic office.[36] Gerhard von Rad rightly criticized this view: 'It is simply not true that in Jeremiah we find genuine prophetic testimonies and more general religious expressions side by side; on the contrary, it is precisely the confessions that arise out of the center of his being a prophet.'[37] And yet von Rad, guided as he was by form-critical categories, was very sensitive to the fact that these confessions are not oracular, but have the form of human words directed upwards to God, and on those grounds maintained that 'we do not in any way hear Jeremiah speaking as a prophet here, in the old sense of that word'.[38] As his final qualification suggests, von Rad recognized that if these 'non-prophetic' confessions emerge from the centre of Jeremiah's prophetic office, then the concept of prophetic witness in Jeremiah must be 'reformulated'. The same goes for Jeremiah's role of intercessor, which breaks the Mosaic mould. In von Rad's words once more, 'Jeremiah as mediator does not merely have the people facing himself, so as to endure suffering from them – no, he carries their entire misery inside himself.'[39]

Jeremiah 14

Jeremiah 14 opens with a word about a drought. The opening verses reveal two notable features. First, the response of the people is disproportionate, particularly the way the servants in verse 3 respond

---

[36] Skinner 1948: 201–230.

[37] Von Rad 1983: 97.

[38] Ibid. 90.

[39] Ibid. 98. Not all scholars believe we are hearing a personal voice at all. For some, the confessions speak with a liturgical voice such as one hears in a psalm of lament, devoid of any personal significance (Reventlow 1961); but Timothy Polk has shown that Jeremiah in his confessions is representative 'in all the bewildering admixture of transparency and opacity, of the actual people we meet in daily life', and that the 'self' of the speaker 'remains fully engaged in the representative task' (Polk 1984: 80–81).

to their failure to find water with 'shame' and 'humiliation'. Secondly, an unusual image is used in verse 3:

> They go to the cisterns but find no water.
> They return with their jars unfilled.

This image has been used once before, in 2:13:

> My people have committed two sins:
> They have forsaken me,
>   the spring of living water,
> and have dug their own cisterns,
>   broken cisterns that cannot hold water.

It is hard to escape the conclusion that the drought, though no doubt a real drought, symbolized the nation's apostasy.[40]

An appeal for mercy follows in verses 7–9, but the speakers are not identified. 'Although our sins testify against us, do something, LORD, for the sake of your name. For our backsliding is great; we have sinned against you.' Who is speaking? This is plainly a prayer of the people for mercy, whether for rain or for forgiveness. And yet, the people are not actually saying these words here; it is Jeremiah who is speaking, and it may be that after all this is his prayer, of intercession, on behalf of the people. It may even be a prayer on his own account: after all, Jeremiah too is a member of the people, and suffers the effects of the drought as much as anyone. Just as the voices of Jeremiah and God blended in chapter 4, so we see his voice and the people's blended here.[41]

The prayer itself, by appealing to the LORD's *name*, alludes to the covenant relationship set out in Exodus 34:6–7, and is asking God to act in accordance with his nature by forgiving their sin. And yet there is an element of danger to this appeal, since God names himself in Exodus 34 not only as one 'forgiving iniquity and transgression and sin', but also as one 'who will by no means clear the guilty'. No doubt Jeremiah's own repentance, in so far as he speaks for himself

---

[40] The drought imagery in ch. 14 has the same marital overtones of ch. 2, and the allusion to divorce in 15:1 further strengthens the link (Jindo 2010: 115–116, 139).

[41] Some scholars see this as an example of a dialogue between Jeremiah and his audience, in which the people's words do not reflect the prophet's views (e.g. Willis 1985, who lists other similar cases, including 14:17 – 15:4). This is compatible with my reading of Jer. 14.

here, is genuine, but by this stage of the book we feel no such confidence about the people, and the next verse (v. 10) confirms our worst suspicions as we hear God announcing to Jeremiah that he will indeed 'remember' the people's iniquities.[42] Finally, in verses 11–12 it becomes clear that the preceding verses really have been an intercessory prayer, just at the very point when this function is being removed.

We are beginning to see in the person of Jeremiah a sort of 'double nature' emerging. Ever since he ate God's words at his commissioning he has been the embodied voice of God, as chapters 4–6 confirmed. By chapter 14 Jeremiah has also become an embattled member of Israel: unlike Moses, who interceded for 'them', Jeremiah pleads for 'us'. So when God bans intercession he sets up a conflict between Jeremiah's two 'natures', a conflict that results in Jeremiah alone feeling the force of Israel's judgment.

However, as our study of Jeremianic discourse might lead us to expect, the situation is more complex than this. As Jeremiah 14:1 makes clear, while it may be Jeremiah's lips moving, it is God's words he speaks, and the reason he prays this prayer is because God put it into his mouth. It is not two but three different voices that combine here. As a word from the LORD, we might interpret the prayer as follows: Jeremiah is praying on the people's behalf as God instructed him to do, with the purpose of criticizing their insincerity. Their words are being thrown back in their faces as a prelude to a speech of judgment.

How do we interpret this very Jeremianic blurring of speakers? Jeremiah is speaking the people's words to God, exposing their sinful hypocrisy. And at the same time he is also speaking for God, passing down words of divine judgment to the people. And Jeremiah, the man in the middle, shares both the suffering of the people and the anger of God. What was initially God's pain over Israel's sin in chapters 2–3, resulting in Israel's suffering at God's hand in chapters 4–6, is all brought together in chapter 14 in the one person of the prophet. This is not an easy place to be, and as the pressure begins to grow unendurable, Jeremiah will begin to speak more and more for himself as well.

---

[42] Polk (1984: 89) has pointed out a neat subversion here of Ps. 79:8–9: 'Do not remember against us our former iniquities; / let your compassion come speedily to meet us, / for we are brought very low. / Help us, O God of our salvation, / for the glory of your name; / deliver us, and atone for our sins, / for your name's sake!' (ESV).

We must not think of the prophet as suffering all this on his own account, however. The internal conflict that wracks him is nothing less than what Heschel calls the pathos of God. Jeremiah 14 continues with another word of judgment in which Jeremiah is forbidden to intercede, as God has decided to compound the drought with war and plague. Out of this word of judgment comes a new word:

> Speak this word to them:
> 'Let my eyes overflow with tears
>   night and day without ceasing;
> for a great blow has shattered
>   my virgin daughter, my people,
>   a horrific, critical injury.
> If I go out to the field,
>   look – those slain by the sword!
> if I enter the city,
>   look – those ill from famine!
> For both prophet and priest
>   travel to a land they do not know.'
>
> (Jer. 14:17–18)

Once again we face an identity crisis: Whose eyes are overflowing with tears? The mention of 'my virgin daughter, my people' in verse 17 makes them God's eyes. But the language is vividly anthropomorphic, and verse 18 is full of all-too-human surprise. One can only conclude that we have here yet another occasion – and 4:19–22, 6:10–12 and 8:18 – 9:2 are like it – where not only are God's words being spoken by Jeremiah, but God's emotions are being felt by Jeremiah.[43] This is prophetic mediation in reverse: Jeremiah is forbidden from presenting the people's pain to God, but he is here being commanded to present God's pain to the people. It seems likely that the people will be untouched by this, given their track record, and so bring down further judgment on themselves. But the one person who will by no means remain unaffected is Jeremiah himself. Here he is, filled with supernatural anguish over the prospect of the punishment that he himself has just announced being carried out against Judah.

---

[43] On Jer. 8:18 – 9:2 in particular see Polk (1984: 108–113), Biddle (1996: 28–31) and Henderson (2007: 132–133), who argues that in 9:1–2 we hear first Jeremiah's heartbreak and then the LORD's anger; two contrasting reactions to the people's rebellion.

And who is Judah? A people that includes Jeremiah himself. The Christological shape of Jeremiah's ministry is inescapable, and we shall return to this in due course.

While Jeremiah's complaints and God's answers in Jeremiah 14 have served to focus attention on the terrible fate awaiting Judah and the divine pain this fate elicits, the next cycle of complaints and answers, in chapter 15, move the focus onto Jeremiah's personal sufferings. The conjunction of these chapters is no accident, as it draws Jeremiah's personal suffering into the picture of the people's sin and punishment.[44]

Jeremiah 15 and beyond

In Jeremiah 15 things only get worse for the prophet. God announces the reversal of Abraham's blessing in verse 8 – 'I will make their *widows* more numerous than the sands of the sea' – but the only listener who seems to be touched by this is Jeremiah, in verse 10: 'Alas, my mother, that you gave me birth, a man with whom the whole land strives and contends! I have neither lent nor borrowed, yet everyone curses me.' While the word of the LORD announces a future judgment on the people, Jeremiah is experiencing that judgment in the present.

Thus Jeremiah's identity as a representative sufferer starts to become explicit. God replies in the next few verses that Jeremiah will not be killed, but he will be a tool for their judgment. Jeremiah knew this already, from his call in chapter 1, but now he knows from experience, and it is bitter indeed, as his confession in verses 15–18 makes clear. The word rendered 'mirage' in verse 18 (*'akzāb*) may mean something more like 'deception' or 'lie'[45] – a piece of brutal honesty unrelieved by any of the hope that more detached reflection might permit:

> You know, LORD!
> Remember me and watch over me;
>   take vengeance for me from my persecutors.
> Do not, out of slowness to anger, take me away;
>   know that I bear on your account reproach.
> Your words were found, and I ate them.

---

[44] Polk 1984: 78.

[45] So Philip Johnston (2010: 301), though his suggestion that Jeremiah is rebuked for this and must repent is not as convincing.

> Your words became my joy
> and my heart's jubilation,
> for *I am called by your name*,
> LORD God of Hosts.
> I did not sit in the circle of revellers and make merry;
> because of your hand, alone I sat,
> for with indignation you had filled me.
> Why has my pain become unending,
> my *wound* incurable,
> *refusing to be healed*?
> You are to me like a mirage,
> *an untrustworthy spring*.
>
> (Jer. 15:15–18)

There are three remarkable phrases in this confession, remarkable because we have heard them before, but not from Jeremiah. It was the people who said 'we are called by your name' (14:9);[46] it was the people who were shattered by a wound (14:17) and who said 'there is no healing for us' (14:19); and it was the people, throughout chapter 14, to whom God was a spring that failed.[47] Jeremiah has become the representative Israelite who suffers in his body the judgment God has announced for the nation. In a mounting series of ironies Jeremiah suffers this judgment at the hands of the very Israelites he represents, and precisely because he dwells among them as one filled with the word of the LORD. And the reason the eating of God's words was delightful to Jeremiah was because he was 'called by your name' – that is, because Jeremiah was God's bride, his true Israel (cf. Isa. 4:1). That Jeremiah alone was delighted by God's nearness and did not merit judgment is enough to make his sense of betrayal completely understandable. In the words of the parable, the citizens of Judah have eaten sour grapes but it is Jeremiah's teeth that are set on edge (Jer. 31:29).[48]

Yet it is not as if God is unaware of the injustice or unresponsive to it. His reply in verses 19–21 explains that Jeremiah must embody

[46] The Hebrew expression 'called by your name' is formulaic; in all the OT this is the only time an individual uses it (Polk 1984: 88).

[47] The word 'waters' brackets this unit, making a clear allusion back from 15:18 to its previous occurrences in 14:3. On the imagery of water in Jeremiah see Holt 2005.

[48] Hannes Bezzel (2009) draws similar conclusions. While his account of the composition-history of the chapter is overly speculative, his observation that Jeremiah is 'not suffering in spite of but because of God's mercy [on Israel]' (70) is valuable.

the word of the LORD in their midst precisely so that they may
express their antagonism towards it and show that they deserve to
be judged by that word ('they shall turn to you but you shall not
turn to them', v. 19). The LORD forcefully reminds Jeremiah that
this was what he was commissioned to be; however, he ends this
bracing reply with not one verb of deliverance, as was the case in
chapter 1, but four – 'save and deliver', 'deliver . . . redeem'. Just as
Jeremiah's experience of abandonment becomes representative of
the abandonment the people will suffer, so the promise of his return
to the protective presence of God should be read as the beginnings
of hope for the people.[49]

For the prophet, however, such words were cold comfort, and
did little to alleviate the injustice of his present suffering. His final
confession is a grim illustration of the extent to which his message
and life have merged:

> You deceived me, LORD, and I was deceived;
>   you strong-armed me and won.
> I am a perpetual joke;
>   they all mock me.
> For whenever I speak, I yell:
>   'Violence and destruction!', I shout.
> For me the word of the LORD equals
>   reproach and derision all day long.
> But when I say, 'I will not call him to mind
>   or speak anymore in his name,'
> there is in my heart something like a fire
>   burning, bottled up in my bones.
> I am weary of containing it.
>   I cannot win.
>
>   (Jer. 20:7–9)

For many interpreters this amounts to 'a crisis in the prophetic
mission', a mission that turns out to be under God's curse.[50] And yet
we must not forget that, as 15:16–17 implies, even Jeremiah's feelings
of betrayal are God's own feelings.[51] The resisting of the word of the
LORD by its speaker, clearly implied by 20:9, should be seen not as

---

[49] Ittmann 1981: 26; McConville 1993b: 73.
[50] Diamond 1987: 77–78.
[51] Smith 1990: 14.

the prophet temporarily absconding from his role as an embodiment of the word of the LORD, but as a living out of the tension that exists within the word of God itself – a tension that was first seen in God's appeals to his bride to return to him in chapter 2, and will be seen once more in the poignant poetry of chapters 30–31. The fact that the word of God which fills Jeremiah causes him unbearable pain to speak, but must be spoken perforce, is for us a window onto the divine nature. As Stulman puts it, 'in the book of Jeremiah the text *transforms* the person of the prophet into the message itself, so that the two – the person and the message – now coalesce and articulate together the poignant *dābār* ('word' or 'event') of the LORD'.[52]

It is not just in his confessions that Jeremiah's life is his message, for as we have seen, the discourse structure of the book co-opts all of its words into service as the word of the LORD. This means that the many chapters of biography later in the book, with hardly a divine oracle to be found, are to be read in the same way as the prophet's confessions: as the word of God through the life of Jeremiah. Jeremiah's life was never meant to be anything less than a total embodiment of judgment and promise.

As the book moves into its second half the prophet's life is now displayed from outside rather than inside. What happens to Jeremiah is an outward expression of what happens to the word of the LORD. Like Jeremiah, it is opposed and stifled; like him, it proves impossible to destroy; like him, it survives beyond judgment to speak afresh to the exiled fugitives. In short, Jeremiah in chapters 37–44 is depicted as 'one who endures the same destiny as the word of God which he proclaims',[53] and his suffering no less than his survival is experienced in solidarity with God.

The one section of the book from which the prophet is virtually absent is the final movement, the OAN, in which Jeremiah features as writer rather than speaker (51:60). It may be that with the addressees of these oracles so far removed from Jeremiah in distance and perhaps time as well, the physical presence of the speaker cannot be a factor in the way it was earlier in the book.[54] Though not framed as a 'letter to the nations', these oracles convey the presence of their speaker in much the same way that the letter to the exiles did back in

---

[52] Stulman 1998: 138, italics original.

[53] Ibid. 139.

[54] The original addressees, one presumes, were the prophet's compatriots, but in the written book of Jeremiah these oracles achieve an international audience.

chapter 29, namely, as an authorial voice to which a life is attached. For the exiles of chapter 29 that life was known to them by personal experience; for the readers of the OAN that life has been presented to them in the preceding chapters, and is therefore known by way of a literary persona, as the prophet Jeremiah can only henceforth be known to the following generations of his readers.

Questions about the speaker, his words and his deeds revisited

We are now in a position to return to the questions raised earlier about the speaker, his words and his deeds. First, does the prophet have any words of his own? Was von Rad right to distinguish between the oracles of Jeremiah the prophet and the free expressions of Jeremiah the man?[55] At a formal level he was of course correct to save the description 'prophetic oracle' for a revelation of the type that is so often prefaced with 'Thus says the LORD'. And yet we have seen that Jeremiah the prophet had no words that he could truly call his own. What von Rad calls 'free lyric poetry', 'a poetic impulse which exists quite independently from prophecy',[56] should be seen in the light of Jeremiah 1 as God's appropriation of all of Jeremiah's words – his lyric poetry, his sermons and speeches, his personal responses and even rebellions against his prophetic calling – as part of the divine word the prophet was created to convey. Certainly, the book's compiler drew no distinction between 'prophetic' oracles and 'lyrical' confessions by the way he arranged them, with the confessions placed, undifferentiated, among the more conventional oracular material. The book of Jeremiah stretches our preconceptions about the forms prophetic speech may legitimately take, and no more so than in the case of Jeremiah, to whom 'the word of the LORD came' as it never had to any prophet before, forming him into a creature of the word through and through.

This disagreement with von Rad should not be exaggerated, however. While he does not class all Jeremiah's words as prophetic speech, he is far from dismissing them. Instead, he treats the confessions as part of Jeremiah's life, or *bios*, which for von Rad 'now takes on the authority of a witness. His suffering soul, his life bleeding to

---

[55] 'The only part of the passage that is divine speech, that is, prophetic proclamation in the strict sense of the term, is the answer of Yahweh. After all, it is very clearly said that the actual words of Jeremiah's confession mark the abandonment of his prophetic office!' (von Rad 1983: 90, on Jer. 15:16–20).

[56] Von Rad 1965: 201.

death in God's task – all this becomes a pointer towards God.'[57] This brings us to our second and third questions: Does Jeremiah's life, his deeds as well as his words, belong in a Jeremianic theology of the word of God? I have concluded that it does, and not just as God constrains Jeremiah to act. Even when it was being freely lived, all of Jeremiah's life was prophetic – his unsolicited words and deeds alike having been captured and pressed into service as the word of God. It is in this sense that von Rad would treat Jeremiah's 'free speech' as prophetic, distinguished from his deeds only in that it was explicitly verbal.

What does this discussion suggest as we formulate a theology of the speaker of the word of God? Jeremiah does not merely speak the word of God; he *embodies* the word of God in the sense that everything he says and does is a declaration of the word of God among his people. This is not to say that deeds, for all that they may speak louder than words, speak with greater clarity: they must be interpreted in words before their import is clear. The 'word of God' does not mean the words and deeds of God; it means the message those words – and deeds – convey. In the life of Jeremiah, God's word, his message, is made concrete and immediate to those who hear (and see) it. And in so far as God conveys himself – his character, his will, his inmost thoughts – by his word, we might say that in the life of his prophet God makes himself present to his people. It is the word of God, not Jeremiah, that we hear when Jeremiah speaks. And it is the word of God, not Jeremiah, that we see when Jeremiah acts. Jeremiah's life is one great act of divine self-communication.

In the light of these reflections the conclusion at the end of our discussion of Jeremianic discourse needs to be modified. I claimed there that 'it is Jeremiah's life we see, but God's voice we hear'; though this remains true at a superficial level, it is more accurate to say that not only is it God's voice we hear; it is God's life we see as well. Whether we parse the confessions as divine oracles or human complaints is immaterial, for they, together with every word and deed of the prophet, count as divine self-revelation.

Concluding reflections

What is so special about speech? Spoken words convey nuances of meaning by the expression of the voice and, if the speaker can be seen,

---

[57] Von Rad 1983: 98.

by gestures and so forth; but in general there is not much that speech can add to the meaning of the written word. And yet there is one fundamental difference – the presence of the speaker. Speech has the power to draw people into relationship with an immediacy and ease the written word cannot rival. While it is true that virtual friends may fall in love over the Internet without ever meeting, nevertheless business executives will fly around the world rather than teleconference, because of the importance of 'the personal touch'. The advent of the virtual age has shown us how dangerously easy it is to reinvent oneself as a different person in order to take advantage of strangers. But once we come face to face, pretence becomes a far riskier business. The speaker in the book of Jeremiah puts a face on the word of God and in so doing strips away any possibility of pretence on either side.

1. *The word of God is not a written document but the living speech of God himself.* The written words of Jeremiah aim by every means possible to connect the reader back to the original speech events by which the word of God came to the prophet. Not only the voice of God, but all the other voices in the book, including the prophet's and even the narrator's, are reframed to present God's voice to the reader as directly as possible. One result of this relentless focus on the original speech of God is the retraction of the prophet's own voice, making him a transparent vessel for the words of God. However, the constant focus on the prophet's life and works in the book – unique to Jeremiah – shows us the crucial importance of the speaker of the words, God's chosen instrument by which he makes himself known to his people.

2. *God's words are no less God's words for being spoken by his prophet.* Jeremiah's commissioning makes it very clear that the word of God when Jeremiah speaks it is just as powerful as it would have been coming from God himself, unmediated.

3. *The speaker in the book of Jeremiah is a creature of the divine word.* The first chapter of Jeremiah shows us a person whose very being is constituted by the word of God. Of course Jeremiah is not the Word incarnate, but the way in which the divine word is presented as touching his ontology, his being, provides a significant prefigurement of the full-blown Word Christology of the New Testament. Jeremiah is a product of the word of God, filled with the words of God, and as those words pour out of him they cause God to be present in judgment and hope. From this starting point, what can we say more precisely about the relationship between the speaker and the word?

4. *Just as the word of God determines the words of God, so it determines the speaker.* The speaker is not himself the word of God; his life with all its words and deeds is analogous to the words from which the word of God, the message, is constituted. These 'words' of the speaker's life, when rightly heard, convey the word of God to the hearer, and it is that divine word by which we determine what these 'words' truly mean. This is the sense in which the speaker is defined by the 'words' he speaks and does, and because he is a creature of the word of God, each one of his words, whether he meant them as words of obedience or words of rebellion, words of public proclamation or words of private reflection, are taken into service as the words of God, whence their true meaning derives.

Another way of expressing this relationship is to say that *the speaker of the word of God is the words of God embodied.* The chapters we sampled demonstrate what it looks like when a prophet is made by God into a word-shaped person. The message he conveys makes his life unbearable, not simply because the message is a distressing one, but because the message is, in some sense, an essential part of his being. He eats God's words, they enter his bloodstream and his bones; and when he opens his mouth, God's words come out – not because God forces him to speak them, but because there is nothing else in him to come out. His fellow countrymen hate him simply because they hate God's words. He feels God's pain because God's words are inside him and they cannot bear the touch of evil. Now there is of course a degree to which this sort of language is metaphorical: we would not say, for example, that Jeremiah ate God's words in a literal sense.[58] But the passages we have examined here strongly resist being classified as metaphor through and through. Just where metaphor stops and bald description begins I do not think we can say, but there is without doubt some true sense in which Jeremiah is – not the word of God made flesh – but the words of God embodied.

5. *Embodiment is a form of authentication.* It is deeply significant that Jeremiah is not simply an empty conduit for divine revelation: what the word of God does in him and to him makes his life in itself an act of divine self-communication. As a result the word of God in

---

[58] On the question of just how the word of the LORD came to Jeremiah we must be somewhat agnostic, but it is probable that the mode of delivery was varied. The language of vision is used once or twice (e.g. 38:22), and in the fascinating episode of Jer. 40:1–6 the word of the LORD comes to Jeremiah through a Deuteronomic-sounding oracle from the captain of Nebuchadnezzar's guard.

Jeremiah is not a mere set of assertions, demands and promises, for
it carries with it a demonstration of its truthfulness and power. In
the forming of Jeremiah into a prophet we see embodied the power
of the word of God to create; in his suffering we see embodied the
power of the word of God to judge; in his survival we see embodied
the power of the word of God to save. The fate of the speaker demonstrates, as a type of prophetic proclamation, the truth of the word
he makes present by his life.

6. *Embodiment anchors the word among its hearers.* At first
glance it seems entirely unnecessary that God should choose to
make himself present to his hearers through a speaker who also
happens to be one of them, who embodies not only the words of
God but also their audience. Were Jeremiah simply to stand over
against the people and address them from the divine council as
God's emissary,[59] his message could be understood perfectly well.
However, it turns out that this cannot do justice to the word of
God in its particularity. This is because God does not stop loving
his people in order to judge them, but suffers with their suffering
through the suffering of Jeremiah. Despite Judah's relegation to the
status of one of the nations, God never stops addressing her as bride
and daughter. And by refusing to withhold his love, the reverse is
also allowed to happen: we see Jeremiah suffering with God's own
suffering at his rejection by the people he loves. In the end, a God
who shares his people's suffering and judgment proves to them by
this that his victory over all that stands against him may become
their victory too. The word of God would be a different word if it
addressed his people from a distance, disengaged; to be what it is, it
must come to them embodied as one of them, fully engaged with the
objects of its address. Another way of putting this is to say that *the
speaker of the word has a double nature; in him the word of God dwells
among his people.*

7. *The speaker is embodied in written words in the form of his
persona.* The discussion so far begs the following objection: surely
Jeremiah did not have to be present in person for the word of God
to be heard. In chapter 36, for example, people responded in faith to
Baruch's reading of Jeremiah's written words. However, true though
that may be, it does not alter the fact that the word theology of the
book of Jeremiah is unremittingly incarnational, if we may use that
term in a lessened sense. Thus, although the person of Jeremiah

---

[59] Cf. Jer. 23:16–22.

ceased embodying his words thousands of years ago, he has been replaced in his book by the *persona* of Jeremiah – his person brought to life again not only by the intrusion of his voice into his prophecies as we have seen, but in the extraordinary collection of biographical writings that make up so much of his written words.[60]

8. *Implications for a theology of the word of God.* What does a study of the speaker of the word tell us about the word of God itself?[61] It has been clear from the start that the word of God is not the words per se; it is the message they convey. Now in addition we see that it is a message, made of words, embodied in a life, that makes God present personally among his people. As *spoken* and living 'words' the message the word of God conveys, while disambiguated by language, is not confined to words, but consists of an entire person whose life is an act of divine self-disclosure. And *it is nothing less than this self-disclosure that is the word of God.* This is not to confuse the persons of God and Jeremiah: in the book of Jeremiah the person concerned is the prophet, but it is not prophetic self-disclosure his life achieves; his life is a tool for divine self-disclosure. While we might truly say of the person of the prophet presented to us in the book of Jeremiah, 'he who has seen me has seen the Father', it is quite clear that we see God not *in* the prophet but *through* him. However, nothing more could be done to prepare for the unimaginable self-disclosure of incarnation.

For us, however, everything is written. The word of God is 'confined to words' for us as it never was for those who knew Jeremiah the man. Nevertheless, these written words may still bring us a vivid sense of the person along with his message. What is more, the fact that this person is textually mediated was in one sense always true: it was Jeremiah's words, soon written down, that disambiguated his actions; even in the case of the LORD Jesus the written words

---

[60] 'The repeated manufacture of a scroll underlines . . . the relation between the prophet himself and his recorded words: Jeremiah is present in the words that are read' (Venema 2004: 136, on Jer. 36).

[61] Is it valid to use Jeremiah's presentation in generalized theological reflection, given the uniqueness of his role as an embodiment of his message? First of all we might reply that what Jeremiah teaches us about God is no less true because he alone teaches it in this way; but there are good reasons apart from this why Jeremiah should be unique in this regard, related to the development of prophecy across the OT period. Earlier prophets relay the contents of divine oracles but without reflecting on their nature as the word of God; Jeremiah is one of the earliest to use word formulas with any regularity. Later prophets are not presented as having the sort of intimate, personalized encounters with God that are common earlier; Jeremiah is one of the last to do so. See Meier 2009, esp. chs. 5, 7.

of Scripture (our Old Testament) mediated his identity to his disciples.[62] To the extent that these words bring us a *persona*, we may still affirm that the word of God comes to us embodied in a person. While the existence of written words creates the possibility of later speakers also in some sense embodying an enscripturated word as they proclaim it, a distinction needs to be maintained between us second-hand speakers of the word and those, like Jeremiah, whose life formed part of their message in a way that finds no direct parallel in our experience. Instead, we are naturally drawn to think of the terrible vocation of Jesus: a vocation that, unlike Jeremiah, Jesus freely chose; a vocation that, unlike Jeremiah's, did lead to his being shattered before his enemies.

9. *The Christological shape of the word of God in Jeremiah.* It may seem unwarranted to speak about 'Christology' in a prophet with almost nothing to say about a future king.[63] However, the New Testament writers are not guilty of such narrow etymologizing, and freely mine the Servant Songs of Isaiah for their Christology. Isaiah's servant figure has been identified both with the expected 'prophet like Moses'[64] and with the figure of Jeremiah,[65] forming a group of related 'Christ figures'. Thus, even though the person of Jeremiah is named in the New Testament only by Matthew,[66] and his book is cited only infrequently elsewhere, it should not be surprising that a biblical-theological reading of Jeremiah uncovers Christological patterns that are impossible to overlook, patterns reflected in books such as John's Gospel and Paul's Corinthian letters.[67] Despite the lack of citations – and many theories have been proposed about why New Testament writers chose to cite from the books they did – it is hard to avoid the conclusion that Jeremiah was not least among the books of Scripture that shaped the Christology of the apostolic church.[68] In any case, our interest here is not the way the New Testament uses Jeremiah, but the way in which Jeremiah,

---

[62] So Watson 1997: 1–2.

[63] A few times the LORD is depicted as king of the nations (10:7, 10; 48:15), and a future David is mentioned thrice (23:5; 30:9; 33:21).

[64] E.g. Hugenberger 1995.

[65] Blank 1974: 126–127.

[66] Matt. 2:17; 27:9; and especially 16:14, where 'some say' that Jesus is Jeremiah *redivivus*.

[67] See e.g. Shead 2000; Peterson 2012.

[68] 'It is clear that Jeremiah's cruciality for New Testament faith consists not in particular citations but in the imaginative redescription of the crisis of Jerusalem according to the large purposes of YHWH' (Brueggemann 2007: 192).

read as Christian Scripture, generates Christology on its own account. From our readings of Jeremiah 1 and 14 – 15 the following sketch provides a beginning.

The speaker of the word is one with God. He embodies the word at the level of his being; his words are God's words, his feelings, God's feelings. His whole life is the message, embodying the judgment and promise he came to announce. In him God makes himself present to his people.

The speaker of the word is one with Israel. He is the Moses who was to come, an intercessor who, unlike Moses, 'carries their entire misery inside himself', feeling with equal force the horror of their sinfulness (just as God does), and the horror of their impending doom (just as they should).

The speaker of the word is torn by his double nature. As a prophet he bears God's name and delights in his word; as a Judean he is cut off and God is closed to him. And yet this inner conflict is an expression of his God-given call, and the pain it generates is no less than God's own pain. By his solidarity with condemned Israel he was always going to suffer from the message of divine wrath he brought them; but that he would suffer judgment alone, at their hands, is both unsurprising, given their hatred of the word of God that he embodied, and unnecessary, if God had really wanted to spare him. More than unnecessary, it is unjust, and this proves almost too much for the speaker to bear.

God's eventual raising up of the speaker of the word is a sign of hope for the nation. Unjust as the speaker's sufferings might have been, it was only because he was one who delighted in God's word that an assured salvation awaited him beyond his suffering. In his oneness with both God and the people the prophet points the way out of Judah's present darkness, though whether anyone can follow him there is a moot point. This element of Jeremiah's Christology is barely hinted at in the text, and at this stage is only evident by bringing the context of Christian Scripture firmly to bear on our reading. However, Jeremiah's theology of salvation emerges with perfect clarity in the second half of his book, as we shall see in due course.

There are many obvious points of contact in the Gospels, such as Jesus' use of Psalm 22 at his crucifixion, a confession that serves very much the same function as Jeremiah's own. And yet, even more than the textual echoes, it is the insight Jeremiah provides onto the whole structure and nature of the Christ's incarnate existence that enriches our Christology. For example, no part of Scripture expresses with greater poignancy just how hard it is to stand between and represent both a holy God and a sinful humanity. Jesus' suffering in his final week was but the last, most trying stage of a long road that began with a stable in Bethlehem, and with a slaughter of children. Not a moment of Jesus' life was untroubled.

Perhaps the best example of a text that does not cite Jeremiah but expresses its distinctive word Christology in almost every line is John's prologue:

> He was in the world, and the world was created through
> him,
> yet the world did not recognize him.
> He came to his own,
> and his own people did not receive him.
> But to all who did receive him,
> he gave them the right to be children of God,
> to those who believe in his name,
> who were born, not of blood,
> or of the will of the flesh, or of the will of man,
> but of God.
>
> (John 1:10–13 HCSB amended)

Jeremiah can still be present to us in his words, just as Jesus is present to us in the words of the Gospels. But unlike Jesus who, being the true Word of God, can be present to us in transforming power in the person of his Spirit, Jeremiah was just a man. And his experience proved that there is nothing in the combination of divine words and prophetic speaker that compels hearing of the word of God. For that matter, even the preaching of Jesus Christ could be and was rejected by many who listened to it. We can go still further. Not only is the combination of God's words and God's speaker not enough to evoke receptiveness in a listener; it may not even be enough to convince listeners they are listening to the words of God in the first place. The whole question of how one knows when it is a prophet speaking is fraught with difficulty, and I shall tackle this problem in the next chapter.

Nevertheless, though words embodied by their speaker may not be sufficient to bring the word of God to us, the book of Jeremiah is convinced that they are ultimately necessary. For the words of God to communicate his message fully, that is, to communicate his person under the form of speech, a speaker who embodies those words in his person must speak them. The words of Jeremiah can address us as the word of God not just because of their content, not just because they are being spoken, but because of the way they come to us, embodied in and by their speaker.

Chapter Four

Word and hearers

The word of God, I have argued, is a message spoken by God – spoken, not written – that comes to a prophet. The words of which that word is made up are then spoken by the prophet in turn and either rejected by the listeners or perhaps received; and if received, what the listeners hear is the word of God, even though it was not God himself whose voice they heard. The word of God is not a disembodied message, and the words of Jeremiah communicate the word of God through the way they come to us, embodied in and by their speaker. However, we should not think that being suitably embodied is all that is required for the word of God to be received as the word of God by those who hear it. For a communication act to be effective, a successful speaker is insufficient. A successful hearer is also needed.

Earlier we saw the abundance of word language in Jeremiah. Alongside this we find an equal abundance of hearing language. The verb 'to hear', *šm'*, is used in all its forms more often in Jeremiah than anywhere else in the Old Testament. A lot of this language is negative, referring to God's words that the people do not hear. What they do hear instead is not pleasant: they hear evil voices, military trumpets, horses, cries of panic and destruction, wailing, the cry of a woman in labour, a voice in Ramah lamenting, Ephraim grieving, reproach and shame. There is hardly a silent moment.

In a book filled with so much noise the problem of the hearer presents itself in a very particular way, arising even before the question of true understanding comes into play. The hearers of Jeremiah's day first had to decide which speaker to listen to. For they lived in a world of multiple, conflicting prophetic voices, and the epistemological problem of how one can know that one is hearing the word of God was for them especially acute. Of course, for us readers of the book there is no problem. That Jeremiah's words are a communication to us of the word of God is the first datum with which the book presents us. But for the original hearers of Jeremiah the rival prophetic messages that confronted them were

147

often plausible and theologically grounded, and choosing between them posed a grave dilemma.

The bulk of this chapter, then, is devoted to a study of the prophets and their listeners. In a closing section I shall add to this picture from material that concerns the people in isolation. Ultimately, the aim is to carry our Jeremianic theology of the word of God one step further, by reflecting on the word of God as it appears to its hearers and the role of the hearers in completing the communication process. What, for example, do we conclude about the nature of the word of God from the fact that, despite its nation-toppling power, it is able to be rejected by listeners?

The hearers' dilemma

Our starting point is not Jeremiah but Deuteronomy, the source of so much of his theology. For it is in Deuteronomy that we find perhaps the only explicit guidance for testing prophets. There are two relevant passages. One is is Deuteronomy 13:1–5, which concerns a prophet who calls on the people to worship other gods – an obvious false message – and backs it up by a sign or wonder that comes true. The people are not to be taken in, but must put that prophet to death. The other is Deuteronomy 18:18–22:

> I will raise up a prophet for them from among their brothers, one like you. I will put my words in his mouth, and he will tell them whatever I command him. And if there is someone who does not listen to my words that he speaks in my name, I myself will hold him accountable. However, if a prophet presumes to speak in my name a word I have not commanded him to speak, or speaks in the name of other gods, that prophet shall die. If ever you ask yourself, 'How can we recognize the word the LORD has not spoken?' – the word a prophet speaks in the LORD's name that does not happen or is not fulfilled, that is a word the LORD has not spoken. The prophet has spoken it presumptuously. Do not dread him.

The person addressed is the hearer disposed to believe and thus fear, and the final goal of the injunction is what hearers are to do once they have identified a prophetic word as false, namely, not to be in fear.[1] To this hearer the law declares that a true prophet's words

---

[1] This is the reading reflected in Neh. 6, as shown by David Shepherd 2005.

must be listened to as if it were God speaking; the counterfeiting of God's voice, or its identification with false gods, is a capital crime. This raises the problem of how to tell when a prophecy is false, and the solution of verse 22 is to wait and see whether it is fulfilled. If it is not, then the prophet (or perhaps the prophecy) should no longer be a source of fearful anticipation (it seems to be a prophecy of doom that the text has in mind).[2] These guidelines are quite narrow; although interpreters have traditionally read a test for true prophecy out of the negatives of verse 22, no direct guidance is given here for judging when a prophecy or prophet is genuine. It may be that a prophecy that is fulfilled is genuinely from the LORD,[3] but though the text leaves room for such a possibility, it makes no such actual claim.

A more secure inference is that the prophecy in question is one that cannot be declared false on theological grounds alone (cf. v. 19, 'in my name'). No waiting is required in the case of a heretical message, as verse 20 indicates. Deuteronomy 13:1–5 is even stronger: even if a prophetic call to turn away from the LORD is accompanied by a sign or wonder that comes true, that call must be rejected; the situation will be a divine test of their obedience.

As a test for false prophecy Deuteronomy 18:22 leaves a lot of ground uncovered. For example, not all prophecy is predictive; many prophetic words are general and hard to substantiate; even true prophecies may not eventuate if the subject repents or God changes his mind (cf. Jer. 18:7–10).[4] More troublesome, however, is the apparent incompleteness of the law in the areas it does cover. First, there is no guidance for how the hearer should respond to a prophecy before events either confirm or invalidate it. And secondly, if a prophecy remains unrealized, how long does one wait before

---

[2] The pronominal suffix suggests it is the word rather than the prophet they are being told not to fear. And yet the translation 'do not dread it' (based on the argument that *ygr*, the verb of which *gwr* in this verse is a by-form, means fear of things to come) only exacerbates the problem that when the prophecy is shown to be hollow, there will be nothing to fear in any case. It is less problematic, then, to see this as referring to the prophet (as do the majority of English versions); however, this might imply that a false prophecy destroys the speaker's future credibility as a prophet, which is also problematic (Meier 2009: 207–217); Meier suggests (213) that 'the word', singular, refers to a single prediction, which need not undo a prophet's reputation if his track record is good enough. Cf. Craigie 1976: 263: 'the criteria represent the means by which a prophet gained his reputation [over time] as a true prophet'. Against Meier, however, v. 20 suggests the prophet in question has no future.

[3] As Sweeney 2005: 79 argues.

[4] Crenshaw 1971: 49–52.

deciding to stop worrying about it? These are not idle questions, as Jeremiah's situation illustrates.[5]

When Hananiah prophesied that God would deliver the people from captivity within two years, not seventy, Jeremiah's response was reminiscent of the 'wait and see' test from Deuteronomy 18:22 (Jer. 28:9). Presently, I shall argue that Jeremiah had something rather different in mind;[6] whatever the case, however, the hearers were in a quandary. If they waited and Hananiah's prophecy did not come true, they could safely ignore Hananiah – but this would tell them nothing about whether to believe Jeremiah if his prophecy still had not come true. And in any case, time was running out: whom should they believe at that moment? They could not afford to do nothing. They had to make the difficult choice to submit to the Babylonian imperium or to resist, and the choice they made would depend on whom they believed in that moment.[7]

To understand this confrontation and its implications, one must be familiar with the intense debate between Jeremiah and the prophets up to this point. Jeremiah's own covenant message is recorded in chapter 7.

The covenant preaching of Jeremiah and the prophets

Jeremiah's covenant preaching: 'Disaster!'

The prophets, Jeremiah included, preached a common message: Honour your covenant obligations. Indeed, this is virtually the definition of a prophet's role as emissary of the divine suzerain. For it was ever the case that God's people, knowing the covenant promises he had made them, tended to forget the responsibilities that went with them.[8] The sermon at the temple gate recorded in Jeremiah 7

---

[5] J. Tigay sees Deut. 18 as applying to mantic prophecy, which relies on quickly falsifiable natural predictions, such as the finding of lost animals (1 Sam. 9:6), and not to classical prophecy whose long-range and contingent predictions were not subject to verification; nevertheless, he suggests that Jer. 28:9 applies Deut. 18 to a classical-style prophecy of well-being (Tigay 1996: 178).

[6] Sharp (2003: 152–153) and others rightly question the connection between Jer. 28 and Deut. 18.

[7] Overholt 1970: 93. The reduction of Jeremiah's and Hananiah's argument to a question of timing is much more pronounced in the MT than in the LXXV; on the distinctive emphases of the earlier edition see Wells 2007.

[8] Deut. 26:16–19 succinctly expresses the obligations on both sides (Williamson 2007: 96, 113).

is therefore programmatic for Jeremiah's ministry. In this sermon Jeremiah exposes the nation's complacent trust in the divine blessing implied by the existence of the temple (v. 4) and presents their treatment of God and one another in terms of breaches of the ten commandments (vv. 5–9). The fact that they cynically exploit God's kindness by completely disregarding their obligations toward one another makes their sins particularly despicable (vv. 10–11), and points to a future in which God will bring down the consequences of covenant unfaithfulness on their heads (vv. 11–15).[9] Although verses 5–7 have promised a full restoration of the covenant relationship as soon as the people show by their behaviour that they have repented, this promise is quickly drowned out by the unstoppable tide of their rebellion. Repentance was never to be. 'Disaster', or 'evil' ($rā'â$),[10] was announced as early as Jeremiah 1:14, and was the single word most characteristic of Jeremiah's preaching:

Then the LORD said to me, 'Out of the north *disaster* shall be poured out upon all who live in the land.' (Jer. 1:14)

Raise a banner toward Zion,
flee for safety, do not delay,
for I bring *disaster* from the north,
and a great destruction.

(Jer. 4:6)

Hear, O earth!
I am bringing *disaster* on these people,
the fruit of their own plotting;
for to my words they have not given heed,
and as for my law, they rejected it.

(Jer. 6:19)

By the end of the first half of Jeremiah the sense of conditionality has gone, and the second half of the book begins in chapter 25 by announcing judgment with no qualification, in view of the nation's persistent refusal to repent.

---

[9] There is a sharp irony in the fact that the nation is hiding from God's demands in the temple, and it effectively turns the very place in which faithfulness ought to have been reinforced into the place where unfaithfulness is justified. This irony will re-emerge in the context of Jeremiah's polemic against the prophets.

[10] A word Jeremiah uses two to five times more frequently than any other prophetic book (counting the Twelve Prophets as a book).

The prophets' covenant preaching: 'Peace!'

We hear very little from the prophets themselves, but we can recon-struct the core of their message through the words of Jeremiah. We need to be careful in the way we do this, as Jeremiah's words about the prophets are far from neutral (an issue I shall take up below), but we do have summaries by Jeremiah of the prophets' message that are widely accepted as unvarnished paraphrases of their words. In the case of chapter 28 the words of the prophet Hananiah himself are recorded. Jeremiah's favourite word for summarizing the prophets' message was 'peace' (*šālôm*):

> They have healed my people's wound glibly,
> claiming, '*Peace, peace,*'
> though there is no *peace*.
>
> (Jer. 6:14)

But I said, 'Alas, LORD God, the prophets keep telling them, "You will not see the sword, and famine will not come to you. Indeed, I will give you certain *peace* in this place."' (Jer. 14:13)

This message of peace was not plucked out of the air, but had its roots in the message of Isaiah, who had prophesied in Jerusalem a century earlier. Isaiah predicted a future in which a Davidic ruler would establish peace across the earth, in which the LORD would make peace with the citizens of Zion, and keep them in perfect peace. The salvation of Jerusalem was not just a distant hope in Isaiah's thinking, but an immediate reality, as he counselled king Ahaz to trust in God and resist the Assyrians: 'I will defend this city to save it, for my own sake and for the sake of my servant David' (Isa. 37:35; cf. Isa. 7:9). And indeed Jerusalem was miraculously delivered from the Assyrian army. A century later it seemed plain to most people that at the foundation of the royal covenant lay God's promise to preserve Jerusalem. And if that meant resisting Assyria a century before, why should it not mean resisting Babylon in the present? It came down to the question of which foreign policy the nation should pursue. Jehoiakim was installed as king by Egypt to serve their inter-ests, and a decade later Zedekiah was installed by Babylon to serve *their* interests. It would be very good to know if God would stand behind a rebellion against the northern foe, just as he had in Isaiah's day. The answer of the prophets was an emphatic yes.

The similarity of their message

Research over recent decades has made plain the extent of Jeremiah's own dependence on Isaiah.[11] As table 4.1 demonstrates, Jeremiah can turn to Isaiah to support both his words of judgment and of promise. For Isaiah did not prophesy unqualified rescue. He left no doubt that Assyria was God's tool for judgment, and that this boded ill for unfaithful Jerusalem and its citizens (Isa. 1:7–9; 29:1–4). There was hope, but not at the cost of ignoring sin.

Table 4.1 The influence of Isaiah on Jeremiah's preaching

Oracle	Contents	Source
Jer. 5:15–17	Description of the invading 'nation from afar'	Isa. 5:26–29
Jer. 4:31; 6:24	Judah's pain like a woman in labour	Isa. 13:8
Jer. 6:27–30	Judah's punishment like the smelting of metal	Isa. 1:21–26
Jer. 23:20	'The anger of the LORD will not turn back'	Isa. 5:25; 9:12, 17, 21; 10:4
Jer. 25:12–13	Babylon/Assyria will be judged by God in the end	Isa. 14:25–27
Jer. 23:1–8	A Davidic branch will arise in the future	Isa. 11:1–16

By the time Zedekiah came to the throne, Babylon had already inflicted a defeat on Jerusalem, and exiled its king and upper classes. Every prophet would have seen God's wrath in this disaster. But this only made the choice between Jeremiah and the other prophets more difficult: both could claim that their message was consistent with the great prophet Isaiah; both agreed that God's commitment to his covenant implied the ultimate salvation of Jerusalem; and both recognized that God's judgment had fallen. By the time Jeremiah and Hananiah came to blows, in the fourth year of Zedekiah, the difference between them could be seen as coming down to a single question: Have we been punished enough? Hananiah, whose name means 'the LORD is gracious', said, 'Yes we have: it is time for God to show mercy and fulfil his promise. We shall have peace in two years.' Jeremiah replied, 'No we have not: our position before God is so dire that Isaiah's promise to Ahaz does not apply to us. We shall have no peace for two generations.'

In the face of those choices it was the hearers' task to recognize the word of God.

[11] See Holladay (1989: 47–50), Sweeney (2005: 78–93) and especially the careful work of Ute Wendel (1995), who shows that Jeremiah was a much truer pupil of Isaiah than Hananiah was. For the use of Isa. 15, 16 and 24:17–18 in Jer. 48 see Meier (2009: 174–177).

The Jeremianic distinctive

While the two rival messages shared much in common at a super-ficial level, Jeremiah's assessment of the people's spiritual state seems to have been unique, as we see in some of his more polemical descriptions of the prophets' message (e.g. Jer. 8:8–13; 15:5–6). In particular, Jeremiah drew on the Mosaic covenant as reflected in the book of Deuteronomy. One passage that influenced him strongly was Deuteronomy 29:16–21, and in particular, verse 19: 'When someone hears the words of this oath, he may bless himself in his mind, thinking, "Peace will be mine, even though I follow my own stubborn heart so that the well-watered may sweep away the dry."'[12] 'Following one's own stubborn heart' is a phrase used only here in all the Pentateuch, and Jeremiah quotes it eight times in the first half of the book to describe the nation.[13] That the stubborn-hearted person of Deuteronomy speaks a word of peace is a suggest-ive detail in view of Jeremiah's choice of that word to characterize the false prophecy of his day. There was something about both the prophets and their hearers, a 'stubbornness of heart', that kept Jeremiah's messsage from veering into optimism.

Jeremiah's reliance on Deuteronomy, seen throughout his prose and poetry alike, is no accident.[14] Theologically, it accords with Jeremiah's calling to be a 'prophet like Moses', and it anchors his prophetic ministry in the law, whence all true prophecy derives. Clements rightly elevates this feature of prophetic literature to a principle, 'the principle that all prophecy must be understood and interpreted in the light of, and against the background of, the Mosaic *torah*'.[15] The Mosaic law thus provides the theological norm

---

[12] Reading the difficult last phrase with McConville (2002a: 412) as expressive of the person's determination to worship fertility gods.

[13] Jer. 3:17; 7:24; 9:14; 11:8; 13:10; 16:12; 18:12; 23:17. The phrase is almost always used in parallel with the verb meaning 'hear' or 'obey': 'they did not hear or stretch out their ears' (7:24; 11:8); 'not obeying my voice' (9:13). Its only other use in the OT is in Ps. 81:12.

[14] The nature of this reliance is much debated, partly owing to scholarly disagreement about whether Jeremiah draws on Deuteronomy or vice versa (McConville has mounted an argument for an early Deuteronomy that I consider to be based on good reading practices: McConville 1993a: 45–64; 2002a: 21–40). For a concise account of the relationship see Holladay (1989: 53–63).

[15] Clements 2007: 37. Jeremiah as preacher of the law is a particularly strong feature of Calvin's interpretation: 'although prophets were from time to time raised up, still it was fitting that the superiority should remain with Moses, lest they should decline in the smallest degree from the rule of the Law' (Calvin 1950b: 408–409; cf.

against which to assess the vaildity of any prophetic utterance, and prevents prophecy from being fatalistic by placing it within a covenant framework in which repentance can always turn curse into blessing.[16]

At the same time, a strong continuity with earlier prophecy, especially that of Amos and Hosea, can be detected in the way Jeremiah's message unfolds.[17] Like them, Jeremiah begins with a call to repentance and a return to covenant obedience, and arrives at a point of no return, when judgment becomes unavoidable, the covenant unworkable. For none of these prophets, however, is this the last word, and in the way Jeremiah applies both the justice and the mercy of God as revealed in the Mosaic law he shows himself to be in the tradition of 'his servants the prophets' (Jer. 25:4) whom the LORD dispatched to an intransigent nation throughout its history.

Jeremiah against the prophets

Should the so-called 'false prophets' be rehabilitated?

As we have seen, our only source of information on the prophets of Jeremiah's day is their great opponent, Jeremiah himself. This fact has aroused scepticism among many scholars, who do not feel that such a polemical portrait ought to be trusted. Were these prophets really as disreputable as their opponent Jeremiah makes out? so lacking in integrity? Were the motives of the pro-Jeremiah authors of this book really so pure? And as soon as a double standard is suspected, scholars are quick to pounce on any number of odd features in the text as indicators of competing and contradictory viewpoints hidden beneath the surface of the text as we now have it. In the words of Carolyn Sharp, 'it is particularly in the last decade or so that the ideological underpinnings of these prophetic conflicts in the book of Jeremiah have begun to be seen for what they are'.[18]

Such a conclusion is a good example of a hermeneutic in which the

---

Tarrer 2009). Calvin's insight can be embraced without accepting his occasional descriptions of prophets as teachers of the law and no more (Moberly 2006: 77). Cf. also Brueggemann 1997: 633–635.

[16] It is therefore inadequate to assert, as Marvin Sweeney does, that Jeremiah's attack on the temple in Jer. 7 and Isaiah's support of the temple in Isa. 7:1 – 9:6 reflect conflicting ideologies (Sweeney 2005: 81–82). Each prophet has applied the same Mosaic standards to a different social, political and theological situation.

[17] See especially Lalleman-de Winkel 2000.

[18] Sharp 2003: 105; cf. Job 2006: 166.

text's theological claims are deemed ideology, and power struggles and ulterior motives are assumed to lie behind the production of most of the biblical literature. For Sharp, the prose of Jeremiah bears the marks of a long struggle between two groups of traditionists, representing the respective interests of the Judeans and the Babylonian exiles, to shape the message of the book. Attempts at a more harmonious reading are 'wholly inadequate to the task of accounting for significant literary and theopolitical tensions in the prose material'.[19] One of the goals of the present chapter is to begin to show that the very real theological tensions present in Jeremiah's material on prophecy can be accommodated within a single theological framework.

This is not to deny that Jeremiah is openly polemical, and though I do not believe this polemic is theologically awry, it nevertheless makes recovery of the underlying historical particulars more contentious. For this reason it is worth establishing the intrinsic likelihood of the extremely negative portrait we find in Jeremiah by reference to the chapters that describe Josiah's reform (2 Kgs 22 – 23). These chapters set out in gruesome detail the deeply ingrained idolatry, syncretism, cult prostitution, illegal sanctuaries, child sacrifice and occultism that pervaded every level of society, all manned and run by priests appointed by the crown specifically to conduct idolatrous worship (2 Kgs 23:5), together no doubt with the attendant prophets, diviners, soothsayers and visionaries that such pagan cults routinely employed (2 Kgs 23:24; Jer. 27:9). Such levels of paganism are entirely credible, and the narrative concludes with the information that, in spite of Josiah's (short-lived) reforms, 'the LORD did not turn away from the heat of his fierce anger, which burned against Judah because of all that Manasseh had done to arouse his anger' (2 Kgs 23:26). We may conclude from this that much of the priestly establishment created to serve the royal cult, including the prophets, remained as a thorn in the nation's side.[20]

Certainly, Jeremiah paints a vivid picture of national institutions shot through with idolatry (Jer. 2:26–28; 7:9–10). To this he adds social injustice and abuses (Jer. 6:13; 7:6, 9), and last but not least a false estimation of what lay in the future (Jer. 5:12; 6:14;

---

[19] Ibid. 157.

[20] While many scholars consider the account of the finding of the law book in 2 Kgs 22 partisan and unreliable (Cogan and Tadmor 1988: 296), few doubt the intensity of the pagan worship Josiah sought to eradicate from the Jerusalem temple and beyond; cf. Japhet 1993: 1019–1020.

7:4, 10). The people as a whole were guilty of all these things, but their leaders, and especially the priests and prophets, were guilty of the added sin of leading the people in this direction (7:8), so that they were especially culpable for the nation's fate. To speak in the name of the LORD is no guarantee that the words spoken will not be an expression of debased Mosaic religion or even unvarnished paganism.

There is one sense in which Jeremiah does not consider his opponents 'false prophets' at all, namely, in what we might call a professional sense. A prophet is simply one who claims to speak in God's name. Whether the message he or she brings comes from a vision of the divine council, or from an oracle given by the LORD, or is fabricated, people are doing the job of a prophet when they preface a speech with, for example, 'Hear the word of the LORD.' 'Prophet' was a job title, and it is not until the Bible was translated into Greek and Aramaic at the end of the Old Testament period that the label 'false' was added to distinguish between those who really spoke for God and those who only claimed to do so.[21] Nevertheless, there are good grounds for adding the label 'false', as Jeremiah 23 reveals.

The verdict of Jeremiah 23: 'Falsehood'

Jeremiah 23:9–40 contains the longest treatment of prophecy in the Bible, and it falls within the section of Jeremiah that proclaims judgment upon the nation's leaders. First, the Davidic monarchy is systematically dismantled; then, in the first part of chapter 23 the image of shepherds is used to denote the kings, priests and prophets who have led the nation astray; by contrast, Jeremiah then announces God's future provision of shepherds and a king who will care for a restored Israel filled with righteousness.[22] In that context the prophets are identified as the single group whose failure is more responsible than any other for bringing about this situation. Five times in this unit Jeremiah tags these prophets with their most distinctive trait: 'falsehood' (šeqer).

Of particular significance as we come to chapter 23 is the oracle of 5:12–14. In it God announces that he is going to activate the prophets' words, with disastrous results:

---

[21] The term 'false prophet' (Gk. *pseudoprophētēs*) is a coinage of the Septuagint, found only in Jer. 6:13; Jer. 26 – 29 (eight times); Zech. 13:2.

[22] Jeremiah's reflective appropriation of Isaiah's royal hope is strategically placed in 23:1–8 (Sweeney 2007).

They have lied about the LORD
and said, 'Not so!
It won't come upon us, disaster,
nor sword nor famine shall we see.'
The prophets will prove to be wind,
the word not in them;
this will in fact be done to them.
Therefore, thus says the LORD God Almighty,
because you [pl.] have spoken this word:
I am about to set my words
on fire in your [sg.] mouth;
these people are tinder,
and it will consume them.

(Jer. 5:12–14)

The sword and famine the prophets have named will be their nemesis and the people's downfall. Like matches in the hands of proverbial little boys, the prophets' words look to burn the whole country down. Ironically, the fire their dead words have ignited is the live words of God in Jeremiah's mouth (cf. 14:13–16).

Jeremiah 23 has a richness and complexity that repays close reading, but for our purposes a synthesis of the argument will suffice here; in due course we shall return to examine verse 22 in detail.

Jeremiah's attack on the 'falsehood' of the prophets is in the first instance a powerful piece of moral theology, as it traces the deep interconnections between beliefs, actions and the society they engender.[23] In Jeremiah's rhetoric the character of the prophets is visible in their false religion (vv. 9b–12), their moral depravity and their seduction of the people (vv. 13–15). These are not three distinct evils, but three dimensions that a person's character will inevitably possess who has turned from covenant faithfulness. Of these dimensions, it is unfaithfulness towards God that lies at the root of the others, and infects all of the person's speech and behaviour with a moral taint that is real and present even in the absence of outward immorality.[24] If such a person should begin to speak for God as a prophet, his or

---

[23] Those scholars who conclude that evaluating falsehood hinges on the contents of the message and not on the person of the prophet (e.g. von Rad 1933; Berridge 1970: 34, n. 52) fail to do justice to the moral dimension of false teaching in Jeremiah's thought.

[24] The prophets were ostensibly worshippers of the LORD, but their lives turned even their true words about him into lies (cf. Moberly 2006: 61, on Jer. 7:8–10).

her misrepresentation of God becomes a source of unfaithfulness in others, and so attracts a special opprobrium. This is the nadir of the prophets' depravity: they actively encourage the people in evil, and actively prevent them from turning back to God (v. 14b). Just as Jeremiah was a product of the divine words that filled him, so the prophets are products of the pollution that fills their minds and sets their whole lives on an evil course (v. 10).

With the shift in focus from the prophets' character (vv. 9–15) to their empty message and the listeners who lap it up (vv. 16–22), three significant issues surface. First, the strong predisposition of the hearers to accept the lies of the prophets, as if bewitched,[25] and to despise the word of God (v. 17), makes the contest between Jeremiah and the prophets an extremely uneven one. Secondly, the most basic criterion of genuineness is invisible. Only God and (presumably) the prophet know whether he has 'stood in the council of the LORD' (vv. 18, 22), or been 'sent' by God (v. 21). The result, in Jeremiah's case, is a vivid apprehension of the word of God (vv. 18–19).[26] This criterion is not beyond scrutiny, for it may be detected indirectly, according to whether the contents of a prophetic message lead the hearers to turn to God and away from evil (vv. 21–22).[27] However, discernible though the mendacity of the prophets may be, their hearers are deaf to the false notes the prophets sing. Thirdly, given the failure of Jeremiah's message to turn the hearers to God, a question must hang over his own prophetic ministry. Is truthfulness sufficient to mark words as prophetic, or must they be efficacious as well (v. 22)?

The remaining oracles (vv. 23–40) have no reply to give to this question other than a fresh proclamation of the superior power of the word of the LORD. That the people cannot discern the truth about their prophets is immaterial in the end, because the word of God will take care of itself, and them too. Powerful as the prophets' lying words are to seduce the willing nation (v. 27),[28] the word of God will sear and pulverize these prophets together with their words, as it threshes the stolen words of verse 30 out from among the truthful

---

[25] Following Fischer's apt translation of v. 16 (Fischer 2005: 1.684).

[26] On these verses see Holladay 1986; Moberly (2006: 74–75, 80–81).

[27] Against Berridge (1970: 35): 'For the people, however, no means lay at their disposal for distinguishing between the "true" and the "false" prophet.'

[28] They may be truly self-deceived, believing themselves sent from God (like the prophets of 1 Kgs 22 – cf. Williams 2002), but this is a deception for which they are entirely culpable. Cf. Osuji (2010: 385) on prophetic self-understanding.

word of verse 28.[29] God is hidden from them, but they are not hidden from him.[30] By chapter's end the prophets, priests and people form a single group whose rejection of Jeremiah's hard words is the very thing that will bring those words down on their heads. The reader comes to this chapter knowing with the gift of hindsight that Jeremiah proved to be right. However, for listeners – even an ideal listener inwardly disposed to accept Jeremiah's words – the ground for trusting Jeremiah grows more and more difficult to stand on the longer the words themselves are not fulfilled.[31] Who can be blamed for heeding the prophets of peace when the prophets of doom are ignored with impunity for decade after decade (25:3–7)? Robert Carroll's complaint about this chapter should not be brushed aside:

> I simply do not understand how readers can follow the arguments of Jer. 23.9–40 that 'the prophets of Jerusalem' are to blame for the destruction of the people and then when they arrive at Jer. 25.1–7 not *see* the blatant contradiction that is entailed in the claim that the people's destruction is due to their not listening to the prophets![32]

Jeremiah 23 provides strong reasons for not trusting the prophets, but, like Deuteronomy 18, it does not address itself directly to the problem of verifying when a prophet is genuine; it seems to assume that a simple reassertion of the message should suffice. The difficulties surrounding the task of telling true prophet from false are crystallized further in the narratives of Jeremiah 26 – 28, which we shall examine in some detail.

---

[29] In view of my earlier suggestions about the word of God versus the words of God, it is interesting to note that v. 28 provides a unique instance in Jeremiah of the *word* of God in the sense of the whole message being used with a verb of speech. At the risk of special pleading one might speculate as to whether the equally unique language of power applied by v. 29 to the word of God betrays an oracle in which the word of God is being envisioned exclusively in terms of its effects.

[30] Skinner 1922:198–199; Brueggemann 1988: 205; Fischer 2005: 1.698.

[31] Meier 2009 presents a number of indicators of prophetic reliability that are fairly constant across the OT. Of these, Jeremiah's objectionable message (193–200) and minority status (201–207) must outweigh the failure of his words to come true (207–218). McKane (1986: 361) puts an opposing case.

[32] Carroll 1999: 77, italics original. Carroll's argument supposes that Jeremiah's distinction between prophets whom God 'sent' (25:4) and the rest is ideological posturing; for the bulk of Jeremiah's hearers a supposition like this would have carried considerable weight.

The hearers' dilemma: Jeremiah or Hananiah?

Jeremiah 26 – 28 shows how Jeremiah's preaching looked to its hearers and describes their reactions, not in order to make us wonder whether Jeremiah is really a true prophet (we already know he is), but to show how the word of God does its job of tearing down and building up in the face of rejection by its hearers. Not before it has triumphed over its opponents and destroyed their false ideas of peace (chs. 26–29) will the word of the LORD be ready to proclaim God's true peace (chs. 30–31).

Jeremiah on trial (Jer. 26)

In Jeremiah 26 we find ourselves back in the temple listening to a sermon very similar to the one heard in chapter 7. It may even be the same sermon in brief, for it holds out the hope that God will repent of his plan to judge, though it is expressed negatively this time. The sermon resulted in Jeremiah's immediate arrest. Two groups moved against him (vv. 7–8), one identified as 'the priests and the prophets', and the other, 'all the people'. They wanted Jeremiah's death, not because he called for their repentance, but because he predicted that the temple and city would be destroyed, and he predicted it in the LORD's name, that is, he said it as a prophet.[33] It is unclear from their reaction in verse 9 which was the greater crime: speaking as a prophet, or speaking against the temple and city; however, it was the former – assuming it to be false prophecy – that attracted the death penalty according to Deuteronomy 18:20.[34]

Verse 10 introduces a new group, 'the officials of Judah', who come from the king's house to act as judges in the case (as indicated by their taking their seat in the entry of the gate). In the same way that Jeremiah typically pairs 'the priests and the prophets', 'the officials' are typically paired with 'the king(s)'. We soon discover that at least some of them were sympathetic to Jeremiah, for verse 24 reveals that the family of Shaphan the court secretary was protecting Jeremiah (cf. 39:14). Jeremiah 36:12 lists more officials who were sympathetic. In chapters 37–38 (a decade later) 'the officials' will be

[33] We should not make too much of the fact that the 'if' has disappeared from the charge sheet in vv. 9, 11: it is an entirely natural representation of Jeremiah's words by an angry audience. Jeremiah reminds them of it in his reply (v. 13).
[34] Twenty years later, when Babylon was at the city gates, the capital offence of sedition would also have been a plausible charge to lay at Jeremiah's feet for this speech.

portrayed as implacable enemies of Jeremiah. However, the narrator reveals nothing of this: all we know of the officials up to this point is that they stand under God's judgment together with the kings, priests and prophets (2:26; 4:9; 24:8).

Curiously, in verse 11 the group labelled 'all the people' seems to have changed sides and joined with the officials in their judgment seat, so it is these two groups to whom Jeremiah presents his defence in verse 12. As a result, 'all the people', having shouted in verse 8 for Jeremiah to die, end up telling the priests and prophets in verse 16 that he does not deserve to die. Jeremiah's defence (vv. 12–15) is no defence at all. It is framed by two references to God's having 'sent' him, which is language the book reserves for a true prophet, and the second of these is strengthened by an adverb: 'truly the LORD sent me to you' (v. 15). Yet Jeremiah does not bring any of the criteria from chapter 23 to bear on this claim, but simply proclaims his message once more, with the rider that if they kill him it will be one more nail in their coffin.

How, then, do we read the verdict of the officials that Jeremiah is not guilty 'because he has spoken to us in the name of the LORD' (v. 16)? First, it throws some light on the accusers' motives in verse 9, suggesting that it was Jeremiah's message they found objectionable rather than its claimed point of origin, which is only now being presented to them as a reason to spare him. Secondly, the officials seem to have accepted at face value Jeremiah's claim that 'the LORD sent me' (v. 12). It is unlikely that they believed every such claim uncritically; given that they were familiar with Deuteronomy 18:22 – and these officials would have known the newly discovered lawbook Shaphan had read to Josiah (2 Kgs 22:10) – they must have known that speaking in the name of the LORD does not guarantee the truth of a prophecy. Taking the text at face value, the simplest conclusion is that they already believed Jeremiah to be a prophet, and the last verse of the chapter adds further support to this. Despite this, a certain amount of ambiguity surrounds the response of this enigmatic group. That some of these officials were convinced by the contents of Jeremiah's prophecy we learn in chapter 36, but the author does not see fit to present us with any of this argument here. Instead, the narrative paints a picture of the word of God being its own defence, extracting belief from the group who held Jeremiah's life in their hands.

After the trial a new group steps on stage: 'some of the elders of the land'. As preservers of the communal memory they cite two cases that may be compared to Jeremiah's. The first (v. 18) is interesting not only for its citation of Micah,[35] but for the fact that the event prophesied did not in fact come about. There is no 'if' in Micah 3:12, but by its nature there was a contingency attached, and when the people changed their ways the contingency came into operation (we see this at work in Jonah as well). The case of Micah therefore supports Jeremiah's prophetic status in two ways: it shows that Jeremiah's message is consistent with previous prophecy, and it shows that a true prophecy can be accepted as such without historical verification.[36] The second case the elders cite is also of a prophet whose message tallies with Jeremiah's. No moral is drawn from it, but its function appears to be to explain why 'we are about to bring great disaster upon ourselves' (v. 20b). Yes, it was true that Micah's word of judgment had not eventuated, but it was the king's response that made all the difference on that occasion. Given Jehoiakim's response to Uriah, a rescinding of the divine word cannot be expected this time.[37] Two points of connection to Jeremiah are made: Uriah 'prophesied in the name of the LORD', and 'in words like those of Jeremiah' (v. 20). As with the officials in verse 16, none of this proves Jeremiah was sent from God – on the contrary, it carries conviction only if one already believes either that everyone who speaks in the name of the LORD is a true prophet, or that Jeremiah's message bears the stamp of truth. His judges do not attempt to establish the genuineness of his calling any more than Jeremiah himself does.

Three final observations are relevant to our enquiry. First, the one group who seems genuinely convinced of Jeremiah's status is not really a 'group': the elders are mentioned twice more in neutral contexts (19:1; 29:1), but do not feature as objects of judgment oracles. None of the other groups involved, even the officials, are shown to have taken Jeremiah's words to heart, and this vindication of the prophet serves to place every hearer we encounter from now on in the wrong.[38]

---

[35] It is the first occurrence in the Bible of written prophecy being cited: cf. Andersen and Freedman 2000: 111–116.

[36] It should be remembered that Deut. 18 seeks to expose false prophets, not identify genuine ones. For Carroll, however, Deut. 18:20 is 'effectively negated' by allowing repentance to exonerate a prophet (Carroll 1984: 390). Against Carroll see Clements (2007: 35, n. 3): when a prophecy is a divine warning, heeding it does not make for a failed prophecy.

[37] Cf. Clements 2007: 39–43.

[38] Keown et al. 1995: 33.

Secondly, in verse 24 'the people' seem to have changed sides yet again. The strange vacillations of the people in this chapter are no accident. They are a tragically wavering group throughout the book. From the people's point of view there seems to be what we might call a hermeneutic of trust at work when someone opens a speech with 'thus says the LORD'. Ironically, Jeremiah seems to be the only prophet who is not afforded this trust by the people. For those of suitably depraved character, the vocation of lying prophet must have been tempting indeed.

Finally, although the question of Jeremiah's authenticity as a prophet is central to the chapter, there is no discussion of how one might establish that a prophet is really speaking for the LORD. This is unexpected in view of the wealth of material in chapter 23. Jeremiah does not present his good character, or argue for the genuineness of his calling, or point to the Mosaic orthodoxy of his message. Even the argument of consistency with earlier prophecy is entered in after the verdict, like a group of 'talking heads' providing post-match analysis. If it is true to say that the aim of chapter 26 is not to make us wonder whether Jeremiah is a true prophet, but to show us how the word of God does its job in the face of rejection, then its message is that the word of God needs no defence, and will prevail of its own power in its own time. In the context of chapter 23 an additional implication of Jeremiah's failure to present either his person or his words as evidence for his legitimacy may well be that it would have been a futile exercise. The only parts of chapter 23 reflected here are its closing affirmations of the superior power of the word of the LORD.

Hananiah on trial (Jer. 27 – 28)

By the time of Jeremiah's public conflict with the prophet Hananiah (chs. 27–28) the first wave of exiles together with king Jeconiah (Jehoiachin) had already been deported to Babylon, along with treasures from the palace and temple. Just such a despoilment and partial exile had been prophesied by Isaiah (39:6–7), and it would have been natural to conclude that the Babylonian judgment prophesied by Isaiah had thereby been fulfilled, and that it was time for God to show mercy and restore the nation, as he always had before.

As chapter 27 opens, Jeremiah is given another symbolic action to perform. The audience is not Judah but the nations of the earth. Together with the symbolic action performed in Babylon at the end of chapter 51, this is the only time we are told that non-Israelites were one of the audiences of Jeremiah's prophecy, an apt reminder of his calling here at the start of the book's second movement. The LORD is God of all the nations of the earth, and the language he uses for Nebuchadnezzar in verse 6 – language of election, messianic language (cf. Isa. 45:1) – is ominously reminiscent of his warning in 18:7–10 that his people should not be complacent about their place in his plans. Jeremiah warns the nations not to heed the lies (*šeqer*) of their prophets, dreamers and sorcerers before he turns his attention to Zedekiah, so putting the king firmly in his place at the end of the international queue. Jeremiah's initial speech to the king (vv. 12–13) reinforces Judah's relegation to the level of the other nations ('as the LORD has spoken concerning any nation that will not submit'), and his subsequent command not to heed the prophets is delivered in words identical to verses 9b–10, except for two additions that strengthen his denunciation of the Judean prophets (see table 4.2 below).

Table 4.2 Parallel prophecies in Jeremiah 27

To the other nations' kings (Jer. 27:9–10)	To Judah's king (Jer. 27:14–15)
As for you, do not listen to your prophets [etc.] who are telling you, 'You will not serve the king of Babylon.' For it is a lie they are prophesying to you,	Do not listen to the words of the prophets who are telling you, 'You will not serve the king of Babylon.' For it is a lie they are prophesying to you.
	For I did not send them – oracle of the LORD – but they are prophesying in my name lies,
with the result that *you will be removed far from your land,*	with the result that
I will banish you and you will perish.	I will banish you and you will perish, *you and the prophets prophesying to you.*

The extra warning in verse 10 about removal from the land turns out to be preparing for a hopeful codicil in verse 11: that the nations may yet remain unexiled if they bow to the Babylonian yoke. There is no such hope for Judah, only an extra measure of blame for its prophets, against whom an entire oracle is then delivered (vv. 16–18). One cannot help but feel that it is their prophets who have cut off Judah's hope that exile might be averted. The words 'do not listen to them . . . it is a lie they prophesy' are repeated for a third time in verse 16, with a new false prophecy spotlighted: the speedy return of the looted temple vessels. It is transparently obvious that Jeremiah's challenge in verse 18, 'if they are prophets, and if the word of the LORD is with them, then let them intercede', does not reflect a shadow of doubt in his mind about their genuineness, for all that it appears (incidentally) to be a genuine test of the true prophet. This rhetorical flourish provides a valuable insight into Jeremiah's style of public debate.

The last four verses (vv. 19–22) give Jeremiah's counter-prophecy: God will not restore them before Babylon has returned and taken the rest of the treasures. But the great bulk of Jeremiah 27 has been concerned to show that Judah's prophets are the least effectual of all the prophets of the nations, and that Judah's uniquely bad prognosis can be put down to their behaviour. This double message – our prophets have only made things worse for us; do not listen to them! – becomes an important guide for reading the following chapter.[39]

Hananiah is introduced in 28:1 with the full narrative regalia a prophet deserves. His prophecy is couched in flawless language, and comes in the form of direct divine speech. It is every bit as authoritative as Jeremiah's prophecies, and is amenable to theological justification, though it is not supplied with one (vv. 1–4). It is even accompanied by a symbolic action, the breaking of Jeremiah's yoke, combined with an interpretative word straight from God (v. 10). Politically this is no mere shoring up of the status quo, for he prophesies the return of the previous king – which must have been awkward for Zedekiah! The one problem with Hananiah's speech is that it repeats the discredited prophecy of 27:16 almost verbatim.

Jeremiah's response in verses 5–9 appears to be his own personal reaction rather than a new word from God, and he is quick to point out to Hananiah that his (Jeremiah's) natural wish for a happy outcome is hardly likely to be fulfilled:[40]

> However – please listen to this word I now speak in your hearing and in the hearing of all the people: the prophets who came before you and me, from earliest times, prophesied to many lands and against great kingdoms war, famine and pestilence. And the prophet who prophesies peace? It is at the fulfilment of the prophet's word that the prophet whom the LORD has sent will be truly known. (Jer. 28:7–9)[41]

---

[39] The compiler of the M edition has worked to connect ch. 28 as closely as possible to ch. 27 by adding the words 'in that same year'; his hermeneutical intentions are quite clear.

[40] The term Jeremiah uses in v. 6 for the hoped-for 'establishing' of Hananiah's word is one associated with covenant faithfulness and God's resultant restoration of the people (*qwm*, 11:5; 23:4–5; 33:14; 34:18; 35:16).

[41] In my translation of Jer. 28:9 I have departed from conventional renderings,

Once again, none of the attributes of a true prophet as gleaned from chapter 23 is brought to bear to determine the origin of Hananiah's words. Hananiah's character is not attacked, nor his leading of the people astray (in contrast to the treatment of the prophets in 29:23). It is quite possible that Hananiah's life was outwardly unimpeachable. It is often supposed that Jeremiah, unable to demonstrate Hananiah's falsehood by any other means, is adapting the Deuteronomic 'wait and see' policy here.[42] So he gently tests Hananiah's claim while waiting for a new revelation to settle the matter (v. 12).[43] And yet the link to Deuteronomy 18:20 is tenuous. Is Jeremiah really turning a test for false prophecies of doom into a test for true prophecies of hope? The assumption that he is brings all sorts of interpretative difficulties in its wake, and there are clues in the text that point us in a different direction.

First, the link to chapter 27 – and especially the way 27:16 paints 28:3 as a lie – makes it unlikely that Jeremiah's eirenic tone and inclusive language ('you and me', v. 8) betray uncertainty as to Hananiah's genuineness.[44] In view of the setting and the hostile audience (v. 5) it is more likely that Jeremiah seeks to win a hearing, which is entirely in keeping with his character when not constrained to speak God's words (20:7-9). Not only this, but I shall argue that Jeremiah is not trying to convince the people at this point; he is testing them.

Secondly, as a piece of rhetoric the effect of 28:6-9 is virtually identical to the more concise 27:18. On each occasion Jeremiah expresses a wish he knows is vain, and throws down the gauntlet

which read the word 'truly' as qualifying the verb 'to send'. Unlike in 26:15 the term appears at the end of the sentence here, where it is more naturally read as qualifying the main clause verb 'be known'. The following interpretation of the verse is unaltered either way, though it is somewhat strengthened by this translation choice.

[42] Stulman considers this 'a long-standing prophetic tradition that holds that words of approbation are less likely to be true than words of woe' (Stulman 1998: 75), though just how vv. 8-9 demonstrate the existence of such a tradition he does not explain.

[43] In his helpful reading of this passage Childs (1985: 133-139) rebuts the traditional view (W. Zimmerli, G. von Rad, J. A. Sanders) that true prophecy is a matter of judging correctly how God's revealed will applies to the present moment (a view, by the way, Osuji [2010: 390] misattributes to Childs himself), so that Jeremiah cannot be certain about his old message until the new revelation of v. 12. However, Childs retains the idea of a test in v. 9, simply shifting it from a test of Jeremiah's self-understanding to a test of God's plan.

[44] Numerous prophetic counter-claims left no evidence of self-doubt in Jer. 23, and there is no reason to think from the narrative to this point that Hananiah should be an exception. Could the word inside him make Jeremiah constitutionally incapable of such uncertainty (against Brueggemann 2007: 70)?

to the prophets, full knowing they will not succeed in the test. Hananiah will no more bring peace by his prophecy than the prophets of chapter 27 will intercede successfully.

Thirdly, Jeremiah makes a counter-claim in verse 8. Standing before them all, his own conviction signalled by the yoke bars on his shoulders, he moves the conversation back onto the international stage, as if to remind Hananiah that the international impact of prophetic words of judgment has always been borne out by the turmoil of their wider world. There is surely an allusion here to Jeremiah's fighting words in chapter 27, with their strong international flavour. This amounts to a claim by Jeremiah to be a true judgment prophet, prophet to the nations, heir of the great prophets of the past. Hananiah picks up the gauntlet in verse 11 by extending his word of peace to the nations.

Fourthly, there are good grounds for seeing in verse 9 a second counter-claim by the prophet. The fact that verse 9 is framed positively, setting it apart from any of the Deuteronomic criteria, opens up the possibility that Jeremiah is not being entirely negative here. The use of the passive 'will be known' begs the question 'Known by whom?' It seems doubtful that it could be the people; they already believe Hananiah to be from God, and Jeremiah to be bogus, and one cannot imagine that an act of fulfilment will alter their opinion. By nature they have neither the ability nor the desire to know God or the truth. The vagueness of this word continues: Which prophet does Jeremiah mean? Hananiah? Any prophet? If we lay aside the idea that Jeremiah is constructing a (not very) Deuteronomic test, another possibility opens up, for the vocabulary of the LORD's 'sending' someone 'truly' occurs on just one other occasion, and that within the same unit of the book: 'for the LORD has truly sent me to speak all these words in your hearing' (26:15).[45] If we were to see in our verse a reference by Jeremiah to himself, then the fact that Jeremiah is about to make his own first šālôm prophecies (29:7, 11) ceases to be troublesome, as does the fact that he has already offered up words of hope by this time, such as the word to the good figs in chapter 24. More profoundly, this permits an answer to the question 'Known by whom?' For at the fulfilment of Jeremiah's hopeful word, and for the first time, God 'will give them a heart to know that I am the LORD' (Jer. 24:7).

---

[45] The only uses of the verb 'to know' in chs. 26–28 are also in these two verses, referring to knowledge of the truth about the prophet.

On this reading, just as Jeremiah claims to be the true prophet of judgment in verse 8, so in verse 9 he claims to be the true prophet of *šālôm*. Just as verse 8 began in tactful inclusiveness, so verse 9's initial vagueness allows any prophet who predicts *šālôm*, including Hananiah, to come into consideration; however, in Jeremiah's thought the qualifier 'at the fulfilment of the prophet's word' tacitly rules out all but himself, a fact the final phrase confirms more formally. In making this claim, Jeremiah implies that the deafness of the hearers to the word of God will be reversed when the *šālôm* he prophesies comes to pass, so that they will at last know which prophet was sent by God. Lastly, the emphatic final position of 'truly' suggests that at present Hananiah is falsely known by the people as a prophet sent by God.

Jeremiah once again makes no attempt to prove that Hananiah is wrong, or that he himself is right. He proposes a test of authenticity no more than he did in 27:18.[46] He simply, as he did in chapter 26, reasserts the word he has already been given, and adds nothing to it (29:11b) until God gives him a new word. This new word (vv. 13–14) makes Hananiah responsible by his rash words for increasing the suffering not only of Judah but of the other nations too. We readers hear this word at the stage of its committal; it is then telescoped together with a new word, heard at the stage of its delivery (vv. 16–17). In view of Jeremiah's diplomacy at their first meeting the final word from God in verse 16 is salutary, not simply because of the extreme penalty, but because of the use of the rare word 'rebellion' (*sārâ*). The word is a clear reference to Deuteronomy 13:5, where death is prescribed for the prophet who urges apostasy and backs it up with a sign or wonder. This is a word of judgment whose swift execution provides the first time in the book when we see a word of destruction actually destroy something. It is no accident that Jeremiah's message of peace begins in the very next chapter.[47]

---

[46] Moberly (2006: 105–109), whose 'rereading' of Jer. 28 has important similarities to my own – notably, in his conclusion that 28:9 does not function as a criterion of discernment – points out that Jeremiah's failure to refer to v. 9 in vv. 15–17 shows he was not thinking of it in terms of a test; and that the lack of a Messenger Formula before v. 15, together with its similarity to Jeremiah's words of 7:4, 8, shows that it is Jeremiah's own clear insight, requiring no revelation to establish it.

[47] The final chapter in the unit Jer. 26 – 29 proclaims Jeremiah's message of a peace (*šālôm*, v. 7) that is inextricably tied to the peace of Babylon, and warns in the strongest of language against the false prophets infecting the exilic community, with their message that Zedekiah's monarchy should be the focus of the exiles' hope. These prophets receive the full treatment of Jer. 23: diviners and dreamers (vv. 8–9), out of

Synthesis

How does such a reading fit the larger context of chapters 26–28? Jeremiah 26 painted a vivid portrait of 'the people' as a group who were swayed by the trappings of prophecy, so much so that they even swung over to Jeremiah's side as they remembered the way he had spoken 'in the name of the LORD our God'. And yet what they want to hear always wins out in the end, so that the scandal of Jeremiah's unpatriotic, anti-temple message evidently turned them back against him by the end of the chapter. In his defence Jeremiah had nothing to offer save the word he had spoken in the first place, and the two groups who spoke in Jeremiah's favour seemed to do so on the basis of no evidence, as if the word of God had compelled their support. In chapter 27 the king has changed but the other characters remain the same. Jeremiah's message of submission to Nebuchadnezzar functions here as the backdrop to a simple message about the prophets, repeated three times: 'Your prophets have only made things worse. Do not listen to them: they are prophesying lies.' Jeremiah has pressed the message upon three audiences in turn: the kings of the surrounding nations, then Zedekiah, then 'the priests and all the people'. This last group then forms the audience in chapter 28 for Hananiah and his thrice-condemned message, and the obvious question is whether they will listen to him, or whether they will recognize that he is prophesying lies. Jeremiah's reply in verse 8 adds nothing to what he has said, but simply points the listeners back to his words in chapter 27. He quietly presents himself as the true prophet, but provides no 'thus says the LORD' and no sign. Hananiah's response contains everything Jeremiah's did not, and at Jeremiah's departure a break is created in the narrative. So a test has been created 'for the priests and all the people'. Will they again be swayed by the trappings of prophecy, and be seduced by the message they want to hear, so that they reject Jeremiah's claim to be the true prophet, a claim supported (as ever) by no more and no less than the words of God themselves? This question the narrator does not answer directly. Instead, we are given a second encounter between the prophets, at which we are not told that anyone else was present. In it, the two

step with the prophets of old (v. 19), morally licentious (v. 23), working against God's true prophet (vv. 24–28) to build faith in a lie (v. 30). In the end, however, Shemaiah is depicted in identical terms to Hananiah: the word 'rebellion' (sārâ) closes out both their judgments (28:16; 29:32), on the same basis each time: 'he prophesied to you though I did not send him and so made you trust in a lie' (28:15; 29:31).

general messages of chapter 27 are made particular and applied to Hananiah: 'You have only made things worse for everyone, and now we shall have an iron yoke . . . you have made the nation believe a lie, and so you must die.' The fact that the people failed the test is therefore revealed in passing, as the reason why Hananiah's fate must be so harsh.

If the connection to Deuteronomy 18:20 is weaker than often believed, the connection to Deuteronomy 13:1–5 may be stronger. It is odd that Jeremiah 28:16 should find Hananiah guilty of a crime (*sārâ*, 'rebellion') that according to Deuteronomy 13:2 involves a sign that takes place (Hananiah's did not) and encouragement to worship other gods (which Hananiah apparently did not give). Presumably the author of Jeremiah 28 considered that persuading the nation 'to trust in lies' removed any distinction between the faith of Judah and the idolatrous faith of the other nations whose prophets preached the same message. The spiritual adultery of which the nation was accused under a Yahwistic king like Jehoiakim implies the same equation (25:5–7). Be that as it may, another point of connection lies to hand, namely, that when a prophet underscores his false message with a sign, 'the LORD your God is testing you to know whether you love the LORD your God with all your heart and with all your soul' (Deut. 13:3b). The hearers of Jeremiah's words failed that test, but the prophet whose lies brought them down proved no match for the word of God. These two chapters are dominated by the theme of the culpability of the prophets.

Four observations emerge from these chapters that are significant for our study. First, there is no false prophecy in the book of Jeremiah that is not demonstrably false to the prophet Jeremiah, even the theologically defensible words of the respectable prophet Hananiah – yet the same cannot be said of the people. They cannot truly know whom God has sent until God's word gives them that knowledge, without which they will be blind to the signs that mark a prophet as false.

Secondly, for those with eyes to see, the basic and invisible truth about false prophets – that the LORD has not sent them – may be discerned from the words they speak. In the first instance it will be evident when their words reflect a distortion of revealed Mosaic faith; beyond this are the evil consequences of such speech in the lives of prophet and hearers alike. Modern interpreters cast their nets too narrowly, and regard their catch too benignly, when they suggest that a false prophet 'invoked an otherwise decently good theology but at the wrong time, supporting leaders and people when they needed a challenge'.[48] For Jeremiah the prophets, like the people who listened to them, were 'stubborn of heart', disposed to turn away from covenant faithfulness and true knowledge of God, whence flowed their lies.

Thirdly, while every false prophecy in Jeremiah was demonstrably false even without a special word from God to establish its falsehood, there are hints that the corollary does not apply, that is, that some true prophecies may be fully recognized as the word of the LORD only after their fulfilment. Jeremiah's 'wait and see' criterion in 28:9, though not required for the exposure of false prophecy, may point to the need for patience in the matter of true prophecy.[49] This is borne out in 32:8, where Jeremiah's response to Hanamel's duly predicted speech is, 'Then I knew that it was the word of the LORD.' As a result of both this and the previous point, Jeremiah's only defensive strategy in all the encounters described here is simply to restate the true words of God over against the false. No other attack on false prophecy is ultimately necessary; no other defence of true prophecy is possible.

Does this mean that there is a middle category of prophecy that one might characterize as 'false but unrecognizably so', or 'provisionally true depending on the response it evokes', or 'true in general but not in this particular'? Logically there is a space for such a category between the demonstrably false and the as-yet-unconfirmed true, but not in the book of Jeremiah. Either prophets are sent from God or they are not, and whether or not this fact can be plainly demonstrated, the hearer is expected to be attuned to the truth as it is expressed in the prophet's words and actions.

From the viewpoint of the hearers we might say that when a false prophecy fails, those who believed it are not enlightened by its failure; and when a true prophecy is fulfilled, those who believed it, or who were touched by its fulfilment so that they came to believe it, are confirmed in their faith so that they can speak in a new way of coming to know that it was the word of the LORD.

---

[48] Sanders (1977: 31), in criticism of the consensus of his day; he goes on to argue for a 'monotheising' that marks true prophecy.

[49] It is possible to make generalizations from Scripture about features that tend to be associated with true and false prophecies (recently, Moberly 2006; Meier 2009: 180–218; Osuji 2010: 369–394); however, the asymmetry that exists between godly and ungodly hearers on the one hand, and true and false prophecies on the other, tends to make these exercises somewhat unsatisfactory.

This raises an acute tension. Hananiah's refusal to accept Jeremiah's prior prophecy was not tolerated, even though Jeremiah's words could not be verified humanly, any more than Hananiah's could. There is no test by which one can invariably and publically verify that what one hears are the words of God, yet one is held responsible for putting one's trust in them if they are, and rejecting them if they are not.

Finally, the word of God through Jeremiah has been powerful enough to take Hananiah's life, but seemingly not powerful enough to make him hear and obey the word of God.

For Jeremiah at this stage the score stands as thirty-five years of prophecy, one fulfilment. Yet, sobering to realize, those who will not give heed to his words stand condemned, and none more so than the nation's leaders, especially the prophets, who were trusted to communicate God's words to the nation. Jeremiah's message about the false prophets and their hearers is well expressed in the book of Lamentations:

> Observant prophets saw for you
> vain whitewash.
> They did not expose your iniquity so as
> to overturn your captivity;
> instead they visioned you oracles
> vain and obscure.
>
> (Lam. 2:14)

In due time the true word of God was shown to be true by its historical fulfilment, and the lies of the prophets were burned up like straw. But by then it was too late for the nation.

'The people' in Jeremiah's preaching

Our study of the prophets has already produced a good portrait of the group called 'the people' (or 'my people'). Their initial indictment for spiritual adultery has been compounded in Jeremiah 26 – 29 by vacillation, credulity and resistance to the word of God. They have turned their back on the God who called them into being, leaving them fools:

> For dense are my people;
> me they do not know.

173

> Foolish children are they,
>   devoid of sense they are.
> Wise are they at doing evil,
>   but at doing good they're clueless.
>
> (Jer. 4:22)

Jeremiah 5:21–31 is an important oracle that fleshes out this portrait. The people have eyes but do not see, and ears but do not hear (v. 21); they have no fear of God (v. 22); their heart is 'stubborn and rebellious' (v. 23); their sins have kept God's blessing at bay (v. 25) – and although the word of God is not mentioned in the list of blessings, we shall see that it belongs there. This has made them easy targets for their leaders (v. 26), who exploit them ruthlessly (vv. 27–28). Worst of all, their sense of the good has so atrophied that they love it when their leaders abuse their trust:

> A bleak horror
>   has appeared in the land:
> the prophets prophesy in falsehood,
>   the priests rule by their power,
>   and my people love it that way;
> but what will you do when it ends?
>
> (Jer. 5:30–31)

In the same way that the prophets deceived themselves with their visions in 23:26, the people are willing accomplices in their own undoing. 'They take hold of deceit; they refuse to return', says Jeremiah 8:5, using the same rare word 'deceit' that elsewhere describes the prophets' 'lying' visions. This does not mean, of course, that the people are unable to understand what Jeremiah tells them; Jeremiah 26:7–9 is a good example of their comprehension. But they do not like what they hear, and so reject it. To use the categories established in chapter 1 of this book, they hear and understand Jeremiah's words, but do not hear them as the word of the LORD.

They are therefore bemused to hear that God is going to judge them, and they cannot understand what they have done wrong: 'When you announce all these words to this people, they will say to you: "For what reason has the LORD spoken all this great disaster against us? What is our iniquity? What is our sin that we have committed against the LORD our God?"' (Jer. 16:10). It would be interesting to know what made them this way. Whether they sinned because they did not know God or whether they lost their knowledge of God because they sinned is a chicken-and-egg question; whatever the answer, the fact of the matter is that they are both sinful and ignorant, and this situation is self-reinforcing, as ignorance leads to more sin, and more sin deepens ignorance. Jeremiah 6:10 uses images of uncircumcision and repugnance to explain that rejecting God and his word is not a neutral act: it desensitizes one to God's voice so that one cannot easily return to a state of awareness (cf. 9:5–6, 25; 17:14–15):

> Look! uncircumcised is their ear
> and they cannot pay attention.
> Look! the word of the LORD is their reproach;
> they do not delight in it.
>
> (Jer. 6:10b)

Not only does disobedience desensitize, but we may also infer that obedience sensitizes a hearer. For to say the word of God is a *reproach* to someone means that it condemns them and they do not like it. This suggests (moving back through the verse) that *paying attention* means being careful to obey, and that a circumcised ear is one that is receptive to God's words and thus disposed to obey, leading to a situation where the word of the LORD brings commendation rather than curse. This amounts to symmetrical positive feedback, whereby an initial disposition is reinforced by the situation it creates. As Jesus put it, referring to the word of God, 'whoever has, more will be given to them, and they will have more than enough. But whoever does not have, even what they have will be taken away from them' (Matt. 13:12).

Jeremiah's failure as a prophet

It is ironic that falsehood, so empty of real value or power, exerts so much stronger a pull on the people than does truth. And not only is it ironic; it is troubling. How can we speak of the power of the word of God if it is so readily resisted by its hearers? Once a person steps onto the downward spiral of rebellion and consequent spiritual deafness, it seems that the words of Jeremiah are powerless to bring them back. And yet bringing them back was precisely what Jeremiah's words presumed to do, as we see in this programmatic declaration: 'Thus says the LORD: "I am about to shape disaster against you and devise a plan against you. Turn now, each from their evil way, and make good your ways and your deeds"' (Jer. 18:11). Jeremiah was not alone in this, for according to 25:3–7 no genuine prophet in Israel's history ever turned back the nation. Almost identical language is used to summarize the message that was prophesied throughout Israel's history, but never heard: 'The LORD sent you all his servants the prophets with great persistence – though you did not hear or make any attempt to hear – saying, "Turn now each from their evil way and from the evil of their deeds!"' (Jer. 25:4–5a). It is clear from the language of these verses that the intention of prophecy was not potential obedience but actual obedience; in Moberly's words, 'prophetic speech is response-seeking speech'.[50] There seems to be a fundamental gulf between what prophecy intended to do and what it actually did.

This failure is very deep, for it undermines the nature of prophecy itself. If prophecy were no more than 'speaking truth to power', we would not be troubled, but when a word that claims to be God's own word impotently urges the hearers to change, then its divine origin, or at least the interest of its divine speaker in seeing his will done (which amounts to much the same thing), is called into question.

The self-undermining nature of failed prophecy is brought out with particular sharpness in the controversial Jeremiah 23:22, which blames the prophets for the people's continued rebellion. The first difficulty is the little-discussed one of translation, because the initial 'if', taken as a condition, ought by normal usage to be describing a real condition:[51] 'if they stand in my council they will proclaim my words'.[52] However, unless one thinks the prophets got to choose whether they stood in the divine council, this is an unreal condition, and the 'if' should be read as a wish introducing a conditional sentence without apodosis: 'O that they had stood in my council!'[53] The next two verbs would then read naturally as purpose

---

[50] Moberly 2006: 52. Fischer (2005: 1.698) draws a helpful parallel to Deut. 4:10.

[51] '*Im* introduces real conditions elsewhere in the Bible (e.g. Jer. 14:18; 15:11; 37:10); DG §121b even includes the present verse in his list of examples. As indicated, the verb sequence (*qatal* – *yiqtol*) would convey a present and future setting.

[52] It is just possible that the 'wrong' conjunction has been used (cf. Ps. 73:15; DG §122 *Rem. 2*); however, it would be unusual for the protases in this case to have conjunctions in front of them. Nevertheless, the following is not impossible: 'But if they had stood in my council / they would be proclaiming my words to my people / and turning them from their evil way / and from the evil of their deeds' (cf. Deut. 32:41; Jer. 23:33 AV).

[53] DG §155a, *Rem. 1*. A less likely possibility is that the conditional 'if' conveys a

or result clauses.[54] In context the verse is not expressing a wish so much as an unfulfilled possibility, expressed as an incomplete sentence:

> If they had stood in my council
> that they might proclaim[55] my words to my people
> and might turn them from their evil way
> and from the evil of their deeds . . .

The context supplies the completion of this sentence: 'then things could have been very different'. Perhaps the people's decline would have been reversed before it became terminal. The point is moot, but the culpability of the prophets is not.

The second difficulty with this verse is widely recognized. If having stood in the divine council makes a prophet's message effective, the constantly ignored Jeremiah must surely be relegated to false prophet status.[56] Perhaps, in that case, the third line of verse 22 should be read as referring only to a desired or potential turning of the people.[57] So Moberly has correctly argued that the syntax of the verb allows the rendition 'they would have sought to turn them from their evil way'; my proposed translation leaves room for this,

---

question: 'Have they stood in my council?' (cf. Jer. 3:5; 5:22; but in these verses an interrogative heads the previous parallel line).

[54] Which such forms commonly are in non-indicative prose (Exod. 7:26) and poetry (Ps. 86:17).

[55] The word is *šmʿ*, 'to hear', in its causative (hiphil) stem, so that one might render 'caused my people to hear'; however, from the usage of hiphil forms in similar contexts it is clear that the focus is on proclamation, speech rather than hearing per se, albeit proclamation that is effective in the sense of being physically heard. An example is 5:20–21, where the same causative is used to make people hear a message they 'do not hear, though they have ears'.

[56] Carroll (1986: 463) argues that this verse is an ideological *tu quoque* (so are you) that delegitimizes any and every prophet against whom it is used. However, McKane rightly points out that this is not a 'test of success' for the prophets of peace (McKane 1986: 1.584; cf. also Fischer 2005: 698). For scholars of an earlier generation the point of the comparison between vv. 18, 22 was Jeremiah's consciousness of being in the presence of God, though – and Carroll misreads Skinner at this point – the incommunicableness of this experience meant that it could not be an objective test of the true prophet (Skinner 1922: 195–196).

[57] 'The argument of v. 22 is not: if they had stood in the council they would have been *successful* in turning people from their evil ways, as if Jeremiah's lack of success would be "evidence" that he was not privy to the words of the divine council. The focus is the nature of the words to be spoken. If they had heard the council deliberations, their words would have been of such a nature as to (potentially) turn the people from their evil ways' (Fretheim 2002: 337–338, italics original).

without actually implying it.[58] However, this line of argument ultimately fails to rescue the verse.

The reason for this is that grammatically the form of the second and third verbs is identical, so that if we read *turn them* as potential but not actual we ought logically to read *proclaim* in the same way. This could work if we had translated 'to proclaim' maximally as 'to make [someone] hear/obey'; but this is an overtranslation (see n. 55). The syntactic relationship of the third and fourth lines is inescapable: if the prophets had stood in God's council the result would have been God's true words ringing in the people's ears and turning them away from the evil (or disaster) that not only lay under their feet (v. 22) but hung over their heads in the form of God's coming wrath (vv. 19–20). This blaming of the prophets for the people's rebellion is fully in keeping with chapters 27–28.[59]

Setting aside wider issues for the moment, this provides a more balanced reading of the chapter. What the false prophets achieve in verse 14 (and using the language of our verse) is certainly actual: 'they strengthen the hands of evildoers, so that no one turns from his evil'. One would naturally expect the reverse in verse 22: if they had spoken to the opposite end, the opposite effect would have been produced. What of the fact that this has not happened in the case of Jeremiah? In the wider context, to grasp the nettle of verse 22 does no more than replicate the sting delivered elsewhere by the self-undermining failure of true prophecy.

For the ignored calls to repent in 18:11 and 25:5 represent not only a failure of intention, but what seems to be a flat contradiction with the book's claim that the word of God can uproot and plant nations and kingdoms at will (1:10), and that, when set over against the empty words of the prophets, the word of God is like a fire and a hammer (23:29). Verses like 23:29 have been hard for interpreters to accept unqualified, given the apparent powerlessness of Jeremiah's

---

[58] Moberly 2006: 86–88. As with the previous translation, however, the primary function of the verbal (*yiqtol*) form seems to be the expression of unreality, and if there is an added modal sense of intention or desire in the verbs of proclamation and turning it must be supplied by the reader.

[59] One might perhaps read v. 22 as envisaging that if all the prophets had spoken with a single voice the people would have repented. It would not then be making an absolute claim about the effects of true prophecy, but rather about the people's need for an unmixed signal. However, Jeremiah does not say, 'that *we* might turn them from their evil way'. Further, in view of what it finally took to turn stubborn-hearted listeners into hearers, this is theologically inadequate.

preaching to offset the effects of false words of prophecy.[60] Yet the mutually undermining nature of an irresistible word of God and an all-too-easily resisted prophetic proclamation should have begun troubling readers before ever they reached chapter 23. The value of Jeremiah 23:22 is that it brings these conflicted elements of Jeremiah's theology unashamedly into direct contact with one another. Significantly, the fact that the word has been overpowered by windy prophets and foolish people does not make the author embarrassed to claim both that the word has unlimited power to compel repentance, and that it always and inevitably brings it about. Various diachronic and sociopolitical reading methods can be brought to bear to dispel the tension we feel here, but our chosen reading method demands that we accept it, and live for the moment with the mystery of how such a powerful word can not only have so little effect on its audience, but remain free of self-doubt into the bargain.

> Declare this in the house of Jacob
> and announce it in Judah:
> 'Do hear this,
> foolish people and mindless!
> Eyes they have, but do not see,
> ears they have, but do not hear.'
>
> (Jer. 5:20–21)

Jeremiah's failure to defend himself

Jeremiah's rhetoric provides a tremendously rich field for study. His poetry is vivid with striking images, biting epigrams, impassioned appeals; his sermons are rich with tradition, argument and dire consequence. And yet Jeremiah put none of this rhetoric to work in his own defence, either when he was on trial or in his dispute with Hananiah. It would be an argument from silence to move from this point to deny the general value of apologetics and rational argument, but the particular conclusion holds, namely, that Jeremiah placed little confidence in reasoned argument as a way of convincing the hearers to accept his words. On the positive side, he clearly places every confidence in the power of the word of God to defend itself and commend itself. This may seem somewhat pigheaded in view of thirty-five years of scepticism from the people, but despite his bitter

[60] So e.g. Dubbink 2004: 31.

complaining and profound suffering, Jeremiah's confidence in the power of the word of God never seems to have wavered. Even at the very end, in Egypt, he was still aggressively asserting, 'then they will know whose word will stand: mine or theirs!' (Jer. 44:28). The more we search for a way out of our impasse, that the word of God does not seem to be penetrating its hearers, the more we are thrown back onto the word: it is that or nothing.

The partial successes of the word

In Jeremiah 26 – 28 the word of God succeeded in penetrating its hearers on two occasions. The officials were convinced to release Jeremiah, albeit for rather obscure reasons, and they do not seem to have been changed themselves by his message. Secondly, Hananiah duly died. We might say of these modest success stories that the word looked after itself in the first instance, and was fulfilled in the second. We do not know how many of Jeremiah's audience were convinced by this that he had been speaking from God; it is consistent with human nature that the number may have been few.

Over the next fifteen chapters of Jeremiah we see the word of God save a handful of people, including Jeremiah. However, the principal way in which the word came true was in the destruction of the nation – a mighty act of power. The partial nature of this success must not be avoided; from his call Jeremiah was appointed not only to tear down but to build up, and God's guarantee to watch over his word to perform it (1:12) seems hollow in view of the very lopsided nature of the results.

Concluding reflections

I began this chapter searching for a way to complete the journey the word of God must take if it is to succeed as a word, a communication, and not just break up into words; the journey from its divine origin through its human speaker and into a receptive listener. Despite some small successes, the result of this search must be declared a failure. The word of God, an irresistible force, has come up against incurably deaf listeners, an immovable object. Jeremiah's preaching, in fact all the preaching of all the prophets, has utterly failed to turn the nation back to God. Does this mean the word of God has failed?

The distinction between word and words may help to clarify this question. The word of God comes to the prophet, who speaks God's words. In combination with their prophetic speaker those words present God's person to the listeners under the form of speech, and if the listeners find those words sweet to their lips (to use the metaphor of Jer. 15:16) they will become hearers, not merely of the words of Jeremiah, but of the word of God, which will enter and transform them from within, as we see so vividly in the example of Jeremiah himself. If, however, those words are distasteful to the listeners (to use the metaphor of Jer. 6:10) they will reject the words, and in doing so desensitize themselves even further to the word's allure; the blandishments of the false prophets will be all they can stomach. In this case the word of God, refused by the listener as a word of transformation, of life, will become to that listener a word of destruction, of death. Yes, the word of God fails to penetrate, but the word of God does not fail. It does precisely what God told Jeremiah at his call it was going to do; it sounds over nations and kingdoms to uproot and to tear down.

And yet this explanation fails to disguise the critical dissonance between the power of the word to judge and the intention of the word to turn the nation back to God. Is it enough to suggest that the word failed to penetrate ultimately because God stepped in to prevent the people from hearing it? There is perhaps a hint of divine hardening in verses like Jeremiah 25:7, but it is far from conclusive.[61] Jeremiah does little to alleviate the tension between a word that calls its hearers to turn and be saved, but that becomes a word of destruction to them.

Our study of the middle chapters of Jeremiah has shown that the hearers of the word had two tasks to perform if they were to be transformed from within rather than destroyed from without: the task of recognition, and the task of reception.

In a world of competing prophetic voices they need first to recognize the words of God *as* the words of God. It would seem that nothing much can help them with this. Criteria do exist for exposing false prophets, and even without equivalent criteria for proving true prophecies there is a path to discernment that lies through being inwardly attuned to the truth.[62] However, while the criteria available

---

[61] For Calvin, 'it is He who deceives false prophets, that by them he may inflict just vengeance on the reprobate, who eagerly go in search of their destructive deceits' (Calvin 1950b: 1.446, commenting on Deut. 13:1 and, *inter alia*, Jer. 28:8–9).

[62] Moberly uses the word *integrity*: 'the recognition of Micaiah [in 1 Kgs 22] as speaking the truth also requires a certain kind of integrity (a degree of honesty, openness) on the part of those who need to do the recognizing' (Moberly 2006: 126).

to evaluate would-be prophets are of value to those who already
have the word within them, Jeremiah does not even try to convince
deaf hearers of the truth of his words; he simply repeats them and
leaves them to do their own work. Despite this, the hearers are held
fully accountable for their failure to recognize the words of God
for what they are. This situation of double-bind finds an analogy
in the relationship between the people and the prophets: while the
prophets shamelessly lead the people away from God, the people
shamelessly collude in being led. Both groups are held fully responsible for the ensuing disaster. If the people are to recognize the words
of God, it is not logical proofs that will convince them, but a basic
inclination towards the word, expressed in Jeremiah by a range of
metaphors of taste.

There is then no separation between recognition and reception,
or the will to obey. We can separate these two acts of the hearer in
theory, but in practice they go together. The fact that the Hebrew
word 'to hear' can also be used to mean 'to understand', 'to agree'
and 'to obey' may contribute to the lack of distinction between
these two tasks within the text, but Jeremiah is quite clear that the
very appetite for the word of God that leads to the recognition that
it is indeed the word of God is the same appetite that inclines the
hearer to obey it. The speaker can do little to make his words more
palatable; either the word of God will, in its own power, refresh the
appetites of a rebellious listener, or nothing will.[63]

Unfortunately, it seems nothing will. At least that is the experience of Jeremiah over thirty-five years of preaching. It is not that his
preaching has been deficient, or that the people need more convincing; the imagery of blindness and deafness is imagery of permanence. As Jeremiah 17:1 says, 'the sin of Judah is inscribed with an
iron stylus; with a diamond point it is engraved on the tablet of their
heart'. The words of Jeremiah were never going to do anything other
than accelerate the downward spiral of disobedience and deafness.
And yet if the word cannot bring about the repentance of its hearers,
it will be seen to be less than the word of God.

We can only conclude that if the hearers are utterly impermeable
to the word by nature, deaf to it beyond any cure or remediation,

---

[63] Earle Ellis extends this idea into the hiddenness of the word in Scripture: 'the
Word of God in Scripture is never truth available, to be picked up at one's own option
like pebbles on a beach. It is always either truth hidden or truth revealed' (Ellis 2000:
276).

then the word will not achieve its intention by more of the same. It will have to break into the hearer in a fundamentally new way, with a radical and new exercise of its power, quite different in nature from the blunt power that tears down the nations of the world. It is no accident that between his condemnation of false prophets in chapter 23 and his admission of failure in chapter 25, Jeremiah is given a word of hope:

> I will give them a heart to know me, that I am the LORD,
> and they will be my people, and I will be their God
> because they will return to me with all their heart.
>
> (Jer. 24:7)

Significantly, this word of hope is offered not to the people of Jerusalem, but to the defeated exiles. It is our task in the following chapter to investigate how the word of God exercises its power to transform the hearer.

Chapter Five

Word and power

We come to a new chapter having hit a snag in our exploration of Jeremiah's theology of the word of God. We have seen the word of God come to the prophet as a spoken message, the words of which are then spoken by the prophet in turn, emanating from him together with all the elements of his character and life as a communication of God's person under the form of speech. When these words are received, what the listeners hear is the word of God.

Disconcertingly, all this turns out to be insufficient to the task. The word of God, notwithstanding its power and truth, failed to penetrate the deaf ears of its listeners. Refused by the nation as a word of transformation, it became instead a word of destruction to them; a powerful word, indeed, but unfortunately not the right word. For God's word included a call for repentance, and a promise of planting, and as long as this word appears to fail in its stated intention, its power must be called into question.

We therefore come to this chapter with two questions in mind, both regarding the power of the word of God. First, can we accept Jeremiah's confidence in the power of the word of God in the face of the rejection it evokes? Secondly, there is the even more fundamental question, around which we have been skirting since the beginning, of just what we mean by attributing power to the divine word in the first place.

The power of the word of God to transform

That the word of God has real power to transform a hearer at all is established in the person of Jeremiah. His call and commissioning show Jeremiah to be a total product of the indwelling divine word, which word determines his thoughts (15:16), emotions (15:16; cf. 23:9), words (1:7–9) and actions (1:7; 2:1; etc.). The extent to which he is under the control of the divine word is revealed in Jeremiah's confessions, as we saw in chapter 3 of this book (esp. Jer. 20:7–9).

Having the word of God within him in this way makes Jeremiah a person of power. This is clear from the contrast between the false prophets on the one hand, described in 5:13 as 'wind' because the word was not in them, and Jeremiah on the other hand, described in the next verse as a person from whose mouth God's words would emerge as a fire to consume the people. The power is not Jeremiah's, but God's, and it is closely related to the truth of the words Jeremiah speaks. This is well illustrated by the theme of the effectiveness of the prophet's intercession. In 27:18 Jeremiah uses effectiveness of intercession as a proof that prophets truly have the word of the LORD within them: 'if they are indeed prophets and if the word of the LORD is with them, let them entreat the LORD of Hosts'. The implication is that their entreaties will be effective because the words they bring before God are his own. Previously in the book God had repeatedly told Jeremiah not to intercede, saying 'Do not offer up a cry or a prayer on their behalf, and do not entreat me, for I will not be listening to you' (7:16; cf. 11:14, 'I will not be listening to them'). Here the prophet is being told the will of God beforehand so that he will not intercede ineffectively, implying negatively this time that when a prophet intercedes, God acts. The power and truth possessed by prophetic words are no less than the power and truth of God himself.

This is expressed most succinctly in Jeremiah 1:12, where God tells Jeremiah, 'I am watching over my word to do it.' In general, the ability of God to do what he says is taken for granted, but his limitless power is argued for indirectly in the first half of the book by the weaving of creation language into the argument (4:23–26; 5:22–24; 10:12–16). The most explicit causal connection between God's power to create and his power to judge is made in 5:22:[1]

> It's me you do not fear? – oracle of the LORD –
> In my presence you don't writhe?
> I who set the sand as a boundary for the sea,
>   an ancient barrier it may not transgress;
> they toss themselves, but cannot prevail,
>   its waves roar, but do not transgress.
> This people has a heart rebelliously insurgent;
>   divergent, they have gone away.
>
> (Jer. 5:22–23)

---

[1] Creation language is also used to underwrite promises of future hope (31:35–37; 33:20–22).

In the second half of the book God's ability to do what he says is confirmed by historical events, and language of fulfilment is met with increasing regularity,[2] culminating in Jeremiah's final prophecy to the Egyptian refugees, that God's word will stand into the future (44:28-29).

In short, the reader is meant to see right from the initial account of Jeremiah's commissioning that God's word is easily powerful enough to overcome the defences of any human being. For a theological reading of the type proposed here, only one conclusion is possible: the successful resistance to the prophetic word displayed by the nation must be a sign not of the thwarting of the divine word, but of God's self-restraint. And it also follows that if God is indeed true to his word, then his word must not be fulfilled solely through the judgment of those who reject it, but also through turning its hearers back to God, as it was intended to do. Somehow judgment and mercy must find a way of being realized together.

Fugitive words of hope

Hope takes shape in Jeremiah's preaching slowly and mysteriously. After his commission to build and to plant (1:10) the first hints we have that God's word will not exert its power in unalloyed judgment come in the guise of small oracles of hope bobbing on the tide of destruction that sweeps through the first half of the book. In none of these oracles is there a hint that exile might be avoided, and always the words of promise are brief, uttered only to be swallowed up by the bitter realities of the present.[3] Almost imperceptibly these promises of future salvation grow more frequent, more unconditional and more comprehensive, until three significant words of salvation are offered near the end of the book's first movement (23:1-4; 23:5-8; 24:4-7). Hope is then put on hold while Jeremiah does battle with the prophets, but once the false peace they offer has been dismantled, and the seventy-year exile is before them as

---

[2] In 29:10, 30:24 and 33:14 the verb 'confirm, fulfil' is used; in 39:16, 40:1, 3 and 44:28-29 we find the verb 'to bring about', a form used over thirty times in Jeremiah with God as subject, most commonly in the phrase 'I am going to bring evil upon'.

[3] Jer. 3:14-18; 12:14-17; 16:14-15; 22:4; 23:1-4; 23:5-8; 24:4-7; 29:10-14. Also note the refrain 'but I will not make a full end of you' in 4:27; 5:10, 18; 46:28. The immediate function of these hopeful words seems to be to remind the people that the God who is justly destroying them is still faithful to his promise to be their God, a faithfulness that serves to underline their faithlessness all the more strongly.

a living reality, God is finally ready to announce his true peace plan. Jeremiah 29 picks up the word 'peace' (*šālôm*) four times to announce that the exiles' peace is to be found in seeking the peace of Babylon (v. 7), and that God's plans for their peace involve a return to the land (vv. 10–11). The key phrase 'I will restore your fortunes' is introduced in verse 14, picking up the vocabulary of turning from chapter 3, where it was used to expose the incurable fickleness of the nation.

By the time we arrive at the Book of Consolation in Jeremiah 30 – 31 we already know that there will be no simple word of hope, no avoiding judgment, no peace without something radical being done about the people's faithlessness.[4]

Overcoming the failure of the word: Jeremiah 30 – 31

Jeremiah 30 – 31, traditionally known as the Book of Consolation, consists of a cycle of six poems, or songs, framed by an introduction and conclusion, and followed by four further oracles.[5] The unit takes as its starting point the seeming failure of the prophetic word: nothing God has done, no words of instruction, no acts of loving care, no deadly judgments, no offers of forgiveness, have had the least effect on these hardened sinners. More of the same would be futile. There are no simple solutions left.

The preamble announces the subject of the Book of Consolation: the restoring of fortunes (v. 3). The idea of reversal contained in this expression is conveyed in the way the poems are written. They are contrary, given to unexpected turns and surprise endings. Yet they are carefully constructed, as Barbara Bozak and others have shown.

---

[4] As Hetty Lalleman has shown, this development in Jeremiah's message – the loss of hope that the people might turn of their own accord and be saved – is best understood against the background of a prophetic tradition dating back to the eighth century, rather than as a later interpolation by exilic or postexilic deuteronomists (Lalleman-de Winkel 2000: 148–163).

[5] Mostly following the careful exegetical work of Bozak 1991. Her structure is not without its problems, especially in the section 31:23–40, and Bob Becking in particular has put forward a strong case for adding 31:23–25 as a seventh 'Thus says the Lord' unit, and dividing the remaining verses into three prophecies headed by 'Behold, days are coming' (Becking 2004a: 52–72). My preference is to distinguish the seventh unit from the preceding song cycle, and to give more independence to the oracle of 31:35–37, as elaborated below.

Table 5.1 The structure of Jeremiah 30 – 31: the song cycle – 'a new thing'

	Stanza	Audience	Theme
Preamble	30:1–4		The hope of restored fortunes
Song 1	30:5–7	male	Forgiveness is not enough
	30:8–11		
Song 2	30:12–15	female	Justice is not enough
	30:16–17		
Song 3	30:18–22	male	Mediation is not enough
	30:23 – 31:1		
Song 4	31:2–3	female	God's unquenchable love . . .
	31:4–6		
Song 5	31:7–9	male	. . . is shown to the judged
	31:10–14		
Song 6	31:15–17	female	and mourning turns to joy
	31:18–20	male	
	31:21–22	female	
Epilogue	31:23–26	the land	Fortunes restored

Table 5.2 The structure of Jeremiah 30 – 31: gazing into the future – 'a new covenant'

	Unit	Opening[6]	Theme
Promise 1	31:27–30	BDC	A new Israel
Promise 2	31:31–34	BDC	A new forgiveness
Guarantee	31:35–37	TSL	A hope as solid as the earth
Promise 3	31:38–40	BDC	A new life with God

The song cycle

The first song begins with a verse spoken by the people. In direct contrast with the hope sounded in verse 3, these people are in dire straits (v. 5). Whose voice terrified them? Was it God's voice, in judgment? Babylon's voice, in victory? It does not say. The rest of the song is spoken by the LORD, but he keeps switching between talking to Jeremiah, or talking to himself, and talking to Jacob, though most English versions have smoothed this out.[7] This is a very elusive

---

[6] BDC = 'Behold, days are coming'; TSL = 'Thus says the LORD'.

[7] Much literary criticism of Jer. 30 – 31 is governed by judgments about the text's coherence or lack thereof, with shifts in speaker, characterization, theology, etc. being taken as indications that small independent oracles were assembled into a loosely organized patchwork. To the extent that synchronic reading succeeds in finding coherence between these units the argument for their original independence is weakened (cf. Becking 2004b). The type of theological reading I undertake here therefore has implications for more traditional literary criticism.

poem. In verse 6, for example, the seemingly obvious question about whether a man can give birth is unsettled by the lines that follow: 'Why have I seen every man with his hands on his stomach like a woman in labour?' Is it simply an image of military defeat as it was in 4:31, or could there actually be some sort of impossible life emerging? In verse 7 it becomes clear that what is on view is the great coming day. It is a dark day, but as through a rift in the clouds a shaft of light enters. Against all the odds, with as much likelihood as a man falling pregnant, hope will emerge from despair.

The second half of the song pictures this hope (vv. 8–10). It is the sort of national life Jacob ought to have enjoyed in the past, and the reversal involved is suggested by picking up the terms 'terror' and 'no peace' from verse 5 and reversing them at the end of verse 10. The poem has come to a natural end, except that it does not stop there. The last word is not 'peace', but vigorous punishment. When? Will God punish now? After the return from exile? Is this a second exile? It does not say. There are no simple solutions left. Yes, God could forgive. He could save and restore. But what then? What will he do when they cuckold him again? Forgive once more and repeat the cycle?

The second song is addressed to the female Zion. Its first half describes her incurable injury, picking up images from earlier in the book (e.g. 6:7; 14:17; 15:18), and its climax at the end of verse 14 is uniquely harsh. No longer is it enemies sent by God who are responsible for her terrible injuries (cf. 6:23); here God describes himself as the enemy, to the point of attributing their cruelty to himself. Even making allowance for poetic hyperbole it seems that in view of a people whose 'iniquity is great, and sins numerous' there is simply no room for mercy any more. Verse 15 concludes with an emphatic single line: 'I have done these things to you'.[8] The destruction wreaked by the word of God upon its deaf hearers was always part of God's good plan.

What has happened to the glorious salvation of the first song? We have been told in no uncertain terms that incurable means incurable, and there is no room for hope. And yet, verse 16 starts so paradoxically that many translations omit the first word. '*Therefore* all who devour you shall be devoured.' The word 'therefore' (*lākēn*) usually

---

[8] All the force of ch. 25 is reflected here, with its demonstration of the inevitability of judgment. Some have read this oracle as God's assertion that he will give the comfort to Israel that others did not, but the incurableness of her wounds and their God-inflicted nature make this improbable. Cf. Brueggemann 1985.

heads the announcement of judgment following an indictment, but although nothing about Judah has changed, God is now suddenly a saviour, for no good reason. And by using what amounts to a non sequitur (cf. 16:14; 32:36), the illogicality of God's plan of salvation is underlined: the unreasonableness of his mercy.[9] In verse 17 a reason is supplied, but it does no more than state the problem in even stronger terms: first, God will cure the wounds he has just told them were incurable; secondly, the wording of verse 17b – 'For they call you Banished one; / "Zion? No one looks out for her!"' – suggests that the mockery of Zion's enemies has aroused God's love.[10] The LORD has determined to act in complete and inscrutable freedom, because he loves his people in defiance of all that is just and reasonable.

In effect, this song declares that justice is not enough. The LORD ought to cast his people off. But in the face of all that seems reasonable he decides to restore his abandoned Zion. And in order to do this he will cure the incurable.

The third song finally introduces the thematic phrase 'I will restore their fortunes'. The first half of the song (vv. 18–23) describes Jacob's future blessings, introducing a new element in verse 21. A prince will 'draw near' – a priestly activity – with a directness that would normally be impossible. And with the mediation of this royal, priestly figure, a covenant relationship will be sustained (v. 22).

Despite this hint of a mediator the poem cannot rest, and God's wrath resurfaces in verses 23–24:

> The burning wrath of the LORD will not turn back
> until he [or it] has accomplished and fulfilled the intentions
> of his heart.
> In days to come you will comprehend this.
>
> (Jer. 30:24 = 23:20)

---

[9] McConville 1993b: 94–95. The translation value of *lākēn* here is not perfectly clear, but even if it were rendered 'indeed' or 'however' (Becking 2004a: 182–183), the sense being conveyed would be one of paradoxical unexpectedness (Brueggemann 1985: 422; Fischer 2005: 2.132). Eugene March's definition of *lākēn* remains sound: an emphatic term signalling that 'the preceding words make what follows necessary or understandable' (March 1974: 284).

[10] The contents of the enemy's speech also suggests that God's honour is being called into question, and if this were Ezekiel we would expect God to declare his salvation was for his name's sake. However, the focus of v. 17b is on Zion the humiliated one, not God the slighted one. '[W]hat Yahweh himself will say in v. 14 about Israel, the covenant partner, Yahweh finds intolerable on the lips of anybody else' (Brueggemann 1985: 426).

This is the same word that Jeremiah saw from the vantage point of the divine council (23:18–20), and in that context it referred to the disaster of exile, which would result in the people finally understanding what God's will for them had been. In its present context it carries a new layer of meaning.[11] For although judgment is certainly God's intent, his deepest intent according to these poems is the restoring of fortunes (vv. 3, 18) and the establishment of a covenant relationship. The bracketing of this recycled vision by covenant formulas in 30:22 and 31:1 is particularly suggestive. Somehow, God's wrath will accomplish the restoration of a relationship with his covenant people. How will this happen? It does not say. Yet it is the first hint that national death in Babylon is more than simply the consequence of apostasy, but also the means of renewal. The destruction of the unhearing nation by the word of God was not a misstep to be undone by God's new plan, but the means by which the ultimate intention of the word would be realized.

The message of this song is that while God will bless his restored people with the mediation of a priest-king, it will not be enough to create and sustain a covenant relationship. On the other hand, God's wrath might be.

The fourth song is short but crucial. Its first stanza remembers the exodus generation; its second stanza (31:4–6) applies the lesson learned to the exiles. In the book of Exodus Israel survived the sword on two occasions, beginning with their escape from Pharaoh's army (cf. Exod 5:21; 15:9; 18:4). The second time was after the apostasy of the golden calf when God appointed the Levites to kill their fellow Israelites (Exod. 32:27), but some, thanks to Moses' intercession, 'survived the sword'. Jeremiah's song questions the basis on which such undeserving people find favour and rest. Its answer is that God loved them (v. 3), which is the reason given in Deuteronomy for his choice of such an unimpressive people in the first place (Deut. 7:7–8). God's love is even more fundamental than his election. And the way this will work out is explored in a series of 'again' statements in verses 4–6, in which rich blessing is enjoyed by the undeserving, because of the profound mystery of a God who never stops loving. Did Israel deserve any of this? Of course not. For if there is to be any hope for the future, then the bottom line has to be God's freely given love.

---

[11] The reuse of 23:19–20 here should be seen as one more instance of the technique of reversal, a frequent device in this song cycle.

The fifth song paints a picture of the recipients of God's love. In its first stanza we hear the sound of Jacob returning from exile. The great salvation that God promises in answer to their prayer (v. 7) comes to a very unusual group. A normal 'assembly' (*qāhāl*, v. 8b) would consist of priests, leaders and warriors, but verse 8 presents a collection of males whose disabilities exclude them from public worship, who have the sign of death on their bodies, together with women who are at their most helpless, yet who bear the seeds of new life.[12] And these lowliest of condemned exiles return, in verse 9, with weeping. The nature of God's love is that he pours it out precisely on people such as these. It is to the condemned, the weak, the contrite that God gives his living water (v. 9); it is these he preserves from ever stumbling again, whom he adopts, nurtures and honours.

The second stanza explores the implications of the fact that it is the judged who receive life. Because they are judged, they experience life as ransomed people (v. 11). God rescues them at his own expense from slavery. He does not do it impersonally, but binds himself to them as a kinsman redeemer. And it is as a redeemed people that the remnant experiences joy and blessing in verses 12–14. The images here, of both Deuteronomic and Edenic blessing, are not allowed to obscure the fact that it is people who languished (v. 12b), who mourned and sorrowed (v. 13b), to whom these blessings come.

The central message of this song is that only the judged can know true joy. This is not the thoughtless triumphalism that marks false worship both then and now, but the inexpressible joy of the judged and weeping exile.

The sixth song is the climax of the cycle, as its three stanzas indicate.[13] Nowhere else in Scripture is God's compassion portrayed with deeper pathos. In two images we are shown the depth of the divine yearning to bring his children back. The first (v. 15) plunges us into an experience of inconsolable grief, creatively reworking the tradition of Rachel's dying sorrow (Gen. 35:16–20) into an image of a mother keening over her dead children. But God tells the mother of the dead nation to dry her eyes. Verse 15 concisely ends, 'There is not', to which God twice replies, 'There is' – 'there is a reward' (v. 16), 'there is hope' (v. 17). The second image is of

---

[12] Bozak 1991: 84–85.

[13] The second appearance of the formula 'Thus says the LORD' in v. 16 introduces God's reply to Rachel rather than a new song (Becking 2004a: 69–70).

Ephraim, rocking in grief (v. 18), overcome by shame.[14] Judged and convicted by his God, Ephraim, like the prodigal son in the parable, is deeply ashamed. But also like the prodigal son he is met in his shame by incomprehensible love. It is hard to overstate the intensity of the passion of verse 20, from its poignant opening question to the closing language of a visceral love so strong that it causes physical pain:[15]

> A son dear to me – is that Ephraim?
> A darling child?
> Indeed, whenever I have spoken against him,
> my thoughts would dwell on him still.
> And so I moan in my gut for him;
> I will have such compassion on him! says the LORD.
> > (Jer. 31:20)

The persona of Jeremiah is absent from these songs, but it is not needed here to depict the pain God suffers in his own person at the destruction of Ephraim by his word.

The final stanza (vv. 21–22) depicts a road back to God, a road that virgin Israel is being urged to walk down without turning aside. It makes its first point by a pun, using a rare word for 'guideposts' that is the same as the word in verse 15 translated 'bitter'. Rachel's bitter weeping is a guidepost, or sign, that they are on the right track. But there is a final, characteristic twist, as verse 22 raises the problem of faithlessness again, and provides a famously cryptic answer:[16]

> How long will you turn this way and that,
> O daughter of turning?
> For the LORD has created a new thing on the earth:
> a female will encompass a man.
> > (Jer. 31:22)

---

[14] Lundbom 2004a: 442–443. To slap the thigh was a way of expressing emotion which one cannot hold in, which demands some sort of physical outlet.

[15] The LXX translators were evidently troubled enough by the anthropomorphism that they removed it completely (Becking 1994: 163). On Jer. 31:20a, Lundbom (2004a: 446) draws an apt comparison with Saul's emotional questioning of David at Engeddi (1 Sam. 24:16).

[16] The language of turning in 31:21–22 is reminiscent of the calls for repentance in ch. 3, and yet in the context of the song cycle it is clear that any hope the people might turn of their own accord, so that judgment is averted, has disappeared.

What will prevent a people that has been brought back to life by God's undeserved love, even a grieving people, from rebelling again? From being exiled again? The reply contains no translation difficulties, but modern versions and commentaries have suggested dozens of alternatives. The sentiment may be a simple one such as 'virgin Israel will embrace her God', but this would be a very obscure way of putting it.[17] One cannot help but suspect that the couplet is being intentionally elusive, at least in part. Certainly, it is allusive, in three different ways. First, the verb *create* and the noun *female* hark back to Genesis 1:27, suggesting a new creation.[18] Secondly, the final line balances the opening gender reversal of 30:6, so that the song cycle is bracketed by two reversals of nature. Thirdly, whatever it means, this surprising couplet appears to be providing a surprising answer to the question 'How long will you waver?', namely, that she will not actually waver very long. Out of his passionate and paradoxical love for hardened sinners, by some tremendous but mysterious reversal of the natural order, God will solve the problem of human faithlessness. How? What will he do? The answer is as mysterious as the song cycle's ending.

This reversal does not mean that the word has failed up till now. The destruction of deaf hearers by the word was always part of God's plan; its result is tremendous pain both for the nation and for the God who loves them; but the broken people that emerge from this destruction to receive the blessings of the covenant are somehow alive to God and to joy in a way they have never been before. There is a deep mystery here, which we take with us into the prose conclusion of the Book of Consolation.

The epilogue. In the preamble God had promised to 'restore the fortunes of my people' and 'bring them back to the land that I gave to their fathers' (30:3). The song cycle then explored the difficulties of this and showed that 'a new thing' would be required. In the final stanza (31:21–22) virgin Israel began a return journey, and the epilogue now depicts her destination – indeed, the destination of the entire song

---

[17] Stulman (2005: 270) has argued for this view as convincingly as any, taking his cues from images of a dysfunctional family pervading this sixth song. For Bernhard Anderson the 'man' (a son) represents not God, but new life in the land of (Virgin) Israel, when a new age supersedes the old (Anderson 1978: 477; cf. Diamond 2003: 590). Patristic exegesis saw here a reference to the virgin Mary carrying the infant Christ in her womb (discussed and rejected by Calvin 1950a: 4.113–115).

[18] The word for *male* in v. 22 is not the word used in Gen. 1; it is a term for a strong man or warrior.

cycle – by picking up both the phrase 'restore the fortunes' and the focus on land with which chapter 30 began.[19] The images and language used ('once more', v. 23; cf. 31:4–5) express continuity with an imagined idyllic past. A place is set aside (v. 23) wherein a new life can be enjoyed by an entire people (v. 24), who seem to be none other than the weak and thirsty of the song cycle (v. 25).

Finally, Jeremiah wakes from the delightful vision by which God brought him the words referred to in 30:4. By this framing device the songs are further bound together, as words the prophet saw.

Gazing into the future

The Book of Consolation ends with a group of oracles introduced by the formula 'See, days are coming', borrowed from 30:3, where it signalled God's intention to restore his people's fortunes. Here at the end this formula introduces visions of a radically new future for the people of God. The sense of discontinuity with the present is strengthened by the phrase 'no longer', used in each oracle (vv. 29, 34, 40),[20] and the reference to 'the house of Israel and the house of Judah' (vv. 27, 31). From now on it is the ideal, universal people of God that is on view.

The first oracle (vv. 27–30) contains the book's greatest concentration of language from Jeremiah's commissioning (v. 28). All of Jeremiah 1:10 is included, but it is joined onto the language of watching from 1:12, language linked with Jeremiah's specific commission to Judah. This is a by now familiar identification of God's people as one of the nations Jeremiah was to tear down and build up, but here its significance is reversed. It is as one of the nations that Israel will now experience God's love. No more a narrowly ethnic Israel, God's future ideal people will be a remnant from every nation. Lastly, this new Israel is promised in verse 29 that they will no longer die for their parents' sins.[21]

---

[19] These verses are not part of the song cycle because (1) the inclusio of 30:5 and 31:22 excludes them; (2) they are more prosaic in style; (3) they address the land, not its human audience (the м edition has expanded the Messenger Formula, which also sets the verses apart somewhat). They are not part of what follows, however, because of their verbal links to 31:3, and the explanatory power of treating v. 26 as a closing word to match the opening of 30:4. For alternative possibilities see Becking (2004a: 71–72 and n. 50).

[20] See Becking 2004a: 235–237.

[21] We might see in the background here the judgment of 2 Kgs 23:26 that Manasseh's sin prevented Josiah's reforms from turning God's wrath away from Judah.

These two new departures amount to a radical reconfiguring of the covenant relationship. Previously, Israel were called out from among the nations and addressed en masse with promises and commands; their general rejection of these led to national disaster. It was not that no individual ever responded to God in obedience and faith; Jeremiah himself is a prime example of an individual inclined towards God. And yet it was never the godliness of the few but always the sinfulness of the many that determined the nation's future, her godly and ungodly together, as Jeremiah's own Egyptian destiny demonstrates. With this oracle, therefore, the covenant relationship is effectively put onto a new footing, so that henceforth a new Israel drawn from every nation will relate to their God on an individual basis, each member dying for his or her own sin.

The negative framing of this promise draws attention once more to the as yet unresolved problem of sin, whose potential to destabilize future arrangements has been a discordant theme throughout the song cycle. The climax of the cycle was its cryptic announcement that God was creating a new thing in the earth (v. 22). And the second appended oracle (vv. 31–34)[22] picks up the adjective *new* – its only other use in the book – as if to bring to its message all that those songs conveyed: something radically new, mysterious, transforming, overwhelmingly joyful, like a new creation.[23]

It opens with an extraordinary statement of discontinuity, which focuses not on Israel's sin but God's faithfulness. The force of verse 17 may be paraphrased as follows: 'Remember how I brought Israel to myself, with what depths of grace and compassion, of steadfastness that no infidelity of theirs could shake ... the new covenant

---

[22] For a fuller treatment see Shead 2000; Williamson (2007: 146–158). For the historical appropriateness of locating a word like this in the late pre-exilic period see Lalleman-de Winkel (2000: 166–208).

[23] Many interpreters, rightly concerned about past and present persecution of Jews in the name of Christ (Lohfink 1991), are quick to point out that *new* could mean *renewed*, that the details which follow are essentially Mosaic, and that the phrase 'not like the covenant I made with their fathers' is ironic (Holmgren 1999: 75–104). However, in its context it is hard to sustain such a reading of the term 'new' (Shead 2000: 41–42; cf. Dumbrell 1984: 175). That being said, the view that 'Jews belong to the old covenant now nullified and Christians are the sole heirs of the new covenant' is, as Brueggemann rightly argues, a complete misreading of a text that offers a new and discontinuous word to the very people who broke the old (Brueggemann 1991: 69–71). At the same time, Brueggemann's judgment that Heb. 9:15–22 and 10:16–17 misreads Jeremiah and so 'provides a basis for a Christian preemption of the promise' (73) does not take seriously enough the scale of the transformation anticipated by Jer. 31:33–34, which was not realized by the 'glad obedience' of the exilic community (70) – as both Malachi and John the Baptist were later to show.

will not be like that.' This startling discomparison is made intelligible by the song cycle, with its message that God's grace and mercy and justice of old are no longer adequate. To overcome the inbuilt faithlessness of the people the new covenant will have to far outstrip what has gone before in its manifestation of divine love and power.

What, then, will this new covenant look like? The syntax of verses 33–34 yields a series of three linked statements followed by a reason that qualifies all three as a whole:[24]

31–32	NOT like the old covenant?
33a	But THIS is the covenant:
33b–34a	1. Law on heart *followed by* relationship *followed by* universal knowledge,
34b	2. BECAUSE I will forgive.

While it was possible for individual Israelites to affirm that they had God's law on their heart (Pss 37:31; 40:81), Jeremiah makes it plain that the people as a whole were unalterably fixed against the law: 'sin is engraved on their heart with an iron stylus' (Jer. 17:1). In the new covenant God will overwrite an original sinful text with his own words, and he will write it on their 'heart', singular. That is, he will write it not only inwardly, but universally. Law on the heart will then enable a relationship. The formula 'I will be their God and they will be my people' reflects formal language of marriage and adoption.[25] Israel will become God's bride and remain faithful because his law will be written on her heart. The third clause moves in a new direction, bringing to the surface the note of universalism present in the singular 'heart' (and also in v. 28). Everyone will know God, not just an elite group.[26] Here at last is an arrangement by which each person will not die for his or her own sin, for all will live by their own

---

[24] As I have argued elsewhere (Shead 2000: 37–41). Fretheim (2002: 443), by contrast, takes the 'because' of v. 34b as qualifying only v. 34a.

[25] Sohn 1999.

[26] Somewhat surprisingly, this verse does not say 'no longer will teachers teach'. Not only do neighbours not usually teach, but what they do in Jeremiah has been entirely negative up to this point (against Becking 2004b: 173), turning 'no longer will they teach' into another ironic comparison whose purpose is to underscore the universality of this unmediated knowledge (Shead 2000: 39). This verse does not contradict the hope of Jer. 3:15 that shepherds will teach the people true knowledge in the latter days.

righteousness, placed within them according to the terms of the new covenant.

The hope of an inwardly transformed people has been expressed before (24:7), but not until now is the basis of this hope expressed. The climax of the oracle (31:34b) is introduced by the particle 'because' (*kî*), which qualifies all of the last two verses. Here is an entirely startling and novel claim: the inner transformation that no covenant promise, legal code, or prophetic preaching ever achieved will now be effected by divine forgiveness. God will not forgive them because they have become godly; they will be made godly by virtue of God's act of forgiveness.

This is a perplexing claim. In two distinct ways it runs counter to other Old Testament discourse about forgiveness. First, it is abnormal for forgiveness to precede the sinner's turning to God. The sacrificial system illustrates the normal way of mending breaches, in which a sin is followed by some form of repentance or restitution, whether inward or ceremonial, followed by atonement and forgiveness.[27] Even if we see these as unintentional sins committed by a person generally disposed to obey, a proper order of events remains. Jeremiah's only previous use of the word 'forgive' makes the point that the refusal of his hearers to turn back to God placed them beyond forgiveness:

> Roam through the streets of Jerusalem,
>   see and know!
> Search her squares to see
>   if you can find a man,
> if there is one who does justice,
>   who seeks faithfulness,
> that I may forgive [*slḥ*] her.
>   . . .
> They have made their faces harder than rock;
>   they have refused to turn.
>
> (Jer. 5:1, 3b; see also v. 7)

Secondly, and even more difficult, is the suggestion that forgiveness will transform the forgiven people into faithful covenant partners. Nowhere else do we find an expectation that forgiveness makes the forgiven person less inclined to reoffend; on the contrary,

---

[27] Cf. Lev. 4:20, 26, 31, 35, which use the same verb as Jer. 31:34, *slḥ*.

Israel's history suggests that forgiveness generates complacency.[28] In Jeremiah's words, 'the heart is crooked above all things; it is incurable – who can know it?' (Jer. 17:9).

One possible solution to these difficultes would be to give the conjunction *kî* (for) a different sense, such as 'indeed', but this is not the natural reading and only creates further problems.[29] Some take the conjunction in a weakened sense, seeing forgiveness as a 'sure sign' that the old situation of sin and judgment is past, and as the 'basic ground' of the entire new covenant promise.[30] Yet this still begs the question of what it looks like to make forgiveness the basis of the promise to transform them inwardly. Our starting point is that of William McKane, that *kî* is causal and that 'the logic of the connection is unclear'.[31]

To clarify this logic requires a closer examination of the verse in question: 'They shall all know me . . . for I will forgive their iniquity, and I will remember their sin no more' (Jer. 31:34). There is nothing normal about the forgiveness of 'iniquity'. The word describes evil behaviour whose guilt attaches to the perpetrators and brings about their destruction.[32] Regular sacrifice is required to cleanse the sanctuary and the priests of the guilt that attaches to them as a result of the people's iniquity (e.g. Num. 18:1), but there is no sacrifice to atone for the iniquity of wilful sin, for which the sinner must be 'cut off'.[33] Only the scapegoat on the Day of Atonement can carry away the collective iniquity of the people (Lev. 16:21–22). Nevertheless,

---

[28] E.g. Jer. 7:3–12. It may be true that forgiveness can at times work transformatively upon a forgiven person (Brueggemann 1991: 72, n. 53), but not in Israel's case, for the people are pathologically hardened against grace.

[29] *Kî* can sometimes have an asseverative force ('indeed'), and it is just possible that the verse may be paraphrased as follows: 'They will all know me – indeed, I will [be able to] forgive them now that they have a heart that turns back to me whenever they sin.' However, once God put his law on their heart the people would not need forgiveness, at least not the extraordinary sort that would merit the attention v. 34 gives it; the verse would have to be referring to the one-off forgiveness entailed in the return from exile, except that we would expect a different form of the verb in that case (*weqatal*, as in 32:37–41). That the argument of vv. 31–34 can be dismissed as ironic has been refuted by Fẹmi Adeyẹmi, though he too begs the question of what it means that forgiveness will 'cause the nation to have . . . an intimate relationship with Yahweh' (Adeyẹmi 2006: 58–59).

[30] Rudolph 1967: 202.

[31] McKane 1996: 822.

[32] Koch 1999; cf. Exod. 20:5.

[33] E.g. Lev. 19:8; 1 Sam. 3:13–14. That the occasions on which iniquity may be atoned for by sacrifice (Lev. 5:17; 22:15) are borderline cases of diminished responsibility confirms the general rule (Koch 1999: 559).

the LORD did at times extend an extraordinary forgiveness on appeal, a forgiveness apart from law, offered out of his divine goodness. The first time we see forgiveness of iniquity broached was after the golden calf incident. In his definitive self-revelation to Moses (Exod. 34:5–7) God identified himself as one who 'bears' iniquity,[34] which emboldened Moses to intercede for the people:[35] 'If now I have found favour in your sight, O LORD, may the LORD go with us. Though this is a stiff-necked people, forgive [*slḥ*] our iniquity and our sin, and make us your inheritance' (Exod. 34:9). Subsequent appeals to God to forgive iniquity are infrequent, and usually base themselves on God's self-revelation to Moses: for example, Numbers 14:19 appeals to his steadfast love, and Psalm 25:11 to his name.[36] However, while Jeremiah's preaching began with a call for the people to acknowledge their iniquity and throw themselves on the mercy of a merciful LORD (Jer. 3:12–13), the people's intransigence was such that God eventually forbade the prophet to make any appeal on their behalf:

> This is what the LORD says concerning this people:
>   They dearly love to wander;
>   their feet they don't restrain.
>   So the LORD does not accept them.
>   Now he will remember their iniquity
>   and punish their sins.
>   Then the LORD said to me,
>   'Do not pray for the welfare of this people.'
>
> (Jer. 14:10–11)

Even extraordinary forgiveness was denied them, for as the song cycle in chapter 30 makes quite clear, the long pattern of sin and

---

[34] The verb used indicates of a human that they will 'bear' the consequence of their iniquity; i.e. be punished (e.g. Exod. 28:43; Lev. 5:1; Num. 5:31). When used of God it suggests that he arrests sin's consequences (e.g. Mic. 7:18), but even as a synonym for forgiveness (Pss 32:5; 85:3) the sense is more of a decision not to punish than to grant a full pardon.

[35] Whether God's response to Moses in Exod. 34:10 is taken to be a new and unconditional covenant (Fretheim 1991: 305–310) or not (Williamson 2007: 108), neither it nor the unconditional patriarchal covenant to which Moses alludes both here and (more directly) in Exod. 32:13 contains guarantees of forgiveness. Although forgiveness is a corollary of God's unconditional promise, Jeremiah demonstrates the difficulties raised by offering it.

[36] See further Lev. 26:36–45; 2 Sam. 24:10; Pss 32; 51; 65:3; 78:32–39; 79:8–9; 85:1–2; 103:8–13; 130.

forgiveness could not continue. Forgiveness had done nothing to fix the problem of sin-inscribed hearts. It is all the more startling, then, that God promises his now-judged people he will 'remember their sin no more' – a direct reversal of Jeremiah 14:10, and an explicit allusion to Exodus 34.[37] Whatever is going on in the new covenant, it is inadequate to explain it simply in terms of a compassionate wiping out of past debt; there is nothing new about that, and when it has been done in the past it has solved nothing.

These theological and contextual considerations allow us to draw some positive conclusions about the nature of forgiveness under the new covenant. First of all, however extraordinary the forgiveness of iniquity may have been, God is now making it an ordinary and foundational provision of his new covenant. As opposed to previous covenants which specified that a breach would not be forgiven (e.g. Josh. 24:19–20), God has now stipulated that his divine identity as one who loves and forgives (Exod. 34:6–7) will be what determines the covenant relationship, not the people's tendency to reject that love. It is not adequate to say, as many commentators do, that this covenant-sanctioned forgiveness is an 'amnesty', or a 'fresh start', or a 'broken cycle that permits Israel to begin again', or even an act of divine grace in which threats of punishment are replaced by a promise to forgive.[38] There is a divine self-giving involved that goes far beyond this, and it is to the way God gives lovingly of himself that we must look as we consider the claim that forgiveness will now have power to transform the forgiven as it never has before.

Secondly, the context of chapters 30–33 makes it clear that just as the exile is God's great act of judgment, so the return from exile is the corresponding act of transforming forgiveness. The magnitude of exile (for Jeremiah's hearers it was to be permanent) is likewise matched by the magnitude of the ensuing forgiveness, which will permanently define the people. In Terence Fretheim's words, 'The return from exile is a newly *constitutive* event for the people of Israel and the new covenant is an accompaniment integral to that event.'[39]

---

[37] The collocation 'forgive + iniquity + sin' is found only in Exod. 34:9; Jer. 31:34; 36:3; 50:20 (Fischer 2005: 2.174).

[38] Allen 2008: 357; Keown et al. 1995: 135; Brueggemann 1991: 72; and Lundbom 2004a: 471 respectively. Naturally, these scholars have more to say than this; e.g. Keown et al. speak of hearts 'polished smooth by forgiveness' that 'cannot turn to sin again' (135). However, the nature of this forgiveness (as opposed to the forgiveness offered previously) tends to go unexamined.

[39] Fretheim 2002: 442, italics original. Cf. prophetic language of return as a second exodus.

Return from exile is thus placed at the logical starting point of the renewal process, which prevents the conclusion that experience of exile will of itself turn hearts permanently to God.[40] Of course they will be repentant in exile, as they always have been,[41] but by their return the people's responsiveness will be made permanent. That is to say, God's act of bringing his people out of their captivity will be instrumental for their inner renewal. This rather mysterious equation is left unexplored until the Babylon oracle of chapters 50–51, but already Jeremiah has been laying the groundwork for his readers to see that the exile he has in mind would not end with the edict of Cyrus in 539 BC, and that the inauguration of the new covenant lay beyond what we know of as the postexilic period.[42]

Thirdly, in contrast to the 'eternal covenant' passage of chapter 32, where return to the land is the initial act that is followed by inner renewal, return in 31:33–34 is the outward component of a single, complex act. Return signifies and effects the act of inner transformation. And because the true power of new covenant forgiveness is exerted inwardly, universally and individually, it is not exhausted by the initial act of bringing back a people. With the end of exile it is proper to speak of a new era beginning, the era of the new covenant, in which God's self-giving forgiveness continually recreates corrupt hearts, generation after generation. Return is finally a paradigm for the definitive reorientation of a sinner by the power of new covenant forgiveness. The passage does not say that the writing of *tôrâ* on the heart makes that person sinless;[43] what it does is keep them in permanent relationship with God.[44]

In the previous oracle (Jer. 31:29–30) God broke new ground by ending the arrangement under which the iniquity of rebellious parents blighted their offspring's lives (cf. Exod. 20:5). Now in this oracle his extraordinary propensity to bear a person's iniquity has deepened to the point where it has become a profound forgiveness of that person, a transaction that heals (to use the language of the song cycle) and purifies (as Jer. 33:8 will put it).[45] Between them, the

[40] The same logic is presented in a linear fashion in Jer. 32:37–41.

[41] E.g. 1 Kgs 8:33–34, 46–50, where forgiveness is also linked with restoration.

[42] Jer. 50 – 51 and the theme of the unended exile are discussed below.

[43] For a discussion of the relationship between this and the Mosaic *tôrâ* see Adeyẹmi (2006: 65–70).

[44] So Fretheim 2002: 450.

[45] It is the language of purification that the letter to the Hebrews picks up to draw its contrast between the covenant that purifies the flesh and the covenant that purifies the conscience (Heb. 9:13–15).

two oracles in Jeremiah 31:27–34 have taken up the foundational theological statement of Exod. 34:7 and shown how forgiveness under the new covenant is a new and powerful expression of God's character. From the depths of his being God speaks into the being of his sinful people, and by drawing them into his own life he remakes them.

The two oracles that conclude the chapter reinforce these conclusions. Against the possibility that any residual sinfulness in the people might lead to their undoing, God swears by the creation itself that Israel will never go into exile again – need never go into exile again (vv. 35–37).[46] Effectively, the problem of faithlessness will finally be resolved. Israel is referred to as a nation rather than a people (v. 36), another indication that Israel by now has come to stand for something more than a single ethnic group.[47] Finally, verses 38–40 offer a vision of the city, the central point of God's creation. The images in these verses are physical and geographical but, just as in verse 24, it is the people they aim to characterize. This city includes the most unclean of people and practices. The hill of Gareb has not been found by archaeologists,[48] but its name evokes uncleanness: 'the hill of festering rash'. Even the notorious valley of Hinnom, the valley of the dead and of child sacrifices, will be 'holy to the LORD, never to be uprooted'. This is the culmination of an ever-expanding hope. God will create a new universal people; he will create a new heart for them through a new forgiveness; he will embrace them to himself in all their filth, so cleansing them for ever. While sinlessness is not a feature of 31:31–34, such hints of a new creation as are present in verses 35–40 seem to envision a world that will ultimately be cleansed of all sin.

[46] The extra Messenger Formula in v. 37 is difficult. In the LXX v. 37 follows directly from v. 34, and functions as the conclusion of the unit 31:31–34; it lacks the Messenger Formula but contains the phrase 'declares the LORD' after its opening line. If the verse was moved to its current position to create the M edition, 'declares the LORD' may have been upgraded to a Messenger Formula to keep it distinct; it is just as possible, however, that LXXV contains the secondary revision, and the Messenger Formula was removed to bring the verse into a closer relationship with vv. 31–34. Whatever the explanation, vv. 35–37 are bound closely together by their subject matter.

[47] The term 'nation' in Jeremiah describes the nations in general, or one of them, such as Babylon, or Judah conceived of as one of these sinful nations (e.g. 5:9; 27:13; 31:7; 36:2). Almost never is it a neutral description of Judah (possibly 7:28; 33:24).

[48] King 1993: 69.

Summary

According to Jeremiah 30, forgiveness is not enough. But the new covenant would seem to be offering a new type of forgiveness, a forgiveness that does not simply declare the people right with God, but makes them right with God. This forgiveness inwardly recreates them so that their heart, the seat of their will, inclines by its new nature towards God and not away from him. Such a radical intervention creates a door to the word of God in the hearers through which the word enters to transform them rather than destroying them from without. As a regenerative word that breaks through where the prophetic word had always failed before, the new covenant is entirely new. The forgiveness it promises, as the song cycle revealed, will be the ultimate demonstration of God's love.

This new word does not involve the retraction of the old word, the word of judgment that destroyed rebellious hearers. On the contrary, there are hints in the Book of Consolation that these two words are in fact the same (30:24; 31:8, 15). God's new forgiveness transforms precisely because it is a new creation, a new life emerging from the death of the unresponsive nation. The power of this word of new creation cannot be contained by the old categories. The Israel this word creates will be one drawn from all nations, knowing God as individuals, and experiencing his love in a renewed creation. No word of forgiveness as traditionally conceived (Lev. 4:10; etc.) can achieve this. Only a word that suffers the tearing down of the object of its love in order to build it anew can work such a salvation.

Finally, it should be said that while the reading I have offered makes considerable theological mileage from what amounts to a number of hints and general indications within the text, its conclusions are borne out in the rest of the book of Jeremiah. Just as the theology of the person of Jeremiah was contained in germinal form in the opening chapter, only to sprout and grow in what followed, so the Book of Consolation initiates a new departure in the book's word theology, in which the power of the word to tear down and to build up becomes evident in new ways.[49]

---

[49] While the phrase 'new covenant' occurs in the OT only in Jer. 31, it is not the only passage that describes the new covenant. Other images and phrases are used elsewhere by Jeremiah and others to describe the same realities (cf. Lalleman-de Winkel 2000: 201–208). Some of those images stress continuity; some stress ethnic Israel. That is to say, radical discontinuity does describe the new covenant, but it is not the only thing that describes the new covenant. Making too much of the language used

The remainder of the section spanning chapters 30–34 provides further oracles of future hope for Judah, but sets them firmly within the historical context of a nation whose covenant-breaking heart (ch. 34) still needs to be broken open by exile. To complete our study of the power of the word to rebuild we must move to Jeremiah 50, but on the way there we shall pause briefly to see the destructive power of the word in action, in what I have called Jeremiah's 'third movement'.

Judgment realized, hope deferred: Jeremiah 35 – 44

The third movement opens with a memorable display of the shape of Judah's hope (ch. 35). For the first time obedient hearing is embodied in someone other than the prophet, but by their outsider status the Rechabites stand for a national hope that remains distant, and provides no escape from a national judgment that has been inevitable since Jehoiakim's day (cf. 25:3–5; 35:14–15). The following chapter opens with the only other use of the phrase 'to forgive iniquity and sin' outside Exodus 34:9 and Jeremiah 31:34, but here the impact is quite different: 'Perhaps the house of Judah will hear all the disaster I am planning to inflict upon them, so that each one of them will turn from his disastrous way. Then I would forgive their iniquity and sin' (Jer. 36:3). In ironic contrast to the new covenant promise the goal of this huge offer is entirely negative. It serves only to highlight how far beyond redemption the people have placed themselves.

From this point we see the battle of the second movement played out again, but with different combatants. In one corner stand not prophets but kings, and in the other, not Jeremiah but the word itself, written and spoken. Just as Jeremiah the prophet emerged from the conflict of chapters 26–28 to speak even more powerful words of judgment and hope (ch. 29), so the word of the LORD emerges from its battle with Jehoiakim (ch. 36) stronger than ever. This time the battle is played out to the bitter end. The message is not hope deferred but judgment realized, as the word fulfils its long-promised work of tearing down the nation. When it comes, the account of the fall of Jerusalem in 39:1–10 is remarkably matter of

in this passage can oversimplify the biblical message. Nevertheless, it is no accident that this language of discontinuity, this image, is the one taken up by Jesus at the Last Supper and then adopted by the writers of the *kainē diathēkē*, the New Testament.

fact.[50] The horrific events it relates are the more affecting for their detached tone, and the final picture of the poorest in the land taking over the property of the dead and exiled rich brings to mind the stark prediction of 6:12: 'their houses shall be turned over to others, fields and wives as well'.[51]

By the end of the movement the word of the LORD is both realized and unrealized. As a word of judgment it has been realized in devastating completeness, and yet the judged remnant in Judah are as closed to the word as ever. We knew by the end of the previous movement that the hope of chapters 30–31 was to be deferred to the other side of judgment, but here we are on the other side, and hope remains all but invisible. To see hope come alive again we must journey to Babylon with the exiles. For the readers of chapters 37–44, who stand where the prophet stood, Babylon remains a remote evil. Jeremiah and the Egyptian refugees are under judgment, in a salvation-historical cul-de-sac. And yet even in judgment the word does not dry up; the door remains open for God to turn the hearts even of these idolaters. The Egypt oracles in chapter 46 will strengthen that note of hope. Only in Judah itself is every note of hope extinguished, for the future now lies among the nations, and when it comes, the fall of Babylon will spell hope for people of every nation on earth.

New life out of death: Jeremiah 50 – 51

The last movement of the book is unique to the M edition of Jeremiah. Positioned as they are, the OAN (chs. 46–51) broaden the horizons of the work from the exiled remnant of Judah, whose dismal circumstances occupy the closing chapters of the LXXV, to the destruction of the nations by the word of the LORD, and the rebuilding of a people from among the nations by that same word. By his rearrangement of

---

[50] Stulman 2005: 319.

[51] So Weiser 1982: 348. The passage is repeated in fuller form in ch. 52, and it is clear that in neither case does the author seek to perpetuate a 'myth of the empty land' (Carroll 1992). The images of depopulation are intended to convey theological truths, and the text, read as a whole, clearly does not intend readers to imagine that nobody remained in Judah. On the other hand, the belief that life in Jerusalem soon returned to normal after 586 BC, and that those in villages at some distance from Jerusalem were 'probably completely unaffected' (Barstad 1996: 81) is highly unlikely in view of archaeological evidence that 'the impact of the Babylonian campaign on population density in Judah was indeed enormous' (Stipp 2010: 141). A theologically sensitive reading similarly excludes the possibility that Jer. 39 undermines confidence in Jeremiah's prophetic credentials by its dissonance with 38:2 and other verses (against Roncace 2005: 119–123).

the individual oracles the author has carved out a route for the word beginning in Egypt, where the narrative of chapter 44 left it. From there the word travels, bringing down proud nations and crushing them – as it did Judah – for their enmity towards the LORD, until finally it arrives at Babylon, erstwhile agent of the LORD's judgment and now universal enemy, whose fall brings the whole book to its narrative and theological climax.[52] The M edition strengthens this climax by adding words of restoration to several of the oracles,[53] thus strengthening the hope of life beyond judgment for the nations, presumably as part of the new Israel.

The Babylon oracle of chapters 50–51 has often struck scholars as inconsistent with the pro-Babylon stance of earlier material, especially chapters 27–29 and 39–40, so that many regard it as late and inauthentic.[54] David Reimer's solution is to recognize the theme of Babylon's punishment as authentically Jeremianic, but to take it as 'a secondary development' in Jeremiah's thought.[55] The unifying factor was Jeremiah's hope for a future life in the land, so that 'when Babylon threatened, the hope was best served by submission; with Babylon's fall, return to the land and the future it held was paramount' (267). This is an astute observation, but it is first of all a theological one, and need not reflect a lapse in time. Already in 25:12 the eventual demise of Babylon is flagged, and the shape of Jeremiah's theology has allowed for this from the beginning, as we have seen. In particular, the fact that God's plans to tear down his people were only a first step makes an ultimate reversal of Babylon's fortunes all but inevitable.[56]

[52] This progression echoes the list of nations who drink the cup of God's wrath in 25:17–26, a list to which the M edition has appended Babylon (25:26b). John Hill has suggested that this list also reflects the history of Israel, beginning in Egypt and ending in Babylon (Hill 1999: 195–196). For a more detailed demonstration of the way the M edition takes words spoken against Jerusalem and applies them climactically against Babylon, see Gosse 1986.

[53] Egypt, 46:26; Moab, 48:47; Ammon, 49:6; only the restoration of Elam, 49:39, was already present in the LXX.

[54] 'It is difficult to see how Jeremiah could have been advocating submission (27) and yet *at the same time* (cf. 51.59) have been proclaiming 51.1–14 or 51.25–40' (Carroll 1989: 816, italics original). Against the view that chs. 50–51 are a hodge-podge of tacked-on material, a case of quantity over quality (Duhm 1901: 360), Kessler 1999 has demonstrated their integral function in the book's structure; Holt 2003 has gone a step further, arguing that they form an inclusio with chs. 2–4. On the theological coherence of these chapters with the rest of the book see the insightful discussion in McConville (1993b: 138–142).

[55] Reimer 1993: 260.

[56] Besides which, Hill has demonstrated that Babylon is not portrayed in a com-

The opening verses of the oracle set it in precisely this theological context, first by naming the gods of Babylon (50:2) and bringing the spiritual dimension of her fall to prominence. The LORD may have used Babylon as a tool for judgment, but he alone remains king of kings. Secondly, language of reciprocity and reversal runs through the entire oracle, beginning with verse 3:

> For against her has arisen a nation from the North,
>   it will make her land a desolation.
> And there will be no inhabitant in her;
>   from man to beast they've fled; they've gone.
>
> (Jer. 50:3)

Hitherto, a nation from the north has been Judah's nemesis, and Judah has been the empty wasteland (e.g. 4:7; 25:9; 32:43; 44:22); but in a great reversal the destroyer is destroyed, laid waste with the very same desolation she[57] inflicted on God's people.

Similar reversals run through the next hundred verses. It is not my intention, however, to examine the entire oracle. The more restricted goal of the present chapter is to explore the power of the word, and specifically its power to create a new people of God. To this end our focus is on what John Hill calls the 'secondary theme' of the oracle, namely, the relationship between Babylon and Judah.[58]

Israel's new covenant life comes through Babylon's death (Jer. 50:4–20)

The structure of the Babylon oracle is a matter of scholarly disagreement,[59] but the interweaving of material concerning Babylon's judgment and material concerning the Judean exiles is not. The first two words concerning the exiles, 50:4–8 and 50:17–20, may be read as frames for the unit 50:4–20. The opening is strongly reminiscent of chapter 31:

---

pletely hostile way in chs. 50–51, but is in many ways likened to Judah: a 'more benign view undermines the perception of Babylon as an essentially alien figure opposed to both Yhwh and Judah' (Hill 1999: 160).

[57] Masculine images tend to be used of Babylon the aggressor, and feminine images of Babylon under judgment (Hill 1999: 167–168; cf. Reimer 1993: 203–208).

[58] Hill 1999: 172–180.

[59] Significant studies include those of Aitken 1984; Bellis 1995; Kessler 2003. There is a helpful survey and discussion in Keown et al. (1995: 357–364).

> In those days and at that time, declares the LORD,
> >the people of Israel shall come,
> they and the people of Judah together,
> >weeping as they go,
> >and the LORD their God they shall seek.
> Of Zion they shall enquire,
> >faces turned to this road.
> 'Come, let us bind ourselves to the LORD
> >in an eternal covenant that will never be forgotten.'
> >>(Jer. 50:4–5)

The naming of Israel alongside Judah points to the universal return from exile envisaged in Jeremiah 31:28; the weeping echoes the fifth song of consolation (31:9), and the enquiry after Zion and its road echoes the fourth and sixth (31:6, 21). With the destruction of the destroyer a renewed Israel enters the age of the new covenant.

The following verses (50:6–8) look further back, picking up an image from chapter 2:

> Israel was holy to the LORD,
> >the first of his harvest; all who ate of it became guilty;
> >evil came upon them.
> >>(Jer. 2:3)

When holy Israel profaned herself – in the original reversal that got everything started in the first place – she could be devoured with impunity, like a sheep by its predator, and in 50:7 her enemies present themselves as God's agents of righteous judgment.[60]

As the oracle turns to address Babylon's judgment it becomes clear that it has been prompted less by her attack on Judah than by the gleeful way she went about it, which was offensive to God (vv. 11–13). There are the beginnings of a mystery here. Somehow Babylon's judgment, which is only loosely connected to Israel, is the catalyst for Israel's salvation. And the second Israel stanza goes on to explore this connection more carefully, beginning in verse 17 where Israel the lost sheep has become Israel the devoured sheep, eaten by the lions of Assyria and Babylon.

The consequence of this ('therefore', v. 18) is that the predator

---

[60] This is a further indication of the thematic cohesiveness of chs. 27–29 and 50–51.

will be punished and the sheep drawn from its belly and returned, alive, to graze on the pastures of Carmel and Bashan, Ephraim and Gilead (v. 19). The climax, like verses 4–5, is strongly reminiscent of the Book of Consolation,[61] and like verse 4 it begins with an eschatological phrase and features a search. However, where the focus of the earlier stanza was Israel's repentance, God's forgiveness as the cause of that repentance is the focus here:

> In those days and in that time, declares the LORD,
> iniquity shall be sought in Israel,
>   but there will be none,
> and the sins of Judah,
>   but they will not be found,
>   for I will forgive the remnant I left.
> (Jer. 50:20; cf. 31:34b)

In a great reversal the profane sheep of verse 6 has ended up holy again, and somehow the death of Babylon has catalyzed it. On the historical level, it was the fall of Babylon that resulted in the exiles being able to return. At the level of imagery it is the death of the ravaging lion that allows the sheep to be drawn alive from its belly and returned to safe pasture. We are left with a strong feeling that, at the theological level also, the judgment of Babylon has some causal connection to the renewal of Israel, that out of Babylon's death comes Israel's life – a life, moreover, purified of iniquity and sins. As in chapter 31 this new life is the product of forgiveness; here we see that God's life-giving forgiveness comes through death. How does the death of Babylon result in the removal of Israel's iniquity? There is no reason it ought to, no reason the death of the beast must be followed by the sheep's extraction, dead or alive.

Already Babylon is beginning to emerge as a symbol of judgment, of death itself, and it may be, if we press a little harder, that when death is destroyed, the life that forgiveness forges is not like the previous one. As the apostle Paul would later say, 'sown in corruption, raised in incorruption; sown in dishonor, raised in glory; sown in weakness, raised in power' (1 Cor. 15:42–43). And here Jeremiah's call to be prophet to the nations comes into sharp focus. For Babylon was the scourge of all the nations, not just Israel, and her downfall can bring hope and life to the nations as well.

---

[61] See further McConville 1993b: 143–144.

211

Israel's new life brings life to the nations and death to Babylon (Jer. 50:21–46)

The remainder of chapter 50 can be divided into two blocks, verses 21–32, 33–46.[62] In the first of these the LORD conducts a cosmic battle against Babylon, who is now revealed as 'the hammer of all the earth' (v. 23), and 'the arrogant one' (vv. 29–32). Her total destruction is no more than her world-destroying and God-despising proclivities deserve. It is with the second block, however, that Israel's fortunes come into focus once more:

> Their redeemer is strong,
>> the LORD of hosts his name.
> He will vigorously pursue their case,
>> so that he may give rest to the earth,
>> and unrest to the inhabitants of Babylon.
>
> (Jer. 50:34)

The way in which Israel's redemption achieves rest for the earth and unrest for Babylon is spelled out in the rest of the poem, which reaches its climax in two altered quotations: verses 41–43 quote a passage from chapter 6 depicting the fall of Zion, but reapply it to Babylon. Israel's deadly judgment has now become Babylon's. The language of purpose in verse 34 indicates that Israel was redeemed precisely so that this could happen. And then verses 44–46 quote a passage from chapter 49 depicting the destruction of Edom, and apply that to Babylon as well.[63] Babylon's downfall means salvation for the nations, and again, according to verse 34, the root cause of this is God's redemption of Israel and Judah, his new covenant people.

There is no historical connection between Judah's return from exile and the emancipation of other subject nations; presumably, the point of this oracle is that Israel's rebirth spells life for the nations by virtue of their inclusion in this newly constituted people of God.

[62] Cf. Keown et al. 1995; Fischer 2005; Allen 2008.

[63] Van der Toorn (2007: 194) argues that the borrowing is in the other direction: 'almost every verse [of Jer. 49:7–22] has a correspondence, often literal, elsewhere in the prophets or in the Book of Jeremiah itself'. He concludes from this that the OAN are a scribal anthology created by *relecture* (the reuse of old prophecies) 'to make the prophet speak again, posthumously'. His broader argument does not lend itself to considering literary reasons for such *relecture*. Alice Ogden Bellis (1999: 192–199) offers a more considered examination of Jer. 50:39–46.

Babylon as a cosmic symbol (Jer. 51)

The transformation of Babylon into a cosmic symbol starts in Jeremiah 25, where she begins as a historical entity, but is then bracketed out of the list of nations assigned to drink the cup of God's wrath: 'I made all the nations drink . . . [Jerusalem, Egypt, Uz and nineteen others] . . . all the kingdoms of the world which are on the face of the earth. And the king of Sheshak will drink after them' (Jer. 25:17–26). Babylon is referred to in code,[64] stripped of her historical name and location and set apart from every other nation, 'unknown and timeless'.[65]

In Jeremiah 51:7 the cup of God's wrath returns, this time describing Babylon herself as the source of the nations' torment, until the moment God broke her. In verse 9 we are reminded of the exiles who were to seek the welfare of the city (29:7), as they recognize that Babylon's wound is now incurable and it is time to return home (cf. 29:7, 14). And so in a series of poems bracketed by 51:1–2, 33 the threshing of Babylon is depicted with vivid urgency. Her sudden and catastrophic destruction at the hand of the God of Israel, creator of all things (vv. 15–19), will be the occasion for the nations to leave her, 'each to his own country' (v. 9). And as Babylon's final judgment and fall is played out in the remainder of the chapter her transformation into a cosmic symbol becomes overt.

The image of a devoured Israel returns in verses 34–35, the predator this time being a primeval monster which is metamorphosed by God's vengeance into a slaughtered sheep (vv. 36–40), and out of whose maw Israel is then extracted (vv. 41–46). From here Babylon/ Sheshak grows into something truly cosmic, so that her emptied sea, her ruins, her inundation and desolate emptiness (vv. 36–43) add up to an apocalyptic uncreation for the society that dedicated itself to eliminating God's people, and her fall causes universal reverberations as 'the heavens and the earth and all that is in them' sing for joy (v. 48). Against this backdrop the striking words of verse 49 transcend the historical Babylon, who is now a universal enemy, a symbol for death itself and everything in creation that stands opposed to God.[66]

---

[64] Sheshak is 'Babylon' written in an A = Z letter substitution code called *atbash*; also in Jer. 51:41.

[65] Hill 1999: 196.

[66] This in spite of the relatively concrete, historical language of the oracle, as Thelle has shown (Thelle 2009: 216–217).

Babylon is to fall because of the slain of Israel
just as because of Babylon the slain of all the earth have
fallen.

(Jer. 51:49)[67]

The verse conveys a sense of balance: Babylon's crimes against Israel
will not go unpunished. The second line, however, gives the reader
pause. It was not any wrong done to Babylon that caused the death of
the nations; Babylon was simply the instrument of their fall. This may
suggest that Israel is being presented in the first line as the instrument
of Babylon's fall.[68] In context we remember the image of the beast
ripped open so that devoured Israel could emerge alive. This time,
however, because Babylon is pictured as the universal, cosmic enemy,
the embodiment of chaos and death, we read in this verse a tacit claim
that in restoring his people to a new covenant life in which iniquity
and sin are no more, God will destroy death itself. What is Israel's
role in this? Just as her destruction by the word of God was the price
she had to pay for her inquities and sins, so death was the eventual
price Babylon had to pay for her iniquitous destruction of Israel. In
symbolic terms, Israel's resurrection will be the death of Death.

The unended exile

Though this vision of Babylon's fall had a historical fulfilment in 486
BC, around fifty years after the edict of Cyrus and the return from
exile,[69] the overarching perspective of the finished book of Jeremiah
is that Babylon stands and the exile has not ended. Its final chapter
reinforces this by leaving the reader (as it were) numbered among the

---

[67] The verse is difficult (McKane 1996: 1339; Fischer 2005: 2.621); I have followed
most English versions in adding 'because of' (*l*) in the first line, speculating that hap-
lography has removed the preposition balancing that attached to 'Babylon' in the
next line. However, some recent commentators read without it: 'Babylon is to fall,
O slain of Israel, just as the slain of the whole earth fell before Babylon' (Holladay
1989: 400; Lundbom 2004b: 486–487). Even so, Lundbom argues that the verse
conveys a *lex talionis*: Israel should know that Babylon's fall is payment for what she
did to the other nations (esp. Israel). The further implication of Israel's involvement
in Babylon's fall is not clear on this reading, but is still implied by the context and
Israel's prominence in the first line.

[68] The comparison can be avoided by rendering the preposition differently each
time: Babylon will fall because of Israel's slain; the slain of the world fell at the hands
of Babylon (Kessler 2003: 135); but this is to ignore the careful balance of the two
lines (Lundbom 2004b: 483).

[69] When the Babylonian play for independence from Xerxes I (486–465) finally
resulted in the destruction of the sanctuary of Marduk and his statue (Kessler 2003:
195–198).

exiles (52:28–30), grasping at the straws of comfort afforded by the
benevolence of the king of kings to his favourite spaniel (52:31–34)
– Jehoiachin, his life lived out in a foreign land in fulfilment of
Jeremiah's malediction: 'Not one of his offspring will succeed in
sitting on David's throne, or ruling again in Judah' (22:30). This
sense of an unended exile, which can be traced through postexilic
writings and into the New Testament,[70] is palpable throughout the
book of Jeremiah. It is felt in the book's opening and closing verses,
in the relegation of God's people to the status of one of the nations,
in Jeremiah's de-emphasizing of national institutions, in the transforming of Babylon into an idealized, cosmic foe – a foe later readers
could identify with the foreign oppressors of their own time. 'To be
in Babylon is a phrase that describes the situation . . . of those who
live in unnamed lands as part of the diaspora. Babylon is a metaphor
and stands for the place from which all those banished from the land
will return.'[71]

While the return under Cyrus and the rebuilding of Jerusalem
and its temple provided a startling demonstration of the power of
God's word to remake Israel, just as Jeremiah's life demonstrated
the power of God's word to transform a person inwardly, these
demonstrations were no more than an earnest of things to come. A
Jew in the Persian province of Yehud could know the same inward
transformation that Jeremiah knew, and could point to his or
her rebuilt institutions as true fulfilments of God's promise made
through Jeremiah; yet it was to just such faithful believers that the
incompleteness of this fulfilment was plainest.[72]

Conclusion

A theological reading of Jeremiah recognizes that chapters 50–51
tell the same story as chapters 30–31, but from a universal, rather
than an Israelite, point of view. The effect is to illuminate elements
of the new covenant promise that were always present, but come into
sharper focus under a new light. Perhaps most important of these

[70] Wright 1992: 268–272; Hill 2004: 158–160.

[71] Hill 1999: 207; cf. Thelle 2009: 231–232. On the unended exile and the role of
Babylon see especially Hill (1999: 24–35, 117–124, 203–217), from whose excellent
treatment I would depart principally in holding that Jeremiah was the origin, not
simply a contributor (so Hill, 212) to the postexilic belief in an unended exile. To
my mind this does better justice to the entire sweep of Jeremiah's historical message,
especially his conviction that the loss of covenant and election privileges removed the
distinction between Judah and the nations.

[72] E.g. Ezra 3:12; cf. Lohfink 1991: 52–57.

are the cosmic implications of new covenant forgiveness, which are foreshadowed in 31:38–40 but gain fresh clarity when we see that the recreation of a universal Israel will bring about the uncreation of a cosmic Babylon (51:41–44).

According to Jeremiah 51:59–64 the oracle originated in the fourth year of Zedekiah, when its vision must have seemed like escapist fantasy. This date, attached to Babylon's death warrant, balances the date given at the beginning of the movement (46:1–2) to mark the empire's birth at Carchemish. Babylon hovers above all the oracles just as she hovers in and around the whole book. Ultimately, the Babylon oracle serves to give the book of Jeremiah to future generations as their own book of judgment and new life. The throwing of Jeremiah's words into the Euphrates fulfils the commission given him in chapter 1; by the end we have come to understand that the tearing down and building up are linked. There is no gospel without judgment, for only the judged can be saved. But the act of saving them changes the world.

How does the word of God exert its power?

No account of a theology of the word of God would be complete without reflecting on what it means to call the divine word powerful. By story's end many of God's words have been realized, and they act as guarantors for his as-yet-unrealized words of judgment and hope. And yet when it comes to their actual fulfilment, it appears God's word takes a step back and his mighty acts move in to bring about the events predicted by the word. When we speak of the power of God's word, do we simply mean it is true? Or is the word of God itself active in his deeds in some more direct fashion?

Going further, what part do the words of Jeremiah play in this? In what sense does the power of the word of God reside in the words of Jeremiah? Are the prophet's words themselves somehow powerful, or do they point to a power beyond words? When it comes to the exercise of material power in the physical universe, such as the overthrowing of nations, or even less tangible works such as the recreating of human hearts, do Jeremiah's words do anything more than serve notice of a divine plan of action to which human words have no substantial relationship?

The book of Jeremiah indulges in very little direct engagement with this question, so the rest of this chapter will consist of what might be called a 'second-order exercise', reflecting with the help of philosophers and theologians on the nature of the power that the book is so confident fills the words placed in Jeremiah's mouth.

The words of Jeremiah are not magical

Symbolic acts?

It used to be fashionable in the 1970s to infer, from the fact that the Hebrew word *dābār* can mean either 'word' or 'thing', that the Hebrews did not distinguish a word from that to which it refers; that 'to encounter the word was to encounter the reality designated by it'.[73] This led to a magical view of words as powerful in themselves, and scholars who credited the Hebrews with this belief made much of the so-called symbolic actions performed by the prophets. 'When Jeremiah puts a yoke on his neck,' they argued, 'he is letting the *thing* do the work of the *words*.' In fact scholars who proposed this idea often argued that the actions were even more efficacious than the words, and that such actions released 'an event in miniature', 'an inevitable circumstance which nothing can avert'.[74]

These views are now discredited. Just because *dābār* can mean 'word' or 'thing' it does not follow that it always means both, any more than the English word 'set' must always mean 'adjust' (as in 'set a clock') and 'describe' (as in 'set the scene'). Moreover, it is quite clear from the biblical text that neither prophet nor audience viewed the sign acts as inevitably bringing about the future they were depicting.[75]

What, then, is the meaning of Jeremiah's actions of spoiling linen underwear (ch. 13), staying single (ch. 16), breaking pots (ch. 19), burying title deeds (ch. 32), and so forth? Positively, they acted like sermon illustrations, but divinely authorized ones, and by their personal nature they served to draw the speaker further into the process, so that all three elements – words, speaker and hearers – were brought into closer connection. Writing of the loin-cloth episode, Heschel mentions not only a 'didactic' aspect of the symbolic action, but also a 'sympathetic' aspect: 'to let the prophet

---

[73] Isaac Rabinowitz 1972, cited in Friebel (1999: 44).

[74] Bowker 1964: 130.

[75] Friebel 1999: 45. For Hughes Old, Jeremiah's signs 'do more than simply illustrate the word; they confirm and seal the word' (Old 1998: 84), but he does not explain how this happens. Von Rad is surely right to see sign acts as both bound to and unfettered by the accompanying word: 'the prophetic symbolic act is simply an intensified form of prophetic speech. The only difference is that in the case of the sign, it was less important that its full implications should be understood by those who saw it performed. Do not symbolic actions sometimes seem to conceal more than they reveal?' (von Rad 1965: 96).

feel what the decision means to the life and pathos of God'.[76] In the end, the most significant and powerful of Jeremiah's sign acts was his own life. The main conclusion for the present discussion is, however, a negative one: the power of the word of God does not reside in the words as such.

Speech acts?

A more modern view of the power of words is speech-act theory, pioneered by J. L. Austin. It has been explored in a specifically theological context by Nicholas Wolterstorff, and applied to the book of Jeremiah by Gordon McConville.[77]

This theory has significant explanatory power when it comes to the way speech affects relationships between people – for example, the words 'I pronounce you guilty' or 'Yes, I will marry you' can have the power to make their addressee a completely different person. Such words may also trigger a chain of events that leads to a person's incarceration (in the first case) or wedding (in the second). In particular, speech-act theory helps to elucidate what happens when a person speaks. For Wolterstorff, speaking consists not simply in communicating or expressing knowledge but in taking up a certain sort of 'normative stance'. That is, if I tell you something, I have altered the moral relationship between us by obligating you to take me at my word that what I said was true. If you refuse to believe me, then my speech action is undercut. In both directions speech actions are no mere transfer of information; they pack a moral punch.[78]

Of course the identity of the speaker is very important. When a powerful person says 'guilty', then – if I have understood the speaker – something within me is changed by that word, something that would not have changed had the speaker been a person of no account. By extension, God, all-powerful and perfectly trustworthy, only has to say something and it is guaranteed, it is literally as good as done. But speech-act theory on this account, while showing *that* God may be present in some sense by his words, and *why* God's speech is such a true reflection of his person, does not tell us *how* he does what he says he will.[79]

---

[76] Heschel 1962: 118.

[77] Austin 1976; Wolterstorff 1995; McConville 2002b.

[78] Wolterstorff 1995: 84–85.

[79] Timothy Ward's clear account of God's words as speech actions (Ward 2009: 22–34) falters a little when he considers what it means to say that an incorporeal God utters words (35).

In the case of Jeremiah there is a further problem, which is that his preaching, though understood, was not heeded; we might say his speech acts, though successful,[80] were undercut by the hearers. Nevertheless, my argument in this chapter has amounted to saying that they were effective speech acts on the grounds that they produced a hardening in the hearers that triggered their destruction.[81] Again, however, the question remains of what it was that made their destruction actual, and what role (if any) the word played at that point.

In short, speech-act theory tells us what we knew already: that the power of the word of God lies in the power of God and the truth of God. As Jeremiah 1:12 says, 'I am watching to see that my word is fulfilled.' What the theory does not address is the means by which words, whether God's or Jeremiah's, exert causal effects, not only on relationships but on the physical universe. Such is the vehemence with which Jeremiah wields language of the word of God that it comes across as a tool, in and of itself, of divine agency in the world. Is this just a manner of speaking, or does it provide us with a unique insight into divine agency?

'The word of God' uniquely denotes the mode of God's action in the world

At one level, of course, language of the word of God is indeed 'just a manner of speaking'. It is axiomatic that if the uncreated God speaks, he does not do it in the same way humans do. To say that God 'speaks' cannot but be metaphorical;[82] it is a comparison that has elements of both 'is' and 'is not'. The 'is nots' of the metaphor include its creaturely accompaniments such as organs of speech

---

[80] Technically speaking, we would say Jeremiah's speech acts were not just 'illocutory' acts of assertion, promise, threat, etc., but complete 'perlocutions' by which the substance of his speech was transmitted as knowledge to the hearers (Wolterstorff 1995: 33). Indeed, we might go further and say that oracles of judgment have the effect of 'convicting' their recipients as in a court of law, whether they know it or not (Houston 1996).

[81] Scholars have debated whether rejected prophetic preaching can be deemed successful performative speech. For an argument that it can, see McConville (2002b: 26–27), who agrees that the 'performance' of the prophets was to declare, or bring into being, a state of judgment.

[82] A metaphor such as 'God is my rock' involves speaking about one thing in terms suggestive of another. It should function 'both to cast up and organize a network of associations. A good metaphor may not simply be an oblique reference to a predetermined subject but a new vision, the birth of a new understanding, a new referential access' (Soskice 1985: 57–58). The simile 'God is like my rock' is by comparison pale, distant and ineffectual.

and vibrating air, but beyond them there is a real point of reference (the 'is'),[83] so that language of word and speech truly and uniquely describes what God 'actually' does. What is more, I wish to suggest that language of divine speech has a value and a point of connection in the being of God that no other metaphor can replicate. The metaphor 'word of God' denotes a reality that metaphors such as 'signal', 'communication', 'revelation', 'pronouncement', and so forth do not. It uniquely expresses the mode of divine action in the world.

The divine agency debate

This contention raises the vexed question of divine agency, that is, of precisely how the uncreated God acts to bring his creation into being and then to rule it and direct its end (and ours). Contemporary discussions of this question go back to a lecture series given in 1964 by the theologian Austin Farrer. In it he conceived of a point at which God's actions impinge upon his world and cause actions that to us appear freely caused by human (or other) actors. This point of intersection he dubbed the 'causal joint'.[84] Farrer stressed that trying to explain it was both impossible and theologically hazardous:

> God's agency must actually be such as to work omnipotently on, in, or through creaturely agencies without either forcing them or competing with them. But as soon as we try to conceive it in action, we degrade it to the creaturely level and place it in the field of interacting causalities. The result can only be (if we take it literally) monstrosity and confusion.[85]

That is, how can God 'manipulate' matter without possessing 'hands' or some material equivalent with which to do physical work? How can he 'force' things to happen without himself being an energetic force analogous to gravity or magnetism? It is the refusal to identify God with any of the physical or energetic causes of things that makes the so-called 'causal joint' a mystery.

The theologian who has probably worked hardest to find a point

---

[83] '[W]e do not claim to describe God, but to point through His effects, and beyond His effects, to Him. . . . this separation of referring and defining is at the very heart of metaphorical speaking'. 'But the theist . . . can coherently claim that his language is referential or, as we prefer, reality depicting, without claim to definitive knowledge' (Soskice 1985: 140–141).

[84] Farrer 1967: 65.

[85] Ibid. 62.

of intersection is Wolfhart Pannenberg, with his doctrine of the Spirit. Pannenberg conceives of the Spirit as 'a single, all-embracing force field within which physical entities are forms of forces that become independent realities'.[86] By 'force field' Pannenberg has a scientific idea in mind. 'The field theories of science, then, can be considered as approximations to the metaphysical reality of the all-pervading spiritual field of God's creative presence in the universe.'[87] The word 'metaphysical' is significant, for the Spirit is 'infinite, ultimate and non-physical';[88] nevertheless, it is clear that Pannenberg is not speaking analogically. The being of the Spirit is identical to that of an impersonal force field of physics, except that it extends infinitely far beyond the universe in space and time.[89] In making this equation Pannenberg includes the created world within the divine being, and despite his protestations to the contrary, this conception of divine immanence is necessarily panentheistic, as John Cooper has convincingly argued.[90] The idea of the Spirit as a field of force can still be a fruitful one, but only when cast as an *analogy* for the way the Spirit is present to all time and space. As analogy it allows the modality of the Spirit's operation to remain unknown, the 'causal joint' hidden.

A less problematic alternative might be to try to imagine a 'causal joint' between God's acts and their physical consequences which is neither material nor energetic. From a scientist's perspective the problem to be solved is the following:

> How can God exert his influence on, make an input of information into, the world-as-a-whole without an input of matter/energy? This seems to me to be the ultimate level of the 'causal joint' conundrum, for it involves the very nature of the divine being in relation to that of matter/energy.[91]

[86] Pannenberg 1991–8: 2.79–84; cf. 1991: 46; the idea of a force field originates in Stoic philosophy.

[87] Pannenberg 1991: 47.

[88] Pannenberg 1991–8: 1.383.

[89] Pannenberg 1993: 44; cf. Pannenberg 1991–8: 2.84–102; Cooper 2007: 274–276.

[90] Cooper 2007: 259–281. For Pannenberg the universe is within God as part of his being, albeit a tiny part of the divine infinitude. 'In virtue of trinitarian differentiation God's eternity includes the time of creatures in its full range, from the beginning of creation to its eschatological consummation' (Pannenberg 1991–8: 1.405–406). The panentheistic model of divine agency is ably defended by Clayton (1997) and, in my opinion, effectively criticized by John Cooper (Cooper 2007: 319–346) and Vanhoozer (2010: 130–138).

[91] Peacocke 1993: 164.

A starting assumption for advocates of 'non-energetic' divine agency is that it cannot involve intervention in the everyday laws of nature.[92] Instead, we should look to 'causal spaces' in the natural order from within which God may continuously 'interact' with his creation to bring about his purposes without an input of energy. Instead of energy, it is proposed that God brings about change by an input of 'information'. Possible 'causal spaces' include non-linear, chaotic systems whose unpredictable end states can be altered by 'holistic pattern-forming agencies which can be thought of as "active information"',[93] divine control of quantum indeterminacy and 'top-down causation' in which changes made to the system-as-a-whole alter its component parts without interfering with any of them directly. The most important example of top-down causation is the relationship of the mind to the brain.[94]

As with Pannenberg's proposal, these are fruitful ideas, but the picture of divine action they paint is hard to reconcile with Scripture. To begin with, the biblical portrait of a sovereign God who, in Christ, 'carries all things [to their appointed end] by his powerful word'[95] suggests constant divine intervention to uphold natural processes not for their own sake, but in order that they might bring about God's purposes; and should those purposes involve the super-seding of natural 'laws', that would not then be a denial but rather an expression of divine faithfulness.[96] More problematic still is that this model of non-energetic divine agency applies to the providential guiding of events much better than it does to the bringing of things into being in the first place. This is doubly problematic if we suppose, as most do, that creation out of nothing is the basic expression of

[92] 'The laws of nature are not constraints externally imposed upon God; rather they are, in their regularity, expressions of the faithful will of the Creator. God is their ordainer and does not work against them, for that would be for God to work against God' (Polkinghorne 1996: 244–245). For Arthur Peacocke, it is contradictory to see God's both sustaining the laws of nature that give expression to his purposes and abrogating them, as if he could not make them do what he wanted to in the first place (Peacocke 1993: 141–143).

[93] Polkinghorne 1996: 247.

[94] For Peacocke and others the mind is an emergent property of the physical brain, whose firing neurons cause its thoughts, but not in such a way that the mind can be reduced to those firing neurons; it transcends them in a relationship of 'super-venience', by which thinking can exert effects on our bodies (Peacocke 1993: 161; cf. Clayton 1997: 257).

[95] For this reading of Heb. 1:3 see O'Brien (2010: 56–57).

[96] It is just as likely that 'the laws that we formulate at specific periods' are approximations of 'the divine world order' that underlies them, and which God controls (Pannenberg 1991–8: 2.44–46; cf. Polkinghorne 1996: 251).

God's creative activity, and God's sustaining of his universe is an act of continuous creation (the technical term is *creatio continua*).[97] It follows, then, that one conceives either of *creatio continua* in a non-energetic way and so leaves unexplained the world's energetic coming-into-being out of nothing, as if the world were independent of God for its existence in the first place,[98] or of creation out of nothing in the same 'non-interventionist' way as *creatio continua*, so that the universe is nudged into existence from within the being of God, a non-energetic reorganization, or self-limitation, of the divine essence. In one way or another the God of the causal spaces is related to the world just as panentheistically as the universal force field of the Spirit.[99]

As with the force-field model, the model of God as the world's mind is a valuable analogy, so long as it remains just that. It is valuable not because it explains how God acts in the world, but because it takes a fundamental idea and shows how it can be consistent with the nature of the universe as we experience it. The idea in question is that mind (and by extension Spirit) can do real work in the world of matter and energy while yet remaining distinct from it. More importantly for our purposes, this discussion brings into focus a collection of things that are neither matter nor energy: ideas, mind, spirit, language, relationship; and it helps us to conceive of these things as real without being either material or even 'creaturely' in the sense of being native to us. They are properties of humans, but they were properties of God first, and when they act as causal agents under human direction they do so in a derivative manner, and point us to the reality of divine causation on a cosmic scale.

Of all of these invisible properties it is *word* that principally serves as divine agent in the Bible. Vanhoozer transfers the concept of divine agency into the linguistic domain by speaking of a 'communicative joint', and by an analogical (non-material) reappropriation of the words 'matter' and 'energy' within a speech-act framework:

---

[97] 'By creating, therefore, God gives existence to something; and by conserving it, God continues to give it existence' (Doran 2000: 167). In this connection the use of 'word' for the mode by which God sustains all things according to Heb. 1:3 is suggestive.

[98] Doran 2000.

[99] See Clayton 1997: 238–240. John Polkinghorne's views (e.g. Polkinghorne 1994: 77–81), which are more orthodox than those of panentheists such as Peacocke and Philip Clayton, do not escape some of the difficulties raised here, in my opinion. All God's activity in the universe cannot be 'from within' without some form of panentheism.

'God's call is effectual precisely in bringing about a certain kind of understanding in and through the Word. The Word that summons us has both propositional content (matter) and illocutionary force (energy).'[100] Vanhoozer stops short, however, of attributing full causal effectiveness (perlocutionary force) to the word, something for which he brings into play the illumination of the Spirit. Jeremiah, on the other hand, does not mention the Spirit – a peculiarity to which we shall return presently – but conceives of divine agency entirely in terms of word and speech.

Speech as the mode of divine agency

We are now ready to consider the metaphor of divine speech, and the light it might shed on the mode of divine agency in the world, that is, on what it might mean that Jeremiah attributes to the word of God the power to tear down and build up nations.

We could suppose that the term *speech*, when applied to God's work of creating as opposed to his work of communicating, is to be treated as a metaphor that refers merely to the divine will, a metaphor in which the speech element is incidental, an 'is not'. In other words, the language of divine word and speech is a code for some other, undisclosed, mode of action by which God creates. But this possibility I wish to dismiss straight away. The Bible's use of speech language in regard to the activities of God is not only ubiquitous, but dominates descriptions of his creative work, his revelatory work and his saving work. As Creator, God makes; as Revealer, he manifests; as Saviour, he shows mercy – among other things – but he speaks in all these capacities. Verbs of speech convey God to us in every mode in which we experience him. And more than this, with the noun *Word* he conveys to us his person in the form of the incarnate Son. It follows that as soon as we concede that there is a real point of reference that makes *speech* a suitable term to describe God's communication of propositions to us, then we are bound to use it to describe his other activities in respect of us as well, and even to describe (with suitable humility) his internal relations as three

---

[100] Vanhoozer 2002: 118 (by 'matter' Vanhoozer signifies 'information', not physical matter). Of course this is only to restate the problem, for the communication of ideas to humans still involves actual matter and energy, so that when Vanhoozer suggests we 'change pictures and think not of a causal but of a *communicative* joint and . . . identify the point at which communication takes place as *interpretation*' (119, italics original), he has not solved the causal joint problem but only pushed it back a step.

Persons in one God. If some of God's speech is speech, then all of it is.

Alternatively, we might suppose that when God speaks words of creation, for example, he is declaring an intention to create, but not directly creating by the instrument of those words. For words make declarations about things, but do not do physical work upon inanimate objects. Indeed, the physical phenomena of speech – vibrations in a physical medium such as air – are entirely accidental. Instead, God fulfils the intention to which his speech gives expression by performing some sort of physical operation on the material universe.[101] We might appeal for this supposition to Genesis 1, where we not only have descriptions along the lines of 'God said, "Let there be light," and there was light' (Gen. 1:3), as if it was the words themselves that did the creating, but also 'God said, "Let there be an expanse between the waters . . ." So God *made* the expanse' (Gen. 1:6–7); or, 'God said, "Let the water swarm with living creatures . . ." So God *created* the large sea-creatures' (Gen. 1:20–21). Now this is well and good, as far as it goes, but it does not go far enough. For as our previous discussion has shown, to say that God performs some sort of direct physical operation on the material universe by exerting power over matter in a manner analogous to the effects of energy would be to admit a panentheism that confuses the Creator with his creation. God is uncreated Spirit, he is not energy, or any other created substance. In short, *how* the uncreated God brings into being and sustains the material universe is a mystery beyond our comprehension, and to say that he *makes* it has no explanatory power at all. It is no more or less satisfactory than to say that he *speaks* it.

There is therefore no reason why we should not suppose, in full and humble acknowledgment of the analogical limitations of the statement as forced upon us by our creatureliness, that when the category of speech is used of God, it truly denotes words that do not merely declare, but effect the contents of that declaration in the material universe. These would not be words as we know them – airy vibrations that carry meaning and some types of power to such living creatures as can understand them – but the transmaterial speech of an uncreated Spirit that is understood, or complied with,

---

[101] This is the implied position taken by Buist Fanning (2000: 850), who takes his lead from von Rad in suggesting that the references to God's creating by his word are shorthand for words plus deeds, emphasizing the effortlessness of the divine creative action.

or conformed to by every atom of the material universe. Barth was right, 'the Word of God does not need to be supplemented by an act. The Word is itself the act of God.'[102] Elihu, if we may depend on his words (and I think we may), puts it like this:

> God thunders wondrously with his voice,
>   doing great things, we know not what.
> For to the snow he says, 'Fall to earth.'
>
> (Job 37:5–6a)

The ensuing speech of God reinforces this idea (Job 39:27), as do the Psalms (e.g. Pss 29:3–9; 33:6–9).

Now it may be objected that a speech which both declares and effects the contents of that declaration is fundamentally unlike any speech we know, to the extent that the use of speech language to describe it is unhelpful. But this is clearly not a problem for the biblical authors, who freely use speech language to describe divine activities that cannot possibly be confined within the boundaries of human speech acts. Evidently there is, in the provident wisdom of God, a relatedness of human and divine speech such that, by conceiving of God's person and works in the language of speech, one is led into true knowledge of the person of one's Creator and Saviour. Indeed, if anything the comparison ought to be the other way around: if any speech is true speech, it is God's speech, of which human speech is the shadow, a creaturely and derivative reflection of an eternal, divine activity.[103]

The all-embracing scope of the powerful word in Jeremiah

Returning to Jeremiah, it is clear that for him God's saying of a thing and his doing of that thing are one and the same. It is more difficult to gain a sense of whether the identity of God's speech and action in Jeremiah comes simply from a belief in God's trustworthiness, or whether it also comes from a belief in the power of words

---

[102] 'Mere word is passive, act is an active participation in history. But this kind of distinction does not apply to the Word of God. As mere Word it is act. As mere Word it is the divine person, the person of the LORD of history, whose self-expression is as such an alteration, and indeed an absolute alteration of the world, whose *passio* in history is as such *actio*' (*CD* I/1: 144).

[103] Cf. Athanasius, for whom the creation of humans as *logikos* (rational) reflects the fact that 'the correspondence between God and human speech about God is built right into the relationship between creature and creator' (Work 2002: 37; cf. Heschel 1962: 271).

in themselves when God speaks them. There are a few hints that
the latter may be the case: first, the occasional references to God's
word as being not only heard but seen (Jer. 2:31; 23:18); secondly,
an interesting variation on the phrase 'I am going to bring evil
upon'. God uses this phrase seventeen times in the book, but once
(25:13) God says, 'I am going to bring *all my words* upon that land,'
substituting the words for the reality they denote. Thirdly, there are
verses like 36:3, in which the people will 'hear all the evil I am planning to do to them' when the scroll containing judgment oracles is
read out. English versions often render it 'hear *about* all the evil',
which is correct, but the connection in Hebrew between the word
and the deed is more direct than this.[104] This is not because of a
supposed Hebrew mentality concerning the power of words, but
because of the nature of the God who speaks and – I would go so
far as to suggest – because of a belief in the intrinsic power of the
divine word.

These arguments are far from conclusive, but whatever his
thoughts on its mechanism Jeremiah's views on divine agency are
clear: the human words are not powerful, but the divine word is.
And because the word is powerful, the human speech acts of which
the book is composed, powerless in themselves to effect the reality
of the declarations they make, add up to a divine message that, in
God's own power and timing, truly topples nations and kingdoms,
and truly creates nations and kingdoms anew.

Perhaps the single most striking feature of Jeremiah's theology
of the word is its all-sufficiency. Nowhere does he use the language
of spirit. Instead, Jeremiah speaks in terms of words – *tôrâ*, or
law – written on the people's heart. This is not the way theologians traditionally describe acts of divine regeneration. Vanhoozer,
for example, has this to say in his discussion of the power of the
word:

> Does it follow that the effectual call supervenes on the
> preached word? No, for this proves too much. Not everyone
> who hears is automatically united to Christ. . . . We need the
> illumination of the Spirit for that. Not for nothing has the
> Reformed tradition discussed the effectual call in terms of
> both Word and Spirit. . . . For the Spirit comes to the Word

---

[104] Hebrew can express the idea of hearing the fact of something, i.e. hearing about
something, by the use of *šm'* followed by *l* and an infinitive (e.g. Neh. 13:27).

when and where God wills. The Spirit 'advenes' on truth to make it efficacious.[105]

How is it that Jeremiah can give expression to what theologians term 'the effectual call' entirely from within the category of the word and the words of God? We shall return to this question in chapter 7; for the moment it is enough to reiterate one of the conclusions of the present chapter, namely, that Jeremiah has no conception of an ineffectual word. For him, God's communicative acts are intrinsically and ineluctably causal. This is not to deny the role of the Spirit in divine agency (remember Pannenberg's analogy); after all, the metaphor of speech requires breath/spirit as the medium for the words. However, it does warn us against drawing a line between word and Spirit such that we say, 'Thus far, the word is at work in the hearer; but from here the Spirit takes over.' There is no point in the conversion of a hearer, or in the creation of the universe, for that matter, where word is not the active causal agent of God's will.[106]

Vanhoozer's discussion of God's effectual call limits itself to the relational effects of divine speech. Nevertheless, he makes brief reference to the traversing of the distance between God and the world in 'the form of a communicative act: Jesus Christ, the Word of God made flesh', and raises the question – only to defer it – of the possibility of rethinking other Christian doctrines, including creation, 'in terms of God's communicative action'.[107] Jeremiah provides us with a resource for just such rethinking.

Concluding reflections

We began this chapter with two questions: What account can we give of the power of the word of God in the face of its massive rejection by the hearers? And how does the word of God exercise its power in any case; what is the connection between the power of the word (such as it is) and the power of the words (if indeed they have any)? The answer spans the second half of Jeremiah, with the grand vision of chapters 25, 30–31 and 50–51 (theologically, they comprise

[105] Vanhoozer 2002: 121–122.
[106] Vanhoozer's choice of the word 'advene' is, *inter alia*, an attempt to acknowledge this.
[107] Vanhoozer 2002: 124.

a single vision) enclosing narratives that bear witness to the deadly effectiveness of the word within Jeremiah's lifetime.

The failure of the prophetic preaching announced in Jeremiah 25:3 turned out to be no failure, but the exercise of a ministry of destruction. As 25:7 explains, their disobedience was 'in order that ... you might bring disaster on yourselves'. Only by first being a word of destruction can the ultimate intention of the word of God be realized: the intention to build and plant a nation for God. As the song cycle in the Book of Consolation tells it, such is the depth of human rebellion that nothing short of a complete cosmic upheaval will suffice to root it out. And it was in just such an upheaval that the power of the word of God was finally felt by Jeremiah's listeners, as their world was brought down around them with crushing finality.

And yet, the miracle of the Old Testament gospel is that the God who uproots does so not in cold anger but in painful love. If the first word was one of uncreation, the second word was one of divine self-giving. God promises to remake Israel from within by an act of forgiveness that amounts to drawing them into his own life, one by one. Such forgiveness cannot be confined within the boundaries of the old Israel, but spans the ruined world. So radical is this remaking of Israel that the whole fabric of the cosmos is caught up in it, and the age of the new covenant will, by virtue of a word of forgiveness, be the age of new creation, the age when death is no more.

The era of the new covenant

Unlike the word of judgment, the word of promise remained unrealized, with the transformation of a few lives (Baruch, Ebed-Melech) the only concrete sign of its power. For the 'new testament' people of God the situation is both the same and utterly changed. Jesus is revealed through the witness of the Gospel writers as the true Israelite (Matt. 1 – 4) whose life paid in ransom (Matt. 20:28) will inaugurate the new covenant era, and bring a new Israel into a heavenly kingdom:

> For this is my blood that establishes the covenant; it is shed for many for the forgiveness of sins. But I tell you, from this moment I will not drink of this fruit of the vine until that day when I drink it in a new way in my Father's kingdom with you. (Matt. 26:28–29 HCSB altered)

The power of new covenant forgiveness, seen in the words of the Last Supper, had already been symbolized in the curing of the paralytic (Matt. 9:1–8), a work of 'resurrection' power that Jesus displayed as a sign of the forgiveness he came to bestow.[108] That God's self-giving extended to the point of death made it an act of power that, in fulfilment of Jeremiah's vision, was able to release the life of many trapped in death: 'The hour has come for the Son of Man to be glorified. I assure you: unless a grain of wheat falls into the ground and dies, it remains by itself. But if it dies, it produces a large crop' (John 12:23–24 HCSB altered). The resurrection of Jesus inaugurated the new covenant era, in which an Israel drawn from every nation (Acts 2:5–11) received forgiveness and a resulting transformation by the Spirit (Acts 2:38; Rom. 8:1–9). To be in Christ is to be a new creation (2 Cor. 5:17).

And yet the final victory over death experienced by Jesus Christ still lies in the future for the Israel gathered around him (Rom. 8:10–25), and the New Testament epistles are written to a people still in exile (1 Pet. 1:1), still sinful,[109] still passing through the death Jesus passed through, but assured by his resurrection that their hope for 'a better country' (Heb. 11:16) will not be in vain. The logic of new covenant forgiveness – that once unleashed there will be no stopping it until it has unmade the world – is the logic that determines the end point not only of Jeremiah, but of the New Testament and of world history. The return from exile, begun at the resurrection, is completed in John's vision of an Israel from every nation guided to springs of living water, their weeping eyes dried (Rev. 7:17). And it is to Jeremiah 50 – 51 that John turns for his description of the end of human society as we know it, the society whose beginnings are depicted in Genesis 11. The symbolic action performed by Seraiah in Jeremiah 51:63–64 is repeated by an angel in Revelation 18:21, and with the fall of Babylon – standing in the first place for Rome, and then for every society opposed to the rule of God, and for the forces of evil and death that rule in God's stead – the prophets and saints whose blood was found in her are raised to join the heavenly triumph (Rev. 18:24 – 19:4).

---

[108] On paralysis as a sign of death and Jesus' miracle as an act of resurrection, see Bolt (2003: 102–115). On new covenant forgiveness in the Gospels more generally, see Peterson (2012: 53–55, 57–58).

[109] So that Carroll is right – up to a point – to say of Jer. 31:31–34 that 'the utopian society characterized by this metaphor of *bĕrît* [covenant] does not and cannot exist' (Carroll 1986: 614).

The power of the word

To say that God's word of promise is not yet fully realized, but remains promise, is not to say that its power lies partially dormant. The power is in the word, and is released in its fullness when the word is spoken. The act of power by which history will end and a new creation descend is nothing more or less than the very same word of judgment and promise already spoken.[110]

How can this be? The New Testament has both illuminated and deepened the mystery of divine agency by revealing that God's self-giving went so far as to create an 'ontological joint', a word-made-flesh, and that it is this Word we proclaim – which Jeremiah proclaimed – when the promises of God are declared.

However, this does not alter the fact that we cannot explain the mode of divine agency in any mechanical or scientific way. The word of God is not like a horse, whose power can be described in terms of muscles and metabolism and mechanics. The only proper way to describe the power of the word of God is to declare the contents of the word of God, for the power of the word of God is that it does what it says. And it does what it says because of whose word it is. And because the word is a divine Word, it need only be spoken in order to be done – not just because God is true, but because his speech in and of itself effects the contents of its declaration. The God who speaks cannot be separated from the speech he utters.

In the lectures on which the present book is based I began by 'speaking about' the word of God and its relationship to the words of Jeremiah; I continued by 'speaking about' Jeremiah, the word-shaped speaker of the word of God, and by 'speaking about' the hearers, irreversibly fixed in their rejection of the word of God. But one cannot 'speak about' the power of the word of God in the same way. One can speak about the *effects* of its power, broken cities and returning exiles, but the word itself is powerful not as it is spoken about, but only as it is spoken.

Finally, what of human words? The words of Jeremiah were not magical, and there was nothing intrinsically powerful in them, no more than there is in any human speech. Yet because the human words Jeremiah spoke were no less than divine words put into his

---

[110] Ultimately, it was the resurrection of Jesus that vindicated all God's words, and, as Pannenberg has argued, 'the fate of Jesus Christ is the anticipation of the end, and thus the [definitive] revelation of God' (Pannenberg 1969: 143; Biddy 2005: [24]–[28]).

mouth by God, they communicated a word of power. The word to which Jeremiah's words added up was a word of love, a word in which the divine speaker inflicts death upon his beloved bride, a death infinitely painful to himself, but endured because it makes possible a word of forgiveness so powerful that it draws her alive from death's clutches, reborn, weeping for joy, a new people from every nation, whose birth destroys death itself. Those are human words, but when God speaks those words, he makes himself present in a word whose power no power can resist.

Up to this point I have been stressing the fact that the word of God is spoken, not written, and that in their written form the book of Jeremiah always refers to the words of God, or the words of Jeremiah. It is now time to consider Jeremiah's theology of the written words.

Chapter Six

Word and permanence

The final strand of Jeremiah's word theology I propose to explore is actually the first strand of his word theology that we encounter as we come to his book. As Jeremiah 1:1 points out, we are not actually hearing the words of Jeremiah at all; we are reading them. For Jeremiah is dead, and all the techniques discussed previously for enhancing the orality of his written words cannot conceal the fact that they are in fact written, not spoken. If it is true that the word of God is by definition a spoken word, then the fact of written words needs explanation. It should not be surprising by now to find that Jeremiah pursues the theme of the words of God written further than any other Old Testament prophet.[1] The most significant written document to which the book of Jeremiah refers is the book of Jeremiah itself, identified by an inclusio in 1:1 and 51:64 as 'the words of Jeremiah', and closely identified in 1:2 with the word of the LORD.[2]

Writing in Deuteronomy

As has so often been the case, we find the book of Deuteronomy in the background of Jeremiah's interest in the written word.[3] Not only is the *tôrâ* it proclaims a written *tôrâ*, just as the words of Jeremiah are written words, and not only does Deuteronomy narrate acts of writing, as does Jeremiah in chapter 36 and elsewhere, but the significance of this writing down is also explored in Deuteronomy. There are five major acts of writing in the book of Deuteronomy,[4]

---

[1] The theme, naturally enough, is prominent in Ezra-Nehemiah and Chronicles, also in Deuteronomy, Joshua and Kings.

[2] Within this book several smaller books are contained: the 'book' of chs. 30–31; the 'book', or letter, of ch. 29; the 'book', or title deed, of 31:6–15; and the 'book', or scroll, of ch. 36, also mentioned in 45:1. One Hebrew word covers all these items.

[3] Fischer 2005: 2.743.

[4] I pass over the references to a written certificate of divorce, judging this act of writing to be of a different order to the others.

the first of which is God's act of writing the ten words on two tablets of stone. Speech is followed by writing, followed by withdrawal of the divine presence. 'And he declared to you his covenant, which he commanded you to perform, that is, the Ten Words, and he wrote them on two tablets of stone' (Deut. 4:13; cf. Deut. 5:22; 9:10; 10:4). The second act of writing is the people's act of writing on their doorposts. It is the last in a chain of commands that emerge from and refer back to a single antecedent phrase, suggesting that the writing of the words was to have been an expression of the internalization of the law, the rewriting of stone letters on human hearts: 'These words that I command you today shall be on your heart . . . You shall write them on the doorposts of your house and on your gates' (Deut. 6:6, 9; cf. Deut. 11:18–20). The third act of writing is the king's act of writing for himself a copy of the law, in the presence of the priests, so that he may learn to fear the LORD. Fourthly, as mentioned repeatedly near the end of the book, the law is written down for the purpose of bringing its curses to prominence in the event of national disobedience.[5] Even the written song of Moses functions to serve as a witness against the people.[6] The event that precipitates Moses' writing down of the law is his imminent departure and transfer of leadership to Joshua, a situation that may perhaps be compared with God's writing down of the Ten Words. The fifth and final act of writing is found in just one verse, Deuteronomy 30:10, which describes obedience to written laws among returned exiles whose hearts the LORD has circumcised so that they will love him.[7]

We can summarize these acts of writing down as follows: written words replace spoken words when the speaker is gone – long gone. They act as a witness in the absence of the speaker, usually to hold people accountable and bring God's judgment upon them (Deut. 31:19). The act of writing words, together with the act of reading them, is a way of remembering and internalizing them, and it is always possible through reading them that one may turn to the LORD from the heart.

---

[5] Deut. 27:3, 8; 28:58; 29:20, 21; 31:9, 19, 22, 24. Regarding Deut. 27, and its message that this is a people under threat, if not sentence, of curse, see Barker 1998.

[6] Though the first two references to the lawbook written by Moses and deposited by the Levites next to the ark for the purposes of septennial reading (31:9, 19) are not negative, the third reference (31:24) is negative, and casts its shadow over the previous two.

[7] The relative ages of this verse and its parallels in Jeremiah are disputed but immaterial to this discussion. However, the idea of law written on the heart (Jer. 31:33) would seem to be a development beyond Deut. 30:10.

Jeremiah and writing

As with Deuteronomy, the value of the written word for Jeremiah lies, in the first instance, with the fact that it lasts a long time (Jer. 32:14), as opposed to a speaker who must eventually die. Writing makes the spoken message permanent.[8]

This permanence is particularly important when the truth of the spoken word is not yet verified by events. The book of Jeremiah itself is written down so that when the word of God is fulfilled it will be seen for what it is. Apart from Jeremiah 1:1, the references to the writing of the book are all in its second half, beginning with Jeremiah 25:13, in which the written prophecy of Babylon's fall is mentioned. That written prediction also closes out the second half (51:59–64), where it is not only read, but thrown into the river in a sign act that depicts the power of those words, as written and read, to bring about God's promised judgment. In the same way we see promises of future hope being written down until such time as they are fulfilled (30:2–3; 32:13–15). There is an example of this process already at work in chapter 26, as the written words of Micah play a part in the debate over the validity of Jeremiah's words.

Written words do more than simply attest to the truth, however, for when the words of the book are read, their listeners may hear the word of the LORD. The prime example of this is Jeremiah's letter to the exiles in chapter 29. Jeremiah entrusted the letter to one of his supporters, who carried it to Babylon and, we may safely assume, read it aloud to the recipients (as is explicitly stated in the case of the scroll Seraiah took to Babylon). The text of the letter is in the form of oracles in which God speaks in the first person (29:4, 8, 10, 16–17, 21, 25, 31); in fact, the Messenger Formula 'thus says the LORD' is used more often here than in any other chapter of Jeremiah. Clearly, the word of God can come to hearers through the prophetic words spoken by another in his name. Hence the confident opening of verse 21, 'Hear the word of the LORD'.[9]

As a result, written words can fulfil a prophetic ministry in lieu of the prophet himself. The contents of Jeremiah's letter are instructive

---

[8] The use of writing to 'cement in' somebody's future is used in Jer. 22:30 of Jehoiachin: 'write this man down as childless'. Writing down can serve truth or lies equally. In Jer. 8:8, for example, the pen of the scribes produces deception.

[9] One of Jeremiah's opponents, Shemaiah, also spoke at a distance by letter (Jer. 29:25).

here. As we saw earlier, Jeremiah did not bring the criteria of true and false prophecy to bear either on the defence of his own prophetic ministry (ch. 26) or on the conflict with Hananiah (chs. 27–28). But in his letter he systematically takes the Babylonian prophets to task at the level of their character (v. 23), the deceitful contents of their message (*šeqer*, v. 21), its negative effect on the community ('made you trust a lie', v. 31), the fact that God did not send them (v. 31), and the specific doom each prophet will face from the fulfilment of the true prophetic word concerning them (vv. 21, 32). Are we seeing the message of Jeremiah's letter being strengthened as much as possible – by additions of the Messenger Formula as well as by polemic – in order to compensate for the absence of the prophet whose presence would normally add strength to his message? Ultimately, of course, only the fulfilment of the events described will carry complete conviction (cf. 23:20; 30:24 – 'in latter days you will understand it').

Finally, the role of Baruch, the writer of Jeremiah's words, is uniquely prominent. His role becomes the focus of attention in chapters 32, 36 and 45. This latter chapter is particularly interesting, as it links his scribal work with the actions of tearing down and uprooting mentioned in Jeremiah 1:10. Baruch's particular legacy in the narratives attributed to him is his preservation of the person of Jeremiah through biography.[10] The written book of Jeremiah preserves his person, his works and his words together.

In short, Deuteronomy's conception of written words is taken up and extended by Jeremiah, in which words initially spoken are written down so as to last into the future. By lasting they will stand to bear witness to the truth and faithfulness of God when his words come to be fulfilled. By being read out they expose listeners to the possibility of hearing the word of the LORD, even in the absence of the prophet who speaks and embodies the word that came to him from the LORD. They allow the hearers to encounter the prophet in his literary persona, to receive his prophetic ministry, to observe his person and works as well as his words. All these themes come together in one of the most important sustained treatments of enscripturation in the Bible, Jeremiah 36.

[10] Di Pede 2004.

Jeremiah 36

Context

Are the acts of writing depicted in Jeremiah 36 historically plausible? This question has long vexed scholars, who are unable to agree on the answer. On the one hand, there is almost no extra-biblical evidence that prophets in the ancient world committed their messages to writing. Karel van der Toorn argues (by analogy with Assyrian practices) that some prophetic oracles were recorded and archived in the temple, so that priests could keep a careful eye on what was being prophesied under their noses.[11] However, he does not consider that the sort of oracles typically found in the Bible would have been archived in this way; they have the quality of sympathethic reminiscences produced well after the event. The claim that Baruch wrote at Jeremiah's dictation is unparalleled, dictation not being among 'the usual practices and techniques of the scribal craft',[12] and may safely be dismissed as a rhetorical gesture aimed at attaching prophetic authority to the words of the text.

On the other hand, the force of van der Toorn's argument is greatly weakened the moment one allows that the literature of the Bible and the practices it records may include peculiar, even novel, aspects. As Joachim Schaper has shown, there is positive evidence for such aspects as the suggestion in Habakkuk 2:2 that at least some Hebrew prophecies were written not just for archiving but to be publically proclaimed.[13] In the case of Jeremiah 36, the fact that archaeological finds have not (so far) yielded comparable acts of writing should not weigh against the biblical account, so long as its character is judged to be generally reliable.[14] Moreover, where Jeremiah's structure of repetition with variation betrays scribal hearsay and reinvention to van der Toorn,[15] I have tried to demonstrate that a coherent organizing spirit underlies the book,

[11] Van der Toorn 2007: 178–188.

[12] Ibid. 186.

[13] Schaper 2009; cf. Jer. 29:1. Certainly, the collecting of prophecies into books, such as those mentioned in Dan. 9:2, was quite unique to Hebrew culture, as far as we know (Schellenberg 2010: 289), and to posit unique causes behind such unique results is not unreasonable.

[14] Notwithstanding its theological (ideological) colouration, the biblical testimony to the events in Judea during the seventh to sixth centuries, and to Jeremiah's role in them, is coherent and historically impressive, and deserves as careful a hearing as any comparative sources – all of which have their share of ideology.

[15] Van der Toorn 2007: 195–199.

whose distinctive form does not require generations of scribal creativity. While it is true that my reading arises out of a commitment to take seriously the theological claims the text makes about itself and the world, it must be remembered that the text presents itself as a human artefact produced by a historical process that includes – by the text's own accounting – a history of scribal activity. My differences with van der Toorn, therefore, do not reduce our respective starting commitments to comparative and theological readings respectively, but ultimately rest on the question of how most satisfyingly to read the text in front of us as a historical document. Thus, for example, Mark Leuchter, working from starting commitments comparable to van der Toorn's, has presented a strong case that an archive of Jeremianic material 'was very likely preserved by the prophet and his colleagues, which would have made copies of Jeremiah's oracles available for public reading and consultation'.[16]

Exegesis

The account begins with a 'word' coming to Jeremiah from the LORD, in which he is commanded to write down all the 'words' the LORD had previously spoken to him. The hearing language of verse 3 suggests that the reading out of these written words has the potential to turn the hearts of the people in the same way that direct prophetic proclamation does.

In verse 4 Jeremiah writes by the hand of another, just as he will speak through the mouth of another when those words are read. But the narrative goes to great lengths to preserve the chain of evidence (as police dramas like to say). First Jeremiah proclaims words to Baruch,[17] then Baruch writes what comes from Jeremiah's mouth, then what comes from his mouth are God's words, then God's words are the ones he previously spoke to Jeremiah. This entire chain of evidence is then repeated in verse 6, but this time Baruch does the proclaiming of the writing of what came from Jeremiah's mouth, which were God's words. The episode concludes in verse 8 with a fascinating breach of this chain, where Baruch does as Jeremiah commanded by 'proclaim[ing] from the scroll the words of the LORD in the house of the LORD'. Just as 'Jeremiah's dicta-

---

[16] Leuchter 2006: 171.
[17] *Qr'* is used in v. 4 with its meaning 'summon', but in v. 18 Baruch uses the word with the sense 'proclaim' when he recounts the events of v. 4 to the officials.

tion to Baruch' can be simplified to 'Jeremiah writing', so 'Baruch's reading of Jeremiah's proclamation of God's words' can be simplified to 'Baruch's proclaiming of God's words'. (I have used the word 'proclaim' to indicate that the same Hebrew word covers both Jeremiah's act of dictating and Baruch's act of reading, as well as Jeremiah's acts of preaching earlier in the book.)

The second major episode in the narrative takes place a year later (v. 9), with what is presumably at least a second public reading of the scroll by Baruch. This time the expression used, in verse 10, omits not Jeremiah but God from the chain of evidence. Just as the narrative of Jeremiah is constructed so that often we cannot tell whether it is Jeremiah or God *speaking*, so the distinction between God's words and Jeremiah's *written* words is blurred in this narrative. In fact, it is more than blurred. In verse 11 the words of Jeremiah read are not heard as such by Gemariah, but as the word of the LORD. The narrative brings the two expressions as close together as possible:

Then Baruch read by means of the scroll [*bassēper*] the words of Jeremiah, in the house of the LORD, in the chamber of Gemariah the son of Shaphan the secretary, which was in the upper court, at the entry of the New Gate of the LORD's house, in the hearing of all the people, and Micaiah the son of Gemariah, son of Shaphan, heard all the words of the LORD [coming] from the scroll [*mē'al hassēper*]. (Jer. 36:10–11)

There is a curious variation in the preposition used with the scroll at the point of reading and the point of hearing. While the prepositions in question each have a wide range of meaning, a strong case can be made for the above translation. Baruch read the words 'in' the scroll, or perhaps 'by means of' the scroll;[18] but Gemariah heard the words 'from' or 'coming from' the scroll.[19] The implication of this

---

[18] The preposition *b* exhibits its usual broad range in Jer. 36: locative ('in', v. 9a); directional ('into', v. 9b); point in time ('on the day', v. 6); kind of time ('by night', v. 30); adverbial ('with ink', v. 18); verbal (v. 25); elsewhere we see it conveying operative (34:4) and partitive senses (34:7). Of these meanings only the adverbial/operative 'he read *by means of* the scroll' or the locative 'he read *in* the scroll' are possible, despite the majority of Bible versions and commentators glossing the phrase '*from* the scroll' (Condamin 1920, Holladay 1989 and Fischer 2005 are exceptions). Reading is described this way whether the words are said to be Jeremiah's (v. 10) or God's (vv. 4, 6, 8).

[19] The compound preposition *mē'al* is used in Jeremiah to denote spatial movement away from; e.g. the people's removal *from* the land; Nebuchadnezzar's

is that writing was conceived of as an act of catching spoken words, like butterflies in a net, and that reading was the act of releasing those words from their written form to be heard once again. What is more, the words inked onto the leather leave the scroll as Jeremiah's words, but arrive as God's words in the ears of the listeners.

From this point in the narrative we begin to see the effects of the reading of the words. Micaiah's response was to report to the scribal officials in the temple. The phrasing of verse 13 is quite indirect: 'he reported to them the words he had heard when Baruch read by means of the scroll in the people's hearing'. The response to this indirect report was interest, but when they heard the actual words read, their response was dread, a conviction that reporting this to the king was essential, and a curiosity about the source of the words. 'How did you write these words?', they ask in verse 17, 'from his mouth?' And Baruch replies, 'From his mouth he proclaimed all these words to me, and I wrote them upon the scroll with ink.'[20] The chain of evidence is confirmed, and the immediate response created by the words themselves is justified after the fact by reasoned enquiry. This permits the inference that the words, like Jeremiah's preaching, have a self-authenticating power, and proofs only strengthen the faith of those who have arrived at belief by another route.

From verse 19 the chain of evidence gets one step longer, and the written Scripture no longer has its hand held either by its human author or the witness who wrote down his words. The same double process occurs as it did previously: an indirect report to the king followed by the reading of the scroll itself, which now fills the slot in the narrative occupied previously by Baruch. It is not Baruch, but the scroll Jehudi fetches this time. The response of the king is described in elaborate detail, and the entire emphasis of verse 24 falls upon the lack of dread or tearing of garments. This response forms a contrast with the dread of the earlier hearers, and also with the tearing of clothes that was the response of king Josiah when he heard the book of the law read out in 2 Kings 22:11.[21]

---

departure *from* the city; the removal of a yoke *from* Jeremiah's neck. The exception is Jer. 36:21, where no movement is involved: the officials are standing *back from* the king. On the other hand, *min* without *'al* in ch. 36 is broader, including temporal (v. 2) and mental (v. 3) as well as spatial senses of 'from'.

[20] In cuneiform texts the expression 'from the mouth' is used to indicate authorship in a broad sense (van der Toorn 2007: 43), but in the context of Jer. 36 it clearly means authorship by dictation.

[21] The close literary relationship of Jer. 36 and 2 Kgs 22 – 23 is undeniable (e.g. Venema 2004), and serves to strengthen the main thrust of Jeremiah's narrative.

The final episode of the chapter begins with the coming of a new word of the LORD to Jeremiah, in which he is instructed to go back to the start of the process and write 'all the former words that were on the former scroll' (v. 28). Then follows in verse 29 a new oracle delivered for Jeremiah to speak against the king. We are not told that this oracle was written down at that time, though we find something similar in Jeremiah 22:19. The final verse is important for two reasons. First it shows Baruch writing the words of the old scroll on a new scroll, but Jeremiah's involvement is as active as ever. This is not a form of independent scribal activity such as is postulated for so much of the literature of the Old Testament in its present form, but another direct enscripturation of prophetic words. Secondly, we see that the instruction of verse 28 is exceeded and many similar words are added, with a suggestively vague use of the passive voice. Of course there was no word in verse 28 against such additions, and the extra word that intervenes is a hint of more to come, but the specifying of extra words is important. Theologically it is the final nail in the coffin of anybody – even a king – who thinks he or she can gag the words of God. And historically it provides the key to the process that underlies the canonical book of Jeremiah as it exists today – or, to be precise, the two canonical forms of Jeremiah, Hebrew and Greek, as they exist in Western and Eastern churches respectively.

Above all, this is a chapter about the preservation of spoken words to be spoken again. That the act of writing also fixes spoken words in a new way is significant, but it misses the mark to read the chapter primarily as an exposition of this idea.[22] The question at its heart is how to preserve speech without loss, how 'to prevent writing from becoming mere nostalgia for a presence we can no longer touch and a voice that we can no longer hear'.[23]

Further, in the light of Deut. 1:5 and Hab. 2:2 we may understand the act of public reading in Jeremiah to give the written words a legal force, as if they were a witness against their listeners (so Schaper 2009: 145).

[22] Against Goldingay 1994: 204: 'Spoken words are all very well, but they can be lost in the wind; a person cannot necessarily be held to them. Putting things in writing makes them definite and fixed.'

[23] Brummitt and Sherwood 2011: 53; cf. McConville 2002b: 25–26. Holt draws an interesting parallel between the rewriting of the scroll in Jer. 36 and the regiving of the *tôrâ* to Moses in Exod. 34, which she judges works as an intertext to give 'a surplus of meaning and authority' to Jeremiah's narrative (Holt 2007: esp. 182–186).

A theology of the written words according to Jeremiah 36

In a tight chain of events, God's speech is conveyed by a prophet's lips, recorded by a scribe's hand and read off the page as divine speech again. For Jeremiah it is the speaker who provides the crucial link between human words and their divine author. In contemporary scholarship, however, the focus is very much on the scribe, and the role he played as author of the words read, which were subsequently rewritten by other scribes to be read again. Before engaging some of these modern debates, it will help to set out clearly Jeremiah's understanding of the relationship between author, scribe and written words. Five links make up the chain:

1. The prophetic authorship of the words is crucial to their status as divine words.
2. There is a complete identity between spoken and written words.
3. In written form they are always words, never word.
4. When read, they have the same power as the words originally spoken by the prophet.
5. The hearer of Scripture read may hear the word of the LORD in the same way as the hearer of prophecy spoken.

Words pass from God to prophet to scribe in unbroken succession. And having done this, they can equally be described as the prophet's words or as God's words. In the same way, that which Baruch writes can be called the writing of Jeremiah, and as Jeremiah can be said in chapter 36 to write a scroll by the hand of Baruch, so by extension we may think of his writing the book as a whole by Baruch's hand;[24] but this all depends on the chain of authorship. To put it another way, the enscripturated words the reader reads were written by the prophet in whose body they burned, *and* they were written by the scribe who carefully composed them; the blurring of hands, prophetic and scribal, reflects the blurring of voices, divine and human, and this is the case precisely because God is the author of the whole. The prophetic words written count as God's words written in a unique way by virtue of their authorship.

Through the act of writing, divine words take up residence on paper, and by means of their inscribed presence amongst us can be proclaimed again and again, venturing forth into the world to do their job of tearing down and building up. The voice we hear is not

---

[24] See my discussion in chapter 2 of the phrase 'this book'.

the voice doing the reading; it is the voice of the prophet who first spoke, and it is the voice of God whose words the prophet spoke. Written words enable the word to be heard into the future, and, more than this, enable the word to shine more brightly than ever it did by preserving it until it can be illuminated by its eventual fulfilment.[25]

Prophetic proclamation and public reading are equally proclamations of the words of God. To the extent that the prophet's words came to their hearers embodied by his person and works, so the written words can come embodied in the record of the prophet's person and works. Of course it is not necessary that there be a literary presence of the prophet – his words can speak with perfect clarity in his absence. And yet it is worth noting that completely disembodied voices are the exception: Isaiah's and Ezekiel's lives enter their message by symbolic actions in the same manner as we have seen in Jeremiah, as well as more prosaically,[26] and the same goes for the Book of the Twelve through the life of Hosea at the start of the collection.[27] The antitype to which the prophets point is a Word made flesh whose person, works and words come to us together, as an inseparable whole.

The response when the word of the LORD is heard by either means is dread and repentance. This response is generated by the word in its own power, not through a reasoned evaluation of the word as divine – indeed, such a process of reasoning is possible only to the mind already transformed by the word in its own power. To hear the words is to hear the word. By the same token, in Jeremiah 36:29 the king's rejection of the words counted as rejection of the word, by which he was therefore destroyed.

The message of Jeremiah 36 is clear; what is less obvious, however, is whether we should read this as Jeremiah's normative account of enscripturation, applicable whenever the word of God is committed authoritatively to writing. In favour of normative reading is the similarity we have already noted between the account of Jeremiah 36 and the understanding of written words found not

---

[25] On the written word as preserving speech for later 'iteration' see Watson (2010: 127–131).

[26] See e.g. the discussion of Ezekiel's persona by James Robson (2006: 193–212).

[27] Hosea is an apt opening to the Book of the Twelve for other reasons also, as summarized by Seitz (2007: 234–235). Hosea's prophecy opens up a canonical reading of the Twelve as a single book, a reading by which we 'are made to stand before the Twelve and see the word go forth, address generations, enclose the prophets in a history larger than themselves, and then reach out and locate us in its grand sweep – in judgment and in mercy – before that same holy God' (Seitz 2007: 245).

only throughout Jeremiah, but in Deuteronomy and associated books (such as Kings). The idea that the words of an original author (the speaker) are preserved in writing so they may be spoken again runs throughout these texts, and Jeremiah 36 subjects this idea to a precise dissection, rather than adding any truly novel elements to it.

Against normative reading stand a host of modern challenges to ancient notions of authorship, writing, and the prophetic origins of Scripture. We shall now consider two of these challenges as a way of 'testing the links' in the chain connecting God and Scripture.

Two modern challenges to the 'Jeremiah 36 paradigm' of enscripturation

The topic of Scripture is a vast one, and even an introductory treatment would double the length of this book. In any case, the doctrine of Scripture is somewhat peripheral to my main topic of enquiry – the word of God – for as we have seen, 'the word of the LORD' is an expression reserved in Scripture (though not in systematic theology) for oral communication. It is no accident that when Jeremiah 36 brings the topic of Scripture to the fore, it does so precisely to illuminate the connection point of Scripture and the spoken word of God. And it is this question of connection to which I shall confine my discussion, in particular, the connecting 'chain' that runs from God to the prophet to the scribe to the written words. To do this I have enlisted the assistance of two biblical scholars who have, each in his own way, challenged traditional ways of thinking about the phenomenon of enscripturation. Karel van der Toorn, whose work we met earlier, has made an important contribution to our understanding of the link between prophet and scribe,[28] and John Goldingay has raised significant questions about the link between scribe and Scripture, especially on the matter of how normative the model of Jeremiah 36 ought to be.[29] However, before turning to these scholars it will be useful to remind ourselves of some features of the first link, between God and the prophet.

From God to the prophet

It is important to recall at this stage the complex nature of the relationship between the words Jeremiah receives from God – words he

[28] Van der Toorn 2007.
[29] Goldingay 1994.

now hears, now ingests, now sees – and the words he then utters as the word of the LORD. This is not a simple matter of dictation, but of Jeremiah's 'translating' the message that comes to him in words that may or may not be identical to the words received, but that correspond to the controlling word, or message (Jer. 32:6–8 is a perhaps trivial case in point). Even more complex are those words not apparently given by God at all, especially Jeremiah's words of confession, which we find woven through the oracles from God. And yet we saw (in chapter 3) that the word of the LORD came to Jeremiah in such a way that it formed him into a creature of the word, whose every thought, word and deed was taken up into his message, becoming in its own way a 'word' from God. Thus we conclude that, both in the case of words from God Jeremiah respeaks, and in the case of words spontaneously arising within him, the word of the LORD determines the words of Jeremiah to the extent that Jeremiah's words can be fully identified with the words of God. This link gives a key to those that follow.

From prophet to scribe: Van der Toorn and the 'scribalization' of prophecy

While the job of prophets was to speak the word of God, the Bible is written: it is a scribal production. Van der Toorn's study of ancient scribal practices reveals the following salient points. First, in stark contrast to modern notions of authors as original, even inspired, thinkers whose writings express their individuality, ancient authors wrote as anonymous craftsmen skilfully giving voice to the common values of the (scribal) community. Although anonymity was the norm, authorship was sometimes invoked, for example where the author claimed direct contact with the divine, but as a way of asserting authority rather than authenticity.[30] Secondly, scribes not only wrote and archived texts; they were custodians who read them publically, explained them and elaborated upon them.[31] Thirdly, discoveries from Mesopotamia and Egypt provide evidence for a number of different modes of text production. While texts were routinely copied with extremely high levels of accuracy,[32] scribes did much more than reproduce texts: they *produced* texts in various ways. They transcribed oral sources, doing so with a creativity that

[30] Van der Toorn 2007: 27–42.
[31] Ibid. 51.
[32] Ibid. 126.

increased as the distance from the oral performance increased; they composed new texts of their own; they made compilations, creating aggregations of originally separate oral or written texts; they expanded existing texts with their own additions, not bit by bit in the course of copying the text, but on the occasion of creating new editions, into which the scribes' oral explanations were inserted, or to which new introductions and conclusions were added.[33] Fourthly, the fact that oral prophecy was turned into writing by scribes, using a full suite of creative text-production techniques, meant that the spoken authority of the prophets soon became an enscripted authority, and this precipitated the so-called 'scribalization' of prophecy, whereby prophets began to write their messages, turning prophecy into a written medium.[34] The notion of revelation therefore shifted, being applied to the written text in itself rather than to the divine imparting of words to a speaker.[35] This new paradigm of revelation can be dated to the twelfth century BC in Mesopotamia, and in Israel, to the emergence of Deuteronomy during the seventh century BC: 'Until Deuteronomy, the written word had been an aid in the oral transmission of the tradition; Deuteronomy stands for a reversal of roles: it turns oral exposition into a handmaid of the written text.'[36]

As we saw earlier, Van der Toorn's work is shaped by his decision to let comparative material from surrounding cultures determine his reading of the biblical text, and this makes him rather sceptical of a number of the claims Scripture makes about itself. Specifically:

> It is highly unlikely that Jeremiah took the initiative to put his oracles on record, and it was certainly not at the command of God. Prophets, as we have seen, were not in the habit of writing their messages; nor were they accustomed to dictating them to others.[37]

The prophet as author and the scribe as his secretary is a phenomenon van der Toorn is willing to concede on occasion,[38] but certainly not in the case of any literature that does not explicitly claim to be direct divine speech. In particular, the Confessions cannot be

---

[33] Ibid. 110–137.
[34] Ibid. 203.
[35] Ibid. 205–207.
[36] Ibid. 211–227; quote from 225.
[37] Ibid. 186.
[38] Ibid. 38, 111.

anything other than a scribal creation: 'The trouble . . . resides in the fact that these texts, if indeed authentically autobiographical, are truly unique. There is nothing like them in the ancient Near East. No one kept this kind of personal diary.'[39] In addition to the priority he gives comparative literature, van der Toorn depends on specific literary reconstructions of the Bible's prehistory in constructing his account of the emergence and growth of the Old Testament in the scribal schools. Any modification to these starting commitments – such as allowing that there were unique aspects to the emergence of written texts in Israel, or engaging in historical reconstructions which are less suspicious of the Old Testament's theological claims – will naturally cast doubt over a number of van der Toorn's conclusions.

Nevertheless, these problems do little to diminish the cogency of van der Toorn's central thesis. Whether we conclude that a book such as Jeremiah was written down during or long after the prophet's lifetime, whether we discern in it large or small amounts of creative writing, compilation and expansion, the book as it stands is a scribal creation from beginning to end. This is not a new thought, of course: from the outset we have noted that the book of Jeremiah is an elaborate narrative about the prophet written by one or more scribes. What van der Toorn helps us to do is think through the implications of this state of affairs for Jeremiah's (and our) theology of the written words.

'From the prophet's mouth'

Jeremiah 36 insists that what Baruch wrote was 'from the prophet's mouth', and verse 18 in particular is hard to read in any way other than as a dictation, within a single short time period, of twenty years of prophecies. Certainly, the first twenty chapters of Jeremiah read like Jeremiah's words direct from his mouth. Apart from the framework of Disjunctive Headings marking major section breaks, and one short narrative about Jeremiah in the third person (19:14 – 20:3; also 18:18) the only voice we hear in Jeremiah 1 – 20 is the voice of Jeremiah, or the voice of God through Jeremiah.

However, the hand of Baruch becomes much more prominent from Jeremiah 26 onwards, as the focus shifts from Jeremiah's words to his deeds, and we feel that we have moved from autobiography into biography. Can we still refer to these later parts of the

---

[39] Ibid. 189.

book as 'the words of Jeremiah'? Chapter 36 itself is a good example: the voice we hear is the narrator's, with just a few verses that count as words of Jeremiah. Can we extend the idea of Scripture conveyed by Jeremiah 36 to Jeremiah 36 itself?[40] The phrase 'from the prophet's mouth' is repeated in Jeremiah 45:1, a chapter that locates itself chronologically with chapter 36; however, these references serve to bracket a long narrative which gives little indication of having been dictated to Baruch. Even the 'autobiographical' sections of the book provide us with only indirect access to the prophet, for whether or not the oracles were dictated, their current arrangement and overall thrust is the work of the narrator who wrote the book's opening verses and Disjunctive Headings.[41]

If we recognize that the actual author of the book of Jeremiah is the scribe and not the prophet, can the link from prophet to scribe be sustained only by investing Baruch with some sort of prophetic status himself, a 'scribalized' prophet? We might escape from this conclusion by supposing that Baruch composed under prophetic supervision, but if later scribes continued to expound and expand the message, then the link is broken anyway. Their written commentary may have been a faithful representation of the original message, but at such a distance from 'the prophet's mouth' they cannot be considered more authoritative than any other interpreter, unless we postulate the prophetic Spirit at work in them also. The problem with this line of thought is that Jeremiah 36 and 45 give us no grounds for supposing that Baruch was anything other than a scribe, the authority of whose words was entirely dependent on their identity with the words spoken by Jeremiah the prophet. The narrative explicitly excludes Baruch as a source of prophetic words in his own right.[42]

Once again the way forward is to be found in the relationship of the word and the words, remembering that the link between God and prophet is forged by having the word of the LORD determine the words of Jeremiah to the extent that Jeremiah's words can be

---

[40] Cf. Pamela Scalise's suggestion that the contents of the scroll in Jer. 36 point to events outside chs. 1–20 'so that the reader will recognize that the completed book has the same purpose as the first scroll' (Scalise 2007: 307).

[41] Cf. Martti Nissinen's useful distinction between the literary genre 'biblical prophecy' and the living phenomenon of 'ancient Hebrew prophecy' (Nissinen 2004: 28–31).

[42] An older school of thought saw prophets' disciples as prophets themselves, creating within their community traditions whose emergence is recorded in the prophetic books as we now have them (e.g. McKane 1979: 186; cf. Schultz 2004: 160).

fully identified with the words of God. Can we conceive of a scribal 'translation' of the prophet's words along similar lines?

We must begin by returning to our discussion of the book's opening verse, which suggests that every word in the book that follows is one of the words of Jeremiah, whether Jeremiah is reported as having said it or not. The scribal author makes no attempt to conceal his presence. He is not embarrassed to claim that the entire book of Jeremiah consists of Jeremiah's words, that it is 'from his mouth', even as he (the scribe) openly and freely composes much of the book. We can conclude only, as we did before, that Baruch's words are so determined by the prophetic word that they count as words of the prophet. Supervision does not account for it. Even if the final book was produced with Jeremiah's imprimatur, other prophetic books almost certainly were not signed off by their eponymous prophets. Nevertheless, they too claim, presumably without intent to deceive, to convey not only the general tenor of the prophet's message, but his words, suggesting that the prophetic word has determined the words.[43]

We have rejected the idea that scribes are separately inspired as prophets, receiving as it were fresh words directly from God. We must also reject the idea that they are simply preachers of the prophetic word, because preachers can never let go of Scripture's hand in the way Scripture, having been written down from the prophet's mouth, can then function *in loco prophetis*, that is, as canon. Rather, in the same way that the prophet translates God's words, the scribes translate his, and the correspondence between the translation and the original is such that the translated words are the words of the original speaker – not in an exact one-to-one correspondence, of course, but in the sense that the more the translated words are pressed for meaning, the closer draws the message of the whole, the 'word', to the message of the original. The 'translation' can be said to reproduce the prophet's words to the extent that this is true of it.

Baruch cannot be called a prophet like Jeremiah because the word of the LORD does not come to him as to a prophet. He receives no new revelation. And yet the words he writes are considered to be the words of the prophet, which is to say, the words of God, and when they are read the listeners hear the word of the LORD. Baruch is not a

---

[43] Titles vary, but generally identify the entire contents of the book with the revelation that came to the prophet: 'the vision of Isaiah' (Isa. 1:1), 'the words of Amos' (Amos 1:1), 'the word of the LORD that came to Micah' (Mic. 1:1).

prophet, but the words he writes are words of a prophet; their nature requires some sort of divine involvement at the point of his scribal activity, a 'concursus' by which perfect congruence is secured.[44] At this point we have moved beyond the book of Jeremiah, which does not reflect on what it takes for a scribe's words to count as coming 'from the prophet's mouth', and therefore equating to the words of God.[45] However, some sort of divine intervention in the scribal act is required if the nature of the book of Jeremiah as a scribal production is to be reconciled with the claims the book makes about itself in part (Jer. 36) and in whole (Jer. 1:1). The alternative is a purely secular view of scribal activity, which forces the conclusion that the words in the Bible are those of the scribes and nobody else, irrespective of the presence of prophetic words behind them. As we shall see, the result is a 'stretching' of the label *prophet* so that it comes to apply, in a derived sense, to those who write the words of God. The editors of prophetic books are prophet-like, 'driven by a "prophetic impetus"', as Annette Schellenberg puts it.[46]

In short, Baruch writes from Jeremiah's mouth, and it is this insistence on the correspondence of the scribal product with the prophetic word on which the status of Scripture as divine words is grounded. We may accept van der Toorn's conclusion that there has been a 'scribalization' of prophecy, but only in a lessened sense: this is not a 'scribalization' that makes a prophet out of the scribe. Baruch remains a Joshua to Jeremiah's Moses. In principle there is no reason why a growth of scribal activity leading to Bible formation cannot coexist with a continuing flourishing of oral prophetic activity.[47]

From scribe to Scripture: Goldingay's 'model of scripture' as inspired word

The final link in the chain of Jeremiah 36 points us beyond the book of Jeremiah to the Bible as a whole. Can the idea of Scripture as

[44] 'Concursus' describes the Spirit's activity 'exercised in, through and by means of the writer's own activity', with the result being both a free, spontaneous human text and a divinely elicited and controlled text (Packer 1958: 80).

[45] Scribes may write lies (Jer. 8:8–9) as easily as write 'from the prophet's mouth' (cf. Carroll 1993); its connection to the prophetic word secures writing as truthful.

[46] Schellenberg 2010: 287.

[47] Though a number of her conclusions seem to me too speculative, or based on models too far removed from Israelite culture to be convincing, Susan Niditch has presented a strong case for the in-principle coexistence of oral and written 'texts' during the era of Bible formation (Niditch 1996; see also Andersen and Freedman 2000: 112–116).

prophetic words be applied to non-prophetic books? Most of the Old Testament is not Prophecy by genre;[48] it is Proverb, Hymn, Law, Narrative, and so forth. James Barr argued in the 1970s that evangelical views of Scripture were flawed precisely because (among other things) they operated on a prophetic paradigm that could not be applied to much of the Bible's literature. To assert that proverbs or narratives were given by God as if they were prophecies would be to adopt a dictation model of inspiration.[49] Vanhoozer argues against this by stepping back from the prophetic paradigm, arguing that verbal inspiration can be upheld without it: 'the primary purpose in stressing the verbal aspect of inspiration is to make a point about the final product, not the process, of inscripturation'.[50] While agreeing with Vanhoozer that the product is what counts, I would like to offer an argument in favour of re-examining and retaining a prophetic paradigm, with the help of Jeremiah. A natural conversation partner for a venture of this kind is John Goldingay.

In a major study Goldingay argues that the various models theologians use to construct a doctrine of Scripture (e.g. authority, inspiration, revelation) fit the way *parts* of Scripture function better than they do the whole.[51] Thus we see in biblical Narrative a witnessing tradition, in biblical Law an authoritative canon, in biblical Prophecy an inspired word, in biblical Apocalyptic an experienced revelation – and we need to be aware of the partial nature of these categories before we 'stretch' them to apply to the whole Bible.[52]

So long as inspiration is defined narrowly to mean speech 'under divine prompting' by which prophets 'speak words framed by God rather than by them', argues Goldingay, we can recognize it as the special feature of Prophecy, the genre in which 'inspired word' finds its natural home. We can still affirm that all Scripture is 'inspired',

---

[48] I have capitalized the word when it refers specifically to the written genre we find in the Bible.

[49] Barr 1984: ch. 3. Cf. Barton 1988: 71; McCormack 2004: 60, n. 9.

[50] Vanhoozer 2002: 136–137.

[51] Goldingay 1994.

[52] Narrative e.g. is not a genre at home with terms such as authority, revelation and inspiration (ibid. 15). For Goldingay, biblical historians such as Luke worked as other historians do, and 'God's involvement with them . . . did not bring with it the gift of additional hard facts' (40). The meaning of events emerges only with time for reflection and in the light of subsequent events (53). Elsewhere he does concede that the Former Prophets might well have an element of 'revealed history', to the extent that their authors drew on 'insights derived from the prophets' interpretation of events' (294). But he maintains between prophet and historiographer a professional distance.

but in a broader sense of that word. 'Statements about inspiration can be too specific to apply comfortably to scripture as a whole or too general to provide a satisfying account of the Prophets in particular.'[53]

At this point Goldingay complicates his argument by pointing out that not all the prophets' words partake of inspiration to the same degree. Sometimes the words they use are their own, not given directly by God, and yet God stands behind those words too, speaking through words not his own, so that we may call them prophetic and inspired.[54] In coming to this view Goldingay stresses that, strictly speaking, it is the people who are inspired rather than their writings. He is still happy to speak of the result as 'verbally inspired' even if the mode was not 'verbal inspiration'.[55] By this he appears to mean a text whose meaning emerges providentially from its constituent words, words human authors are allowed to choose by an act of divine 'self-denial'.[56]

This paves the way for a general view of Scripture as inspired word, in which the 'stretching' of the label from its prophetic origins has attenuated some of its force, so that we cannot speak of words being given by God to the author as to a prophet.

> To affirm that wisdom books and psalms are the word of God may imply that here we may have recourse to the classic notion of God providentially working through the human personality so that words devised by a human author are words that express the mind of God and fulfill God's purpose – a notion that is less well fitting to prophecy itself.[57]

Nevertheless, Scripture as a whole resembles prophecy in its effectiveness and its ongoing meaningfulness.[58] Thus the narratives of Scripture 'share the characteristics of the word of God that scripture itself attributes to prophecy. The gospel story does its work and brings new life to people.'[59] To call it God's word tells us how to read it.

---

[53] Ibid. 205.
[54] Ibid. 223–236.
[55] Ibid. 232.
[56] Ibid. 216–219.
[57] Ibid. 260.
[58] Ibid. 253.
[59] Ibid. 256.

Goldingay's views as they relate to the present discussion are well summed up in the following quotation:

> We must not 'generalize in univocal fashion the concept of inspiration derived from the prophetic genre and assume that God spoke to the redactors of the sacred books just as he spoke to the prophets,' any more than we should flatten the notion of inspiration so that the way it applies to such redactors determines the way it applies to prophets. The experience of evangelists and psalmists was unlike that of prophets. Their words are just as much God's words, just as effective and relevant, but they did not come to and through their writers in the same way.[60]

Prophetic speech or prophetic book?

Goldingay makes a strong case for treating all Scripture as the word of God in terms of its force and impact on the listener, irrespective of its genre or how it came into existence in written (let alone spoken) form. However, the point at which the present study of Jeremiah may cast some light onto the questions he raises is that of the *words* of God – in particular, the written words of Scripture.

The first difficulty with Goldingay's model of prophecy as inspired word is that it is so dependent on the imagined situation of a prophet's receiving and then speaking words from God. As Goldingay himself points out,[61] prophecy as speech is silenced by the writing down of prophetic words. The fact that prophetic books contain so much that is not 'inspired word' in Goldingay's narrow sense of the term only strengthens the conclusion that his category 'prophecy as inspired word' is not strictly a model of Scripture at all, but a model of speech.[62]

What is more, if we examine the situation of Jeremiah's receiving words from God it is not at all clear how those words came to him. Words were 'put in his mouth' (Jer. 1:9), but as we have seen, this does not reduce to dictation, vision or other conscious experience;

---

[60] Ibid. 254, and citing P. Ricœur.

[61] Ibid. 107.

[62] As Stuart Weeks observes, prophecy 'involves the mediation of a message to its addressee within the context of a specific circumstance. To publish, or even to preserve that message outside its original context is something different from prophesying' (Weeks 2009: 269). His subsequent surmise, that it is historiographic in its motivation, is open to question.

the prophet's spontaneous confessions are also framed as words of God, placed directly within Jeremiah by virtue of his constitution as a prophet. Even some of the oracles give the appearance of being literary compositions, borrowing their contents from oracles previously given, while presenting themselves as God's speech.[63] Along with the sermons, the book of Jeremiah identifies all these speeches (now written words), variously received by the prophet, as the words of God.[64] In short, an 'inspired word' understanding of prophecy formed by an imagined experience of a prophet's receiving an oracle does not actually fit the Bible's own account very well.

The objection might be raised, that the idea of prophecy conveyed by the prophetic book is an artificial one, serving to secure prophetic status for a derived, scribal product. However, we have no way back to the actual experience of the prophet other than through his book. We either accept, with suitable care, the book's claim to have preserved 'the words of Jeremiah', or (with Robert Carroll and others) we give up all claims to knowledge of the historical individual, and construct our idea of prophets and prophecy from a more suspicious reading of biblical data under the control of comparative evidence.[65] As it stands, the book of Jeremiah both connects us to the prophet and sets us at a distance from him. As a scribal product it does not give us the prophet's words with unmediated directness, but instead we receive them through Baruch. Thus if we wish to hold onto a type of literature called 'Prophecy', we cannot characterize it (as Goldingay does) in terms of the experiences and living speech of a prophet, but only in terms of the literary genre which mediates that person to us.[66]

---

[63] E.g. Jer. 49:7–22, most of which corresponds more or less literally to verses elsewhere in Jeremiah and beyond.

[64] Goldingay's illustration of prophetic words not directly from God, namely, the formula 'Thus says the LORD', is unfortunate, for in many cases God does indeed speak the words 'Thus says the LORD', quoting himself in the third person in the process of instructing Jeremiah what to say (Shead 2002b: 32–44). The separation of speech into words directly from God and human words that become 'in some sense part of the word of Yahweh' (Goldingay 1994: 235) is difficult, and the distinction has no bearing on the way the authors of the book of Jeremiah conceive of them.

[65] From a purely generic point of view, 'a definition of prophecy should not *a priori* exclude the literary products that emerged from the scribal interpretations of prophetic words. Rather, these should be considered secondary prolongation of the prophetic communicational process' (Nissinen 2004: 25).

[66] At the outset Goldingay foresees the problem of oversimplifying the complexity of biblical books by reducing them to one or two categories, but believes the benefits of this simplification justify it (1994: 14). However, the consequence of this step – namely, the shift of focus from Scripture to a theoretical precursor of Scripture – can

Thus we might say that from the prophet's viewpoint, or that of an observer, the 'mode of reception' of God's words varies, but from the divine viewpoint God's 'mode of superintendence' of the prophet's subsequent speech does not. It is always *direct*: that is, the words that emerge from the prophet, however he feels them to have been generated, correspond to the words directly placed into him by God; every prophetic discourse is authorized at the level of its words.[67]

What, then, do we mean by speaking of the *book* of Jeremiah as one whose enscripturation follows a 'prophetic paradigm'? We mean that, irrespective of how they came to the prophet, the words given him directly by God were spoken, and then written down, under a divine superintendence by which the words of the book are authorized as the words of God.[68] There remains a difference between prophet and scribe, of course: the words Baruch received came from the prophet's mouth, not directly from God, and – more significantly – God's involvement in Baruch's labours did not come in the person-altering way that secured all Jeremiah's words as words of God. All the same, the identity of Baruch's words with the words of God bespeaks the same degree of divine superintendence over the written words as over the spoken word. In short, when we 'stretch' the prophetic paradigm from the case of the prophet to the case of the prophetic book we lose the immediacy of contact with the divine words as originally given, but we retain the full strength of identification between the written and the spoken words.

From oral to written: recovering a 'prophetic paradigm of inspiration'

To extend a 'Jeremianic' paradigm of enscripturation from the prophetic book to Scripture as a whole means claiming that the

---

be felt in every genre, such as Law, which in its present narrative setting does not perform quite the same legislative function it (presumably) once did.

[67] The language of superintendence and authorization comes from Wolterstorff 1995: 41–42; my point of departure from his treatment concerns the degree of superintendence involved in authorized divine discourse, which, as I argue, operates by definition at the verbal level in prophetic discourse.

[68] Just as the mode of inspiration felt by the prophet as he spoke cannot be fixed, neither can the mode of the scribe's 'inspiration' be fixed. As we saw in our discussion of van der Toorn's work, some sort of divine underwriting or 'concursus' may be inferred as necessary during the writing-down process, but whether the scribe experienced this as a mental and spiritual 'inspiration', or experienced only the toil and strain of writing well and carefully, matters not.

psalmist, the sage and the historian wrote the words of God, either because they wrote as prophets (direct recipients of the word of God) in their own right, or because God moved them, as he moved Baruch, to produce canonical translations of prophetic words. The fact that their words are freely chosen and carefully composed should be no more a problem than it is in the case of Jeremiah (the prophet and the book). The problem lies elsewhere: on what basis can we call their books 'prophetic' by origin (in the case of the author) or genre (in the case of the book)?

Prophetic authors

First of all, how does one justify the claim that every biblical author may be considered a prophet? Most Old Testament books are anonymous. There is little or no direct evidence by which to identify their originators as prophets. Some that are not anonymous (e.g. Proverbs, Daniel, Nehemiah) link themselves to individuals who fall well outside the conventional definition of a prophet. And yet we can trace a growing tendency after the return from exile to identify the sources of canonical writings as prophetic, especially the historical narratives of Joshua to 2 Kings. The Chronicler's way of drawing to a close his account of kings' reigns is a case in point; his interest in prophetic enscripturation of history reveals a conviction that the words written and passed down are the very words of God: 'The remaining events of Solomon, from first to last, are they not written in *The Events of Nathan the Prophet*, and in *The Prophecy of Ahijah the Shilonite*, and in *The Visions of Iddo the Seer concerning Jeroboam son of Nebat*?' (2 Chr. 9:29).[69] Whatever one's opinion of the reliability of the Chronicler's references to prophets as authors of histories,[70] it is clear that the later Jewish understanding of biblical historiography as prophetic literature was already well established in the Persian period. Moreover, the fact that Jews, including Jesus, counted the books of Joshua to Kings in the canonical division of The Prophets is in perfect accord with the nature of these books as literature. It is well recognized today that these histories are theological histories, and that they highlight prophecy and fulfilment as major determinants of Israel's history.[71]

By the New Testament period prophets are recognized as respon-

---

[69] Cf. 1 Chr. 29:29; 2 Chr. 12:15; 13:22; 20:34; 26:22; 32:32.

[70] The options are well canvassed by Sarah Japhet (1993: 19–23).

[71] See e.g. Sternberg 1985: 84–128; Long 1994: 76–87, 107; Firth 2009: 45–48.

sible for all Scripture. So for Paul 'the Scriptures of the prophets' (Rom. 16:26) can describe not just a subset of the Old Testament but all Scripture as prophetic in origin; even when the apostle distinguishes the canonical divisions of Law and Prophets (e.g. Rom. 3:21) he presents both as bearing witness prophetically to the Christ, that is, as prophetic in substance.[72] The examples could be multiplied.[73]

How do we account for this strongly prophetic view of the authors of Scripture? Given that a prophet was understood to be one whose own words were the words of God, I would suggest that it was precisely the apostles' confidence in the words of Scripture that led them to speak of their authors as prophets. It is one's verdict about the words that permits the inference about their author.

What manner of prophetic author is implied by such descriptions? Even though his words were only indirectly the words of God, Baruch the writer is a better model than Jeremiah the speaker, in that he was not a prophet by birth and calling, but rather a man whose written words were, on occasion, divinely secured as prophetic words. Like Baruch, the Old Testament's historians, poets and sages 'scribed' the words of God. Sometimes these words were newly given, as if to a prophet proper; at other times they were 'translations' of words originally given prophetically to others; but in every instance the writer was functioning as an 'occasional prophet' in the same lessened sense as Baruch.[74] As with the notion of written prophecy, the notion of an occasional prophet 'stretches' the Jeremianic idea of the prophet as one called and shaped to be a speaker of the word of God.[75] It is in this 'stretched' sense that we apply a 'prophetic paradigm' to the authors of Scripture, recognizing in them people moved for the occasion by a prophetic impulse to write the words of God.

---

[72] I am indebted to Brian Rosner for his insights on the law as prophecy in Paul's thought. See also Watson (2004: 357): 'For Paul [the Torah] is most fundamentally the divine promise, in which God announces an unconditional saving action, universal in its scope, that lies beyond the horizon of the scriptural writers themselves.'

[73] In a different context Acts 3:21–22 suggests an age of prophecy running from Moses to Jesus in which Moses, the first prophet, spoke of Jesus, the last. See also Acts 28:23; Gal. 3:6–8; Matt. 11:13 ('For all the prophets and the law prophesied until John came'); 2 Pet. 1:20–21; Heb. 1:1.

[74] In contrast to those apocalyptic writings of the late Second Temple period that elevate Baruch to prophetic heights greater even than those occupied by Jeremiah (Barton 1999: 306–308).

[75] Occasional *speakers* of prophecy feature throughout the OT in varying form: compare Num. 22 – 24 with Dan. 9.

257

Prophetic books

It is all very well to recognize in the authors of Scripture a 'prophetic impulse', but in what sense is it meaningful to call the result 'prophecy'? The literary genre Prophecy is a varied one, but in every instance the person of the prophet features to some degree, at least enough to establish that the words of the book derive 'from his mouth' in one way or another, the result of words given him directly by God. This is not the case with other literature. Moses is traditionally credited with the authorship of Genesis, but Genesis itself does not assign him this role; the book is not presented as if from the mouth of anyone. Non-prophetic literature has quite distinct formal characteristics, and it would be wrong to treat History, Wisdom, Psalm, Apocalyptic as if they were somehow variations on a prophetic theme. Each form has its own integrity and force, and cannot be understood if not read by its own conventions of communication.

However, as we have seen, the point at which the genre Prophecy should *not* be distinguished from other writing is the mode of divine superintendence by which it came into being. The 'what' of Prophecy may be unique, containing as it does oracles revealed directly as the word of God to a prophet, but the genre Prophecy has no monopoly on the 'how'. We may say of Narrative or Wisdom, and without undermining their generic particularity, that God superintended their authors just as he did the prophets and their scribes, so that the words they wrote counted as the words of God. And that is tantamount to affirming that all Scripture is prophetic, whatever else it may also be (Law, Narrative, History). That is to say, when the label 'prophecy' is stretched to cover all Scripture it does so as an attribute that qualifies the distinctive nature of each form of biblical writing. Thus biblical History corresponds formally to the history writing of the period, and may be read in keeping with its genre; biblical Wisdom shares the features of international wisdom literature, with which it may fruitfully be compared; yet these biblical genres are unique in that they give us *prophetic* history, *prophetic* wisdom, literature whose words and word are the words and word of God.

The obstacle to this view is obvious: many of the 'words' of which these literatures are constructed are patently not divine words, but secular and even pagan. A historian composes using elements he finds about him: court records, annals, folk histories, personal reports, oral traditions. None of these is prophetic either by origin or genre. His work can be examined against other histories and in the light of archaeological discoveries. Similarly, a sage collects wise sayings from many nations, and a psalmist weaves conventional tropes and line forms into a stirring performance. How do we conceive of these secular words counting as divine words? The solution, as ever, is to recognize that the word determines the words.

Using speech-act categories, some scholars would claim divine authorship for this sort of material by classifying it as 'appropriated discourse'. This is a type of double-agency discourse in which God authorizes a pre-existing human discourse to speak for him, as might a person who commits himself to action by seconding a motion. He may not agree with everything in the motion, but authorizes the motion in general as fairly representing his views.[76] And yet we do not see the words of Baruch appropriated in such a rough and ready fashion. God's involvement with the authorial activity of Baruch is extensive enough that the result is as much 'the words of Jeremiah' as are the oracles spoken by the prophet. To count as prophetic an appropriated discourse must find its way into writing under a degree of divine superintendence that permits the words to count as God's.[77]

There is no reason in my opinion that the same high level of divine appropriation cannot be postulated for the other types of literature I have mentioned. The appropriated elements, whether court records or widely circulating sayings, are equivalent to individual 'words' available to the author, elements of his overall 'word' or message. That final 'word' can be readily conceived of as the product of occasional, prophet-like inspiration, and in the context of that prophetic word, the individual words become the words of God. Just as a Jeremiah borrows each item of his vocabulary from a language whose meanings were culturally determined before he began to speak, and weaves those words together into a discourse whose shape gives the necessary precision to the meanings of its constituent words, so it is with the higher-level elements a historian or sage borrows from the surrounding culture. The prophetic discourse into

---

[76] Wolterstorff 1995: 51–54 (cf. Goldingay 1994: 231–236). Some appropriated discourse is also 'deputized' discourse, in which the speaker is deputized by God to speak in God's name; both types of discourse call for divine inspiration of some sort (Wolterstorff 1995: 186–187).

[77] Of course a distinction in the *mode* of superintendence remains between, say, the directness of 'Stand in the gate of the LORD's house and speak all the words I have commanded you to speak' (Jer. 26:2) and the indirectness of 'I have no command from the LORD, but I give a judgment as one who by the LORD's mercy is trustworthy' (1 Cor. 7:25).

which these 'secular' elements have been taken up serves to 'sanctify' them (as John Webster would say) to act as instruments of God's powerful speech:

> Sanctification refers to the work of the Spirit of Christ through which creaturely realities are elected, shaped and preserved to undertake a role in the economy of salvation: creaturely realities are sanctified by divine use. But it is important to emphasise that the divine 'use', though utterly gratuitous, is not occasional or punctiliar. . . . There is an election and overseeing of the entire historical course of the creaturely reality so that it becomes a creature which may serve the purposes of God.[78]

Finally, we should not exaggerate the scribal nature of the written words of God. Across its genres the Old Testament has a marked oral character, grounded as much as anything in the ubiquity of its direct speeches. For Christof Hardmeier the narrative methods of the Bible work 'as an *orality* that is intentionally *written down* as literarily-conceived orality', so that the Bible is what he calls a 'memorial literature'.[79] The words of God were written down to be spoken once more. A proper understanding of the prophetic nature of the written words allows us to hear the spoken word that issues from these words as a divine word, not merely in general import, but down to the very words of which it is constituted.

Concluding reflections

> In many times and in many ways long ago, God spoke to our fathers by the prophets.
>
> (Heb. 1:1)

The mode of revelation does not make a prophet; much less a prophetic book. It is the unmediated directness of the word of God that comes (by whatever mode), and the way in which that word secures the prophetic spoken words and the prophet-like written words *as words of God* that makes Prophecy prophecy in the first instance, and Scripture prophetic in the second. A Jeremianic model of the

---

[78] Webster 2003: 26.
[79] Hardmeier 2005: 396, italics original.

words written locates their prophet-like nature in the words and their connection to the word, and not – against Goldingay – in the writer's experience of receiving the words.

The so-called 'prophetic paradigm' of verbal inspiration is therefore too narrowly conceived of by both sides of the debate (Barr and Vanhoozer, for instance). Following the example of Jeremiah we ought to see the prophetic paradigm embracing not only dictated oracles – words put into the mouth, so to speak – but also recognize the prophetic origins and nature of narratives, paraphrased sermons, wise sayings, psalms and laments, even legal material and commentary. While this discussion has run beyond the confines of Jeremiah, and its conclusions must therefore be received with a measure of provisionality, the paradigm of Scripture towards which Jeremiah points is in the end a simple one: a book may be recognized as prophetic, its author moved by a prophetic impulse, when the words it contains are recognized to be the words of God. This is certainly the claim prophetic literature makes for itself, and the grounds on which this claim rests are equally available to every type of biblical literature.

This conclusion will raise immediate difficulties in the minds of many theologians, who see great dangers in treating inspiration as a property of words rather than their authors; I shall return to this problem in my next and last chapter.

A note on inerrancy

The 'inerrancy' of Scripture is a term to which a range of definitions has been attached, and the book of Jeremiah can be of no help in deciding the proper meaning of a word it does not use. However, it does cast light on some of the ways in which it is helpful and unhelpful to speak of Scripture as being free from error. Positively, Jeremiah teaches that the word determines the words, and that God preserves his word for future generations. This is enough to secure trust that the words we read will lead us into a right understanding of the word and not mislead us through being in error. By virtue of the fact that they do this, they count as the words of God, and we expect truly to hear the word in them, and may press them closely for meaning. If and when some of the words have been damaged or lost, we may use the word – that is, the larger message – as the rule against which to evaluate the soundness of the words in the task of their recovery. Negatively, one may not begin from the fact that the words of Scripture are the words of God and conclude that they must therefore be perfect in every way. For God uses not only the inescapably imperfect languages of humans, but also larger elements that were not in their genesis the product of inspired men and women. These 'found objects' he assembles into a word by which he himself, in all his truth and perfection, can make himself present. The words are God's words because the word they convey is God's word, not because of their individual properties. What Jeremiah does not tell us is whether the capacity for error that attaches to human words was originally realized in the form of actual error. Of course, this is not to say that the Scriptures are bound to contain mistakes; rather, the doctrine of the word of God – more specifically, the doctrine of Scripture – neither requires nor determines an error-free Scripture. A strong form of inerrancy, such as the belief that no erroneous assertions may be found in Scripture, must find its rationale in the doctrine of God rather than the doctrine of Scripture per se. Fred Zaspel's summary of Warfield is instructive here: 'If Scripture in its every detail is the word of God, *who cannot err*, then by the nature of the case it is and must be entirely trustworthy and reliable in every respect.'[80]

A note on translation

When we say that the words are determined by the word, what do we mean by the 'word', or message? It is not enough to equate the 'word' with the general gist or basic idea of a text; it can be no less than the deep, rich message of the whole, to which every word adds its contribution. Therefore, not just any translated word can be called a word of the original. One decides that an individual translated word is the right word when it sharpens, deepens or enriches the message of the whole. This is not a one-way process, of course, because we need the words in order to see the word and we need the word in order to choose the words. Neither is it a futile process, however, for beyond the message of a chapter (say), is the message of the book, and beyond the message of the book is the single, Christ-shaped message of Scripture, and these larger texts within which the text in question lies nested provide reference points that give us a view of the text (or 'word') from without, as it were. A biblical-theological reading of the text provides us with a triangulation point by which to bring the message of the text into focus without, I believe, preventing it from speaking with its own voice; the words, if we give them the

---

[80] Zaspel 2010: 117, italics added.

hearing due the words of God, retain the power to disturb mistaken impressions of the whole.

In other words, Bible translation as an activity is inescapably hermeneutical. It can never be a simple matter of choosing the English gloss with the largest overlap of semantic domain with its Hebrew (or Greek) counterpart. The only final test of the correctness of a word is its effectiveness, taken with the other words chosen, at reproducing the message of the original. And if the result of reading a translation closely, of pressing its words for meaning, is to bring its message into ever closer correspondence with the message of the original, then our confidence in those words as words of God will strengthen.

Chapter Seven

From the book of Jeremiah to the doctrine of the word of God

We have traced Jeremiah's doctrine of the word of God as it unfolds progressively through the form of a story whose main character is the word of the LORD. We have seen the word of the LORD come to a speaker, and shape him into a person whose words are the words of God, an instrument for the breaking and building of nations. We have seen the hearers successfully resist this all-powerful word, unable to hear it as they ought, until it breaks and scatters them by the agency of Nebuchadnezzar. We have seen the word come into its full power as God makes himself present in transforming forgiveness. What is this word of God? It is God's speech, his active presence in the universe, and as concerns his human creatures, it is the means by which he manifests himself as Creator, Judge and Recreator of all.[1]

However, more yet needs to be said before we have fairly reflected the biblical presentation of this doctrine. To begin with, this divine word must be carried to us through some medium, and the nature of this medium will inevitably illuminate the nature of the word. In my previous chapter we examined the medium of the words of Scripture; arguably, however, the medium of the Spirit is more fundamental in elucidating the nature of the divine word. Finally, and most importantly, the personal nature of the word of the LORD as depicted in Jeremiah (prophet and book) is no flight of fancy, but the adumbration of a Word made flesh, in whom God is present among us with devastating immediacy, a painful and redemptive presence that lays bare the core of the divine nature. How should we relate the Word, the words and Jesus Christ in a Jeremianic doctrine of the word of God?

After touching briefly on the question of word and Spirit in

---

[1] Cf. Poythress (2009: 17–22) on the idea that God makes himself present in his speech generally.

Jeremiah, the bulk of this chapter will be devoted to reflecting on Jeremiah's theology in conversation with Karl Barth.

Words and spirit in Jeremiah

Jeremiah has no theology of the spirit. Except for one use in Jeremiah 51:11 to describe the spirit of humans, Jeremiah uses *rûaḥ* (spirit) only to mean 'wind' or 'breath'.[2] This is not because the book is actively anti-spirit, as some have inferred from the tenuous substance of Jeremiah 5:13.[3] On the contrary, Jeremiah transfers language from the domain of spirit to the domain of words in ways that are not tendentious, but neutral and unmarked. For example, the fluttering beginnings of speech conveyed by the word 'hover' (*rḥp*) in Genesis 1:2 is attached there to the spirit of God, but in Jeremiah 23:9 the prophet's bones 'flutter' (*rḥp*) because of God's 'holy words'.[4]

Rather than a negative determination to exclude spirit, for which there is no real evidence, I conclude that it is Jeremiah's positive choice to pursue a theology of word and words that creates this situation. This is borne out when we examine what might be called 'spirit-shaped absences' in the book's theology: points at which we expect the spirit of the LORD will feature, but where we find other language taking its place.

Our expectations come from reading the other prophets, and especially Jeremiah's near-contemporary, Ezekiel, for whom the spirit has a major role in transforming the people inwardly to make them responsive to the prophet's word (e.g. Ezek. 36:26–27).[5] Jeremiah, in contrast, describes both the message received by the hearer, and the transformative effect of that message, by means of carefully differentiated word language.[6] The obvious place to see this in action is

[2] Wind: 2:24; 4:11; 5:13; 10:13; 13:24; 18:17; 22:22; 49:32; 49:36; 51:1, 16. Breath: 10:14; 14:6; 51:17. It is significant that Deuteronomy is even more sparing in its use of spirit language (as are Leviticus and Joshua); however, Jeremiah's non-usage may be accounted for purely from within.

[3] For a balanced discussion see Robson (2006: 153–156).

[4] Deut. 32:11 is the word's only other occurrence, where it describes an eagle fluttering over its young.

[5] 'What Jeremiah sees as achieved by Yahweh writing the Torah on the hearts of the house of Israel (Jer. 31:33) . . . Ezekiel ascribes to the giving of the divine *rwḥ*' (Robson 2006: 262).

[6] In 2 Cor. 3 Paul blends the prophets' imagery, comparing the ink that wrote the old covenant law on stone tablets to the Spirit writing Christ's letter on tablets that are hearts of flesh. Cf. Peterson 2012: 108–110.

Jeremiah's equivalent account of the regeneration of the hearer, the promise of the new covenant.

The absence of the spirit from Jeremiah 31:31–33 is only the first surprise. Just as unexpected is God's promise in verse 33 to write not 'words' but his *tôrâ* (law) on their heart. Why not 'words', if word is so central to Jeremiah? The answer may be inferred from Jeremiah 26:4–6 (cf. also 6:19; 9:13): 'words' are or were spoken, the exclusive domain of the prophet; but law was written from the first, the domain of the priest (cf. Deut. 17:18; 33:10). Similarly, *tôrâ* in Deuteronomy is always a written entity, whether written by the finger of God or of Moses.[7] Law is expounded, observed, followed; but word is always spoken. As priest is to prophet, so law is to word. Law is relational rather than simply proclamatory; mediated rather than directly received.[8]

By writing law on people's heart, then, God makes not prophets, but priests, permanently inclined to obedience, and permanently enjoying an unmediated relationship with the LORD. In view of this it is all the more remarkable that the word of the LORD can ever be said to exist in written form. But it can, and Scripture by virtue of this fact takes the place of the prophet in the economy of salvation.[9]

We are now in a position to reflect on Jeremiah's 'spirit-shaped absences', and to indicate, with due caution, some implications of his decision to replace spirit with words. Consider the effects of *tôrâ*, written words, on the heart. In Jeremiah's thought it makes one a fundamentally different type of hearer. One no longer experiences the address of God's words as distasteful, but as sweet and

---

[7] 'This law' is explained to mean the written text in Deut. 27:3, 28:58, 30:10, and by inference means the same elsewhere (e.g. 4:44; 34:10). Deut. 1:5 is no exception: 'Moses undertook to explain this law' uses a rare verb linked explicitly to writing in its other two occurrences (Deut. 27:8; Hab. 2:2); the written words gain legal force by being read out (Schaper 2009: 144). Deuteronomy supplies no evidence to support the view (e.g. Schniedewind 2004: 188) that *tôrâ* as 'law' meant oral tradition before the Persian period. On 'the book of the Torah' as a phrase coding for Scripture throughout the OT, see Venema 2004.

[8] In Jeremiah writing is always the writing of scrolls, with just three exceptions, all images of permanence. Two of them bracket Jer. 17:1–13, which depicts people who have internalized an anti-decalogue (v. 1), and who will be 'written in the dirt' (v. 13). The image of writing, related as it does to v. 1, conveys permanence; the image of dirt conveys death.

[9] In the broadest sense of *tôrâ* as instruction, all Scripture might perhaps be said to contain law, but law is not what Scripture *is*. It is a record of God's address by which he makes himself present to a hearer; only incidentally does it function as a book of instruction for faithful covenant living.

life-giving. The more one has, the more one wants, as one's obedient listening results in even greater sensitivity to the words proclaimed. In effect, Jeremiah's theology of words inwardly written does much of the same work that a theology of the Spirit does in traditional accounts of *illumination*. Like the Holy Spirit, these words of *tôrâ* do not sit out in front of a person, but enter in because they have remade him or her into a new creation.

Secondly, if we turn from the new covenant to Jeremiah's commissioning, we find another kind of 'spirit-shaped absence' in the account of God's words put into Jeremiah's mouth at his commissioning (Jer. 1:9). Here the ingested words do much of the same work that a theology of the Spirit does in traditional accounts of *inspiration*.[10] God's words, ingested, become a delight to Jeremiah (15:16), they overcome him physically (23:9) and they emerge from him perforce, like living creatures (20:9).[11]

Of course, unlike the Spirit, and unlike the Word of God in its fullest sense, the words of God are not God, and cannot be said to replace the Holy Spirit in a theology of the word of God.[12] Nevertheless, they do much of the same work, and this will prove significant as we move towards an engagement with Barth. Crucial for this conversation will be my previous observation that the words of God are not simply put into Jeremiah's mouth to emerge as the word of God spoken by Jeremiah, but emerge as the *words* of God spoken. This means that in Jeremiah 36 the written words of Jeremiah could equally be said to be the written words of God, not written in the sense of always-written *tôrâ*, but written in the sense of originally spoken words. That is to say, not only do the words of God in Jeremiah's theology do much of the work the Spirit does in

---

[10] God's filling of Jeremiah with words is not quite so marked a 'spirit-shaped absence' as God's transformation of hearts, because 'inspiration' of the prophet by the spirit of God is only prominent in Ezekiel. Nevertheless, it is present to a sufficient degree in other prophets (Robson 2006: 146–160) to make it a meaningful label here.

[11] The central act of God in Jeremiah – the destroying and recreating of his people – may be identified with the spiritual act of *regeneration*, but while God's word that judges, and his words that reinscribe the heart, are part of the process, regeneration as a whole in Jeremiah proceeds from the prior act of divine forgiveness.

[12] God, his word and his words are not an analogy to be pressed into a trinitarian ontology of speaker, message and speech, even though the idea communicated by breath and by words is similar: both are the medium of the message. Both versions of the speech analogy, though sanctioned perhaps above all other ways of speaking about God's actions in the world, fail utterly to the extent that we conceive of them as impersonal. We do not find a Trinity of Persons anticipated in the book of Jeremiah, though in the prophet's person(a) we have a human embodiment of the words of God.

other formulations, but they provide a point of connection to God from within the written text of Scripture.

To summarize: though an explicit theology of the spirit of the LORD is absent from Jeremiah's thought, it is effectively represented in word language, and more particularly, 'words' language, both words spoken and especially words of God written on the human heart. Despite its limitations, the great strength of Jeremiah's substitution of words for spirit is the light it can throw on our thinking about the relation between Scripture and the Spirit.

The Word, the words and Jesus Christ: Jeremiah in conversation with Karl Barth

As we move from Jeremiah to the doctrine of the Word of God, Karl Barth makes a natural choice of conversation partner, as he arguably excels above all other theologians in the single-mindedness with which he makes the Word of God the organizing centre of his dogmatics. Barth's dogmatic theology is famously unsummarizable, and I shall make no claim to comprehensiveness in the following discussion. Instead, I would like to draw attention to a major stream of thought within Barth's word theology, and reflect on it with the help of Jeremianic categories.

Some salient features of Barth's doctrine of the Word of God

The following aspects of Barth's word theology are especially pertinent to the discussion.

1. The term 'Word of God' is a proper description of three things: Jesus, the Bible and proclamation. But Jesus is the Word of God in a unique way: it is only in Jesus that God is directly present, coming himself and speaking to us. Scripture and proclamation are not God, so they can only be the Word of God in a derivative, though real, way.

2. The Bible is a fully human document whose authors, the prophets and apostles, point to Christ the Word of God as witnesses to divine revelation. However, 'what we hear in the human expression is more than a human expression. What we hear is revelation, and therefore the very Word of God.'[13]

3. Barth explains how the Bible can be called the Word of God

---

[13] *CD* I/2: 473.

by drawing an analogy with the way Jesus is God and man: his two natures are not mingled up, but held together. The Bible is fully human, error-prone, a child of its times, 'but it speaks to us miraculously as the Word of God'. Again, '[Scripture] too can and must – not as though it were Jesus Christ, but in the same serious sense as Jesus Christ – be called the Word of God'.[14] Barth will not permit the thought of some sort of a lesser Word of God inhering in the Bible, as if there was some other Word of God in addition to Jesus. So it follows that the identification of the Bible as the Word of God cannot be a simple identification: it must be a way of speaking about the living presence of Christ in Scripture.

4. It follows from this that when God graciously works in us by his Spirit to create faith,[15] we find that the Bible speaks to us as the Word of God. The presence of the Word of God is not a physical attribute of the Bible itself, but God uses this human witness as his chosen instrument to make the Word of God, that is, Jesus, present to us. This is the sense in which Barth speaks of the Bible's *becoming* the Word of God, and it is in this sense of becoming, of event, that the Bible *is* the Word of God.

5. The role of the Spirit is crucial at every point of this process, and Barth speaks of inspiration as a circle that runs from the inspiration of the author through the verbal inspiration of the biblical witness to the reader, who must be enabled by the Spirit to receive that witness as the Word of God. For Scripture does not have inspiration as a natural property open to examination by all, but inspiration is something that attaches to the Word of God, and this means that the activities of the Spirit traditionally distinguished by the terms *inspiration* and *illumination* are properly to be seen as facets of the single activity of the Spirit of Jesus by which he makes the Word of God known at each stage of its journey from speaker to hearer.[16]

> In the statement that 'the Bible is the Word of God' we cannot suddenly mean a lesser, less potent, less ineffable and majestic word of God, than that which has occupied us in the doctrine of the Trinity and in the doctrine of Christ and of the Holy Spirit. There is only one Word of God and that is the eternal Word of the Father which for our reconciliation

[14] Ibid. 500.
[15] Ibid. 512.
[16] Ibid. 516–518.

became flesh like us and has now returned to the Father, to be present to His Church by the Holy Spirit. In Holy Scripture, too, in the human word of his witnesses, it is a matter of this Word and its presence.[17]

Barth's Jeremianic doctrine of the Word of God

The 'Word of God' does not primarily describe the Bible

An attentive reader will have noticed some immediate points of contact, positive and negative, with Jeremiah's word theology. First, Jeremiah speaks of Scripture as the 'words of the LORD', and the term 'word of the LORD' is reserved for their import, or message, as heard by a receptive listener. This is not to say that the church has been in error over the centuries it has been calling Scripture the Word of God. Terms such as 'revelation', for example, are used productively within theology in a manner quite distinct from their biblical usage. There is much to be gained from a systematic theology that organizes its doctrine of Scripture around the designation 'Word of God'. However, the Jeremianic designation 'words of God' provides us with a complementary organizing centre that not only has some powerful explanatory and clarifying features, but implies a theology in which the idea of the word (or words) of God arguably does (or do) more work than in any alternate systematization.

The Word of God is dynamic

Secondly – and this is to be expected given my reasons for choosing Barth – when Jeremiah *does* speak about the word of the LORD (singular), he speaks about it in ways that find strong echoes in Barth's language of event and becoming. One can imagine Jeremiah nodding when Barth says, 'we cannot regard the presence of God's Word in the Bible as an attribute inhering once and for all in this book as such. . . . Of the book as we have it, we can only say: We recollect that we have heard in this book the Word of God.'[18] Or again, 'The statement that the Bible is God's Word is a confession of faith, a statement of the faith which hears God himself speak through the biblical word of man.'[19] This dynamic word theology, in which the words of Scripture are heard as the Word of God by those whom God has made able to hear them, is completely Jeremianic.

---

[17] Ibid. 512–513.
[18] Ibid. 530.
[19] *CD* I/1: 110.

It is worth remembering that Jeremiah and Barth are not a club of two. This dynamic way of speaking can be found in many theologians;[20] however, it does not characterize their approach to the extent that it does Barth's, whose understanding of the way God speaks in Scripture is so entirely dominated by his conviction that the Word of God is Jesus, a conviction out of which his 'eventism' grows (to borrow a term from Wolterstorff 1995: 71).

The Word of God is Christ

One of the great strengths of this dynamic conception of the Word of God is that it allows us to hold to the tenet that there is only one Word of God, which is Christ – a tenet that is consistent with the argument I advanced in chapter 5 that all speech of God is the same speech. It also finds echoes in Jeremiah's depiction of the word of the LORD as a powerful destructive and creative force.

Moreover, Barth's word theology does justice to the Jeremianic picture of the divine word that emerged in chapter 3, in which God makes himself present to us under the form of (spoken) words. Now a point of difference might seem to arise here, in that the word of the LORD in Jeremiah is obviously not Jesus himself. Yet as the citation that concluded my précis of Barth's word theology makes clear, it is not a matter of Jesus' bodily presence in Barth, either, but Jesus present by his Holy Spirit. And so it is in a real sense for Jeremiah: the Word of God that comes to me as a receptive hearer of Jeremiah's words is the person of Jesus under the form of words. As the New Testament puts it, the prophets spoke of 'the things that have now been announced to you' (1 Pet. 1:12).

The real point of difference between Jeremiah and Barth does not concern Barth's idea of what the Word of God is, but rather his idea of how this Word of God is related to Scripture.

---

[20] A few examples must suffice. Athanasius: the spreading *kerygma*, whose source is Scripture, is 'the *logos* himself, sojourning here by his teaching' (cited in Work 2002: 43). Calvin: the word of God is 'the hand of God stretching itself out to act powerfully through the apostle in every way', as a 'violent force' that 'urges us . . . to give obedience to it' (Commentary on 1 Corinthians, cited in Bloesch 1994: 49). Bonhoeffer: in the word of Scripture there is a 'making present' of Christ in a direct way (Webster 2003: 80–82). Vanhoozer (using speech-act categories): 'While Christ is a fully human and fully divine agent, all we are claiming for Scripture is that it is a fully human and fully divine *act*' (Vanhoozer 2002: 153, italics original).

Jeremiah's un-Barthian doctrine of the words of God

Under a slightly mischievous heading, I wish to subject five tenets of Barth's doctrine of Scripture to a Jeremianic examination. To each of these 'moot points' I believe Jeremiah would offer a Barthian *Nein*!

That the prophets bear witness to divine revelation, like modern preachers

Barth's description of the activity of prophets as bearing witness to divine revelation does not do them justice. While he readily speaks of prophets repeating 'in human words what has first been said by Yahweh Himself',[21] he will never allow divine words to cross over into the domain of human language, as they appear to do in the case of Baruch's reading the words of the LORD from the scroll. There is no difference for Barth in the way in which the words of a modern preacher and an ancient prophet represent God's Word – they are human words with God's commission behind them, which are endorsed by God, which God freely uses to draw near to us in person. Yes, the prophet is unique, but only because of his unique encounter with the Word, not because of the language he uses to describe that encounter to us.[22]

> In this event [i.e. of recollection, discovery, faith and the self-imposing of the Bible] the Bible is God's Word. That is to say, in this event the human prophetic and apostolic word is a representative of God's Word in the same way as the word of the modern preacher is to be in the event of real proclamation: a human word which has God's commission to us behind it, a human word to which God has given Himself as object, a human word which is recognized and accepted by God as good, a human word in which God's own address to us is an event.[23]

---

[21] *CD* I/2: 490.
[22] Cf. *CD* I/1: 102. For Barth the prophets are unique in the sense that they alone proclaim revelation as they encountered it: 'We are reminded that everywhere the Old Testament claims to speak with authority, because it repeats in human words what has first been said by Yahweh Himself. Not every man can do this. Not every man can speak God's Word. For not every man has heard it. But those who have heard it can and must repeat it' (*CD* I/2: 490–491).
[23] *CD* I/1: 109.

To this, Jeremiah replies, 'No.' As we have seen, Jeremiah makes the closest possible identification of the prophet's words with God's words. Not only does the word of the LORD, that is, the message from God in which we encounter him, come to the prophet, but the human words of which that word is constituted are given to the prophet by God, who directly constrains and controls him (Jer. 1:4–19). I shall develop this idea in the following sections.[24]

That Scripture's 'double nature' is a holding together of the (human) words of Jeremiah and the (divine) Word of God

For Barth, just as the humanity of the incarnate Christ was not mingled with his divine nature but coexisted with it, so Scripture in its humanity consists entirely of fallible human testimony to divine revelation, and contains no divine words, but by an act of God's free grace it is heard by us as the Word of God without ceasing to be human words. 'Therefore the miracle which has to take place if the Bible is to rise up and speak to us as the Word of God has always to consist in an awakening and strengthening of our faith.'[25]

> Again it is quite impossible that there should be a direct identity between *the human word of Holy Scripture* and *the Word of God*, and therefore between the creaturely reality in itself and as such and the reality of God the Creator. It is impossible that there should have been a transmutation of the one into the other or an admixture of the one with the other. This is not the case even in the person of Christ where the identity between God and man, in all the originality and indissolubility in which it confronts us, is an assumed identity, one especially willed, created and effected by God. . . . When we necessarily allow for inherent differences, it is exactly the same with the unity of the divine and the human word in Holy Scripture.[26]

---

[24] Members of Christ's kingdom are greater than prophets by virtue of the fact that what they bear witness to is the Word made flesh (Luke 7:24–28); but while the contents of prophetic speech reveal God's word less clearly, prophetic (and apostolic) speech is unique in the directness by which it is determined at the level of its words by the divine speaker himself. The prophets, therefore, stand as counter-examples to Barth's categorization of all (enscripturated) human speech about God as testimony. All the more must Barth be questioned, then, over his assertion that prophets are not deputies, but purely witnesses (Wolterstorff 1995: 68).

[25] *CD* I/2: 512.

[26] *CD* I/1: 499, italics added.

Jeremiah's first point of departure from this statement is not the indirect nature of the identity Barth proposes, but the nature of the two things (italicized) Barth compares. Although Barth seems to be comparing equivalent entities, word and Word, in fact one is written and the other is spoken (or communicated, or living). In Jeremianic terms we would say that Barth has created a doctrine of Scripture whose double nature holds together not 'word' (singular, human) and 'Word' (singular, divine) but 'the words of Jeremiah' and 'the word of the LORD'. The point of connection for Barth, as we shall see, is the illuminating work of the Holy Spirit, who both inspires the authors to write and the audience to hear those writings as the Word of God.

What is quickly apparent is that Barth has no slot in his theology for the *words* of God (pl.).

By contrast, the Jeremianic doctrine of Scripture gives a double nature to the words of Jeremiah and the words of God, both written. And when we compare these entities, we find that we can indeed speak in a meaningful way of a direct identity between them. The identity between the two sets of words (pl.) belongs to a series of similar identities through which the words of God are preserved to be spoken aloud when Scripture is read. For instance, the prominence given to the role of dictation in chapter 36 was paradigmatic, not for the method of composition of the book, but for the level of Jeremianic authorship the reader is expected to see in and behind words written by his scribe, whether those words were dictated by the prophet or freely composed. By extension – and here is the most basic identity – we are expected to see a commensurate degree of divine involvement in the words Jeremiah chooses to speak in God's name. The nature of this identity is well illustrated by Jeremiah 37:2 and 43:1, which bring the words of God and the words of Jeremiah together in a manner that does not find a comfortable home in the first volume of Barth's *Dogmatics*:

> But neither he nor his servants nor the people of the land heard the words of the LORD that he had spoken by the agency of [*bĕyad*] Jeremiah the prophet. (Jer. 37:2)

> Jeremiah finished speaking to all the people all the words of the LORD their God, all these words with which the LORD their God had sent him to them. (Jer. 43:1)

Here is a holding together, with uncomfortable directness, of the words of Jeremiah – once spoken, now written – and the words of God – once spoken, now written.

We are now ready to construct a Jeremianic version of Barth's threefold taxonomy of the Word. The first form of the Word of God we encounter is proclamation, the message of Jeremiah by which God makes himself present to his people. The second and derivative form is Scripture, properly speaking the words of God by which the spoken Word is preserved for subsequent speaking and hearing.[27] The ultimate form (faintly adumbrated in Jeremiah through the person of the prophet) is Jesus Christ, the Word become flesh, in whom God is directly manifest. Each of these has in its own way a double nature, and we must now, under our next 'moot point', reflect on the nature of the 'direct identity' of the human and divine in the written words themselves. This will lead us to reconsider Barth's Christological argument, until now ignored, as we work towards a 'Jeremianic' way of speaking of the Word of God. Only then will we be ready to think about the 'indirect identity' Barth actually proposes, namely, that of Scripture and the Word of God.

That human language is an unfit vehicle for the Word of God
1. *The human and divine words.* Barth insists that the form of human words 'is an unsuitable medium for God's self-presentation. It does not correspond to the matter but contradicts it.' He continues:

> The form of God's Word, then, is in fact the form of the cosmos which stands in contradiction to God. It has as little ability to reveal God to us as we have to see God in it. If God's Word is revealed in it, it is revealed 'through it', of course, but in such a way that this 'through it' means 'in spite of it'. The secularity proper to God's Word is not in itself and as such transparent or capable of being the translucent garment or mirror of God's Word.[28]

This is evidently true in the sense that the creation, including both language and the human mind, is fallen and sinful, and Barth rightly rejects the idea that there could be anything more perfect about the

---

[27] So that while Scripture initially derives from proclamation, ultimately it generates it.
[28] *CD* I/1: 166.

language of Scripture than there is about the fallen, flawed linguistic systems of human culture.[29] (Indeed, if the words of Scripture were perfect they would be untranslatable, like the Qur'an.) Even the created form of the human Jesus of Nazareth was not, in and of itself, the revealing Word of God.[30]

Yet this is where the concept of Scripture as the words of God comes into its own. For the words of God are demonstrably not divine, and their (notional) distinction from the words of Jeremiah lies not in their ontology, but in their origin. Yet when we claim as an attribute of the text that it is in substance the words of God, while we have not thereby divinized the text,[31] we have made an ontological claim in respect of it. Our claim is that it is by these words in particular that God makes himself present to us.

This is perhaps the heart of Barth's departure from Jeremiah's word theology, namely, Jeremiah's conception of human forms by which the word of God comes to the hearers as being produced under a direct divine supervision that is unique to Jeremiah, and that qualifies his words as the words of God. They are not *divine* words in the sense of being other than human in form, and not even *unique* words in the sense that translating them into another language, for example, would render them no longer the words of God, but rather the *particular* words chosen by God to convey the word of God to their hearers.[32] It is as though God makes his selection from Jeremiah's vocabulary, from Baruch's compositions, from the words of the people, and gives those flawed human words to Jeremiah to speak, or perhaps to write by Baruch's hand, so that the words of

---

[29] B. B. Warfield's treatment is open to misinterpretation at this point: though Scripture is human 'in form and quality', 'the confluent operation of the Holy Spirit throughout the whole process *raises the result above what could by any possibility be achieved by mere human powers* and constitutes it expressly a supernatural product' (Warfield 1948: 95, italics added).

[30] *CD* I/1: 323. As Barth points out elsewhere, were we to imagine Christ's human nature being divinized, then 'does not a deified human essence cease to be our human essence, usable as such for the work of the Son of God for us and to us, and accessible and recognisable to us as such?' (*CD* IV/2: 89).

[31] I have chosen the term 'divinized' in reference to warnings by Barth scholars that the consequence of claiming that human words may bear the Word of God is an (unintentional) 'divinizing' of the text (so e.g. Webster 2003: 23; McCormack 2004: 68). However, these warnings are very much tied to the equating of written human words and living divine Word, an equation I have argued we must avoid; therefore I have set them to one side.

[32] The word, or message, that these words convey is all-important in this formulation, for it and it alone determines the extent to which substitute words, such as those in a translation, can be properly described as the words of God.

Jeremiah are indeed God's words, through which God speaks in the created language 'Human', and through which, by a mystery of divine agency, he graciously makes himself present as Word. By virtue of their success at presenting God to us these human words can truly be said to be God's words.[33]

There is a significant correspondence between the ordering power of the words in Jeremiah's theology, in which the text has its being, and the work of the Spirit in Webster's account of Scripture: 'In its ordering by the Spirit's sanctifying work the text has its being; its ontology is defined out of the formative economy of the Spirit of God.'[34]

2. *Analogies from Christology*. For Barth, Christology provides a powerful analogy for his argument: if Christ's divine nature does not in the least dilute or compromise his human nature, how could we begin to imagine that the divine Word of God would detract from the humanity of a Scripture where there is no union of persons involved at all? However, as I have argued, Barth's decision to ask how the Word of God relates to the 'human word' of Scripture is misconceived, because it does not take the double nature of the written words into account. And when the question is suitably reframed, Barth's Christological argument loses its force.

Instead, another aspect of Christology becomes relevant, namely, that while the two natures of Christ are not mixed, yet at the same time the divine nature is truly, actually present in the person of the man Jesus (cf. John 1:14; 14:9). The divine can be revealed from within finitude. The Word of God to us is not Christ in his divinity, the divine *Logos* contained within the human body, but the Word incarnate; it is the Word made flesh that is 'the radiance of God's glory, the exact representation of his being' (Heb. 1:3).[35] 'All of

---

[33] Cf. Ebeling's argument that human language is a gift from God designed to enable the Word of God to be made present in human word-events (Ebeling 1967); on the reception of these ideas in Pannenberg's thought see Biddy 2005.

[34] Webster 2003: 28.

[35] On the fundamental question of what Barth means by 'Jesus Christ' we find mixed signals. Alan Spence argues that Barth conceives of Jesus Christ the Word of God as a divine event, the crucified and risen LORD of the church's proclamation, through which God speaks to us (Spence 2008: 132–133). For Spence this contradicts the classical view in which Jesus is unique because of his *person* rather than the nature of his revelatory action. However, Spence goes too far when he suggests that for Barth 'the word of God constitutes the divinity of the man Jesus' (133); Spence may at this point have identified the Word of God and 'revelation' more closely than Barth does. Henri Blocher provides a useful corrective, reminding us that the Jesus Christ on whom Barth concentrates is 'God the Son *and identically* the man Jesus of Nazareth'.

Christ's activities are thus the actions of the person or hypostasis of the incarnate Christ.'[36]

3. *The human and divine Word.* We feel the force of this Christological analogy in the first instance when considering the double nature of the word of God in Jeremiah's theology. Let us take a step back for a moment. In what identity does the word (sg., spoken) participate for Jeremiah? One might expect that 'the word of the LORD', the message by which God makes himself present, should be identified in some way with 'the word of Jeremiah', the prophet's living speech. And yet, while 'the words of Jeremiah' are mentioned occasionally, referring to written or otherwise abstracted words,[37] 'the word of Jeremiah' never is. Either his speech is heard as the word of the LORD or, if rejected, remains the words of the LORD, unassimilated in the listener's consciousness. Given that the message heard is clearly coming from human lips in human words we may attribute to it a double nature, but if this be so, 'the word of the LORD' does not refer to the divine part of this nature, but to the totality of the communication by which God makes himself present to a hearer.

Taken by themselves, the individual words mean almost nothing; taken together, they combine into a word, a message; when read or spoken, that message becomes what we might call a 'discourse' and communicates meaning.[38] So the words of God taken up on the lips of Jeremiah, and embodied in his person or persona, add up to a message which amounts to an act of divine self-disclosure. God does not reside magically in the inked letters, like a genie in a bottle, but truly manifests himself from within the message they convey by means of the human speaker. We cannot isolate the word of God (divine) by removing the word of Jeremiah (human); as with the

---

The idea that Jesus is eternally pre-existent in his divine nature only, as the *Logos* not yet incarnate (the so-called *Logos asarkos*) is 'deeply distasteful' to Barth even though 'at times, he seems to endorse it' (Blocher 2008: 29).

[36] Spence (2008: 59), summarizing the Chalcedonian Christology of John of Damascus. Against this Barth's argument, as distilled by Bruce McCormack, appears unhelpful: 'If it would be wrong to say of the humanity of Jesus Christ that it is, as such, the *direct* revelation of God . . . then how can we say this of Scripture?' (McCormack 2004: 63, italics original). The humanity of Jesus Christ is never 'as such'.

[37] Jer. 1:1, 36:10 and 51:64 refer to written words; Jer. 26:20 refers to another prophet's speaking words like those of Jeremiah.

[38] See especially Vanhoozer (2002: 127–203), who also uses the term 'embodiment' to characterize the spoken word, both in the form of Christ and of the church (e.g. 158).

incarnate Word, it is the latter in which and by which the former is manifest. As with the divine and human words (pl.), there is a miracle of divine agency by which the human word addresses us as the Word of God.

The final form of the Word, Jesus Christ himself, has been a point of comparison all along. Considered in his own right, what more must one say of him that has not already been said of the prophet Jeremiah?[39] God does not use the human Jesus as a channel through which to be present among us, but himself inhabits Jesus' humanity so that it is taken up without diminution into the Godhead, a full 'hypostasis'. Here, of course, there is no question of an analogy; rather, as we have seen, the self-emptying, or 'kenosis', by which God becomes human in Christ finds an echo in the lesser self-manifestations of proclaimed Word and enscripturated words.[40]

To conclude: as with the double nature of the words, human and divine, so it is with the double nature of the spoken Word. The same mystery of divine agency attaches to both identities: the *words* of Jeremiah are instruments of God's speech, the causal joint of that instrumentality hidden from us, but nevertheless real; those words are set apart from all others by virtue of the use to which God puts them. The same applies to the *word*, or self-presentation, of Jeremiah and of God. One is the instrument by which the other manifests himself. In the case of the incarnate Word himself, if we may reverse the direction of our analogy for a moment we might say that just as the written words are the medium of the spoken message, so the body of Christ – not only its component cells and organs, but its tastes, dispositions, personality traits – is the medium of the incarnate Word. Though his body is fully human, it is the particular body chosen by God to depict, express and communicate his eternal, uncreated Word, God the Son. Might another body have done? Yes, but not any other: it had to be the right one for expressing one particular Word and that Word alone. Is the form of human words 'an

[39] Barth gives a false impression when he states, 'If [Jesus] reveals God, then irrespective of His creaturehood, He Himself has to be God' (*CD* I/1: 406), for the prophets can equally reveal God without being divine. 'The relation of the Son to the Father determines the status of the revelation rather than the other way round' (Spence 2008: 137).

[40] 'In Jesus Christ the word of man was the Word of God. If (*mutatis mutandis*) this is analogically applied to Scripture, then Scripture as "servant" must be reckoned as having the same "kenotic" function, but at the next "lower" interactive level' (Morrison 2006: 237; cf. Work 2002: 61–66).

unsuitable medium for God's self-presentation', as Barth claimed? Perhaps it is, but then so was a human body.

This brings us, at last, to the relationship of Scripture and the Word of God, which I shall address through a fourth 'moot point'.

That a hearer's faith is required before Scripture can be the Word of God to him or her

I have argued that Barth creates a straw man when he imagines binding the Word of God so tightly to the written words of the text that the text is 'divinized'. It is obvious to one and all that the human words are not God's presence in and of themselves; they are the vehicles by which God makes himself present as Word. The real problem lies not with what Barth denies, but what he fails to affirm. The human words of Scripture may be, must be, directly identified with the *words* of God.

However, this still begs the question of how the written words may be called the Word of God. Barth's solution, and it is a worthy one, is to identify its *being* as Scripture with its *becoming* the Word of God in the hearts of Spirit-filled hearers.[41] The starting point is revelation, an event by which God makes himself known in the person of Christ. This event takes place in the believer to whom God discloses himself, which he does by means of the Bible. And so when God chooses to grant faith, the Bible becomes the Word of God to that believer, but – and this is crucial – it is only becoming what it already is, namely, the Word of God by God's eternal decision. Why must being be in becoming? Because if it is not, if things are what they are simply as substances and not out of prior and ongoing decisions and acts, then the incarnation would introduce a basic change into the being of God, undermining divine immutability.[42]

Where Barth remains elusive in this dynamic picture of Being is over the question of its occasionalism. Does God always choose that Scripture become the Word of God in this way? Barth will not exclude the possibility of a positive answer;[43] a Jeremianic theology

---

[41] McCormack 2004: 63–67.

[42] *CD* IV/2: 84–89; cf. McCormack 2004: 74.

[43] For McCormack Barth teaches the negative as well as the positive: 'when and where the Bible does *not* become the Word of God, there God has chosen provisionally, for the time being, not to bear witness to himself in and through its witness *to this particular reader*' (McCormack 2004: 66, italics original). And yet in his section on Scripture as the Word of God (esp. *CD* I/2: 495–537), Barth appears to take pains not to assert the negative. His summation (534) is typical: 'Certainly it is not our faith which makes the Bible the Word of God. But we cannot safeguard the objectivity of

is bolder still, being confident that Scripture never fails to become what it is; however, in strong contrast to Barth, Jeremiah allows that in the case of a deaf listener, in whom God does not work the miracle of faith, the words of God become the Word of God in judgment. A listener's determination that Scripture not be the Word of God has no bearing whatever on its becoming. Scripture becomes the Word of God to us whether we like it or not, whether we even realize it. Jeremiah has no doctrine of the ineffectual word, and by extension there will be no occasion for us to speak of Scripture as a book that is not the Word of God absolutely and without further qualification, for God always freely chooses that it should become and be the Word of God, whether in salvation or in judgment.[44]

This conclusion about the Word of God is difficult to square with the idea that revelation is the act by which God makes himself known as person. How can the Word of God be the Word of God to someone without resulting in the hearer knowing God? For Jeremiah the Word of God can bear down in judgment on a person's life by working in the world at large in fulfilment of God's promise to judge, while revealing nothing of God to the deaf listener; and though the judged may initially be blind to the presence of God in his Word, all will be revealed on the last day.[45] That the promise of Scripture, proclaimed and ignored, might 'become' the Word of God to someone not in hope but in condemnation raises further difficulties, of which Jeremiah is acutely aware (as we saw in chapter 4; cf. Jer. 25:3), but they do not alter the basic truth that the Word of God never falls short of becoming what it is.

And what is it? It is the Word of God, depicted, expressed and communicated by means of the words of God. These words, like the humanity of Jesus Christ, are not a rind to be peeled away in order to taste the fruits of divine revelation within, but are themselves

---

the truth that it is the Word of God better than by insisting that it does demand our faith. . . . For in doing so we maintain that it is the truth of the living God, beyond which there is none other, the power of which we are not allowed to doubt in face of the forces of human subjectivity.'

[44] Cf. D. A. Carson in his critique of Webster: 'whatever the written thing is, it remains that, *even if people ignore it . . . and receive none of God's self-presencing by this means*' (Carson 2010: 247, italics original).

[45] A theme of Jer. 42 – 44 (cf. 42:19; 44:28), but far more prominent in Ezekiel. See also Phil. 2:10–11; Col. 1:20. This aspect of the Word's activity is picked up strongly by Pannenberg (1969: 153–155), though arguably without a sufficiently strong emphasis on the identity of the Word and Christ. Barth himself correctly rejects the idea that the Word is like an impersonal force (*CD* I/1: 110–111).

the stuff of revelation, things created, selected and used by God in a miracle of self-disclosure. By identifying Scripture with the words of God rather than with the Word of God we no longer need to conceive of the dynamic 'event of revelation' transforming 'human words of Scripture into something they otherwise are not'.[46]

That the Spirit's inspiring activity must be attached only to the Word

We have already seen this feature of Barth's doctrine, to which Jeremiah replies with a final 'No'. Barth's concern, rightly, is that the text not be treated as an inspired object and so be separated off from the inspiring God. This happens, he believes, when the doctrine of inspiration is detached from the whole 'circle' of inspiration (running from the initial revelation to the apostle, to the verbal inspiration of the text, to the spiritual opening of a hearer's ears) and concentrated in and limited to one point in that circle: 'namely, to the work of the Spirit in the emergence of the spoken or written prophetic and apostolic word as such'.[47] The result is a degrading of verbal inspiration to verbal inspiredness: 'the inspiration of the biblical witnesses ... can and must be regarded quite definitely not merely as real but as verbal inspiration. But the question is whether it has not been taken out of the circle and regarded as verbal-inspiredness.'[48]

Here, again, the Jeremianic depiction of Scripture as the words of God provides a valuable corrective. For we can conceive of the words of Scripture as God's words, brought into being through the direct operation of the Spirit, having the quality of being God's words in and of themselves, but without thereby making the Word of God a fixed property of the text open to the scrutiny of any and every reader. Indeed, the 'circle' of the Spirit's activity cannot be separated at any point from a corresponding 'circle' of the words (pl.).[49] The same words that come from God to fill the prophet also

---

[46] Thompson 2008: 190.

[47] *CD* I/2: 517.

[48] Ibid. 518. Barth goes on to argue that in many post-Reformation writers this narrowing down of the doctrine has led to the divinity of the Bible being referred to 'without those backward and forward relationships', and the inner testimony of the Spirit is 'separated from the living witness of the Spirit in Scripture' (ibid. 523). Webster agrees, stating that this view of inspiration makes the biblical text 'a revelatory agent by virtue of an act of divine inspiration in the past' (Webster 2003: 36).

[49] McCormack (2004: 62), in his opposing of B. B. Warfield (for whom it is claimed Scripture completes revelation) and Barth (for whom apparently it is the Spirit's work in the hearer that does this) creates a false dichotomy.

fill the parchment in written form, and when they are proclaimed God writes them on the hearts of hearers so that they hear the Word of God.

Ultimately, a Jeremianic word theology allows us to recover illumination and inspiration as two distinct activities of the Spirit without losing the dynamic and personal depiction of the Word of God that Jeremiah (and Barth) makes so much of. As I suggested in my section on words and Spirit, we can speak of the coming of words to Jeremiah and the coming of words to hearers in distinct ways. God puts (*nātattî*) his spoken words into Jeremiah's mouth, an activity that in another theological system would find a close parallel in the act of inspiration. And by emerging from Jeremiah's mouth as the words of God spoken and then the words of God written, they justify the attaching of inspiration to the written text, and they do this without making God an 'attribute' of the Bible.[50] In a quite separate act, however, God puts (*nātattî*) his always-written *tôrâ* onto the heart of the new Israel, an act that lends itself to language of illumination when reframed in terms of the Spirit's activity.

The words are not divine, while the Spirit of course is. But like the Spirit the words come from God, and like the Spirit they point beyond themselves as the instruments of God's self-manifestation in the form of his Word.

In conclusion

While God as Trinity is compatible with Jeremiah's theology, Jeremiah provides us with perhaps the most striking account we have of the unity that characterizes the actions of the three-personed God in the economy of salvation. Though the LORD is the source of all the words in the book of Jeremiah, it is his word that is the book's focus, and for the book's reader the LORD is actually the product of his word.

More narrowly, the ontology of the book of Jeremiah as simultaneously the words of Jeremiah and the words of God sets the text itself as a location of God's activity. It *can* be said to have an inspiredness attaching to it, and yet without either divinizing the text or locating its power to judge and transform the hearers anywhere other than in God's free decision to make himself present as Word through those divine and human words.

In short, the uncompromising use of word as an organizing centre

---

[50] Cf. Barth, *CD* I/2: 513.

for Jeremiah's theology sharpens the double nature of Scripture so that it succeeds at the point where Barth was not always clear – in upholding the Word of God as never anything less than God himself made present among us, without as a result denying to Scripture its unique nature as the very words of God.

Theologies of the words and word of God

All theologies of Scripture face the same challenge: how can one account for the humanity and the divinity of this unique text in a manner that is faithful to the God who has revealed himself by it? As we reflect on the way in which Jeremiah tackles this problem through a careful identifying and distinguishing of word and words, it is worth reminding ourselves that this is not the only fruitful way of going about it. To pick just one recent example, Webster tackles the same problem by a careful analysis of the relationship between Word and Spirit. He is happy to describe Scripture both in terms of its form, the words, and its matter, the Word, both of which are inspired by the activity of the Spirit. What makes Scripture, conceived of as the Word of God, into something that acts dynamically to reveal and save is the work of the Spirit of Christ, through which the Word of God, or Scripture, becomes a field of the Spirit's activity.[51]

Webster's doctrine of Scripture is satisfyingly trinitarian, and it has considerable explanatory power when it comes to accounting for the active presence of God not only in the text as a finished product but also in and through the human processes by which the text was produced, transmitted, canonized and interpreted.

In contrast, Jeremiah's doctrine of the word of God, from which the Spirit is notably absent, might be thought to be asking the category of word and words to do too much, occupying slots that would be more adequately filled by a doctrine of the Spirit. And yet we must respect Jeremiah's non-use of spirit language as a deliberate choice; the advantages of his exclusive word-theology have, I hope, been adequately demonstrated. His position in salvation history obviously excludes a full-blown trinitarian theology, and yet if his book is read as Christian Scripture, a consonance with Christian theology is evident that does no violence to the text's own particular genius.

Turning from theologies of Scripture to the broader doctrine

[51] Webster 2003.

of the Word of God, it is therefore only to be expected that the framework I have constructed from Jeremiah, of speech (divine and human), speaker and hearers, together with the associated questions of power and permanence, finds analogues wherever the act of speaking, or the event of revelation, is used as an organizing principle for doing Christian theology. Examples are as varied as Christoph Schwöbel, who depicts revelation as a process embracing a triune God speaking in the Christ event to disclose himself by the Spirit to recipients with the result that they come to faith;[52] Kevin Vanhoozer, for whom God's self-communicative speech and action, climaxing in the Christ event, draw forth corresponding words and deeds from the church they create, with doctrine, like a stage director, having the task of guiding the church into wise participation in the ongoing drama of redemption;[53] and David Cunningham, who conceives of theology as rhetoric by which a *speaker* engages an *audience* with persuasive *arguments*, these three elements working 'in concert' to move people to embrace a God who cannot be grasped by mere words and logic.[54] All of these schemes share the conviction that doctrine, if it would be faithful to the nature of the God it serves, can never be reduced to statements of fact and abstract ideas, but must always seek to draw persons into a world of speech events by which God reveals himself, addresses us as LORD, and draws us by his Word into an eternal communion of knowing and being.

Jeremiah's doctrine of the Word of God

Jeremiah's model for word theology, organized around the concrete situation of speech events, has a certain inevitability to it, and as we have just seen, lends itself to fruitful elaboration in today's church. And yet his theology, emerging as it does from a complex narrative, has qualities very hard to replicate in the more deliberate and systematic studies of theologians proper. In Patrick Miller's words, we might call this 'theology nourished from below', which he suggests will, compared with conventional formulations, be *concrete*, undercutting the abstractness of much talk about God; *imaginative*, maintaining the mystery of God through the indirectness of poetic speech; and *realistic*, corresponding to the creaturely reality of the

---

[52] Schwöbel 1992.
[53] Vanhoozer 2005.
[54] Cunningham 1990.

world we live in.[55] In the case of Jeremiah we encounter a theology marked by passion and urgency, by direct address, embodied by its speaker. These qualities are not incidental by-products of the form in which his theology is couched. Rather, they are essential aspects of a right doctrine of the Word of God.

The task of the present book has been to read the story of Jeremiah, his compatriates and the downfall of their nation, and to discern within it the story it was written to tell – the story of its main character, the word of the LORD. The threads of this story cannot all be taken up in a neat conclusion, and if we were to try we would find that what we held in our hands was something less than the story we set out to capture. Instead, I would like to point to some of the story's more salutary features.

For many pages now I have been writing about the Word in the abstract, and it is easy to forget just how vivid and impassioned this Word is as it pleads, laments, denounces, declaims, suffers, exults, wonders, hopes, destroys, plants, feeds, transforms. Not as a theological construct, but in the most concrete and immediate of ways, this Word inhabits the story as a person. This is a person whose fire and ardour, whose patience and longsuffering, whose raw, loving power we feel we would know anywhere.

The Word of God would be a different Word if it addressed his people from a distance, disengaged; to be what it is, it must come to them embodied as one of them, fully engaged with the objects of its address. The Word comes embodied in its prophetic speaker in order that we may know the Word, not the speaker, better. The prophet is a window through whom we look in both directions, and though we can draw a fair sketch of Jeremiah himself, it takes some squinting of the eyes to achieve. The Word of God is a message, made of words, spoken and lived out through a person whose life is an act of divine self-disclosure.

To speak this Word takes more than lips; it needs a life. And in the same way, to hear it takes more than ears. The words do not compel by mere force of logic, but commend themselves to the listener's appetite. To recognize them as the Word of God is to receive them in obedient trust.

However, the power to receive the Word lies entirely with the Word, and the fixed anatagonism to the Word that characterizes its listeners makes it inevitable that God's address to them must be

---

[55] Miller 2004: 301–305.

a Word of destruction. The power of this Word cannot be resisted, and as it overwhelms the objects of God's address, like a consuming fire, it reveals itself to have been a Word of loving self-giving from the beginning – a power utterly alien to fallen human sensibilities. The judgment that falls therefore lays the ground for a Word of forgiveness, a Word by which God draws Israel into his own life and, in so doing, remakes the world. The Word of God can never be less that God himself, and so revelation, wrath and redemption are all equally modes of divine self-giving.

By causing his Word to be translated into written words, God provides himself with means to continue putting his words into his people's mouths and for writing them on his people's heart. In written form they are no more than words, but through a divinely secured act of translation they are no less than God's words, and when they are proclaimed, the Word of God through Jeremiah sounds again in all its destructive and creative power. At each stage of this story the words change but the Word remains the same. And at each stage, by the power of God, the unchanging Word of God determines the changing words so that they count each time as the very words of God.

In the lives of his new covenant community this Word continues to make its home on earth. We have seen that when written words are read out, their reader becomes their living speaker.[56] As Jeremiah says to Zedekiah in Jeremiah 38:20, 'Hear the voice of the LORD in what I am telling you.'[57] The Word still speaks, through the embodied proclamation of his covenant partners, to bring a new creation into being.

Expressed in these terms Jeremiah's doctrine of the Word of God is in effect a character sketch, and the character in question comes to life from within the story of the word of the LORD: and because its lineaments in all their individuality are a product of the particular

---

[56] The New Testament takes this a step further: the speaker, the one who proclaims the Word, becomes, like Jeremiah, a vehicle for its embodiment. The apostle Paul is a good example: 'if I come again, I will not be lenient, since you seek proof of Christ speaking in me. He is not weak toward you, but powerful among you.' To be a speaker of the word for Paul is to 'share in the fellowship of his sufferings', to 'have among us the mind that was in Christ Jesus', to have hearers become 'imitators of us and of the Lord' (2 Cor. 13:2b–3; Phil. 3:10; 2:5; 1 Thess. 1:6). The Jeremianic shape of Paul's ministry (1 Cor. 9:16) is nowhere more evident than in 2 Corinthians; cf. Young and Ford 1987: 70–74.

[57] For the translation of this phrase see McKane (1996: 958) and Rudolph (1967: 242).

words by which God has chosen to represent himself, one's delight in the Word must grow out of one's delight in the words. In the language of another age, John Donne captured this relationship with striking effect:

> My *God*, my *God*, thou art . . . a *God* in whose words there is such a height of *figures*, such *voyages*, such *peregrinations* to fetch remote and precious *metaphors*, such *extensions*, such *spreadings*, such *Curtains* of *Allegories*, such *third heauens* of *Hyperboles*, so *harmonious eloquutions*. . . . O, what words but thine, can express the inexpressible *texture*, and *composition* of thy *word*.[58]

It is not always best for doctrine to be as unsystematic as this, but Jeremiah helps us to recognize that a sound doctrine of the Word of God (not to mention other facets of Christian doctrine) needs to find ways of becoming more closely connected to its subject matter than the word 'doctrine' usually allows. The most suitable way of achieving this is through acts of praise and proclamation, which is where doctrine can and should reach its highest pitch of expression.

People of the Word

Doctrine's truths are urgent, passionate truths, and the theologian must cultivate not simply a good eye for a syllogism, but a discerning palate that knows what Christian truth tastes like. The same goes for the biblical scholar who decides to read the Bible as a theological book, as the words of God. Next, we must remember that biblical-theological interpretation is a theological activity, and the professional barrier between the biblicist and the systematician needs to be lowered to help the Bible reader appreciate the whole that determines the parts. By the same token, doctrine has something to learn from biblical studies, and needs to lower the barrier from the other direction so that the parts can determine not only the contents but the form of the whole. Those of us who serve as theological educators in the 'post-Enlightenment academy' should be exploring new and creative ways of blurring the boundaries between the various subdisciplines of Theology.

If only it were as simple as this! It is sobering to see Jeremiah

---

[58] *Devotions upon Emergent Occasions*, Expostulation 19, italics original.

struggling with resentment and anger at what the word of the LORD is doing to him; we see the same struggle with Ezekiel. Part of this seems to have been their subjective experience of God's anger, but only a part. Resistance to the divine Word continues to be an experienced reality, even for those who have been transformed by it. The Word of God does not finish its work until 'death is swallowed up in victory', and so hearing the Word in the words will be a moral matter even for regenerate listeners. Knowledge and obedience can therefore never be separated, for there emerges 'the beginning of true understanding when we reverently embrace what it pleases God there to witness of himself. But not only faith, perfect and in every way complete, but all right knowledge of God is born in obedience.'[59]

To be a good reader of the Bible as the Word of God therefore means being determined oneself by the Word at every point. To be a 'people of the book' will not suffice; we are called to be people of the Word, determined in all our words and deeds by our LORD, Jesus Christ. And it is as the gathered people of God, drawn by his Word into a divine union of mutual self-giving, that we principally experience what it means to have his words written on our heart (sg.). Where Scripture is carefully read and obediently heard, where it is joyously sung, prayed, studied and proclaimed, there God makes himself present in the living and transforming person of his Word, and there he fashions a forgiven people into the words by which his Word will speak to tear down this world, this city of death, and build the eternal city of God.

> I will put my law within them,
>   on their heart I will write it;
> then I will be their God
>   and they shall be my people.
> No longer shall a person teach their neighbour
>   or their brother, saying,
>   'Know the LORD!',
> for all of them shall know me,
>   from the least to the greatest –
>   an oracle of the LORD!
> For I will forgive their iniquity
>   and their sin I will remember no more.

(Jer. 31:33–34)

---

[59] Calvin 1960: 1.6.2; cf. Bonhoeffer 1986: 45.

Bibliography

Abma, R. (1999), *Bonds of Love: Methodic Studies of Prophetic Texts with Marriage Imagery (Isaiah 50:1–3 and 54:1–10, Hosea 1 – 3, Jeremiah 2 – 3)*, SSN 40, Assen: Van Gorcum.

Accordance® (2008), Biblical Database Software for Macintosh, Version 8.1.1. Altamonte Springs, Florida: OakTree Software.

Adeyẹmi, F. (2006), *The New Covenant Torah in Jeremiah and the Law of Christ in Paul*, Studies in Biblical Literature 94, New York: Peter Lang.

Aitken, K. T. (1984), 'The Oracles Against Babylon in Jeremiah 50 – 51: Structures and Perspectives', *TynB* 35: 25–63.

Allen, L. C. (2008), *Jeremiah: A Commentary*, OTL, Louisville: Westminster John Knox.

Andersen, F. I., and D. N. Freedman (2000), *Micah: A New Translation and Commentary*, AB 24E, New York: Doubleday.

Anderson, B. W. (1978), '"The Lord Has Created Something New" – A Stylistic Study of Jer. 31:15–22', *CBQ* 40: 463–478.

Applegate, J. (1997), '"Peace, Peace, When There Is No Peace"', in Curtis and Römer 1997: 51–90.

—— (1998), 'The Fate of Zedekiah: Redactional Debate in the Book of Jeremiah', *VT* 48: 137–160, 301–308.

Auld, A. G. (ed.) (1993), *Understanding Poets and Prophets: Essays in Honour of George Wishart Anderson*, JSOTSup 152, Sheffield: JSOT Press.

Austin, J. L. (1976), *How to Do Things with Words: The William James Lectures Delivered at Harvard University in 1955*, 2nd ed., London: Oxford University Press.

Bacote, V., L. C. Miguélez and D. L. Okholm (eds.) (2004), *Evangelicals and Scripture: Tradition, Authority and Hermeneutics*, Downers Grove: InterVarsity Press.

Barker, P. A. (1998), 'The Theology of Deuteronomy 27', *TynB* 49: 277–304.

Barr, J. (1984), *Escaping from Fundamentalism*, London: SCM.

—— (1999), *The Concept of Biblical Theology: An Old Testament Perspective*, London: SCM.

Barstad, H. M. (1996), *The Myth of the Empty Land: A Study in the History and Archaeology of Judah During the 'Exilic' Period*, SOFS 28, Oslo: Scandinavian University Press.

Barstad, H. M., and R. G. Kratz (eds.) (2009), *Prophecy in the Book of Jeremiah*, BZAW 388, Berlin: W. de Gruyter.

Barth, K. (1977), *Church Dogmatics*, tr. G. T. Thompson and H. Knight, 1936–1967, Edinburgh: T. & T. Clark.

Barton, J. (1988), *People of the Book: The Authority of the Bible in Christianity*, London: SPCK.

—— (1999), 'Jeremiah in the Apocrypha and Pseudepigrapha', in Diamond et al. 1999: 306–317.

—— (2007), *The Nature of Biblical Critcism*, Louisville: Westminster John Knox.

Baumgartner, W. (1988), *Jeremiah's Poems of Lament*, tr. D. E. Orton, 1917, HTIBS 7, Sheffield: Almond.

Becking, B. (1994), 'Jeremiah's Book of Consolation: A Textual Comparison. Notes on the Masoretic Text and the Old Greek Version of Jeremiah xxx-xxxi', *VT* 44: 145–169.

—— (2004a), *Between Fear and Freedom: Essays on the Interpretation of Jeremiah 30–31*, OtSt 51, Leiden: E. J. Brill.

—— (2004b), 'The Conceptual Coherence of the Book of Consolation', in Kessler 2004: 163–179.

Bellis, A. O. (1995), *The Structure and Composition of Jeremiah 50:2 – 51:58*, Lewiston: Mellen Biblical Press.

—— (1999), 'Poetic Structure and Intertextual Logic in Jeremiah 50', in Diamond et al. 1999: 179–199.

Berridge, J. M. (1970), *Prophet, People, and the Word of Yahweh: An Examination of Form and Content in the Proclamation of the Prophet Jeremiah*, BaST 4, Zurich: EVZ.

Bezzel, H. (2009), 'The Suffering of the Elect: Variations on a Theological Problem', in Barstad and Kratz 2009: 48–73.

Biddle, M. E. (1988), 'The Literary Frame Surrounding Jeremiah 30,1 – 33,26', *ZAW* 100: 409–413.

—— (1996), *Polyphony and Symphony in Prophetic Literature: Rereading Jeremiah 7 – 20*, SOTI 2, Macon: Mercer University Press.

Biddy, W. S. (2005), 'Review of Wolfhart Pannenberg on Human Linguisticality and the Word of God', *Ars Disputandi* 5: n.p., online at <http://www.ArsDisputandi.org>, accessed 7 Dec. 2011.

Blank, S. H. (1974), 'The Prophet as Paradigm', in J. L. Crenshaw and J. T. Willis (eds.), *Essays in Old Testament Ethics (J. Philip Hyatt, in Memoriam)*, New York: Ktav, 115–128.

Blocher, H. (2008), 'Karl Barth's Christocentric Method', in Gibson and Strange 2008: 21–54.

Bloesch, D. G. (1994), *Holy Scripture: Revelation, Inspiration and Interpretation*, Downers Grove: InterVarsity Press.

Bogaert, P.-M. (1981a), 'De Baruch à Jérémie: les deux rédactions conservées du livre de Jérémie', in Bogaert 1981a: 168–173.

Bogaert, P.-M. (ed.) (1981b), *Le livre de Jérémie, le prophète et son milieu, les oracles et leur transmission*, BETL 54, Leuven: Leuven University Press.

Bolt, P. G. (2003), *Jesus' Defeat of Death: Persuading Mark's Early Readers*, SNTSMS 125, Cambridge: Cambridge University Press.

Bonhoeffer, D. (1986), *Meditating on the Word*, Cambridge, Mass.: Cowley.

Bowker, J. W. (1964), 'Prophetic Action and Sacramental Form', in F. L. Cross (ed.), *SE* 3.2, TU 88, Berlin: Akademie, 129–137.

Bozak, B. A. (1991), *Life 'Anew': A Literary-Theological Study of Jer. 30 – 31*, AnBib 122, Rome: Biblical Institute Press.

Bright, J. (1965), *Jeremiah*, AB 21, Garden City, N. Y.: Doubleday.

Brooke, G. J. (1997), 'The Book of Jeremiah and Its Reception in the Qumran Scrolls', in Curtis and Römer 1997: 183–206.

Brueggemann, W. (1985), 'The "Uncared" for Now Cared for (Jer 30:12–17): A Methodological Consideration', *JBL* 104: 419–428.

—— (1988), *To Pluck up, to Tear Down: A Commentary on Jeremiah 1–25*, ITC, Grand Rapids: Eerdmans.

—— (1991), *To Build, to Plant: A Commentary on Jeremiah 26 – 52*, ITC, Grand Rapids: Eerdmans.

—— (1997), *Theology of the Old Testament: Testimony, Dispute, Advocacy*, Minneapolis: Fortress.

—— (2006), *Like Fire in the Bones: Listening for the Prophetic Word in Jeremiah*, Minneapolis: Fortress.

—— (2007), *The Theology of the Book of Jeremiah*, Cambridge: Cambridge University Press.

Brummitt, M., and Y. Sherwood (2011), 'The Fear of Loss Inherent in Writing: Jeremiah 36 as the Story of a Self-Conscious Scroll', in A. R. P. Diamond and L. Stulman (eds.), *Jeremiah (Dis)placed: New Directions in Writing/Reading Jeremiah*, LHBOTS 529, New York: T. & T. Clark, 47–66.

Calvin, J. (1950a), *Commentaries on the Book of the Prophet*

Jeremiah and Lamentations, 5 vols., tr. J. Owen, repr. 1850–5, Grand Rapids: Eerdmans.

—— (1950b), *Commentaries on the Four Last Books of Moses Arranged in the Form of a Harmony*, 4 vols., tr. C. W. Bingham, repr. 1852–5, Grand Rapids: Eerdmans.

—— (1960), *Institutes of the Christian Religion*, 2 vols., tr. F. L. Battles, 1559, LCC 20, 21, Philadelphia: Westminster.

Carroll, R. P. (1981), *From Chaos to Covenant: Uses of Prophecy in the Book of Jeremiah*, London: SCM.

—— (1984), 'Prophecy, Dissonance, and Jeremiah xxvi', in L. G. Perdue and B. W. Kovacs (eds.), *A Prophet to the Nations: Essays in Jeremiah Studies*, Winona Lake: Eisenbrauns, 381–391.

—— (1986), *Jeremiah: A Commentary*, OTL, London: SCM.

—— (1989), *Jeremiah*, OTG, Sheffield: JSOT Press.

—— (1992), 'The Myth of the Empty Land', in D. Jobling and T. Pippin (eds.), *Ideological Criticism of Biblical Texts*, Semeia 59, Atlanta: Scholars Press, 79–93.

—— (1993), 'Inscribing the Covenant: Writing and the Written in Jeremiah', in Auld 1993: 61–76.

—— (1999), 'Halfway Through a Dark Wood: Reflections on Jeremiah 25', in Diamond et al. 1999: 73–86.

Carson, D. A. (2010), *Collected Writings on Scripture*, Wheaton: Crossway; Nottingham: Apollos.

Childs, B. S. (1985), *Old Testament Theology in a Canonical Context*, London: SCM.

—— (1992), *Biblical Theology of the Old and New Testaments: Theological Reflections on the Christian Bible*, London: SCM.

Clayton, P. D. (1997), *God and Contemporary Science*, ESCT, Edinburgh: Edinburgh University Press.

Clements, R. E. (1993), 'Jeremiah 1 – 25 and the Deuteronomistic History', in Auld 1993: 93–113.

—— (2007), 'Prophecy Interpreted: Intertextuality and Theodicy – A Case Study of Jeremiah 26:16–24', in Goldingay and Allen 2007: 32–44.

Cogan, M., and H. Tadmor (1988), *II Kings: A New Translation with Introduction and Commentary*, AB 11, New York: Doubleday.

Condamin, A. (1920), *Le livre de Jérémie*, Paris: Libraire Victor Lecoffre.

Cooper, J. (2007), *Panentheism: The Other God of the Philosophers*, Nottingham: Apollos.

Cornill, C. H. (1895), *The Book of the Prophet Jeremiah: Critical*

Edition of the Hebrew Text Arranged in Chronological Order; with Notes by C. H. Cornill, tr. C. Johnston, The Sacred Books of the Old Testament 11, Leipzig: J. C. Hinrichs.

Craigie, P. C. (1976), *The Book of Deuteronomy*, NICOT, Grand Rapids: Eerdmans.

Crenshaw, J. L. (1971), *Prophetic Conflict: Its Effect Upon Israelite Religion*, BZAW 124, Berlin: W. de Gruyter.

Cunningham, D. S. (1990), *Faithful Persuasion: In Aid of a Rhetoric of Christian Theology*, Notre Dame: University of Notre Dame Press.

Curtis, A. H. W., and T. Römer (eds.) (1997), *The Book of Jeremiah and Its Reception*, BETL 128, Leuven: Leuven University Press.

Davidson, R. (1993), 'Jeremiah, the Book of', in B. M. Metzger and M. D. Coogan (eds.), *The Oxford Companion to the Bible*, New York: Oxford University Press, 343–347.

Davies, P. R. (1995), *Whose Bible Is It Anyway?*, JSOTSup 204, Sheffield: Sheffield Academic Press.

Diamond, A. R. P. (1987), *The Confessions of Jeremiah in Context: Scenes of Prophetic Drama*, JSOTSup 45, Sheffield: JSOT Press.

—— (2003), 'Jeremiah', in J. J. G. Dunn and J. W. Rogerson (eds.), *Eerdmans Commentary on the Bible*, Grand Rapids: Eerdmans, 543–616.

Diamond, A. R. P., and K. M. O'Connor (1999), 'Unaithful Passions: Coding Women Coding Men in Jeremiah 2–3 (4.2)', in Diamond et al. 1999: 123–145.

Diamond, A. R. P., K. M. O'Connor and L. Stulman (eds.) (1999), *Troubling Jeremiah*, JSOTSup 260, Sheffield: Sheffield Academic Press.

Di Pede, E. (2004), 'Jérusalem, 'Ebed-Melek et Baruch: Enquête narrative sur le déplacement chronologique de Jr 45', *RB* 111: 61–77.

Donne, J. (1624), 'Expostulation 19', *Deuotions vpon Emergent Occasions and seuerall steps in my Sicknes*, 2nd ed., London: Printed by A. M. for Thomas Jones, Electronic reproduction of original in Henry E. Huntingdon Library, STC, 2nd ed., 7034, Early English Books Online, accessed 29 Feb. 2012, images 231–242.

Doran, C. (2000), 'The Quest for the Causal Joint', *JFSE* 4: 161–170.

Dubbink, J. (2004), 'Getting Closer to Jeremiah: The Word of YHWH and the Literary-Theological Person of a Prophet', in Kessler 2004: 25–39.

Duhm, B. (1901), *Das Buch Jeremia*, KHC 11, Tübingen: J. C. B. Mohr.

Dumbrell, W. J. (1984), *Covenant and Creation: A Theology of the Old Testament Covenants*, Flemington Markets, NSW, Exeter: Paternoster.

Ebeling, G. (1963), 'The Meaning of "Biblical Theology"', *Word and Faith*, tr. J. B. Leitch, Philadelphia: Fortress, 79–97.

—— (1967), *God and Word*, tr. J. W. Leitch, Philadelphia: Fortress.

Eichhorn, J. G. (1803), *Einleitung in das Alte Testament*, 3rd ed., vol. 3, Leipzig: Weidmannischen Buchhandlung.

Ellis, E. E. (2000), *Christ and the Future in New Testament History*, NTSup 97, Leiden: E. J. Brill.

Fanning, B. M. (2000), 'Word', in *NDBT*, 848–853.

Farrer, A. (1967), *Faith and Speculation: An Essay in Philosophical Theology*, London: A. & C. Black.

Firth, D. G. (2009), *1 & 2 Samuel*, AOTC 8, Nottingham: Apollos.

Fischer, G. (2005), *Jeremia*, 2 vols., Freiburg: Herder.

Flint, P. W. (ed.) (2001), *The Bible at Qumran: Text, Shape, and Interpretation*, Grand Rapids: Eerdmans.

Fowl, S. E. (ed.) (1997), *The Theological Interpretation of Scripture: Classic and Contemporary Readings*, Oxford: Blackwell.

—— (1998), *Engaging Scripture: A Model for Theological Interpretation*, Challenges in Contemporary Theology, Oxford: Blackwell.

Frei, H. W. (1974), *The Eclipse of Biblical Narrative: A Study in Eighteenth and Nineteenth Century Hermeneutics*, New Haven: Yale University Press.

Fretheim, T. E. (1991), *Exodus*, Interpretation, Louisville: John Knox.

—— (2002), *Jeremiah*, SHBC 15, Macon, Ga.: Smyth & Helwys.

Friebel, K. G. (1999), *Jeremiah's and Ezekiel's Sign-Acts*, JSOTSup 283, Sheffield: Sheffield Academic.

Gabler, J. P. (2004), 'An Oration on the Proper Disctinction Between Biblical and Dogmatic Theology and the Specific Objectives of Each', in B. C. Ollenberger (ed.), *Old Testament Theology: Flowering and Future*, tr. J. Sandys-Wunsch and L. Eldredge (1831), Sources for Biblical and Theological Study 1, Winona Lake: Eisenbrauns, 497–506.

Gibson, D., and D. Strange (eds.) (2008), *Engaging with Barth: Contemporary Evangelical Critiques*, Leicester: Apollos.

Gibson, J. C. L. (1994), *Davidson's Introductory Hebrew Grammar:*

Syntax, 4th ed., completely revised, Edinburgh: T. & T. Clark.

Gibson, R. J. (ed.) (1997), *Interpreting God's Plan: Biblical Theology and the Pastor*, Explorations 11, Carlisle: Paternoster.

Gignilliat, M. (2010), 'Theological Exegesis as Exegetical Showing: A Case of Isaiah's Figural Potentiality', *IJST* 12.2: 217–232.

Goldingay, J. (1994), *Models for Scripture*, Grand Rapids: Eerdmans.

—— (1995), *Models for the Interpretation of Scripture*, Carlisle: Paternoster; Grand Rapids: Eerdmans.

—— (2000), 'Biblical Narrative and Systematic Theology', in Green and Turner 2000: 123–142.

—— (2003), *Old Testament Theology*, vol. 1: *Israel's Gospel*, Downers Grove: InterVarsity Press.

Goldingay, J., and L. C. Allen (eds.) (2007), *Uprooting and Planting: Essays on Jeremiah for Leslie Allen*, LHBOTS 459, New York: T. & T. Clark.

Goldman, Y. (1992), *Prophétie et royauté au retour de l'exil: les origines littéraires de la forme massorétique du livre de Jérémie*, OBO 118, Freiburg, Switzerland: Universitätsverlag.

Goldsworthy, G. (1997), 'Is Biblical Theology Viable?', in Gibson 1997: 18–46.

Gordon, R. P. (2006), *Hebrew Bible and Ancient Versions: Selected Essays of Robert P. Gordon*, SOTSM, Aldershot: Ashgate.

Gosse, B. (1986), 'La malédiction contre Babylone de Jérémie 51,59–64 et les rédactions du livre de Jérémie', *ZAW* 98: 383–399.

Green, J. B. (2000), 'Scripture and Theology: Uniting the Two so Long Divided', in Green and Turner 2000: 23–43.

Green, J. B., and M. Turner (eds.) (2000), *Between Two Horizons: Spanning New Testament Studies and Systematic Theology*, Grand Rapids: Eerdmans.

Grether, O. (1934), *Name und Wort Gottes im Alten Testament*, BZAW 64, Berlin: W. de Gruyter.

Hardmeier, C. (1993), 'Probleme der Textsyntax, der Redeeinbettung und der Abschnittgliederung in Jer 32 mit ihren kompositionsgeschichtlichen Konsequenzen', in H. Irsigler (ed.), *Syntax und Text: Beiträge zur 22. Internationalen Ökumenischen Hebräisch-Dozenten-Konferenz 1993 in Bamberg*, ATSAT 40. Münchener Universitätsschriften: Philosophische Facultät Altertumskunde und Kulturwissensachaften, St. Ottilien: EOS, 49–79.

—— (1995), 'Jeremia 32,2–15* als Eröffnung der Erzählung von der Gefangenschaft und Befreiung Jeremias in Jer 34,7; 37,3–40,6*', in W. Gross (ed.), *Jeremia und die 'deuteronomistische Bewegung'*, BBB 98, Weinheim: Belz Athenäum, 187–214.

—— (2005), *Erzähldiskurs und Redepragmatik im Alten Testament: Unterwegs zu einer performativen Theologie der Bibel*, FAT 46, Tübingen: Mohr Siebeck.

Hays, J. D. (2004), 'Jeremiah, the Septuagint, the Dead Sea Scrolls and Inerrancy', in Bacote et al. 2004: 133–149.

Hays, R. B. (2007), 'Reading the Bible with Eyes of Faith: The Practice of Theological Exegesis', *JTI* 1.1: 5–21.

—— (2008), 'Can Narrative Criticism Recover the Theological Unity of Scripture?', *JTI* 2.2: 193–211.

Heine, R. A. (2007), *Reading the Old Testament with the Ancient Church: Exploring the Formation of Early Christian Thought*, Evangelical Resourcement, Grand Rapids: Baker Academic.

Helm, P., and C. Trueman (eds.) (2002), *The Trustworthiness of God: Perspectives on the Nature of Scripture*, Leicester: Apollos.

Hendel, R. S. (2010), 'Farewell to SBL: Faith and Reason in Biblical Studies', *BAR* 35.4: 28, 74.

Henderson, J. M. (2007), 'Jeremiah 2 – 10 as a Unified Literary Composition: Evidence of Dramatic Portrayal and Narrative Progression', in Goldingay and Allen 2007: 116–152.

Heschel, A. J. (1962), *The Prophets*, New York: Harper & Row.

Hill, J. (1999), *Friend or Foe? The Figure of Babylon in the Book of Jeremiah MT*, BIS 40, Leiden: E. J. Brill.

—— (2004), 'The Book of Jeremiah and the Unended Exile', in Kessler 2004: 149–161.

Holladay, W. L. (1958), *The Root šûbh in the Old Testament: With Particular Reference to Its Usages in Covenantal Contexts*, Leiden: E. J. Brill.

—— (1964), 'The Background of Jeremiah's Self-Understanding: Moses, Samuel, and Psalm 22', *JBL* 83: 153–164.

—— (1976), *The Architecture of Jeremiah 1–20*, Cranberry, N. J.: Associated University Presses.

—— (1985), 'A Proposal for Reflections in the Book of Jeremiah of the Seven-Year Recitation of the Law in Deuteronomy (Deut 31,10–13)', in N. Lohfink (ed.), *Deuteronomium, Entstehung, Gestalt und Botschaft*, BETL 68, Leuven: Leuven University Press, 326–328.

—— (1986), *Jeremiah 1: A Commentary on the Book of the Prophet Jeremiah Chapters 1 – 25*, Hermeneia, Philadelphia: Fortress.

—— (1989), *Jeremiah 2: A Commentary on the Book of the Prophet Jeremiah Chapters 26 – 52*, Hermeneia, Philadelphia: Fortress.

—— (1990), *Jeremiah: A Fresh Reading*, New York: Pilgrim.

Holmgren, F. C. (1999), *The Old Testament and the Significance of Jesus: Embracing Change – Maintaining Christian Identity*, Grand Rapids: Eerdmans.

Holt, E. K. (1999), 'The Potent Word of God: Remarks on the Composition of Jeremiah 37 – 44', in Diamond et al. 1999: 161–178.

—— (2003), 'The Meaning of an *Inclusio*: A Theological Interpretation of the Book of Jeremiah', *SJOT* 17.2: 183–205.

—— (2005), 'The Fountain of Living Water and the Deceitful Brook: The Pool of Water Metaphors in the Book of Jeremiah', in P. van Hecke (ed.), *Metaphor in the Hebrew Bible*, BETL 187, Leuven: Peeters, 99–117.

—— (2007), 'Word of Jeremiah – Word of God: Structures of Authority in the Book of Jeremiah', in Goldingay and Allen 2007: 172–189.

Houston, W. (1996), 'What Did the Prophets Think They Were Doing? Speech Acts and Prophetic Discourse in the Old Testament', in R. P. Gordon (ed.), *The Place Is Too Small for Us: The Israelite Prophets in Recent Scholarship*, repr. 1993, Sources for Biblical and Theological Study 5, Winona Lake: Eisenbrauns, 133–153.

Hugenberger, G. P. (1995), 'The Servant of the LORD in the "Servant Songs" of Isaiah: A Second Moses Figure', in P. E. Satterthwaite, R. S. Hess and G. J. Wenham (eds.), *The LORD's Anointed: Interpretation of Old Testament Messianic Texts*, Carlisle: Paternoster, 105–140.

Ittmann, N. (1981), *Die Konfessionen Jeremias: ihre Bedeutung für d. Verkündigung d. Propheten*, WMANT 54, Neukirchen-Vluyn: Neukirchener.

Janzen, J. G. (1973), *Studies in the Text of Jeremiah*, HSM 6, Cambridge, Mass.: Harvard University Press.

Japhet, S. (1993), *I and II Chronicles: A Commentary*, OTL, Louisville: Westminster John Knox.

Jindo, J. Y. (2010), *Biblical Metaphor Reconsidered: A Cognitive Approach to Poetic Prophecy in Jeremiah 1 – 24*, HSM 64, Winona Lake: Eisenbrauns.

Job, J. B. (2006), *Jeremiah's Kings: A Study of the Monarchy in Jeremiah*, SOTSM, Aldershot: Ashgate.

Jobling, D. (1978), 'Jeremiah's Poem in III 1 – IV 2', *VT* 28.1: 45–55.

Johnston, P. S. (2010), '"Now You See Me, Now You Don't!"': Jeremiah and God', in J. Day (ed.), *Prophecy and Prophets in Ancient Israel: Proceedings of the Oxford Old Testament Seminar*, New York: T. & T. Clark, 290–308.

Kalmanofsky, A. (2008), *Terror All Around: Horror, Monsters, and Theology in the Book of Jeremiah*, LHBOTS 390, New York: T. & T. Clark.

Kaltner, J., and L. Stulman (eds.) (2004), *Inspired Speech: Prophecy in the Ancient Near East*, JSOTSup 378, London: T. & T. Clark.

Keown, G. L. , P. J. Scalise and T. G. Smothers (1995), *Jeremiah 26 – 52*, WBC 27, Dallas: Word.

Kessler, M. (1968), 'Jeremiah Chapters 26 – 45 Reconsidered', *JNES* 27: 81–88.

—— (1999), 'The Function of Chapters 25 and 50 – 51 in the Book of Jeremiah', in Diamond et al. 1999: 64–72.

—— (2003), *Battle of the Gods: The God of Israel versus Marduk of Babylon: A Literary/Theological Interpretation of Jeremiah 50 – 51*, SSN, Assen: Van Gorcum.

—— (ed.) (2004), *Reading the Book of Jeremiah: A Search for Coherence*, Winona Lake: Eisenbrauns.

Kidner, D. (1987), *The Message of Jeremiah: Against Wind and Tide*, BST, Leicester: Inter-Varsity Press.

King, P. J. (1993), *Jeremiah: An Archaeological Companion*, Louisville: Westminster John Knox.

Koch, K. (1999), '*'āwōn*', in *TDOT* 10: 546–562.

Kremers, H. (1953), 'Leidensgemeinschaft mit Gott im Alten Testament: Eine Untersuchung der "biographischen" Berichte im Jeremiabuch', *EvT* 13: 122–140.

Lalleman-de Winkel, H. (2000), *Jeremiah in Prophetic Tradition: An Examination of the Book of Jeremiah in the Light of Israel's Prophetic Traditions*, CBET 26, Leuven: Peeters.

Lawlor, J. I. (2004), 'Word Event in Jeremiah: A Look at the Composition's "Introductory Formulas"', in Kaltner and Stulman 2004: 231–243.

Legaspi, M. C. (2010), *The Death of Scripture and the Rise of Biblical Studies*, Oxford: Oxford Unversity Press.

Leslie, E. A. (1954), *Jeremiah: Chronologically Arranged, Translated, and Interpreted*, New York: Abingdon.

Leuchter, M. (2006), *Josiah's Reform and Jeremiah's Scroll: Historical Calamity and Prophetic Response*, HBM 6, Sheffield: Sheffield Phoenix.

Lindbeck, G. A. (1984), *The Nature of Doctrine: Religion and Theology in a Postliberal Age*, London: SPCK.

Lohfink, N. (1991), *The Covenant Never Revoked: Biblical Reflections on Christian–Jewish Dialogue*, tr. J. J. Scullion, 1989, New York: Paulist.

Long, V. P. (1994), *The Art of Biblical History*, Foundations of Contemporary Interpretation 5, Grand Rapids: Zondervan.

Longman, T., III (2008), *Jeremiah, Lamentations*, NIBC, Peabody, Mass.: Hendrickson.

Lundbom, J. R. (1975), *Jeremiah: A Study in Ancient Hebrew Rhetoric*, SBLDS 18, Missoula: Scholars Press.

—— (1986), 'Baruch, Seraiah, and Expanded Colophons in the Book of Jeremiah', *JSOT* 36: 89–114.

—— (1999), *Jeremiah 1 – 20: A New Translation with Introduction and Commentary*, AB 21A, New York: Doubleday.

—— (2004a), *Jeremiah 21 – 36: A New Translation with Introduction and Commentary*, AB 21B, New York: Doubleday.

—— (2004b), *Jeremiah 37 – 52: A New Translation with Introduction and Commentary*, AB 21C, New York: Doubleday.

McConville, J. G. (1991), 'Jeremiah: Prophet and Book', *TynB* 42: 80–95.

—— (1993a), *Grace in the End: A Study in Deuteronomic Theology*, SOTBT 1, Carlisle: Paternoster.

—— (1993b), *Judgment and Promise: An Interpretation of the Book of Jeremiah*, Leicester: Apollos.

—— (2002a), *Deuteronomy*, AOTC 5, Leicester: Apollos.

—— (2002b), 'Divine Speech and the Book of Jeremiah', in Helm and Trueman 2002: 18–38.

McCormack, B. L. (2004), 'The Being of Holy Scripture Is in Becoming: Karl Barth in Conversation with American Evangelical Criticism', in Bacote et al. 2004: 55–75.

McGrath, A. E. (1990), *The Genesis of Doctrine: A Study in the Foundations of Doctrinal Criticism*, Oxford: Basil Blackwell.

MacIntyre, A. (1981), *After Virtue*, London: Duckworth.

McKane, W. (1979), *Tradition and Interpretation*, Oxford: Clarendon.

—— (1986), *A Critical and Exegetical Commentary on Jeremiah*, vol. 1, ICC, Edinburgh: T. & T. Clark.

—— (1996), *A Critical and Exegetical Commentary on Jeremiah*, vol. 2, ICC, Edinburgh: T. & T. Clark.

March, W. E. (1974), 'lākēn: Its Function and Meanings', in J. J. Jackson and M. Kessler (eds.), *Rhetorical Criticism: Essays in Honor of James Muilenburg*, Pittsburgh: Pickwick, 256–284.

Marshall, I. H. (2004), *Beyond the Bible: Moving from Scripture to Theology*, Grand Rapids: Baker Academic.

Mauser, U. (1971), *Gottesbild und Menschwerdung: eine Untersuchung zur Einheit des Alten und Neuen Testaments*, Tübingen: J. C. B. Mohr.

Meier, S. A. (1992), *Speaking of Speaking: Marking Direct Discourse in the Hebrew Bible*, VTSup 46, Leiden: E. J. Brill.

—— (2009), *Themes and Transformations in Old Testament Prophecy*, Downers Grove: IVP Academic.

Migsch, H. (1996), *Jeremias Ackerkauf: Eine Untersuchung von Jeremia 32*, ÖBS 15, Frankfurt am Main: Peter Lang.

—— (1997), 'Die vorbildlichen Rechabiter: zur Redestruktur von Jeremia xxxv', *VT* 47: 316–328.

Miller, P. D. (2004), *The Way of the LORD: Essays in Old Testament Theology*, Grand Rapids: Eerdmans.

Milne, B. (2009), *Know the Truth: A Handbook of Christian Belief*, 3rd ed., Leicester: Inter-Varsity Press; Downers Grove: InterVarsity Press.

Moberly, R. W. L. (2006), *Prophecy and Discernment*, Cambridge Studies in Christian Doctrine 14, Cambridge: Cambridge University Press.

—— (2009), 'What Is Theological Interpretation of Scripture?', *JTI* 3.2: 161–178.

Morrison, J. D. (2006), *Has God Said? Scripture, the Word of God, and the Crisis of Theological Authority*, ETSMS 5, Eugene, Ore.: Pickwick.

Mowinckel, S. (1914), *Zur Komposition des Buches Jeremia*, Videnskapsselskapets Skrifter. II. Hist.-Filos. Klasse. 1913. No. 5, Kristiania: Jacob Dybwad.

Neumann, P. K. D. (1973), 'Das Wort, das geschehen ist . . . Zum Problem der Wortempfangsterminologie in Jer. i–xxv', *VT* 23: 169–217.

Nicholson, E. W. (1970), *Preaching to the Exiles*, Oxford: Blackwell.

Niditch, S. (1996), *Oral Word and Written Word: Orality and Literacy in Ancient Israel*, Library of Ancient Israel, Louisville: Westminster John Knox.

Nissinen, M. (2004), 'What Is Prophecy? An Ancient Near Eastern Perspective', in Kaltner and Stulman 2004: 17–37.

Nötscher, F. (1934), *Das Buch Jeremias*, HSAT 7, Bonn: Peter Hanstein.

O'Brien, P. T. (2010), *The Letter to the Hebrews*, PNTC, Grand Rapids: Eerdmans; Nottingham: Apollos.

O'Collins, G., and D. Kendall (1997), *The Bible for Theology: Ten Principles for the Theological Use of Scripture*, New York: Paulist.

O'Connor, K. M. (1988), *The Confessions of Jeremiah: Their Interpretation and Role in Chapters 1–25*, Atlanta: Scholars Press.

—— (1999), 'The Tears of God and Divine Character in Jeremiah 2 – 9', in Diamond et al. 1999: 387–401.

Old, H. O. (1998), *The Reading and Preaching of the Scriptures in the Worship of the Christian Church*, vol. 1: *The Biblical Period*, Grand Rapids: Eerdmans.

Osuji, A. C. (2010), *Where Is the Truth? Narrative Exegesis and the Question of True and False Prophecy in Jer 26 – 29 (MT)*, BETL 214, Leuven: Peeters.

Overholt, T. W. (1970), *The Threat of Falsehood: A Study in the Theology of the Book of Jeremiah*, SBT 2.16, London: Alec R. Allenson.

Packer, J. I. (1958), *'Fundamentalism' and the Word of God*, London: Inter-Varsity Fellowship.

Pannenberg, W. (1969), 'Dogmatic Theses on the Concept of Revelation', in W. Pannenberg (ed.), *Revelation as History*, tr. D. Granskou and E. Quinn (1965), London: Sheed & Ward, 123–158.

—— (1991), *An Introduction to Systematic Theology*, Grand Rapids: Eerdmans.

—— (1991–8), *Systematic Theology*, 3 vols., tr. G. Bromiley, 1988–93, Grand Rapids: Eerdmans.

—— (1993), 'The Doctrine of Creation and Modern Science', in T. Peters (ed.), *Toward a Theology of Nature: Essays on Science and Faith*, repr., Louisville: Westminster John Knox, 29–49.

Pao, D. (2002), *Acts and the Isaianic New Exodus*, Grand Rapids: Baker Academic.

Parenti, A. (1930), *Notae introductoriae et exegeticae in prophetiam Jeremiae*, Romae: Pontificia Universitas Gregoriana.

Parunak, H. Van D. (1994), 'Some Discourse Functions of Prophetic Quotation Formulas in Jeremiah', in R. D. Bergen (ed.), *Biblical Hebrew and Discourse Linguistics*, Dallas: Summer Institute of Linguistics, 489–519.

Peacocke, A. R. (1993), *Theology for a Scientific Age: Being and Becoming – Natural, Divine and Human*, enlarged ed., London: SCM.

Peterson, D. G. (2012), *Transformed by God: New Covenant Life and Ministry*, Nottingham: Inter-Varsity Press.

Pietersma, A. (2007), 'An Excursus on Bisectioning Ieremias', electronic supplement to *NETS*, online at <http://ccat.sas.upenn.edu/nets/edition/ieremias-excursus.pdf>, accessed 1 Mar. 2008.

Piovanelli, P. (1997), 'JrB 33,14–26, ou la continuité des institutions à l'époque maccabéenne', in Curtis and Römer 1997: 255–276.

Polk, T. (1984), *The Prophetic Persona: Jeremiah and the Language of the Self*, JSOTSup 32, Sheffield: JSOT Press.

Polkinghorne, J. (1994), *Science and Christian Belief: Theological Reflections of a Bottom-up Thinker*, London: SPCK.

—— (1996), 'Chaos Theory and Divine Action', in W. M. Richardson and W. J. Wildman (eds.), *Religion and Science: History, Method, Dialogue*, New York: Routledge, 243–252.

Poythress, V. S. (2009), *In the Beginning Was the Word: Language: A God-Centered Approach*, Wheaton: Crossway.

Rad, G. von (1933), 'Die falsche Propheten', *ZAW* 51: 109–120.

—— (1965), *Old Testament Theology*, 2 vols., tr. D. M. G. Stalker, 1957–60, San Francisco: Harper.

—— (1983), 'The Confessions of Jeremiah', in J. L. Crenshaw (ed.), *Theodicy in the Old Testament*, tr. A. J. Ehlin, 1936, IRT 4, Philadelphia: Fortress, 88–99.

Rae, M. A., J. Goldingay, C. J. H. Wright, R. W. Wall and K. Greene-McCreight (2008), 'Christ in/and the Old Testament', *JTI* 2.1: 1–22.

Regt, L. J. de (2004), 'The Prophet in the First and Second Edition of Jeremiah: Increased Dramatisation and the Modern Translator', in S. Crisp and M. Jinbachian (eds.), *Text, Theology and Translation: Essays in Honour of Jan de Waard*, Great Britain: United Bible Societies, 163–175.

Reimer, D. J. (1993), *The Oracles Against Babylon in Jeremiah 50–51: A Horror Among the Nations*, San Fransisco: Mellen Research University Press.

Rendtorff, R. (2005), *The Canonical Hebrew Bible: A Theology of the Old Testament*, tr. D. E. Orton, 2001, Tools for Biblical Study 7, Leiden: Deo.

Reventlow, H. L. G. von (1961), *Liturgie und prophetisches Ich bei Jeremia*, Gütersloh: Gerd Mohn.

Ricœur, P. (1995), *Figuring the Sacred: Religion, Narrative, and Imagination*, tr. D. Pellauer, Minneapolis: Fortress.

Rietzschel, C. (1966), *Das Problem der Urrolle: Ein Beitrag zur Redaktionsgeschichte des Jeremiabuches*, Gütersloh: Gütersloher Gerd Mohn.

Robson, J. (2006), *Word and Spirit in Ezekiel*, LHBOTS 447, New York: T. & T. Clark.

Rofé, A. (1989), 'The Arrangement of the Book of Jeremiah', *ZAW* 101: 390–398.

Roncace, M. (2005), *Jeremiah, Zedekiah, and the Fall of Jerusalem*, New York: T. & T. Clark.

Rosenberg, A. J. (1989), *Jeremiah*, vol. 2: *A New English Translation*, Judaica Books of the Prophets, New York: Judaica.

Rosenberg, J. (1987), 'Jeremiah and Ezekiel', in R. Alter and F. Kermode (eds.), *The Literary Guide to the Bible*, London: Collins, 184–206.

Rosner, B. S. (2000), 'Biblical Theology', in *NDBT*, 3–11.

Rudolph, W. (1967), *Jeremia*, 3rd ed., HAT 12, Tübingen: Mohr (Siebeck).

Sailhamer, J. H. (2002), 'Biblical Theology and the Composition of the Hebrew Bible', in S. J. Hafemann (ed.), *Biblical Theology: Retrospect and Prospect*, Leicester: Apollos, 25–37.

Sanders, J. A. (1977), 'Hermeneutics in True and False Prophecy', in G. W. Coates and B. O. Long (eds.), *Canon and Authority: Essays in Old Testament Religion and Theology*, Philadelphia: Fortress, 21–41.

Scalise, P. J. (2007), 'Baruch as First Reader: Baruch's Lament in the Structure of the Book of Jeremiah', in Goldingay and Allen 2007: 291–307.

Schaper, J. (2009), 'On Writing and Reciting in Jeremiah 36', in Barstad and Kratz 2009: 137–147.

Schellenberg, A. (2010), 'A "Lying Pen of the Scribes" (Jer 8:8)? Orality and Writing in the Formation of Prophetic Books', in A. Weissenrieder and R. B. Coote (eds.), *The Interface of Orality and Writing*, WUNT 260, Tübingen: Mohr Siebeck, 285–309.

Schmid, K. (1996), *Buchgestalten des Jeremiabuches: Untersuchungen zur Redaktions- und Rezeptionsgeschichte von Jer 30–33 im Kontext des Buches*, WMANT 72, Neukirchen-Vluyn: Neukirchener.

Schmidt, W. H. (1978), '*dābhar*', in *TDOT* 3: 94–125.

Schniedewind, W. M. (2004), *How the Bible Became a Book:*

The Textualization of Ancient Israel, Cambridge: Cambridge University Press.

Schultz, R. (2004), 'How Many Isaiahs Were There and What Does It Matter? Prophetic Inspiration in Recent Evangelical Scholarship', in Bacote et al. 2004: 150–170.

Schwöbel, C. (1992), *God: Action and Revelation*, Studies in Philosophical Theology 3, Kampen: Kok Pharos.

Scobie, C. H. H. (2003), *The Ways of Our God: An Approach to Biblical Theology*, Grand Rapids: Eerdmans.

Seidl, T. (1979), 'Die Wortereignisformel in Jeremia: Beobachtungen zu den Formen der Redeeröffnung in Jeremia, im Anschluß an Jer 27,1.2', *BZ* NS 23: 20–47.

Seitz, C. R. (1989a), 'The Prophet Moses and the Canonical Shape of Jeremiah', *ZAW* 101: 3–27.

—— (1989b), *Theology in Conflict: Reactions to the Exile in the Book of Jeremiah*, BZAW 176, Berlin: W. de Gruyter.

—— (2007), *Prophecy and Hermeneutics: Toward a New Introduction to the Prophets*, Studies in Theological Interpretation, Grand Rapids: Baker Academic.

Selms, A. van (1976), 'Telescoped Discussion as a Literary Device in Jeremiah', *VT* 26: 99–112.

Sharp, C. J. (2003), *Prophecy and Ideology in Jeremiah: Struggles for Authority in Deutero-Jeremianic Prose*, OTS, Edinburgh: T. & T. Clark.

Shead, A. G. (2000), 'The New Covenant and Pauline Hermeneutics', in P. Bolt and M. Thompson (eds.), *The Gospel to the Nations: Perspectives on Paul's Mission*, Leicester: Apollos, 33–49.

—— (2002a), 'An Old Testament Theology of the Sabbath Year and Jubilee', *RTR* 61: 19–33.

—— (2002b), *The Open Book and the Sealed Book: Jeremiah 32 in Its Hebrew and Greek Recensions*, HBV 3 / JSOTSup 347, Sheffield: Sheffield Academic Press.

Shepherd, D. (2005), 'Prophetaphobia: Fear and False Prophecy in Nehemiah vi', *VT* 55: 232–250.

Shepherd, M. B. (2011), *The Twelve Prophets in the New Testament*, Studies in Biblical Literature 140, New York: Peter Lang.

Silva, M. (1993), 'The New Testament Use of the Old Testament: Text Form and Authority', in D. A. Carson and J. D. Woodbridge (eds.), *Scripture and Truth*, Grand Rapids: Baker, 147–165.

Skinner, J. (1922), *The Book of the Prophet Isaiah Chapters XL–*

LXVI, in the Revised Version with Introduction and Notes, CBSC, Cambridge: Cambridge University Press.

—— (1948), *Prophecy and Religion: Studies in the Life of Jeremiah,* Cambridge: Cambridge University Press.

Smith, M. S. (1990), *The Laments of Jeremiah and Their Contexts: A Literary and Redactional Study of Jeremiah 11–20,* SBLMS 42, Atlanta: Scholars Press.

Sohn, S.-T. (1999), '"I Will Be Your God and You Will Be My People": The Origin and Background of the Covenant Formula', in R. Chazan, W. W. Hallo and L. H. Schiffman (eds.), *Ki Baruch Hu: Ancient Near Eastern, Biblical and Judaic Studies in Honor of Baruch A. Levine,* Winona Lake: Eisenbrauns, 355–372.

Soskice, J. M. (1985), *Metaphor and Religious Language,* Oxford: Clarendon.

Spence, A. (2008), *Christology: A Guide for the Perplexed,* London: T. & T. Clark.

Sternberg, M. (1985), *The Poetics of Biblical Narrative: Ideological Literature and the Drama of Reading,* ISBL, Bloomington: Indiana University Press.

Stipp, H.-J. (1994), *Das masoretische und alexandrinische Sondergut des Jeremiabuches: Textgeschichtlicher Rang, Eigenarten, Triebkräfte,* OBO 136, Freiburg, Switzerland: Universitätsverlag.

—— (2010), 'The Concept of the Empty Land in Jeremiah 37 – 43', in E. Ben Zvi and C. Levine (eds.), *The Concept of Exile in Ancient Israel and Its Historical Contexts,* BZAW 404, Berlin: W. de Gruyter, 103–154.

Stulman, L. (1984), 'Some Theological and Lexical Differences Between the Old Greek and the MT of the Jeremiah Prose Discourses', *HS* 25: 18–23.

—— (1986), *The Prose Sermons of the Book of Jeremiah: A Redescription of the Correspondences with the Deuteronomistic Literature in the Light of Recent Text-Critical Research,* SBLDS 83, Atlanta: Scholars Press.

—— (1998), *Order Amid Chaos: Jeremiah as Symbolic Tapestry,* Biblical Seminar, Sheffield: Sheffield Academic Press.

—— (1999), 'The Prose Sermons as Hermeneutical Guide to Jeremiah 1 – 25: The Deconstruction of Judah's Symbolic World', in Diamond et al. 1999: 34–63.

—— (2005), *Jeremiah,* AbOTC, Nashville: Abingdon.

Sweeney, M. A. (2005), *Form and Intertextuality in Prophetic and Apocalyptic Literature,* FAT 45, Tübingen: Mohr Siebeck.

—— (2007), 'Jeremiah's Reflection on the Isaian Royal Promise: Jeremiah 23:1–8 in Context', in Goldingay and Allen 2007: 308–321.

Tarrer, S. (2009), 'John Calvin and the Prophetic Curriculum of Jeremiah', *Churchman* 123.1: 29–52.

Taylor, M. A. (1987), 'Jeremiah 45: The Problem of Placement', *JSOT* 37: 79–98.

Thelle, R. I. (2009), 'Babylon in the Book of Jeremiah (MT): Negotiating a Power Shift', in Barstad and Kratz 2009: 187–232.

Thiel, W. (1973), *Die deuteronomistische Redaktion von Jer 1–25*, WMANT 41, Neukirchen–Vluyn: Neukirchener.

Thompson, M. D. (2008), 'Witness to the Word: On Barth's Doctrine of Scripture', in Gibson and Strange 2008: 168–197.

Tigay, J. P. (1996), *Deuteronomy*, JPSTC, Philadelphia: Jewish Publication Society.

Tolkien, J. R. R. (1966), *The Hobbit: Or There and Back Again*, 3rd ed., London: Allen & Unwin.

Toorn, K. van der (2007), *Scribal Culture and the Making of the Hebrew Bible*, Cambridge: Harvard University Press.

Tov, E. (1981), 'Some Aspects of the Textual and Literary History of Jeremiah', in Bogaert 1981a: 145–167.

—— (1985), 'The Literary History of the Book of Jeremiah in the Light of Its Textual History', in J. H. Tigay (ed.), *Empirical Models for Biblical Criticism*, Philadelphia: University of Pennsylvania Press, 211–237.

—— (1998), 'The Significance of the Texts from the Judean Desert for the History of the Text of the Hebrew Bible: A New Synthesis', in F. Cryer and T. L. Thompson (eds.), *Qumran Between the Old and New Testaments*, JSOTSup 290 / Copenhagen International Seminar 6, Sheffield: Sheffield Academic Press, 277–309.

—— (2001), *Textual Criticism of the Hebrew Bible*, 2nd rev. ed., Minneapolis: Fortress.

Treier, D. J. (2008), *Introducing Theological Interpretation of Scripture: Recovering a Christian Practice*, Grand Rapids: Baker.

—— (2010), 'What Is Theological Interpretation? An Ecclesiological Reduction', *IJST* 12.2: 144–161.

Trimm, C. (2010), 'Evangelicals, Theology, and Biblical Interpretation: Reflections on the Theological Interpretation of Scripture', *BBR* 20.3: 311–330.

Ulrich, E., F. M. Cross, R. E. Fuller, J. E. Sanderson, P. W. Skehan and E. Tov (eds.) (1997), *Qumran Cave 4*, vol. 10, DJD 15, Oxford: Clarendon.

Vanhoozer, K. J. (2002), *First Theology: God, Scriptures and Hermeneutics*, Leicester: Apollos.

—— (2005), *The Drama of Doctrine: A Canonical–Linguistic Approach to Christian Theology*, Louisville: Westminster John Knox.

—— (2008a), 'The Apostolic Discourse and Its Developments', in M. Bockmuehl and A. J. Torrance (eds.), *Scripture's Doctrine and Theology's Bible: How the New Testament Shapes Christian Dogmatics*, Grand Rapids: Baker Academic, 191–207.

—— (ed.) (2008b), *Theological Interpretation of the Old Testament: A Book by Book Survey*, Grand Rapids: Baker Academic.

—— (2010), *Remythologizing Theology: Divine Action, Passion, and Authorship*, CSCD 18, Cambridge: Cambridge University Press.

Venema, G. J. (2004), *Reading Scripture in the Old Testament: Deuteronomy 9 – 10, 31, 2 Kings 22 – 23, Jeremiah 36, Nehemiah 8*, OtSt 48, Leiden: E. J. Brill.

Wal, A. J. O. van der (2004), 'Toward a Synchronic Analysis of the Masoretic Text of the Book of Jeremiah', in Kessler 2004: 13–23.

Wanke, G. (1971), *Untersuchungen zur sogenannten Baruchschrift*, BZAW 122, Berlin: W. de Gruyter.

Ward, T. (2009), *Words of Life: Scripture as the Living and Active Word of God*, Nottingham: Inter-Varsity Press.

Warfield, B. B. (1948), 'The Biblical Idea of Revelation', in B. B. Warfield (ed.), *The Inspiration and Authority of the Bible*, Philadelphia: Presbyterian & Reformed, 71–104.

Watson, F. (1996), 'Bible, Theology and the University: A Response to Philip Davies', *JSOT* 71: 3–16.

—— (1997), *Text and Truth: Redefining Biblical Theology*, Edinburgh: T. & T. Clark.

—— (2004), *Paul and the Hermeneutics of Faith*, London: T. & T. Clark.

—— (2010), 'Hermeneutics and the Doctrine of Scripture: Why They Need Each Other', *IJST* 12.2: 118–143.

Webb, B. (1997), 'Biblical Theology and Biblical Interpretation', in Gibson 1997: 47–74.

Webster, J. (2003), *Holy Scripture: A Dogmatic Sketch*, Current Issues in Theology, Cambridge: Cambridge University Press.

—— (2010), 'Editorial', *IJST* 12.2: 116–117.

Weeks, S. (2009), 'Jeremiah as a Prophetic Book', in Barstad and Kratz 2009: 265–274.

Weiser, A. (1982), *Das Buch Jeremia: Kapitel 25,15 – 52,34*, 7th ed., ATD 21, Göttingen: Vandenhoeck & Ruprecht.

Wells, R. (2007), 'Dislocations in Time and Ideology in the Reconception of Jeremiah's Words: The Encounter with Hananiah in the Septuagint *Vorlage* and the Masoretic Text', in Goldingay and Allen 2007: 322–350.

Wendel, U. (1995), *Jesaja und Jeremia: Worte, Motive und Einsichten Jesajas in der Verkündigung Jeremias*, BThSt 25, Neukirchen-Vluyn: Neukirchener.

Westermann, C. (1985), 'The Old Testament's Understanding of History in Relation to That of the Enlightenment', in J. T. Butler, E. W. Conrad and B. C. Ollenburger (eds.), *Understanding the Word: Essays in Honor of Bernhard W. Anderson*, JSOTSup 37, Sheffield: JSOT Press, 207–220.

Williams, P. J. (2002), 'Lying Spirits Sent by God? The Case of Micaiah's Prophecy', in Helm and Trueman 2002: 58–66.

Williamson, P. R. (2007), *Sealed with an Oath: Covenant in God's Unfolding Purpose*, NSBT 23, Nottingham: Apollos.

Willis, J. I. (1985), 'Dialogue Between Prophet and Audience as a Rhetorical Device in the Book of Jeremiah', *JSOT* 33: 63–82.

Wolterstorff, N. (1995), *Divine Discourse: Philosophical Reflections of the Claim that God Speaks*, Cambridge: Cambridge University Press.

Work, T. (2002), *Living and Active: Scripture in the Economy of Salvation*, Grand Rapids: Eerdmans.

Wright, N. T. (1992), *The New Testament and the People of God*, London: SPCK.

Yeago, D. S. (1997), 'The New Testament and the Nicene Dogma: A Contribution to the Recovery of Theological Exegesis', in Fowl 1997: 87–100.

Young, F., and D. F. Ford (1987), *Meaning and Truth in 2 Corinthians*, Grand Rapids: Eerdmans.

Zaspel, F. G. (2010), *The Theology of B. B. Warfield: A Systematic Summary*, Wheaton: Crossway; Nottingham: Apollos.

Zimmerli, W. (1969), *Ezechiel*, vol. 1, BKAT 13.1, Neukirchen-Vluyn: Neukirchener.

Index of authors

Index of Scripture references